SEXUALITY EDUCATION

GARLAND REFERENCE LIBRARY
OF SOCIAL SCIENCE
(VOL. 416)

SEXUALITY EDUCATION
A Resource Book

Carol Cassell
Pamela M. Wilson

GARLAND PUBLISHING, INC. • NEW YORK & LONDON
1989

LIBRARY OF CONGRESS
Library of Congress Cataloging-in-Publication Data

Sexuality education : a resource book / [edited by] Carol Cassell.
Pamela M. Wilson
   p. cm. — (Garland reference library of social science ; vol.
416)
   Bibliography: p.
   Includes index.
   ISBN 0–8240–7899–3 (alk. paper)
   1. Sex instruction—United States.   2. Parent and child—United
States.   3. Birth control clinics—United States.   4. Family life
education—United States.   I. Cassell, Carol, 1936–   II. Wilson,
Pamela.   III. Series: Garland reference library of social science ;
v. 416.
HQ56.S38633   1989
306.7'07—dc19   88-16994
                                                                          CIP

Printed on acid-free, 250-year-life paper
Manufactured in the United States of America

CONTENTS

Editors and Contributors   ix

Acknowledgments   xv

Preface   xvii

Introduction   xix
    Carol Cassell and Pamela M. Wilson

Part I. Sexuality Education in the Family

Overview: Family Education for Sexuality
    Mary Steichen Calderone   3

Sexuality Education for Parents
    Judith Alter   13

Parent-Child Programs
    Jean G. Brown   27

A Gay Child in the Family
    Wayne V. Pawlowski   35

Resources on Homosexuality   46

Sexual Abuse Prevention: Issues and Answers
    Sol Gordon   51

Resources on Child Sexual Abuse Prevention   56

v

National Family Sexuality Education Month
    Carol Cassell   67

Annotated Bibliography: Sexuality Education in the
Family   71

Part II. Sexuality Education in the Schools

Overview: A Perspective on School Programs
    Mary Lee Tatum   95

Family Life Education in a Public School System
    L. Jean Hunter   105

Elementary School Sexuality Education
    Claire Scholz   119

Beyond the Facts: Sexuality Education in Junior
High/Middle School
    Ellen Rosenberg   123

Sexuality Education in Senior High Schools
    Martha Roper   127

Sexuality Education in the Independent School
Setting
    Deborah M. Roffman   137

Human Sexuality in Higher Education
    Michael Hammes   147

Sexuality Education Within Health Education
Curricula
    Sue Steed   155

Family Life Education Teacher Training
    Ellen Wagman   161

School-Based Health Clinics: Improving Adolescent
Health and Reducing Teenage Pregnancy
    Douglas Kirby
    Sharon Lovick   169

Annotated Bibliography: Sexuality Education in the Schools   179

Part III. Sexuality Education in the Community

Overview: Current Issues, Future Directions
Joe Fay   215

Youth Organizations: A Valuable Sex Education Resource
Jane Quinn   223

Resources Available from Youth Organizations   232

The Role of Family Planning/Health Agencies
Janet Alyn   237

The Role of Churches
Esther Walter   243

Sexuality Education: Working with a Community
Susan J. Hart   251

The AIDS Epidemic and Sexuality Education
Debra W. Haffner   257

How to Talk About Evaluation of Sex Education Programs Without Blushing or Stammering
Jesse Blatt   269

Annotated Bibliography: Sexuality Education in the Community   283

Part IV. Model Programs

Family Centered Sexuality Education
Helen Patricia Mudd
Elizabeth Nixon West   307

The Mother-Daughter Experience
    Kathy Hazelwood
    Gwen Killmer   319

Straight Talk: A Program to Increase Family
Communication About Sexuality
    Debby Goodman   325

Feeling Good Workshops
    Gloria Blum   331

Resources on Sexuality and Disability   336

Postponing Sexual Involvement: An Educational
Series for Young People
    Marie E. Mitchell   343

Challenging Youth with Choices: The Life Options
Strategy for Sexuality Education
    Carol Hunter-Geboy   353

Bridging the Gap
    Robert A. Hatcher
    Monica M. Oakley   363

TeenAge Communication Theater
    Elena Love   373

No Is Not Enough: Teen Acquaintance Rape and
Sexual Abuse Prevention
    Caren Adams
    Jan Loreen-Martin   383

A Teacher Training Model
    Peggy B. Smith   389

The Sex Education Coalition: A Model for
Community Interaction
    Joan S. Benesch   403

Resources from the Sex Education Coalition   412

Appendix: Audiovisual Distributors   415

Index   419

EDITORS

Carol Cassell, Ph.D.
Author and Researcher
Past President, American
    Association of Sex
    Educators,
Counselors, and Therapists

Pamela M. Wilson, M.S.W.
Sexuality Education Program
    Consultant
Washington, D.C.

CONTRIBUTORS

Caren Adams
Co-author of *No More
    Secrets: Protecting Your
    Child From Sexual
    Assault* and *No Is Not
    Enough: Helping
    Teenagers Avoid Sexual
    Assault.*

Judith Alter, Ph.D.
Clinical Psychologist
Private Practice
Bethesda, Maryland

Janet Alyn
Education Director
Planned Parenthood of San
    Antonio
San Antonio, Texas

Joan Benesch
Coordinator of the Training
    Institute
Planned Parenthood of
    Maryland
Co-founder, Sex Education
    Coalition
Washington, D.C.

ix

Jesse Blatt, Ph.D.
Research Psychologist
Washington, D.C.

Gloria Blum, M.A.
Feeling Good Associates
Kailua-Kona, Hawaii
Co-author of "Feeling Good
    About Yourself"

Jean G. Brown, M.S.W.,
    A.C.S.W., A.C.S.E.
Administrative Assistant
Family Guidance
    Center/Community
    Mental Health Center
St. Joseph, Missouri

Mary Steichen Calderone,
    M.D., M.P.H.
Founder and Past Executive
    Director
The Sex Information and
    Education Council of the
    United States
New York, New York

Joe Fay, M.A.
Director of Education
Planned Parenthood of
    Central Pennsylvania
York, Pennsylvania

Debby Goodman
Director of Education
Planned Parenthood of
    Central Oklahoma
Oklahoma City, Oklahoma

Sol Gordon, Ph.D.
Former Director
Institute for Family
    Research and Education
Syracuse, New York

Debra W. Haffner M.P.H.
Executive Director
Sex Information and
    Education Council of the
    U.S. (SIECUS)
New York, New York

Michael Hammes, Ph.D.
Assistant Professor
Health Promotion
University of New Mexico
Albuquerque, New Mexico

Susan J. Hart
Health Education Services
    Project
    Supervisor/Educator
South Texas Family
    Planning and Health
    Corporation
Corpus Christi, Texas

Robert A. Hatcher, M.D.,
    M.P.H.
Professor of Gynecology and
    Obstetrics
Emory University School of
    Medicine
Atlanta, Georgia
Senior Author of
    *Contraceptive
    Technology*

Kathy Hazelwood
Director of Education
Panhandle Planned
  Parenthood Association
Amarillo, Texas

L. Jean Hunter
Curriculum Specialist for
  Family Life Education
Alexandria City Public
  Schools
Alexandria, Virginia

Carol Hunter-Geboy, Ph.D.
Human Development
  Consultant
Silver Spring, Maryland

Gwen Killmer
Education Specialist
Texas Panhandle Planned
  Parenthood Association
Amarillo, Texas

Douglas Kirby, Ph.D.
Director of Research
Center for Population
  Options
Washington, D.C.

Elena Love
Education Director
Planned Parenthood
Dallas, Texas

Sharon Lovick
Support Center for School-
  Based Clinics

Center for Population
  Options
Houston, Texas

Jan Loreen-Martin
Education Consultant
Planned Parenthood of
  Seattle-King County
Seattle, Washington
Co-author of *No Is Not
  Enough: Helping
  Teenagers Avoid Sexual
  Assault* and *Sexuality
  Education and Training:
  Theory, Techniques and
  Resources*

Marie E. Mitchell, R.N.
Program Supervisor, Teen
  Services Program
Grady Memorial Hospital
Atlanta, Georgia
Co-author of *Postponing
  Sexual Involvement: An
  Educational Series for
  Young People and
  Parents*

Helen Patricia Mudd,
  A.C.S.W.
Coordinator of Children's
  Services
Catholic Charities Diocese of
  Arlington, Inc.
Arlington, Virginia

Monica M. Oakley, R.N., B.S.N.
Health Care Network
Grand Rapids, Michigan

Wayne Pawlowski, A.C.S.W.
Director of Training
Planned Parenthood of Metropolitan Washington
Washington, D.C.

Jane Quinn, A.C.S.W.
Director of Program Services
Girls Clubs of America, Inc.
New York, New York

Deborah Roffman, M.S.
Sexuality Educator and Consultant
The Park School
Baltimore, Maryland

Martha R. Roper, M.A.
Sexuality Educator/Consultant
School District of University City
St. Louis, Missouri

Ellen Rosenberg
Director, Growing Up Feeling Good Programs
Rockville Center, New York
Author of *Growing Up Feeling Good* and *Getting Closer: Discover and Understand Your*

Child's Secret Feelings About Growing Up

Claire Scholz, M.A.
Psychologist, Family Life Education
Irvington Public Schools
Irvington, New Jersey

Peggy B. Smith, Ph.D.
Associate Professor OB/GYN
Baylor College of Medicine
Houston, Texas

Sue Steed
Health Education Coordinator
Albuquerque Public Schools
Albuquerque, New Mexico

Mary Lee Tatum, M.A.
Teacher/Consultant
Family Life/Sexuality Education Program
Falls Church, Virginia

Ellen Wagman, M.P.H.
Director of Training
ETR Associates
Santa Cruz, California

Esther Walter
Educational Consultant
Des Moines, Iowa

Elizabeth West, A.C.S.W.
Former Coordinator of
    Children's Services
Catholic Charities Diocese of
    Arlington, Inc.
Arlington, Virginia

ACKNOWLEDGMENTS

We gratefully acknowledge the people who helped with the great task of producing this book:

- Our contributing authors, who offered highly professional articles.
- Leigh Hallingby, formerly of SIECUS, who contributed many ideas for bibliographic resources as well as support throughout the project.
- Karen Tracy and Natalie Stewart, who spent many hours typing articles and annotated resources.
- Karin Williams, who provided invaluable assistance in organizing details.

In addition, we acknowledge the use of the following resources that aided in the compilation of the annotated resource sections:

- *Family Life Educator*, a quarterly journal published by ETR Associates, Network Publications, 1700 Mission Street, Suite 203, P.O. Box 1830, Santa Cruz, CA 95061-9979. The Network Publications Catalog was also helpful.
- *SIECUS Report*, a quarterly newsletter published by the Sex Information and Education Council of the U.S., New York University, 32 Washington Place, New York, NY 10003.
- *Sexuality Education: An Annotated Guide for Resource Materials.* Written by Pamela Wilson in 1984 and currently published by Network Publications in Santa Cruz.

We especially thank and recognize Marie Ellen Larcada, our editor, for her enthusiasm and support throughout this project.

PREFACE

This book provides a comprehensive guide to a wide range of sexuality education programs and resources. The framework of this collection is based upon the recognition that the home, the church, the school, and the community have complementary roles to play in this important area of education. Our purpose is to describe a variety of ways to plan and implement sexuality education and to provide in-depth information on the current resources available.

Contributors to this book are experienced educators who are nationally recognized as outstanding professionals in the field. Each contributor describes one aspect of the practice of sexuality education: its goals, theory, planning and development, implementation, evaluation, teacher training, the role of community agencies.

This book is divided into four parts: sexuality education in the family, sexuality education in schools, sexuality education programs in the community, and a section for model programs that runs the gamut from acquaintance rape prevention to special programs for mothers and daughters, to teen theater groups. At the beginning of Parts I–III, we present an overview of the issues involved in the planning and implementation of sexuality education in the setting being discussed. The articles in each section offer practical and useful guidelines for conducting sexuality education and serve as a sound introduction to the subject as well as an update on innovative programs for those who are already involved in the field. An annotated bibliography follows each of the first three sections, listing books, periodicals, and media appropriate for that type of sexuality education. In some cases a list of annotated resources follows a particular article. For example, a list of resources on homosexuality follows the article "A Gay Child in the Family."

This practical book is essential for locating a wide selection of materials to use in the presentation of sexuality education. Educators, counselors, students, administrators, and policy makers in education, health, and social services will find this volume especially helpful in developing programs, identifying references, and establishing guidelines for the provision of sexuality education in both the public and private sectors.

INTRODUCTION

Sexuality is a central and vital aspect of the human personality. According to the American Medical Association, human sexuality "involves what we do, but it is also what we are. It is an identification, an activity, a biological and emotional process, an outlook and expression of self . . . it is an important factor in every personal relationship and every human endeavor from business to politics" (American Medical Association, 1972).

There is a growing awareness that sexuality is so integrated with every other aspect of human life that education in human sexuality is necessarily a life-long process. While sexuality education is an important offering in schools, these courses constitute only a small portion of the sexual learning process. Sexual learning is not an event for youth only but a process spanning life. An integral part of social learning, sexuality education relates to learning sources as diverse as the extended family, the place of worship, work sites, health care services, community and national institutions, social policies, social activists, the media, and the law. All have important roles to play in sexuality education.

Although parents are the primary sexuality educators, research shows that many parents don't feel adequately prepared to discuss sexuality with their children. This lack of preparation needs to be remedied. The Sex Information and Education Council of the United States (SIECUS) states in an annual report, "Sexuality is learned as the result of a process that should not be left to chance or ignorance. . . . It is important that the informal process of sex education within the family be supported by planned, enlightened learning opportunities offering information at appropriate times in the growing period." In accord with that recommendation, many of the programs conducted in communities today are geared to help parents become more comfortable and more effective in their role.

A Brief History

Sexuality education may appear to be a contemporary issue, but, in actuality, interest in the topic can be traced back to the turn of the century when groups such as the American Purity Alliance, the YWCA, and the Child Study Association sponsored lectures and panels on sex-related topics. As early as 1892, the National Education Association and the National Congress of Parents and Teachers discussed sex education in the schools at their annual convention. Throughout the 1920s and 1930s there are periodic references to sex education in printed materials from the U.S. Office of Education that mention the need to teach students anatomy, physiology and hygiene, with a focus primarily on the elimination of venereal diseases. In 1940, U.S. Public Health pamphlets broadly covered sex education methods and suggested a course of study for teachers in the secondary schools. By the fifties, the importance of sex education was widely discussed. The delegates to the Mid-Century White House Conference on Children and Youth declared that well-prepared teachers should avoid emphasizing only the facts about sex and give attention to the total topic. And in 1955 the Joint Committee on Health Problems in Education of the National Education Association published a group of pamphlets referred to as the "sex education series."

In the next decade, the policy of the U.S. Office of Education was to encourage and support family life and sex education at all levels as well as teacher training programs. The founding of two important organizations signaled the emergence of sexuality education as a profession: the Sex Information and Education Council of the United States and the American Association of Sex Educators, Counselors, and Therapists.

In the late 1960s, as more sexuality education classes were offered in the schools, groups of parents opposed to the classes began to organize nationally. In general, these groups have treated "sex education" as a political issue rather than an educational process and tend to sensationalize any education about sexuality with the label "sex instruction." It may be that most new programs in public schools will always meet with opposition from this small, but vocal, minority.

In today's public opinion polls, over 80 percent of all Americans favor sex education in the schools. However, there are many shadings of opinion about the content, the type of instruction needed, and the appropriate grade level for sexuality education.

Despite widespread support for school sexuality education, a study supported by the Centers for Disease Control found that "only about 10 percent of our school students are getting a comprehensive sex education program. The rest get substantially less, or nothing" (Kirby, 1979). Beyond a simple desire to avoid political tension, many schools hesitate to implement courses because they are confused about the goals of sexuality education. Some think that sexuality education is synonymous with pregnancy and disease prevention; others see it as preparation for marriage and parenting; and still others define it broadly and comprehensively.

The diverse titles given to sexuality education programs—family life education, sex education, human growth and development, family life and human development—only add to the confusion. The old term "sex education" is a problem because it evokes the image of a class focussed on sexual behavior. "Sexuality education" is preferable because the word "sexuality" conveys a broader meaning—it is education about the human condition, being male or female, feelings, roles, communication, as well as sexual functioning. The title "family life education" is often chosen by schools because it is less controversial in that it implies the importance of family life and family relationships. Some programs labeled as "family life education" exclude the more explicit aspects of sexuality, focusing instead on self-esteem issues, preparation for marriage, family economics, and parenting skills. However, there is a growing trend for schools, especially elementary schools, to develop age-appropriate, comprehensive sexuality education programs called "family life education." ETR Associates, a non-profit organization in Santa Cruz, California, has helped to popularize this title by forming the Family Life Education Network and publishing the quarterly journal, *The Family Life Educator*. Regardless of the title given to a program, it is important for it to focus on the whole person and include the genital functions as a normal and positive part of being human. In this volume, there is a preference for the term "sexuality education." However, in many cases, contributors use the terms "family life education" and "sex education" interchangeably.

Contemporary Directions

In days gone by, school "sex education" classes usually consisted of a lecture or two on physiology, reproduction, and sexually transmitted diseases. Since the mid-1970s the trend in sexuality education is toward an emphasis on the total person, exploration of values, and development of life skills as opposed to earlier educational efforts aimed mainly at the acquisition of knowledge. Programs today include a focus on the psychological, sociological, economic, and cultural factors that affect sexual attitudes and behavior. Today it is more widely recognized that people have important choices to make about relationships and childbearing. In this context fewer courses treat sexuality education as something necessary only as preparation for marriage and parenthood.

A variety of teaching methodologies are commonly used, with an emphasis on developing critical thinking. Where and when sexuality courses are offered in the schools depends upon the local school system or individual school. In some situations, sexuality education can be found as a separate course, in others the topic is found as a part of a related classroom subject or as a component of a semester course (Bruess and Greenberg, 1981).

Although the schools remain the most common place for sexuality education courses for young people, many different types of organizations—community youth groups, family planning agencies, public health agencies, churches—are now involved in providing sexuality education in a variety of settings. These programs are designed to be a reliable source of accurate information to supplement but not replace the family's responsibility.

Approaches and opportunities for training sexuality educators have been expanded. Many colleges and universities offer single courses and even entire degree programs to prepare future sexuality educators. Professional continuing education programs now exist for school teachers and administrators, health and social workers, counselors, physicians, nurses, and other professionals.

Evidence of the coming of age of sexuality education is the growing amount of good literature and audiovisual materials that has been developed over the last ten years. Not long ago it was difficult for sexuality educators to find a good selection of appropriate materials. Today the educator's problem is often sorting through the many valuable resources available.

There is a rapidly growing tendency for schools to offer instruction in family life/sexuality education in response to the AIDS epidemic, the mounting tide of teenage pregnancy, the alarming percentages of sexually transmitted disease among young people, the rate of marital and family breakdowns, and many other symptoms that arise out of ignorance about sexuality and sexual relationships. It is important for sexuality educators to help school districts think carefully and realistically about their goals. To date, few, if any, sexuality programs have proven that they can reduce sex-related problems. At the same time, there have been no long-term evaluations of K-12 comprehensive programs. It seems reasonable to believe that participation in a responsible sexuality education program throughout childhood and adolescence would have some impact on these problems. Still, this fact has not been proven and there are so many other, often more powerful, influences on adolescents' behavior.

The best and most appropriate reasons to offer sexuality education programs are:

- to help prepare people for upcoming stages of development
- to increase comfort with the topic of sexuality
- to increase the attitude that sexuality is a normal and positive part of human existence
- to provide responsible answers to questions and concerns that arise in an age when the media bombard us with sexual messages
- to increase skills that will enable people to live happy, safe, and responsible lives as sexual beings.

It is a mistake to promote a sexuality education program by promising to reduce problems. First, the program takes on a "problem" focus and second, it is difficult to show significant results. Positive programs are more responsible and more realistic. This is not to say that social problems should not be addressed in the program—they should. For example, age-appropriate information about AIDS must be a part of sexuality education programs around the country. However, it would be a mistake to bombard people with information about AIDS in a vacuum without the balance of a comprehensive sexuality program.

Future Issues

This is a busy time for sexuality educators. A variety of agencies—schools, churches, youth-serving organizations, health and family planning groups, civic groups—are interested in developing programs. Wisely, many of these groups work together with qualified sexuality educators to develop quality programs. It is important for communities to avoid "re-inventing the wheel" and to benefit from the knowledge and experience that have been developed over the last twenty years.

Within the field old and new challenges exist. Sexuality educators are sorting out answers to the following questions:

- How can agencies obtain funding for sexuality programs that do not have a "problem" focus?
- What is the best way to incorporate AIDS education into sexuality education?
- What impact will the fear of AIDS have on the developing sexuality of young people?
- Is it appropriate to promote abstinence as the best choice for teenagers?
- Should programs suggest petting and masturbation as alternatives to sexual intercourse for teenagers?
- As the population of aging citizens increases, how should sexuality educators reach out to that neglected population?

Many of these important issues are addressed in the various sections of this book.

Summary

The contemporary profile of sexuality education is a complex one with a comprehensive view of human sexuality in contrast to the narrow scope and limited content of previous years. These changes did not occur in isolation but rather in response to a changing American society. The influence of two world wars, the work of sex researchers such as Alfred Kinsey, William Masters and Virginia Johnson, and Shere Hite, changes in marriage and family living, and the explosion of the communications industry and the mass media have all been influential in the development of modern sexuality education theory and practice. Moreover, the trend is in the direction of more and better sexuality education programs for persons of all ages. Today there are more quality sexuality education programs than ever before, paving the way for the important work that still remains to be done.

C.A.C.
P.M.W.

References

American Medical Association Committee on Human Sexuality. *Human Sexuality.* Chicago: American Medical Association, 1972.

Bruess, Clint E., and Jerrold S. Greenberg. *Sex Education: Theory and Practice.* Belmont, Calif.: Wadsworth Publishing Company, 1981.

Kirby, Douglas, Judith Alter, and Peter Scales. *An Analysis of U.S. Sex Education Programs and Evaluation Methods.* Bethesda, Md.: Mathtech, Inc., 1979.

Planned Parenthood Federation of America. *Sexuality Education: Definition and Discussion.* New York, 1981.

Part I
Sexuality Education
in the
Family

OVERVIEW:
FAMILY EDUCATION FOR
SEXUALITY
Mary Steichen Calderone

A family is two or more persons, at least one of whom qualifies as a legally responsible adult, who share one domicile in order to care for and about each other. If the family unit comes to include one or more under-age children, then the family's primary task is clear: the nature and quality of the adult guidance, supportive care, and love bestowed on the child(ren) as they mature should be geared to enhancing potentialities of all family members, in the direction of maturation, competence, self-esteem, sense of responsibility, and capacity to give and to receive love.

What relation does the above bear to education for sexuality—that is, to education for becoming and living as a sexual person? If the overall educational process is to be designed to contribute toward a solid infrastructure within each person for successful social living, then integrated with this should be careful designs for development of components for successful *sexual* living as well—in other words, of a benignly oriented sociosexual ambience to grow up in. To engineer so major a paradigm shift, several facts should be recognized and accepted. In order to be integrated as armatures for all family-oriented programs: the normal human baby is born equipped with three major endowments that have been functioning along with the other human body-mind systems since their formation early in gestation and that authenticate its humanness. The three are the baby's *body, mind* and *sexuality.* Need for understanding, acceptance, and development of that third endowment has met with the same fanatic hysteria and uninstructed opposition as once assailed a quite different paradigm shift— one that would "see" the sun not as the 24-hour commuter circling the earth once a year but as the stable, immovable center of our universe.

Body. No other living being normally and inevitably persists in standing erect throughout all but the first year of its life span, thus neatly freeing both hands for the development of all their varied skills—including expressions of tenderness and love. Tilling the fields, training a dog, riding a racehorse, dancing, skating, holding a book, sewing, cooking, typing, computing, designing, and/or constructing buildings or performing surgery—all are uniquely human body/mind skills that require training and mastery.

Mind. The most accomplished great ape or dolphin cannot approach even the simplest human being in gene-wired capacity for learning, language, memory, association, reasoning, writing, inventing, creating, imagining, choosing, deciding, postponing, loving . . . a child goes to school, then to university and to professional school, to learn how to use its mind on behalf of itself and others. Studies show that a supportive home and vigorous, pleasurable preschool learning experience serve to undergird successful achievement of life's skills (Hechinger, 1984). Dreaming, imagining, inventing, reasoning—all such functions take part in how we plan and carry out, sometimes over long lifetimes, the most intricate and subtle projects.

Sexuality. Other mammals are born hard-wired to mate in direct species-specific response to a wide variety of gene programs and of environment-specific signals related to season, climate, and its annual changes, length of day, state of nutrition, and myriads of other factors. Other mammals do not have the mental resources and proclivities that we enjoy—flexibility of choices, mental reasoning power, learning and/or relearning in adult and even in aging adult life. As a result of these species-specific differences, human beings can watch how the animal world does or does not resolve problems caused by fast or slow changes; in animals for which environmental changes have occurred, it may be difficult for humans to detect the way they adapt or, more often, fail to adapt to the changes. Species-specific mating styles vary greatly: some choose a carefully looked-over and suitably behaving mate for life (swans). Others mate at random: the grey whales are recently reported to go into a kind of mating frenzy, with mating contacts one after the other with constantly changing partners in a kind of promiscuous gene-mixing celebration. Both extremes are also seen today among humans, with one great difference: at any time *we* can elect to change our mating behaviors, a realization many are learning how to act upon in these sobering days of AIDS.

Care of the young among animals is another broad area with many variables hard-wired into the species-specific patterns, from being left exclusively to the female with the male never aware of his offspring to the Australian male emu that mates with a series of females, watches as each lays—and leaves—an egg almost directly in front of him, nudges it into the hole he has scooped out in the sun-warmed sand, broods the clutch until all chicks have pipped in the same 24-hour day, then herds them over to the calmly waiting hens each of which accepts a chick she will feed and bring to maturity while he simply returns to his ordinary male life. In the nonhuman mammalian world, no matter what changes in behavior might be indicated by altered circumstances, obedience to the genes is dictated with little variation.

By contrast, over the span of history humans have come to determine their pre- and post-mating behaviors within a wide variety of the socially accepted patterns of monogamy, polygamy, and occasionally polyandry as modified by ceremonial living patterns (often called superstitions by other religious beliefs and observances). And although the original purpose for mating in many primitive societies may have been to have children as resources for one's old age, in the more educated and developed Western societies such aspects as providing legal sanction (for the male at least) to enjoyment of sex for pleasure as well as for order and peace within the social structure have combined to lead to acceptance of such diverse patterns as conventional permanent coupling, legalization of divorce, and serial monogamy.

Where there has been demand for recognition that human females as well as males may seek sex for pleasure *and* sex for procreation, many different ways have co-existed to facilitate such choices. As a result, along with such other factors as lowered death rates, diminished need for manual labor, and the hardening realities of overpopulation and diminishing resources, this has brought to a head the essentiality of worldwide sophisticated, safe methods of contraception.

In many of the more developed societies the fiction has been maintained that children can only grow up "innocent" as long as they remain "ignorant" of the facts of sex, reproduction, sexual pleasure, and other such dangerous subjects until the time that their parents have deemed them ready for such "dangerous" (because suggestive) knowledge, i.e., until they are ready to marry. Characteristically, such westernized societies in ostrich-like fashion convinced themselves that children *would* "wait to be told" about sex before trying it out on their own! This foolishly discounted the myriads of media messages of all kinds that *do* every day reach even pre-kindergartners, proclaiming that sex is the norm and is great to enjoy right now! Even if they were allowed to watch only "Sesame Street," they were sure on Saturday mornings to get the message from the commercials interspersing the comics or from the mail-order lingerie catalogs that invade middle-class homes.

So our kids, at ever younger ages, quite naturally began to do as they saw the adults *did* rather than as they *said*; the teen pregnancies began to climb even as their ages began to lower to include an occasional prepubertal pregnancy. The adult world too late began to realize that things were getting out of hand. Threats were heard from the unread and unscientifically informed, blaming what was happening on "all that sex education they teach in the schools," deliberately ignoring that at most only about 10% of school programs include anything at all on sex-related topics. Thus did poorly educated prejudice join with rank ignorance to stifle all information about the truths of human sexuality, and the combination of negative forces led straight to increased premature motherhood among unprepared young girls who were childishly naive about the realities of procreation. The birthrate soared as did the toll of premature births and deaths, and ever-growing neglect and deprivation plagued the children that children were being forced to bear. For society to emerge from such tragic human havoc requires that public health methodology identify, accelerate, and implement new, effective ways to educate for positive sexual health in parents and children alike (Calderone, 1982). Time is of the essence, for the next generations of sexually violent criminals are already in the ranks.

Reproductivity vs. sexuality. These are two areas of intensive human living that, despite the fact that they involve two distinct body/mind systems, are always lumped together as if they were one. This is despite the long-known simple fact that they function at different periods in the life span with entirely different end-purposes. Their differences in structures and natures serve to characterize them as male or female. For instance, it is unlikely for the male to function normally in reproduction if he does not co-experience sexual desire, while the human female can reproduce many times over without pleasure or even with displeasure. In contrast are the permanent linkages such as the cardio-respiratory systems that are identical in structure and function in both sexes, so that the deterioration of only one can cause its owner's life to crash.

In the late 1970s, it was observed (Calderone, 1983) during amniocenteses that as early as the 17th week of gestation, fetal penises could be seen in erection with a regular periodicity of about 90 minutes. This would be about nine weeks following the beginning of elaboration of testosterone by the embryo's own pre-gonadal cells—the main factor operative in male gender differentiation and

functioning—but that does not alone serve to differentiate the
sexual from the reproductive systems or male from female
sexual functioning. There are striking differences and
similarities. Females are normally reproductive from puberty
to approaching 50; sexually they have been observed to begin
periodic vaginal lubrication from birth (Langfeldt, 1980), to
be able to produce signs of sexual arousal, and even what
appears to be orgasm by simple thigh pressure in the first
weeks or months of life (Kinsey, 1953), and to continue these
responses well into old age. The potent male can remain
reproductive for his entire life span from puberty on, provided
his sexual drive also remains lifelong, or it may wane with
erectile difficulties as the years advance. In any case it has
become vital to recognize any clear distinctions between male
and female generative and/or sexual functions:

Male. Reproductive/sexual/urinary systems: testes, vas
deferens, urethra, prostate, epididymis, seminal vesicles,
penis, olfactory and visual systems, skin, breasts, brain, sexual
memory and association pathways. Hormone: testosterone
(testicles).

Female. Reproductive system: ovaries, tubes, uterus,
vagina (as two-way conduit). Hormones: estrogen (ovaries),
progesterone, pituitrin.

Sexual response system: clitoris, labia, vagina,
G-spot, peri-vaginal and peri-rectal tissues and muscles, anus,
skin, breasts, mouth, olfactory and visual systems, brain,
sexual memory and association pathways. Hormones: adrenal
testosterone; estrogen to maintain vaginal integrity.

From the moment of birth, baby boys continue the 90-
minute schedule of penile erections begun so early in fetal
life. Professionals and parents alike need to open their
minds to the bald scientific proof of sexual functioning as
demonstrated prenatally in humans that will continue
normally throughout the life span. Disarmed by the new
sexual paradigm provided by science, parents and other
caretakers can open their minds to a great truth—the
functioning of the dual systems as God- and nature-given:
sexual beginnings *in utero* and the advent of puberty
signalizing the advent of reproductivity. In this way parents

can come to perceive the twelve pre-pubertal years as nature's way of protecting the development, from birth to puberty, of the capacity for reproduction in safe manner and can teach their children how to become reasonably capable of judging under what circumstances and after what age elective parenthood might make sense. How to meet the needs of the infant, child, or adolescent under their care will thus be greatly clarified and clear the air for acknowledging the valid existence of sexuality.

Such shared knowledge from experts will allow for correction of the erroneous impressions that sexual thoughts, fantasies, or behavior are *per se* "bad" or "dangerous' or "a habit to be punished or broken," paving the way for major steps *away* from the threatening attitudes of fear/anger/sin/punishment *toward* those supporting understanding/acceptance/socialization with responsibility, attitudes generally taken for granted for other normal body functions. Very young children easily accept from loving parents that sex and sex feelings are a part of everybody all their lives, and one of God's many gifts to us. "We want to help you learn the truth about that part of you, so that you can understand how to take charge of yourself in the safe and growing ways that we want for you as you grow up" (Calderone, 1982).

To help accomplish this much, health and education professionals can help families learn the following operative principles:

1. Every baby is born hard-wired to be interested in and to want to explore and understand everything that comes across his or her path. This natural drive can be subverted by negative or indifferent attitudes of caregivers (Landreth, 1967).
2. All the endowments of a baby at birth require gradual, patient, realistic socialization by parents, with the primary goal of supporting their ordained *use* in rewarding, appropriate ways (Brazelton, 1981).
3. The functionings and reactions that commonly occur in all body systems of normal children are there for

specific purposes, so are automatically to be considered "good" and to be respected and protected.

But parents always want to know when sex education should "begin." The simplest answer is the truth, that we have no choice about "when," inasmuch as the process automatically begins at the very moment of birth itself, in terms of the softness and tenderness of the voices expressing welcome and love; warmth and tenderness of the hands in stroking or cleansing the baby's face and body (Blackman, 1980); softness and sweet smell of the breast that is always there for food and comfort; gentleness of the faces whose smiles remain even in the face of the longest crying spells or the foulest diapers.

Bonding begins at birth and is of great significance as seen in the intensity of the gaze or of a ten-day-old baby focusing on its mother's face while responding to her emerging tongue with its own tentative but successful imitative effort (Brazelton, 1981).

Summary

It took well over 100 years before even the educated could accept Galileo's new paradigm of the sun instead of the earth as the center of our universe. Just so will it take time for many modern societies to understand and accept the simple fact that children are born with their sexual and all other systems functional save the one. As the twenty-first century nears, it is ever more vital that everyone learns how to see our children in newer and truer ways, in order to make possible the fresh and effective means for the vital, gradual socialization of sexuality as a universal factor intrinsic to being human throughout the entire life span.

It is also important to be aware that children are not sexual in the ways that they will be as adults but have their own stage-appropriate ways for experiencing and thinking about sex as integral to all other areas of development (Goldman, 1982). They need for us to keep the conversations going as they themselves move toward a more mature understanding of the complexities of the world and its peoples (Calderone, 1982).

Truth and talk are the basics for helping children understand the world they inhabit. Those whom circumstances force to live in crowded facilities can still be helped to develop the will, the strength, and the techniques for surviving, even in crowded rooms with minimum facilities for privacy, comfort, and cleanliness. We owe our children such chances for decency and education, and the three basic moralities—justice, kindness, responsibility— must be lived within family structures before they can permeate outward to the world. All of these elements are essential for positive sexual socialization.

A committee of many denominations and faiths drawn from the clergy once worked on a statement for SIECUS about the sexuality of children. The concluding sentence was: "Parents should be taught to bless, honor, dignify, conserve— and *celebrate*—their children's sexuality."

References

Blackman, N. "Pleasure and Touching: Their Significance in the Development of the Pre-School Child." *Proceedings of the International Symposium on Childhood and Sexuality*. Edited by J.M. Sampson. Montreal: Editions Etudes Vivantes, 1980.

Brazelton, T. *On Becoming a Family: The Growth of Attachment*. New York: Dell, 1981.

Calderone, M., and J. Ramey. *Talking With Your Child About Sex*. New York: Random House, 1982.

Calderone, M. "Fetal Erection and Its Message to Us." SIECUS Report 11: no. 5/6, 1983.

Goldman, R., and J. Goldman. *Children's Sexual Thinking*. Boston: Rutledge and Kegan Paul, 1982.

Hechinger, F. "Changed Lives," review of report on Perry
    Preschool Program. *The New York Times,* September
    11, 1984.

Kinsey, A., W. Pomeroy, and C. Martin. *Sexual Behavior in
    the Human Female.* Philadelphia: W.B. Saunders
    Co., 1953.

Landreth, C. *Early Childhood: Behavior and Learning.* New
    York: Alfred Knopf, 1967.

Langfelt, T. "Aspects of Sexual Development, Problems and
    Therapy in Children." *Proceedings of the
    International Symposium on Childhood and
    Sexuality.* Edited by J.M. Sampson. Montreal: Editions
    Etudes Vivantes, 1980.

SEXUALITY EDUCATION FOR PARENTS
Judith Alter

It has been over a decade since we moved from simply acknowledging the sexual problems and struggles American young people experience to actively exploring strategies for helping children reach adulthood with healthy and fulfilling sexual lives. As is the tendency whenever we are faced with problems that affect the youth of the nation, our major strategy was to turn to the schools to provide a solution. Some see school sex education as the best vehicle to reach the most children, but many parents are reluctant to allow schools, churches, and other institutions to assume primary responsibility for the sex education of their children. They feel the sexual attitudes and behavior of young people should reflect the values of their individual homes. There has been little argument.

Parents, politicians, and educators concur that parents need to be first in charge. Indeed, this is a logical conclusion considering that the greatest influence on a child's developing sexuality and future behavior is the family. Still, parents tell researchers that even though they very much want to be responsible for this critical task, they are either inhibited or feel incompetent. They want help. This brings us to the topic discussed in this article: programs designed to help parents in their role as sex educators of their children.

Beginning early in the Carter Administration, a major emphasis in the field of sex education was given to developing programs for parents. During the Reagan

Administration, that emphasis became one of the few approaches to sex education to retain government support. While other, more innovative approaches to sexuality education have been explored, interest in parent programs has been sustained throughout the eighties. Over the years, research was conducted, parents' needs were assessed, and programs were developed in almost every state in the nation.

Research

The literature of the 1970s and 1980s indicates that most young people receive their sex education from sources other than their parents (Bennett and Dickinson, 1980; Fox, 1980; Thornburg, 1981). In homes where sexuality is discussed, the discussions tend to be infrequent, between mothers and daughters, and about menstruation and the biological aspects of reproduction (Bloch, 1978; McCary, 1978; Roberts et al., 1978). Multiple factors explain this limited communication. Because parents lack appropriate role models, they cannot draw on past experiences when attempting to approach their own children. Parents perceive themselves as being unable to provide adequate education because they feel they don't know enough or because they don't know how to explain what they do know. They feel uncomfortable discussing sexuality and, therefore, postpone it or avoid it entirely. They experience a contradiction between new and old values and are confused about what they believe and what they want to convey to their children. They assume that if their children are interested, they will ask; and they are fearful that providing information will lead to sexual experimentation (Bennett and Dickinson, 1980; General Mills, 1977; Roberts et al., 1978).

Unfortunately, research on the impact of parent/child communication on adolescent sexual behavior is not quite as conclusive. Still, survey data do suggest that parents can influence their child's sexual behavior either by direct verbal communication or by serving as role models (Inazu and Fox, 1980; Lewis, 1973; McNab, 1976; Spanier, 1977). Childrearing practices and parent/child relationships certainly mold a child's personality characteristics and intrapsychic dynamics, which ultimately play a significant role in adolescent behavior. Encouraging studies indicate that both parents and children think parents should be responsible for their children's sex education; both desire more open communication; and parents want assistance and the opportunity to attend structured courses (Block, 1979; Conley and Huff, 1974; General Mills, 1977; Roberts et al., 1978).

Needs Assessment

Attempts have been made to more clearly define parents' needs with respect to teaching their children about sex. Government contracts supported research that involved observation of parent classes, interviews with parents and parent sex education experts, and structured written needs assessments completed by parents and parent sex educators from around the country. These studies conducted at Mathtech, Inc. (a research consulting firm awarded major government contracts to study the impact of sex education) demonstrated parents' need for greater sexual knowledge and greater skills in making use of that knowledge in communications with their children (General Mills, 1977; Kirby et al., 1979; Alter et al., 1982).

Knowledge. Parents report that their needs for knowledge vary depending on the ages of their children. Parents of younger children need to know more about the basics: anatomy, physiology, and sexual development. Parents of older children feel they need to know more about most things, including puberty issues, contraception, and teenage pregnancy.

Skill development. Parents feel a need to learn how to be better listeners, to resolve problems, to answer questions, and to begin and maintain conversations about sex. They express considerable insecurity about communication issues. They also feel that they cannot change old patterns or overcome their own inhibitions without a course.

Adult inhibitions. Particularly significant is parents' strongly expressed need to feel more comfortable with their own sexuality and to understand better their own values about sexuality. Their emphasis and consensus on this need indicate that these more personal issues must be addressed.

Programs

Over the past ten years, existing programs have multiplied. Parent sex education programs can be found throughout the country—in cities, suburbs, and rural communities. They take place in schools, churches, and health organizations, on weekdays and weekends. They range from a few hours' duration to courses stretching over months. Programs are offered to parents of various ethnic groups and to parents with children ranging in age from infancy to eighteen years of age. They are sponsored by federal agencies, private foundations, health clinics, social service organizations, and churches.

We have also witnessed a concerted effort to ascertain whether courses for parents are, in fact, helpful. They appear to be, but evaluation results have been mixed. The Mathtech study revealed that courses increase parents' factual knowledge, help support important attitudes for educating their children, and have a modest impact on parent/child communication (Alter et al., 1982). One of the difficulties in assessing the impact of parent sex education is that programs differ in content and approach. Some educators believe that parent education is best approached as a corollary to children's courses. They keep parents informed about the child's program, hoping that parents will become more supportive of the school program and use the course as a catalyst for family discussion. Other educators offer separate courses for parents, believing that (1) parents can begin their training as sex educators of their children independently of their children's school program, preferably when their children are very young and (2) separate courses offer greater freedom to choose teachers, sponsors, and settings that best meet parents' needs, styles, and values. Those offering separate courses for parents tend to emphasize one of the following issues:

1. *Address parents' conflicted feelings.* Some educators view the major obstacle to parent/child communication about sexuality to be a combination of parents' ambivalence about sexuality and their lack of adequate sexuality education. Courses focus on helping parents resolve their own conflicts and become more comfortable with their own sexuality (e.g., they may remember and analyze their own early information about sexuality).

2. *Provide accurate information.* Many educators believe that parents lack, or feel they lack, adequate information about sexuality and child development. Courses focus on providing this knowledge to parents—knowledge about specific topics and knowledge about how children think and reason (e.g., parents watch educational films).

3. *Teach communication skills.* Other educators contend that the primary problem is that parents do not know how to communicate with their children in general and particularly about sensitive topics. Courses teach communication skills and give parents an opportunity to practice these skills (e.g., they may role-play conversations with their children).

4. *Explore attitudes and values.* Some educators, recognizing that parents are often confused about their own standards and values, contend that parents are unable to teach sexuality because they don't know what they believe or what values they want to convey. Courses based on this premise help parents explore and clarify their own attitudes about sexual issues, so that parents will be better able to explain their values to their children (e.g., they may be asked to identify and prioritize five important values they want to convey to their children).

5. *Address sexuality issues in the home.* Educators recognize that many parents attend courses because of sexuality issues arising in their own homes. A course concentrates on communication with respect to current sex-

related issues in parents' own homes (e.g., parents may be
presented with a dilemma and be asked to decide how they
would approach their child).

While these foci can be discussed as if they are distinct
and separate, they actually overlap with one another. Few
educators implement only one approach; most place more
emphasis on one approach, but also introduce the others.

Problems

Educators have been only moderately satisfied with the
success of their endeavors. In particular, it has been difficult
to fund programs, recruit participants, and maintain
attendance for multiple-session courses. Educators have felt
overwhelmed by complex, multiple goals and limited time.
It's reasonable, then, to review the amount of effort necessary
to expend on courses for parents, compare that with any
observable impact, and reconsider both the approach to
reaching parents and the most important messages they
need to receive.

The logistical issues confronting sponsors and potential
sponsors remain intimidating. Financing a successful
operation is often a challenge. A sponsor must provide a
convenient and comfortable facility, hire and often train a
teacher, provide materials, and back recruitment efforts. The
problem of securing adequate funds overlaps with the
frustration of recruiting participants. To repeatedly fill a
multi-session course for parents, it is advisable to make the
course exceptionally attractive, for example, by providing food
and babysitting, which creates an additional expense.

Even with inducements, recruiting parents to commit
themselves to more than one short evening is difficult. As
much as they may express a need and desire for courses,
parents' actual participation is another matter. Many experts
suggest that ultimately it is the parent least in need who
participates. Regardless, multi-session courses reach only a
handful of parents. Even when a program is financed and
parents are recruited, it is rarely secure. Most programs are

dependent on the efforts of a few key people. If the trained teacher and primary advocate of the program leaves, the program suffers and often disappears.

One may legitimately ask, "Is it worth the effort?" Many programs were developed to help arrest unplanned pregnancies and sexually transmitted disease among young people. Other programs cited increased and more relaxed parent/child communication about sexuality as their goal. It has been difficult to assess whether courses for parents alone have produced any such impact. We do know that courses for parents and children together can increase family communication about sexuality (Kirby, 1984). As mentioned earlier, evaluation efforts reveal that courses do have a positive impact on such areas as factual knowledge. However, it is doubtful that a short course dramatically alters the family's communication style. So the questions remain. Is the modest effect a course has on small groups of parents worth the effort? Are we doing the best we can do? How can we improve and maximize our efforts? In spite of all the questions one thing is clear. The greatest number of parents, community groups, and government agencies find parent sex education to be more acceptable than other types of programs.

Moving Ahead

We have the advantage of drawing on past experiences. The first task, therefore, is to reevaluate the goals and objectives of courses. It is often stated that sex education goals are grandiose and unrealistic. In 1979 and 1980, Mathtech, Inc., was awarded government contracts that reflected the intent of government to support sex education programs. The two primary goals of programs were to decrease unwanted adolescent pregnancies and to enhance a positive and fulfilling sexuality. To do this, educators and researchers established that it was necessary to provide parents with facts about a variety of subjects, clarify and influence their attitudes and values, develop communication skills, and help make them more comfortable with their own sexuality. All in, at the most, 12 hours! The goals and objectives of educators are admirable, but to accomplish anything in a short period of time it is imperative to set priorities.

Parents still lack a basic understanding of child development—psychological as well as physical—and puzzle over their relationship with their child at different points in the child's life. Long before unwanted pregnancies and sexually transmitted disease are a concern, children are establishing relationships and experiencing conflicts that are antecedents to normality and pathology. For example, a young boy whose every wish is granted and who is taught little respect for rules of conduct may, as an adult, have great difficulty respecting a woman's assertive "no." A young girl who has never known privacy and has been repeatedly exposed to sexual situations (e.g., sexual abuse) may have great difficulty with adult intimacy even with a loving partner. A young boy who is not taught to be responsible for his actions may not even think about contraception when he begins having sexual intercourse.

In reaction to the restrictive era when children were raised to be seen and not heard and sex was a dirty subject not to be discussed, some adults adopted permissive and overly indulgent childrearing practices. The American family has changed—more single parent homes, two career households—without giving serious thought to how childrearing practices should be adapted. Too frequently children are not provided with firm boundaries, are not required to control their impulses, do not develop a true sense of autonomy, do not learn responsibility, and are bombarded with confusing sexual messages. On the other hand, many adults, while questioning the inhibitions acquired during childhood, still exhibit their ambivalence about sexuality when unexpectedly confronted at home (e.g., exploding with anger upon discovering a child masturbating). Parents, teachers, and others in constant contact with children need to be reminded of some of the basic principles that govern character formation, such as the need for autonomy, consistency, and security. This is probably the most urgent and universal need, and ultimately, will have the greatest impact on sex-related problems in adolescence and adulthood.

Stage 1: Back to Basics

It is difficult to know where to begin. Parents definitely need to learn about normal physical and psychological development throughout childhood so that they will know what to anticipate as their children grow and develop. In addition, parents need to be reminded of a few fundamental childrearing axioms that will help them raise self-confident, responsible people who also have a positive sense of their own sexuality.

Children need to develop positive attitudes about body and gender. Adults must avoid inflicting shame and anxiety about the human body and bodily functions. They shouldn't threaten children or angrily punish them for sexual curiosity. Parents should convey the message that it is equally wonderful to be a boy or a girl—that there are special opportunities and experiences unique to each sex.

Children learn from confronting and overcoming frustrations. Adults who always take over when children face obstacles or shield them from potentially upsetting experiences interfere with children's developing sense of autonomy, self-esteem, and ability to handle problems independently. Children need to experience frustration and failure in order to learn how to overcome these obstacles. It is a joy to watch a child's delight when he or she finally experiences mastery without assistance.

Children need privacy. Many parents want their children to be spared the inhibitions common in the parents' generation. However, in their attempts to provide a home atmosphere free of hangups about bodies and bodily functions, they may also introduce situations that are often overwhelming, confusing, and not sensitive to the child's current emotional development. For example, parents should maintain reasonable standards of modesty. Locking bedroom doors and wearing clothing in front of elementary school-age children is the best policy. Of course, if a child walks in unexpectedly on a parent changing clothes in the bedroom, it is appropriate to handle the situation calmly and naturally.

Parents need to be parents, not friends, and set standards of conduct. Children develop the capacity to make responsible decisions and to set standards, but the process is not innate; it must be modeled and taught. Even though children will test the limits, they need their parents to be the authority. For example, parents may establish that swearing is forbidden in their home or that dating curfews must be adhered to. Children can learn to set their own limits if parents teach them how. As children move through adolescence and demonstrate a growing maturity, parents should gradually relinquish their control, set standards together with their children, and finally allow their children to establish their own rules.

Children need evidence of the love and respect their parents feel for them. They learn self-respect and develop self-esteem from those around them. Children notice which receives more attention—their strengths or their limitations. They remember when adults enjoy their company and appreciate their thoughts and opinions. Children also need affection at all ages. Touch nurtures self-esteem and prepares children to show love to others.

Parents need to reflect on the messages they convey when they react (or don't react) to their children's exploration and discovery of their own sexuality. For example, response to an infant's discovery of genitals is one of the first sex education lessons the child receives. Parents who ignore their adolescent's obvious display of promiscuous behavior also convey a message.

Children learn about adult relationships through their relationships with each parent and their parents' relationship with one another (or other partners). Positive, loving relationships during the good times and responsible interactions during the tough times will have lasting implications.

Children must realize that parents have private lives from which they are excluded. This can be a particularly difficult issue in single parent homes. Parents need to be careful not to make their children too important and to allow and encourage children to explore interests outside the home.

These reminders need to be heard by as many parents as possible. We hope to see a time when, as a matter of course, every school offers evening presentations covering these issues. Most of the logistical issues that have plagued previous efforts can be avoided if school administrations assume the responsibility for inviting a qualified and dynamic speaker to address the audience at a general Back-to-School night or any other meeting that large numbers of parents attend.

Stage 2: Beyond the Basics

Beyond these basic childrearing guidelines parents do need additional help dealing with specific issues related to sexuality. Educators should still make efforts to recruit parents to programs. Recruitment strategies that have been effective include:

1. Make personal contacts.
2. Conduct a lively session on the topic at a PTA or other parent group meeting to sell parents on the idea of a program.
3. Find parent leaders to assist with recruitment.
4. Conduct the program with existing groups.
5. Work with a co-sponsoring organization that currently serves parents that will assist with recruitment, such as churches.

When conducting programs, it is also important to have realistic goals for the course and an agenda for reaching these goals. What about the different approaches for educating parents discussed earlier?

As critical as it is for parents to explore their own conflicts and become more comfortable with their own sexuality, it is unrealistic to hope to accomplish this during a brief course, and the chances of finding an educator who has been adequately trained to handle this highly charged and very personal topic are slim. Many people in this society have deep conflicts about sexuality that have been with them most of their lives. Parent sex education should not become group psychotherapy. However, any course that explores sexuality has a desensitizing effect on participants. If nothing else, parents will become more used to hearing sexuality topics discussed openly in mixed company.

The list of possible knowledge topics to include in parent sex education courses is extensive—too extensive to cover in a short program. The informational needs of individual parents vary. Fortunately, a wealth of informative books is now readily available and can provide much of the necessary information to parents who are amenable to reading them. Courses should help direct parents to these resources.

An often-cited complaint about teaching communication skills is that much of parent/child communication is nonverbal and that few parents respond well to structured techniques, such as "reflective listening." Once again, it is probably unrealistic to expect family communication to change except in the grossest terms, i.e., some discussion may take the place of no discussion. In some families, that, in itself, will be a major accomplishment. Giving parents actual practice in (1) using sexual words, (2) conveying their specific values, (3) starting conversations, and (4) answering questions is one of the most useful activities any program can provide. When designing programs, educators should be aware of the limitations and pitfalls in any one approach and maintain realistic expectations about what they can accomplish. The adolescent pregnancy problem will not be eliminated by parents receiving 12 hours of instruction. However, educators can build on and strengthen the "Back to Basics" principles while offering parents factual information or practice talking about sexuality or while addressing problems arising in the home.

Today numerous parent sex education (and general sex education) curricula are available to educators. The resource list at the end of Part I describes many excellent curricula. Educators should never start from scratch; they should build on the ideas already developed by pioneers in the field.

In addition to programs, there are other strategies for helping parents become more effective sexuality educators. These include providing (1) reading lists, (2) self-teaching workbooks, (3) video education programs, and (4) media campaigns. Reaching parents can be difficult but well worth the effort. Parents play the most important role in raising their children to be responsible, healthy, and fulfilled sexual beings. Sexuality educators must always support parents in this important role.

References

Alter, J., S. Baxter, D. Kirby, and P. Wilson. *Teaching Parents to be the Primary Sex Educators of Their Children*, Vol. 1: *Impact of Programs*. Edited by A.T. Cook. Washington, D.C.: Government Printing Office, 1982.

Bennett, S.M., and W.B. Dickinson. "Student-Parent Rapport and Parent Involvement in Sex, Birth Control, and Venereal Disease Education." *The Journal of Sex Research* 16, No. 2 (1980): 114-130.

Bloch, D. "Sex Education Practices of Mothers." *Journal of Sex Education and Therapy* 4, No. 1 (1978): 7-12.

Bloch, D. "Attitudes of Mothers Toward Sex Education." *American Journal of Public Health* 69 (September 1979): 911-914

Conley, J.A., and R.S. Huff. "The Generation Gap in Sex Education: Is There One?" *The Journal of School Health* 44, No. 8 (1974): 428-437.

Fox, G.L. "The Mother-Adolescent Daughter Relationship as a Sexual Socialization Structure: A Research Review." *Family Relations* 29, No. 1 (1980): 21-28.

General Mills, Inc. *Raising Children in a Changing Society*. Minneapolis, Minn.: General Mills, Inc., 1977.

Inazu, J.K., and G.L Fox. "Maternal Influence on the Sexual
     Development   of Teenage Daughters." *Journal of
     Family Issues* 1, No. 1 (1980): 81-102.
Kirby, D. *Sexuality Education: An Evaluation of Programs
     and Their Effects.* An Executive Summary. Santa Cruz,
     Calif.: Network Publications, 1984.
Kirby, D., J. Alter, and P. Scales. *An Analysis of U.S. Sex
     Education   Programs   and   Evaluation   Methods.*
     Bethesda, Md.: Mathtech, Inc., 1979.
Lewis, R.A. "Parents and Peers: Socialization Agents in the
     Coital Behavior of Young Adults." *Journal of Sex
     Research* 9, No. 2 (1973): 156-170.
McCary, S.P. "Ages and Sources of Information for Learning
     about and Experiencing Sexual Concepts as Related by
     43 University Students." *Journal of Sex Education and
     Therapy* 4, No. 2 (1978): 50-53.
McNab, S.L. "Sexual Attitude Development in Children and
     the Parents' Role." *The Journal of School Health* 46,
     No. 9 (1976): 537-542.
Roberts, E.J., D. Kline, and J. Gagnon. *Family Life and
     Sexual   Learning.* Vol. 1. Cambridge, Mass.:
     Population Education, 1978.
Spanier, G.B. "Sources of Sex Information and Premarital
     Sexual Behavior." *The Journal of Sex Research* 13, No.
     2 (1977): 73-88.
Thornburg, H.D. "The Amount of Sex Information Learning
     Obtained During Early Adolescence." *Journal of
     Early Adolescence* 1, No. 2 (1981): 171-183.

PARENT-CHILD PROGRAMS
Jean G. Brown

In developing and promoting sex education programs in conservative, rural northwest Missouri, where teenage pregnancy rates were often higher than the national average, our efforts were frequently criticized and blocked by the philosophy that "sex education belongs in the home." Not being opposed to that idea, we explored methods for increasing parental involvement in the sexuality education process. In visiting with parents, it soon became apparent that although they supported the concept of sex education in the home, very few were providing even basic factual information to their children. Several reasons were given for their lack of involvement: (1) lack of information necessary to answer questions; (2) as children, sexuality information had not been provided in their homes and so they had no model from their parents to follow; (3) personal discomfort; (4) perceived discomfort of their children; (5) uncertainty regarding the what, when, how, and why of providing such information. We finally decided that bringing both parent and child together in the same program could be very beneficial in establishing and promoting the parent's successful involvement in the child's sex education.

Primary goals of the parent-child model include: (1) to provide necessary factual information; (2) to explore sexual attitudes, feelings, and values; (3) to promote positive self-esteem and acceptance of sexuality; (4) to enhance parent-child communication on the topic of sexuality; and (5) to strengthen the parent-child relationship.

In this model, where parent and child attend the educational program together, the success of the class depends on the participation of the parent as a "team teacher." The role of the parent must be more than that of chauffeur or chaperone. The parent actively participates in the classroom experience instead of passively observing the child learn. An introductory session, "Parents Night," helps parents understand their role in the class and can promote awareness and acceptance of the curriculum. During this session, the instructor can explain the philosophy of the course, course content, and the role of parents in the sexuality education process both in the classroom and at home. (When only one parent participates with the child, it is wise to discuss the role that the non-participating parent plays in the class experience and ways that this "absent" parent can be better incorporated into discussions at home.) Also in the introductory session, the instructor should strongly encourage parents to share stories from their past, feelings about their own body changes during puberty, experiences during pregnancies and deliveries, and opinions and values.

Parents generally have specific questions regarding curriculum content. They want to know if and how masturbation, intercourse, birth control, and abortion—to list a few subjects—will be presented. They want to know what kind of value position will accompany the facts. Discovering that the instructor will present basic facts, discuss a wide continuum of values, and refer the child back to parents for their specific values is usually reassuring. Parents also want and need reassurance that sexuality education is beneficial rather than detrimental to the child's well-being. (The myth that sexuality education increases curiosity and leads to experimentation still exists.) Other parent questions and concerns include: Can you tell children too much too soon? What if I don't know the answers to their questions? My child never asks questions, how can I get him/her to come to me? What impact do television and media have? How can I help my child deal with peer pressure and learn to make independent, responsible decisions? What if I'm not comfortable with the subject? How can I give my child contraceptive information without making it sound like I'm condoning early sexual activity? In responding to such concerns, the instructor can solicit input from the group in addition to offering his or her own ideas. Building a supportive parent network contributes to a successful class experience and to increased parental involvement in sexuality education.

An advantage of the parent-child model is that parent and child are learning the facts and new communication skills together. This enhances and reinforces the factual learning and skill-building. Learning together establishes a common frame of reference and terminology that facilitates communication on the subject. Parents become more knowledgeable and often more comfortable providing information and answering questions. Thus, parents get established, in their children's eyes, as available and approachable resources.

The groups, which consist of twelve to thirty persons (six to fifteen parent-child pairs), also encourage an exchange of ideas, values, and feelings among parents and youth in a relaxed, nonthreatening atmosphere. The program structure allows for communication not only between parent and child but also with other parents and children. Peer interaction and support are important for both parents and youth. Parent feedback and course follow-up studies indicate that learning and practicing communication skills together facilitates communication outside the program both during and after the course. This is a particularly important outcome of the program because better communication seems to have an impact on the child's future sexual experience. Studies by Lewis and by Spanier suggest that improving communication within families can help reduce adolescents' irresponsible sexual behavior and decrease unwanted pregnancies.

Due to the differences in developmental abilities and informational needs, classes are generally designed for pre-adolescents (nine- to twelve-year-olds) and early adolescents (thirteen- to fifteen-year-olds). Beyond this age segregation, the parent-child model allows for many variations. Instructor and community preferences often determine the class structure. In some instances, classes are segregated by sex, and so mothers usually attend with their daughters and fathers attend with their sons. However, the opposite-sexed parent could attend (i.e., mothers with sons) or a parent substitute (grandparent, adult friend, foster parent, aunt/uncle) could participate. Classes can be totally segregated or can allow for some coed dialogue or shared film viewing when two segregated classes are taught simultaneously. Coeducational programs are especially appropriate for the adolescent population. One or both parents can participate with their child in the educational experience.

Optimum group size is approximately twenty persons, with a suitable range of twelve to fifteen. Classes of fewer than twelve participants may place extra demands on the participants and may detract from the group process; classes in excess of thirty participants may restrict the amount of time that the instructor has for questions and individual attention.

It is important that group activities, films, mini-lectures, discussions, and games be designed to allow parents and children to have fun together as well as to learn. Activities should promote a discussion of (1) facts and (2) the feelings, opinions, and values that correspond to the fact; this establishes communication on two levels between parent and child. Still other activities provide opportunities for joint decision-making and problem-solving.

The parent-child model employs a variety of learning formats. Children need the opportunity to relate to their parent(s) and to peers and other adults; parents also need the chance to relate to peers and other children, as well as to their own son/daughter. Parent/child dyads, small groups of two or three parent-child pairs, groups of youth and groups of parents followed by total group process can accomplish this familial and peer interaction and support. Thus, participants get to observe a variety of communication styles.

Finally, the opportunity to ask anonymous questions is critical for the success in this parent-child educational mix. At the end of each session all participants place a question or comment in a question box. Questions are then answered at the beginning of the next session. This allows children to ask sophisticated questions and parents to ask simplistic questions without embarrassment or identification.

Ten to twelve hours is adequate to cover the necessary curriculum content and is a reasonable time commitment by both parents and youth. This time can be spread over five to six weeks or spent in a more concentrated format (two sessions per week; weekend retreat). Evening sessions are usually necessary for parental involvement.

Courses for preteens and early teens discuss reproductive anatomy and physiology, body changes during puberty, health and hygiene, reproduction, pregnancy, and childbirth. In sex segregated programs, the basic curricula for male and female classes are very similar. It is important that both cover the same topics so that boys and girls learn about the male and female body functions, but some topics are covered more thoroughly in one class than in the other. For example, both classes discuss menstruation, but the girls' class covers it in greater depth. Preteens are generally more interested in factual information regarding normal body changes and how to integrate these changes into their body image and daily living. Opportunities to discuss being different from their friends and coping with body changes (i.e., menstruation, wet dreams) are critical.

Adolescent classes cover, in greater detail, the same basic factual information and additional subjects more appropriate to teenagers. Breast and pelvic examinations, sexually transmitted diseases, teenage pregnancy/parenthood, dating, birth control methods, and sexual decision-making are included in the adolescent curriculum. Early adolescents are more concerned about sexual feelings, the expression of these feelings, dating, and peer relations/pressure. Values clarification, communication, and decision-making skills are emphasized in courses for both preteens and early adolescents.

At the Family Guidance Center in St. Joseph, Missouri, approximately 3,000 people have completed the program since it pioneered in October 1976. Many parents have taken the course with each of their children. Other parents have participated in the nine- to twelve-year-old program and then graduated to the adolescent program. Groups such as schools, PTAs, YMCAs, YWCAs, churches, youth organizations, Girl Scouts, community education programs, and county university extension offices have co-sponsored these classes. Some churches have offered an optional extra class session that provides the church's views on sexuality; both clergy and lay persons have been involved. This endorsement and support lend a credibility to the program that is extremely important when the program is offered for the first time in a new community. The sponsoring organization can identify the needs of the community and can determine which class(es) to offer. (Parent/daughter nine- to twelve-year-old classes are almost always in demand and are readily filled as these parents seem to recognize that puberty is imminent for their daughters and want help providing information for the children.) The sponsoring group can also (1) select an acceptable location and schedule, (2) provide the room, equipment, and refreshments, (3) recruit participants, and (4) handle registration.

The nine counties served by the Family Guidance Center/ Community Mental Health Center have demonstrated much enthusiasm for the project. Several communities offer the programs annually. One community has offered the four courses each year since 1976. A local PTA established an ongoing committee that schedules and coordinates parent-child classes for its school every year. In fact, two staff persons teaching three evenings per week during September through November and January through May were unable to meet the demand for programs. Therefore, we conducted training programs with local education, health, and mental health professionals so that they could conduct programs themselves. Now many of these communities have local resources (e.g., teachers, school nurses, public health nurses, 4-H youth workers, etc.) to provide the desired programs. Labeled as one of the exemplary sex education programs in the country, our program was evaluated during 1980-1982 by an independent research firm, Mathtech, Inc., through a contract from the Center for Health Promotion and Education, Centers for Disease Control. The evaluation proved that participants gained knowledge, became more aware of their values, and increased parent-child communication regarding sexuality. Due to the involvement of both parent and child in the learning process, these benefits are more likely to continue after the course is completed. For many families, participation in the program marked the beginning of a more formal sexuality education process within the family. However, the class format facilitates the continuation of this process as parents become established as resources whom children can consult throughout their adolescent years. Family members have the communication skills and the comfort level to approach questions, issues, and concerns together.

References

Brown, J., L. Peterson, and R. Linebarger. *Parent-Child Sex Education: A Training Module.* St. Joseph, Missouri: Parent-Child Experience, Inc., 1982.

Kirby, D. "The Effects of Selected Sexuality Education Programs: Toward a More Realistic View." *Journal of Sex Education and Therapy* (Spring/Summer 1985): 28-37.

Kirby, D., L. Peterson, and J. Brown. "Joint Parent-Child Sex Education." *Child Welfare* LXI, No. 2 (February 1982): 105-114.

Lewis, R.A. "Parents and Peers: Socialization Agents in the Coital Behavior of Young Adults." *Journal of Sex Research* 9, No. 2 (1973): 156-170.

Spanier, G.B. "Sources of Sex Information and Premarital
      Sexual Behavior." *The Journal of Sex Research* 13, No.
      2 (1977): 73-88.

A GAY CHILD IN THE FAMILY
Wayne V. Pawlowski

"You're what?"

"I'm gay!"

There is probably no other dialogue between parent and child that causes such anger, panic, guilt, and shame for parents. No parent expects to have a gay or lesbian child; and no child expects to be gay or lesbian. But, some children *are* gay and some parents have homosexual children. In fact we know that about 10 percent of our population will grow up to be predominantly homosexual and that this will occur despite the wishes, plans, guidance, and religious beliefs of the individuals and families affected. Yet few, if any, parents seriously contemplate the fact that they could turn out to be the parents of one of that 10 percent.

Parents of young children may have concerns about homosexuality that are expressed by discouraging "sissiness" in boys and "tomboyishness" in girls. As their children grow into teenagers, parents may wonder if their children are masculine or feminine enough. Parents may even go so far as to say, "We don't want any queers in this family!" However, it is a very unusual parent who translates these concerns into conscious thoughts about the probability of having a homosexual child. Any real questions or fears about this possibility are usually left buried unless events or words force them into consciousness. In other words, most parents will not think about homosexuality unless homosexuality makes itself known within their family.

Assumptions of Heterosexuality

Parents raise their children on the assumption that they will be heterosexual, presenting only a heterosexual role model for life and mating. Parents are strongly supported by the larger culture in this regard. With few exceptions, there are no visible, positive, homosexual role models for children. It is true that within the diverse cultural groups that make up the United States, some differences in male-female roles, expectations, etc., may be found. However, the basic model of sexual expression and coupling is almost always heterosexual.

This leaves the 10 percent of children who will inevitably grow up to be homosexual in a very isolated situation. They have received clear messages regarding who and what they are *supposed* to be but as they grow up they slowly realize that they are "different." They do not have feelings of romantic and sexual attraction toward persons of the opposite sex. Try as they may (and most will try *very* hard) they cannot make those feelings happen. As homosexual children become aware of this significant difference, they simultaneously begin to realize that no one has prepared them for this difference; and they have no positive, readily available ways to explore what this difference means. No one is there to answer their newly discovered questions. No one is there to affirm their worth as human beings.

Causes of Homosexuality

But why do some children grow up with this difference? Where does homosexuality come from? How can homosexuality develop in a culture that presents only heterosexual role models? Why does it persist despite the strong sanctions and messages against it?

The answers to these questions are both simple and complex. The simple answer is that no one really knows what causes homosexuality or why it exists. Nor, for that matter, do we know what causes heterosexuality or bisexuality. The complex answer involves all of what we currently "know" and theorize about genetics, fetal development, and human growth and development. As yet, however, there is no clear or final answer to how all of these complicated issues contribute to, or cause homosexuality (if they do at all).

Over the years many theories about the causes of homosexuality have been suggested. These have included unhealthy family dynamics, exposure to homosexuals, early homosexual experiences, early sexual abuse, mental illness, developmental lags/fixations, hormonal differences, and genetic differences. Many of these theories were based upon unstudied or untested hypotheses, generalizations made from therapy-patient populations, unscientific and biased research designs, misinterpretation of earlier writings and research, and a starting premise that homosexuality was bad and/or unnatural and therefore, had to have an unhealthy or pathological cause.

In the past 10 to 15 years all of these old theories have been carefully reexamined under the critical eye of new knowledge and with greater respect for scientific research methodology. The results of this new examination clearly disprove some theories, raise more questions than answers about others, and leave us with the conclusion that none of the old theories by themselves can adequately explain all cases of homosexuality. The best that can be concluded at this time is that there is some evidence for both biological and environmental components. As with all human behavior, however, how and why one person behaves one way and another person with seemingly the same background and experience behaves in another way is a very complicated phenomenon.

One thing, however, can be stated with a fair degree of certainty. That is, parents are not to blame if they have a child who grows up to be predominantly homosexual. In other words, a child does not become a homosexual simply because of something a parent did or did not do. Whatever the cause(s), it appears to be much more complicated and much more powerful than parental influence alone.

Awareness of Early Differences

Most gay men and lesbians report with adult hindsight they knew something was "different" about them when they were growing up. However, because they were children they did not have any way of knowing that what they felt really was different from what most heterosexual children feel. As children, gays and lesbians have no reference point or comparison for their feelings, have no words or concepts to describe them, and therefore, would not typically even think about sharing them with anyone. As a result, these feelings of difference are seldom, if ever, communicated to anyone until adulthood.

This reported "difference," as it is later described in adulthood, appears to be a vague, yet pervasive, emotional and physical attraction to members of the same sex. During childhood this early attraction is not overtly sexual in nature and does not become so until adolescence, the time in life when sexual maturation takes place. Unfortunately, by the time most children reach adolescence and become consciously aware of these feelings, they have been exposed to enough negative messages about sex, in general, and about homosexual sex, specifically, that they learn not to talk with anyone about these feelings.

The Peer Group and Heterosexual Youth

At the same time that sexual feelings become overt and children begin to feel they cannot talk about these feelings, the peer group begins to replace parents and family as the primary source of information and force of socialization. For most young people, the peer group becomes the primary arena for experimentation regarding identity and relationships.

For heterosexual youths the peer group is vast, visible, and accessible. Within it heterosexual youths begin to learn about and practice their newly emerging heterosexuality. They are able to talk about sexual topics, experience emotional attachments and rejection, learn how to talk to and interact with others to whom they are sexually attracted, learn how to date and court someone, and develop a sense of themselves as sexual beings. Heterosexual adolescents take this learning and experience from the peer group context and try it out in other settings. The positive or negative feedback they receive validates their behavior as appropriate, inappropriate, or marginal in a given situation. As a result of this practicing, by the time they are young adults most heterosexual youths have had the opportunity to learn about, experiment with, and integrate many sexual and nonsexual experiences into their own newly developing value systems. These value systems become the foundations for later (one hopes, responsible) sexual behaviors.

The Peer Group and Homosexual Youth

Most homosexual youths, on the other hand, generally have no peer group (or any visible, accessible reference group) in which they can begin to learn about and understand their "different" romantic feelings. Homosexual adolescents have no peer group affording them the opportunity to learn who they are or to help them lay the foundation for later adult sexual behaviors. In fact, within the adolescent subculture, homosexuality is devalued, actively avoided, and frequently persecuted. As a result, rather than finding support and acceptance from peers, most homosexual youths go through adolescence with a profound sense of isolation.

In order to protect their identities and avoid rejection by friends and loved ones, many homosexual youth deny their homosexual feelings or pretend they have heterosexual feelings. As a result they often become masters of disguise in an attempt to cover their sexual feelings, their profound fears, and their confusion. To make matters worse, few, if any, homosexual adolescents are able to find any supportive environment in which to explore who they are. Nor are most able to turn to their families for support or constructive feedback as they attempt to integrate their newly discovered homosexuality into their newly developing value systems and identities.

Unfortunately, most homosexual youths develop their early value systems and identities from societal messages about homosexuality rather than from interactions with others who share their sexual orientation. Examples of these societal messages in the late 1980s have included:

1. The Supreme Court decision upholding the Georgia sodomy laws,
2. The much-publicized notion that AIDS is God's punishment for homosexuals,
3. The negative, often violent, anti-gay graffiti on the walls of public rest-rooms,
4. A community health service's decision to exclude a dial-a-health-question-tape on homosexuality because it is too "controversial,"
5. A university's refusal to recognize a non-political, gay student support group,
6. A state initiative to prohibit homosexuals from teaching in public schools,
7. The many attempts across the country to strike down recently passed laws protecting the civil rights of homosexuals.

These negative societal messages lead most homosexual youths to grow up with a feeling that they are not worthwhile or valued human beings. Even worse, however, is the fact that this unaccepting and negative attitude in our society almost precludes homosexual youth from talking about, learning about, and practicing responsible, adult, homosexual relationships and behaviors until after they "come out," which usually occurs in adulthood. (Coming out is a complicated and involved concept that refers to the process of self-realization, acceptance of one's feelings, and a movement "out" to meet and interact with other gay/lesbian individuals.) Since many homosexual youth will secretly and anonymously experiment with their sexuality *before* they come out, they are left at dramatically increased risk of contracting the deadly and as yet untreatable AIDS virus (this is especially true for boys).

Young Gay/Lesbian Socialization

In most communities "gay bars" are usually the only "known" places where someone can go to meet homosexuals. As with heterosexual singles bars, these night spots do not lend themselves easily to the development of meaningful relationships. Nor do they usually reflect the value systems within which most young people have grown up. Unfortunately, this generally foreign environment becomes the primary arena in which most young-adult homosexuals begin their long-delayed experimentation with and learning about relationships, sexual behaviors, and who they are. Unfortunately, now that the legal drinking age is twenty-one years in most states, gay and lesbian teenagers are left without any place to meet others like themselves. This situation only compounds the homosexual adolescent's isolation and inability to begin the learning and practice that heterosexual adolescents are so easily able to accomplish.

Many young gays and lesbians who begin their "gay socialization" in bars find themselves going through a period of frequent and depersonalized sexual encounters or a series of short, intense, emotional relationships. Unfortunately, these periods usually occur before the young people are able to find a supportive, nurturing, and mentoring peer group in which to share their feelings and gain perspective on their experiences. By the time many young homosexuals find these peer groups, they have been battered by numerous unhappy experiences and often feel disillusioned or cynical. Only after they diversify their activities and friends are these gay men and lesbians able to begin developing a broader and healthier sense of themselves and their world.

Homosexuality in the Family

When parents learn that one of their children is gay or lesbian, they frequently view this as a tragedy; the family has somehow been disgraced. However, the tragedy is *not* that a family has a homosexual member because 10 percent of all families will have homosexual members. Rather, the real tragedy is that family messages about homosexuality are so frequently negative and condemnatory that homosexual children often turn away from their parents for love and understanding. In fact, gay and lesbian children often feel they must turn *anywhere* other than to their families for the love, help, and support that they and all children so desperately need. This is borne out by the fact that the majority of gay men and lesbians do not tell their parents about their homosexuality. Their fear of parental rejection and/or condemnation is, in fact, a realistic one since so many parents do reject their children who come out to them.

Ideal Parental Responses to Homosexuality

What, then, would be the ideal response to homosexuality? In the best of all possible worlds how would parents educate their children about this complex subject?

In a truly ideal world, parents would be neither heterosexist nor homophobic. (Heterosexism is the assumption that heterosexuality is always preferable to everything else; homophobia is an intense, usually irrational, fear and hatred of homosexuality.) Ideally, parents would expose their children in an open and accepting way to information about homosexuality and they would try to have gay men and lesbians be part of their children's lives. In most extended families there are homosexual members. Parents would interact with and talk about these family members openly and positively. If there were no homosexual family members, parents would present gay friends or colleagues as ordinary people with the same diversity of values, aspirations, needs, and goals as all other people.

Children of these parents would learn that:
- When strong sexual feelings and desires begin to surface, some of these feelings and desires may be for members of the opposite sex and some may be for members of the same sex.

- This mix is normal, natural, and a common part of growing up.
- For some people the same-sex feelings will never occur or will fade away almost completely.
- For still others there will always be a mix of same-sex and opposite-sex feelings, either fading or increasing throughout their lives.
- Caring friendships with persons of both sexes and all orientations are possible and desirable.

These parents would emphasize that no matter what sexual feelings and desires a person has at any time:

- *No one* should *ever* exploit, take advantage of, or force sexual feelings or desires onto someone else.
- No one should ever use his or her age, power, or relationship with someone to intimidate or manipulate a person into a sexual relationship.

Simultaneously, these parents in an ideal world would encourage open and accepting communication about all of these issues within the family. In addition, parents would:

- Encourage and respect whatever sexual feelings their children develop.
- Make their children feel good about who they are and what they feel.
- Teach their children the appropriate values and ethics that accompany sexual expression, development of relationships, and acceptance of responsibility.

Realistic Parental Responses

But what can parents who live in the real heterosexist and homophobic world say and do about homosexuality? How can parents be most helpful to potentially gay children? First and foremost, parents should admit that regardless of how open and accepting they are, they probably would prefer *not* to have a gay or lesbian child. This world is hostile to homosexuals, and few caring parents want their children to be the objects of society's hostility.

Taking this as a starting point with no need to apologize for or feel guilty, parents who want to be helpful to a potentially gay child can take as many of the ideal responses as possible and implement them as best they can. At the very least, parents can read about homosexuality so they can be knowledgeable. They can try to be aware of language, jokes, and remarks that are homophobic, heterosexist, or cast homosexuals in a degrading light. They should not allow these words or jokes in their home, and they should be clear as to why they consider them to be unacceptable. Also, parents need to remember that in a basically heterosexual household the subject of homosexuality will not naturally come up. Parents will need to look for and use many different opportunities to discuss homosexuality in front of and with their children.

Beyond these specific suggestions, all other general guidelines for open communication about sexuality within the family can be used. There are many good books available for parents that include suggestions for creating a climate that facilitates honest and open communication about sexuality within the family.

Limitations on the Best of Intentions

At this point it is important to point out that even the most understanding, loving, and accepting parents will have difficulty knowing how best to respond to and be a resource to a gay or lesbian child. Most parents (though not all) are heterosexual and as a result do not have the life experience to fully prepare a homosexual child for life in a heterosexual world. Heterosexual parents do not share their homosexual child's "culture" and as a result most are not able to "enculturate" their child. They cannot fully prepare him or her to confront and survive the homophobic discrimination that gays and lesbians so often experience in the heterosexual world.

A Final Note

As a final note, parents who wonder whether their child is homosexual do not necessarily have to wait for the child to volunteer the information. Parents can approach their child and ask directly, as long as they are willing to hear and accept the real answer and not just be reassured that their child is heterosexual. While most parents may not believe it at the time, they have already done some important things right if their child is able to tell them that he or she is homosexual. Usually if children feel safe enough to tell parents about homosexual feelings, the parents have created a powerful, loving, accepting, and trusting bond, and they have already done much to help their child along an inevitably difficult path.

Much has been written about, by, and for parents of gay men and lesbians. Any parent who is faced with the reality of a gay or lesbian child should contact the National Federation of Parents and Friends of Lesbians and Gays (PFLAG), P.O. Box 24565, Los Angeles, CA 90024 to obtain literature, guidance, and support. PFLAG has chapters in most states and larger cities.

RESOURCES ON HOMOSEXUALITY

Books

Back, Gloria Guss. *Are You Still My Mother? Are You Still My Family?* New York: Warner Books, 1985.

A combination of vignettes about parents of gay people. Provides the outline and content of the author's workshops for families of gay people in New York. Sensitive and moving, yet full of good information and guidance. Gives parents something to help them through the turmoil that accompanies the discovery that a child is a homosexual.

Borhek, Mary V. *Coming Out to Parents: A Two-Way Survival Guide for Lesbians and Gay Men and Their Parents.* Pilgrim Press, 132 West 31st Street, New York, NY 10001, 1983.

Sound, sympathetic, and helpful advice from a parent who has herself been through the experience of her child's "coming out." Includes section on religious issues.

Fairchild, Betty, and Nancy Hayward. *Now That You Know: What Every Parent Should Know About Homosexuality.* New York: Harcourt, Brace, Jovanovich, 1979.

Written by two mothers of gay children, this book is still one of the best available for parents of gays and lesbians. In addition to a great deal of "case" material, it contains information about homosexuality, a review of relevant biblical passages, and an overview of the positions of several churches on the issue of homosexuality. Universally described by parents as "very helpful."

Fricke, Aaron. *Reflections of a Rock Lobster: A Story About Growing Up Gay.* Boston: Alyson Publications, 1981.

Probably the best book available that describes what it is like to grow up gay. After years of turmoil and self-hate, Aaron Fricke "comes out" and winds up taking his high school to court in order to take a male date to his senior prom. He wins. A true, sensitive, moving, sad, yet uplifting, story. A must for anyone who wants to better understand the pain of growing up gay.

Hanckel, Frances, and John Cunningham. *A Way of Love, A Way of Life: A Young Person's Introduction to What It Means to Be Gay.* New York: Lothrop, Lee and Shepard, 1979.

Fills a void that existed in sex education literature for teenagers. Offers a tremendous amount of information about the gay lifestyle and includes chapters on "How to Tell If You're Gay," "Asking for Help," and "Family Relationships and Friendships." Written for all young people but is especially for those who might be confused about their sexual orientation. The authors provide support for young people in this situation without pressuring them to be one way or the other.

Heron, Ann, ed. *One Teenager in 10: Writings by Gay and Lesbian Youth.* Boston: Alyson Publications, 1983.

An excellent book to read after *Reflections of a Rock Lobster.* Gay and lesbian youth tell their own stories about what it is like to grow up "different." Sometimes painful, sometimes inspiring, the stories all touch the heart. These vignettes do not have the depth of *Rock Lobster* but rather provide a broad look at the many complicated situations gay and lesbian youth face while growing up.

Human Rights Federation. *Demystifying Homosexuality: a Teaching Guide about Lesbians and Gay Men.* New York: Irvington Publishers, 1984.

A curriculum that includes classroom techniques, lesson plans, questions, answers, and discussion about the lifestyles, concerns, and sexuality of lesbians, gay men, and bisexuals. Lists community and educational resources.

Martin, Del, and Phyllis Lyon. *Lesbian/Woman*. New York: Bantam, 1983.

Written by a couple who have been together over 25 years. Depicts what it is like to grow up gay, to be a lesbian mother, and to face living, loving, and surviving as a lesbian in a male-dominated world. Provides a review of the gains and setbacks in lesbian culture over the past 10 years.

McWhirter, David P., and Andrew M. Mattison. *The Male Couple: How Relationships Develop*. Englewood Cliffs, N.J.: Prentice-Hall, 1984.

A study of 156 male couples involved in relationships ranging from one to 37 years. Describes six ages and stages of pair-bonding that will also prove valuable to those interested in heterosexual relationships.

SMYAL, ed. *Sexual Minority Youth: An Annotated Bibliography*. Washington, D.C.: SMYAL Library, 1984.

The SMYAL (Sexual Minority Youth Assistance League) bibliography is probably the most comprehensive reference available anywhere that deals specifically with the issue of homosexual youth. It contains both light reading and scientific journal articles and is an indispensable help in finding out what has been published about gay and lesbian youth. It has two sections for youth (fiction and non-fiction), a section for parents and a section for youth workers. It is published by the SMYAL Library, 1638 R Street, N.W., #2, Washington, DC 20009.

Switzer, David, and Shirley Switzer. *Parents of the Homosexual*. Philadelphia: The Westminster Press, 1980.

Written for Christian parents but is useful for parents from any religious background. Looks at the guilt and anger that parents often feel toward their homosexual children, themselves, and even God. Contains an in-depth discussion of biblical references to homosexuality and helps parents find ways to reconcile their child's sexual orientation with the parents' religious beliefs. An excellent resource for parents struggling with religious and spiritual issues.

Audiovisuals

First Dance. Producer/Distributor: Fanlight Productions, Video, 19 min., 1986.

Portrays the case of a Rhode Island high school student who was denied the right to attend the senior prom with his male date. The action takes place in the courtroom as the young man fights for his first-amendment rights. Although the gay adolescent is somewhat stereotyped, the film is an excellent discussion stimulant. Focus is on attitudes rather than information about homosexuality, so facilitators will have to supply facts either before or after the film. For adolescent and adult audiences.

Michael, a Gay Son. Producer/Distributor: Filmmakers Library, 16mm., 28 min., 1981.

A docudrama about a young man, Michael, who reveals his homosexuality to his family. Realistically explores typical family reactions. In a moving session, a family therapist enables family members to honestly reveal what Michael's homosexuality means to them. Requires additional clarification after viewing the film to point out the misinformation that many of Michael's family members believed about homosexuality. For parents and professionals. (White characters.)

On Being Gay: A Conversation with Brian McNaught Producer/Distributor: TRB Productions, Video, 80 min., 1986.

Award-winning author, counselor, and lecturer Brian McNaught talks with enthusiasm and authority about the fallacies, facts, and, most importantly, feelings of being gay in a "straight" world. Can be shown in two separate 40-minute segments. Excellent for parents and professionals. (White characters.)

Pink Triangles. Producer/Distributor: Cambridge
   Documentary Films, 16 mm or Video, 35 min., 1982.

   A film about homophobia, specifically, and
discrimination and oppression, generally. Examines both
historical and contemporary patterns of persecution in which
racial, religious, political, and sexual minorities become
societal victims. Gay men and lesbians from many racial and
cultural backgrounds tell their individual stories.

What About McBride? Producer/Distributor: McGraw-Hill
   Films, 16 mm, 10 min., 1974

   Portrays two teenage boys who, while planning a rafting
trip down a river, discuss McBride as a possible companion.
One of the boys rejects McBride because he has heard that
McBride is homosexual. The ensuing argument brings out
the typical myths and stereotypes about homosexuals.
Although dated, it is a good trigger film for sparking
discussion and thought. For adolescent audiences. (White
characters.)

SEXUAL ABUSE PREVENTION: ISSUES AND ANSWERS

Sol Gordon

The problem of child sexual abuse is serious. Tens of thousands of children are victimized every year, yet our societal reaction tends to be simplistic, superficial, and, at times, outrageous.

Problems in Current Prevention Efforts

Central to the sexual abuse field is the myth: "If you teach kids to say 'no,' the molester will go away." In fact, there is little evidence to substantiate this position. We are now discovering that most abused children have tried to say "no" without success. The message indirectly communicated to these children is that the abuse was basically their fault, because had they said "no" (or used karate), they would have been safe.

Most of the work in sexual abuse prevention is an attempt to isolate this "problem" from the larger issues of the role of parents as sex educators and the need for sex education in the schools. The assumption is this: if educators don't emphasize sex, but stress instead the concept of protecting one's "private parts," school administrators or fanatical opponents of sex education won't be offended. Worst of all, there seem to be few messages for the molester. There is now overwhelming evidence that molesters are aware of their deviant urges and may begin acting them out during their adolescent years when they could still be reached.

A Better Approach

For progress to be made in prevention, American society must develop a commitment to comprehensive sexuality education in both schools and community organizations. This education should portray sexuality as a positive, natural, and important component of the human personality. Most importantly, programs should stress that being touched is a basic need that we all have. Caring touch helps each individual to thrive as a sexual person.

We need to initiate sensible sexual abuse prevention programs within the context of comprehensive sexuality/family life education courses. Essentially, these programs should include the following messages: Some people—mostly males—for reasons that we don't entirely understand, get sexually turned on by children. In many situations, they were themselves molested as children. If they act out—seduce or rape children (yes, we need to use the word rape)—it often becomes a habit that's very difficult to break. It is like having a drug or alcohol problem.

Here's what potential abusers need to know:

1. Sexual abuse is always, always, harmful to the child.
2. It is illegal and will get you into a lot of trouble, including long prison terms.
3. It will mean, if you become addicted, that you will not be able to have a normal, healthy relationship with an adult partner.
4. It is essential that you get professional help.
5. In the meantime, until you can be helped or cured, every time you have the urge to molest a child, go off to a private place and masturbate.
6. Masturbation is a more appropriate outlet for sexual urges than sex with children.
7. Finally, no child can legally give consent no matter what you think, even if you can rationalize your

behavior with the idea that not only did the child consent but it was good for the child.

Of course, there is hardly a school, church, or social agency in the whole country that would be willing to include these messages in their sexual abuse prevention efforts. Unfortunately, too many people believe that society's "sexual permissiveness" is responsible for the problem. However, sexual permissiveness has nothing to do with this behavior. It is also not widely understood that when people feel guilty about sexual thoughts, guilt becomes the energy for the thoughts and obsessive urges. Most people have inappropriate and deviant urges but are able to deal with them in a mature way, either by self-control or masturbation or by achieving "relief" through appropriate sexual behavior.

Parental Role

In the meantime, parents can take responsibility for educating their own children. Even if a child has been abused, a calm parental response can make the difference between the child perceiving the event as an unfortunate incident or a tragedy that will haunt the child for the rest of his or her life. Parents need to teach children that no one is allowed to touch, or play with, or fondle their genitals (penis, vulva, vagina) or anus, or breasts (for girls), and they are not allowed to touch anyone else's. The sexual words must be used. "Private parts" implies that the sexual parts of the body can't be named or discussed. In addition, children must be taught not to go with or take anything from strangers. Then, they must learn to be assertive, to say "no." Children should also know that it's always all right to lie to protect themselves and to say they won't tell and then, when they are safe, to tell an adult they trust.

Educators only confuse children when they use the terms "good and bad touching." We all know that most sexual touching feels good. "Right and wrong touching" is clearer terminology.

Current Problems to Overcome

A frightening over-reaction to fears of sexual abuse is now occurring. Parents, grandparents, teachers, and day-care workers are becoming afraid to touch, hug and kiss children. Children need hugging and touching more, not less. It is essential for their mental health and self-esteem.

Every teenager and adult knows the difference between sexually exploitive touching and loving touching. And no parent need fear that telling their children about sexual abuse will prevent the children from having a normal sex life when they grow up. Children who are loved integrate this information relatively easily.

Apart from the terrible unreadiness and insensitivity of the legal system in handling problems of sexual abuse, there has been a scandalous rise in the number of false accusations (very few made by children under five but quite a few by older children who are sometimes being used for malicious reasons by their parents).

People across the country who have been unjustly accused are now banding together to protect themselves through a new organization called Victims of Child Abuse Laws (VOCAL). In citing this, my purpose is not to deflect attention from the real problem of sexual abuse—for every false accusation, 100 cases are real. However, we must remain aware that even a single false accusation is a serious matter.

Prevention in the Future

It behooves all of us to at least begin taking these matters seriously and move our interventions to a new level. We have to stop putting the onus on the victim and, in the process, provide a network of support for abused children. Professionals are discovering more and more that the abused children who suffer the most are those who told someone and were not rescued. We must make it publicly known that most of the children who have been abused were abused by people they knew and trusted. Every nursery, every elementary school, every PTA in the country must conduct educational programs focused on sensible prevention strategies. To have meaningful impact, audiences must include staff, parents, and children.

References

Caldwell, Bettye M. "How and When to Talk to Your Child About Sex Abuse." *Working Mother* (January 1985).

Carnes, Patrick. *The Sexual Addiction.* Minneapolis: CompCare Publications, 1983.

Finkelhor, David. *Child Sexual Abuse—New Theory and Research.* New York: The Free Press, 1984.

Gilgun, Jane, and Sol Gordon. "Sex Education and the Prevention of Child Sexual Abuse." *Journal of Sex Education and Therapy* 11:46-52.

Koblinksy, Sally, and Nory Behana. "Child Sexual Abuse— The Educator's Role in Prevention, Detection and Intervention." *Young Children* (September 1984).

Special Child Sexual Abuse Issue. *SIECUS Report,* 13, No. 1 (September 1984).

Special Child Sexual Abuse Issue. *IMPACT '85.* Out of print. Ed-U Press, P.O. Box 583, Fayetteville, NY 13066.

RESOURCES ON CHILD SEXUAL ABUSE PREVENTION

Curricula

Anderson, Cordelia, in collaboration with Illusion Theater. *Touch Continuum Study Cards: Sexual Abuse Prevention Educational Study Cards for Elementary Grades.* Santa Cruz, Calif.: Network Publications, 1981.

An excellent supplement to other programs, these large laminated cards are designed so that the teacher may hold them up while reading off the back. One side contains illustrations depicting different kinds of touch; the other side contains discussion questions and discussion points. Examples of the types of illustrations shown are: playful touch, games, kissing, squeezing, wrestling, bullying, trusting your senses, recognizing sexual abuse without touch, helping and talking to someone.

Anderson, Cordelia. *No Easy Answers: A Sexual Abuse Prevention Curriculum for Junior and Senior High Students.* Santa Cruz, Calif.: Network Publications, 1982.

Twenty lessons designed to help students develop skills in communication of their feelings, attitudes, and expectations related to sexuality and sexual exploitation and to teach students protection and prevention skills. It presents ideas from which many other curricula have drawn.

Cooper, Sally, Yvonne Luther, and Cathy Phelps. *Strategies for Free Children: A Leader's Guide to Child Assault Prevention.* Intrepid Clearing House, P.O. Box 02084, Columbus, OH 43202, 1983.

A complete guide to conducting a community-based Child Abuse Prevention (CAP) project involving parents, educators, and elementary-age children. Includes detailed narrative of workshops for children and adults, including commonly asked questions and suggested answers. This guide grew out of workshops done by a National Assault Prevention Center, CAP-STRATEGIES, in Columbus, Ohio.

Gilder, Sharon Allen. *Safety, Touch and Me.* Sexual Assault Service, 751 Rockville Pike, Suite 268, Rockville, MD 20850.

Designed to teach children in grades 4-6 specific prevention techniques to avoid assault. Teaches what to do if assaulted and encourages children to talk with a parent or trusted adult. Available free.

Girls Clubs of Omaha. *Kid-Ability, A Self-Protection Program for Children.* 3706 Lake Street, Omaha, NE 68111, 1985.

Outlines an interactive six-hour workshop for children, which uses skill-building, role-playing and art activities. Materials include an instructor's manual available to those trained to present the workshops, a children's journal, and a volunteer's guide to helping children during the workshop.

Harms, Ruth, Donna James, and Margaret Schonfield. *Talking About Touching: A Personal Safety Curriculum.* Santa Cruz, Calif.: Network Publications, 1984.

This outstanding curriculum was developed to teach elementary school children how to protect themselves from exploitation, particularly sexual exploitation. Emphasizes the importance of teaching children to think independently and encourages the kind of decision-making that will protect them when they encounter a potentially dangerous situation. Incorporates the use of large photographs as teaching aids.

O'Day, Bonnie. *Preventing Sexual Abuse of Persons with Disabilities: A Curriculum for Hearing Impaired, Physically Disabled, Blind, and Mentally Retarded Students.* Santa Cruz, Calif.: Network Publications, 1983.

A set of 8-9 lesson plans is provided for adolescents in each of the four groups named in the subtitle, as well as suggested modifications for younger students. Topics covered include vocabulary, touch, myths and facts about sexual assault, acquaintance rape, reactions and feelings of victims, personal safety, and assertiveness. Includes 20 drawings for use with students. Originally published by Minnesota Program for Victims of Sexual Assault.

Audiovisuals

Better Safe Than Sorry. Producer/Distributor: Film Fair Communications, 16mm or Video, 15 min., 1978.

Tells children, aged 9 to 14, how they can assume more responsibility for their own safety. Narrated by an articulate boy and girl who encourage children to use good judgment in a variety of situations. These situations include being offered gifts by a stranger, getting a strange phone call at home when parents are out, and several others, including potential sexual abuse. (Racially mixed characters.)

Better Safe Than Sorry II. Producer/Distributor: Film Fair Communications, 16 mm or Video, 14 min., 1983.

Television personality Stephanie Edwards talks to a group of young children, aged 5 to 9, about the prevention of child sexual abuse. She communicates to the children in a very simple and straightforward manner. Numerous situations are dramatized and the children are asked to decide how to react to each, based on what they have just been taught. (Racially mixed characters.)

Better Safe Than Sorry III. Producer/Distributor: Film Fair Communications, 16 mm or Video, 19 min., 1985.

Teaches adolescent boys and girls how to handle sexually abusive situations. Presents three dramatized vignettes: date rape, incest, and sexual abuse. Common sense rules for coping with such problems are presented. Also available in Spanish.

Circles: Stop Abuse. Producer/Distributor: Stanfield Film Associates, Filmstrips, Slides, or Video, 50 min., 1986.

Designed for mentally retarded adults, this program uses colored circles to demonstrate appropriate social distance and relationships with other people. Conveys the message that viewers have to protect themselves and that touching must be comfortable to both people involved, at the same time.

Feeling Yes, Feeling No. Producer/Distributor: Perennial Education, 16 mm or Video, 72 min., 1985.

Originated with Vancouver Green Thumb Theater for Young Children. Program One (14 min.) teaches children basic skills that build self-worth, confidence, and good judgment. Program Two (14 min.) reinforces the understanding of "yes" and "no" feelings and teaches children how to recognize sexual assault by strangers. The subject of sexual assault by family members and other trusted persons is introduced in Program Three (16 min.). Program Four (28 min.) explains child sexual assault to adults and gives information on what they can do.

Now I Can Tell You My Secret. Producer/Distributor: Coronet/MTI Film & Video, 16 mm or Video, 15 min., 1984.

Expresses the myths of child abuse. Teaches children to say "no," to "get away," and to "tell someone." Scenes depict a neighbor, Mr. Blaine, who sexually abuses Andrew and then tells him that this is their secret and that Andrew will get in trouble if he tells anyone. Also shows how, after class discussion of sexual abuse, Andrew is able to say "no" to Mr. Blaine and to tell his parents about the incident.

No More Secrets. Producer/Distributor: ODN Productions, 16 mm or Video, 13 min., 1982.

Designed to make grade school children of both sexes aware of the possibility of sexual abuse. The children in the film offer simple but effective methods of dealing with potential and actual abuse. Helps children who are in this situation understand that it is not their fault. While the children in the film are all very mature and articulate for their age, the important messages are relevant for most upper-elementary school-aged children. (White characters.)

Strong Kids, Safe Kids. Producer/Distributor: Network
   Publications, Video, 42 min., 1984.

Oriented toward the home video market, this is
recommended for entertaining and educational family
viewing and for stimulating discussion about child sexual
abuse prevention. Well-known television characters, such as
"The Fonz," the Smurfs, and the Flintstones, appear along
with professional experts, in a playful format that makes a
scary subject non-threatening. A bit long for young children.

Talking Helps. Producer/Distributor: ODN Productions, 16
   mm or Video, 27 min., 1984.

Designed to accompany the film *No More Secrets*, this
film shows educators and parents how sexual abuse
prevention can be taught to children. A teacher demonstrates
strategies for introducing child sexual abuse prevention to
preadolescent children and for building personal safety
skills.

A Time to Tell: Teen Sexual Abuse. Producer/Distributor:
   Coronet/MTI Film & Video, 16 mm or Video, 20 min.,
   1985.

Teenagers in a support group share their experiences and
feelings about being sexually abused. Focuses on one young
woman who was almost involved in date rape and another
who was involved in incest. Through sharing their secrets
with those who can help, teens learn to protect themselves.

Touch. Producer/Distributor: Coronet/MTI Film & Video, 16
   mm or Video, 32 min., 1984.

Shows the fine work of Minneapolis's pioneering
Illusion Theater, founded by Cordelia Anderson, who
narrates along with Lindsey Wagner. Explores the
continuum of touch, from nurturing to confusing to
exploitative, and includes information about sexual abuse and
how to prevent it. Appropriate for children of all ages.

A Touchy Subject. Producer/Distributor: ODN Productions,
   Video, 15 min., 1986.

Designed to help parents talk with their preadolescent children about child sexual abuse prevention. Parents are shown talking to children aged 3, 7, and 10, weaving the information into normal day-to-day events.

Books for Professionals and Parents

Adams, Caren, and Jennifer Fay. *No More Secrets: Protecting Your Child from Sexual Assault.* Santa Cruz, Calif.: Network Publications, 1981.

Each of the 10 chapters answers a question such as: What is child sexual assault? How can I protect my child? What do I say? Can games help teach prevention? What if my child has been assaulted? Will everything be okay after the crisis?

Clark, Kay. *Sexual Abuse Prevention: An Annotated Bibliography.* Santa Cruz, Calif.: Network Publications, 1986.

Comprehensive bibliography including over 250 items on child sexual abuse prevention. Contains annotations for curricula, books, audiovisual materials, and other teaching aids. Carefully researched for current availability and price information.

Kempe, Ruth S., and C. Henry Kempe. *The Common Secret: Sexual Abuse of Children and Adolescents.* Santa Cruz, Calif.: Network Publications, 1984.

Provides factual information as well as insights into the various forms of child sexual abuse. Breaks down the field into seven categories with detailed definitions and background for each: incest, pedophilia, exhibitionism, molestation, statutory rape and rape, child prostitution, and child pornography.

Nelson, Mary, and Kay Clark. *The Educator's Guide to Preventing Child Sexual Abuse.* Santa Cruz, Calif.: Network Publications, 1981.

Contains contributions by 19 leading professionals and provides valuable insights into the complex issues surrounding the problem of child sexual abuse. Topics include: family relationships, community involvement, the schools' role, legal issues, the role of media and advertising, cultural considerations, disabled children, theory and research, and more.

Soukup, Wickner, and Corbett. *Three in Every Classroom: The Child Victim of Incest—What You As a Teacher Can Do.* Santa Cruz, Calif.: Network Publications, 1984.

Teaches educators about sexual abuse and how to deal with the child victim in the classroom. Sections include: defining incest and family dynamics; recognizing symptoms; how to respond to a child victim; a teacher's responsibility in reporting abuse. Originally published by Richards Publishing Company in Gonvick, Minnesota.

Books for Young Children

Bass, Ellen. *I Like You to Make Jokes with Me, But I Don't Want You to Touch Me.* Lollipop Power, P.O. Box 1171, Chapel Hill, NC 27514, 1981.

A story about a young girl who, with the help of her mother, learns to tell a man who works at the grocery store that she likes to joke with him, but does not want him to touch her.

Coalition for Child Advocacy. *Touching.* Santa Cruz, Calif.: Network Publications, 1985.

Helps children learn that while some touch is good, touch that is secret, forced, or resulting from deception is not good. Includes an illustration of the body without labels, which allows parents to teach their children the names they prefer to use for the parts of the body.

Dayee, Frances S. *Private Zone: A Book Teaching Children Sexual Assault Prevention Tools.* Edmons, Wash.: Charles Franklin Press, 1982.

Teaches children, aged 3-9, the general concepts of privacy: that everybody has private parts; when it is permissible for someone such as a parent or physician to touch their private zone, and what to do if someone touches them or asks to be touched in a way they do not like. Although the introduction encourages use of sexual terms, the book avoids them, leaving this to parents' discretion.

Freeman, Lory. *It's My Body: A Book to Teach Young Children How to Resist Uncomfortable Touch.* Everett, Wash.: Planned Parenthood, 1984.

Enables adults and preschool children to talk together about sexual abuse in a way that minimizes embarrassment and fear but emphasizes self-reliance and open communication. Teaches concepts: your body belongs to you and you only share it with someone else when you want to. Also available from Network Publications in Santa Cruz, California.

Girard, Linda Walvoord. *My Body Is Private.* Albert Whitman, 5747 West Howard Street, Niles, IL 60648, 1984.

A mother teaches her child about sexual abuse and methods of keeping one's body private. The child learns to trust her feelings and to confide in those adults whom she does trust.

Gordon, Sol, and Judith Gordon. *A Better Safe Than Sorry Book.* Fayetteville, N.Y.: Ed-U Press, 1984.

An attractive book with illustrations of multi-ethnic children and adults. Informs children (ages 3-9) about sexual exploitation, teaches them how to say "no," and assures them that they have their parents' love and support to talk about and refuse inappropriate advances. Also available from Network Publications in Santa Cruz, California.

Hindman, Jan. *A Very Touching Book . . . For Little People and for Big People.* Durkee, Ore.: McClure-Hindman Books, 1985.

Encourages adults and children to laugh, giggle, cuddle, care, and share. Uses humor and sensitivity to open communications between adults and children about child sexual abuse and protection against it. Highly recommended.

McGovern, Kevin. *Alice Doesn't Babysit Anymore.* McGovern & Mulbacker Books, P.O. Box 25537, Portland, OR 97225, 1985.

Through a story of a babysitter who takes sexual advantage of children, this attractively illustrated book encourages children to tell trusted adults if they are being sexually abused.

Morgan, Marcia K. *A Little Bird Told Me About . . . My Feelings.* Santa Cruz, Calif.: Network Publications, 1984.

A coloring book for children ages 4-10, designed to teach them to identify and trust their own instincts about good and bad touch. Also includes a section for parents.

Stowell, Jo, and Mary Dietzel. *My Very Own Book About Me.* Lutheran Social Services, North 1226 Howard Street, Spokane, WA 99201, 1982.

Workbook that encourages children to fill in the blanks, draw pictures, and answer questions. Provides discussion of private parts of the body, good and bad touching, and the right to say "no." An accompanying Parents' Guide is included at no charge.

Wachter, Oralee. *No More Secrets for Me.* Boston, Mass.: Little, Brown, 1983.

In four vivid and realistic stories, children in abusive situations involving a babysitter, a retired teacher, a camp counselor, and a stepfather take action to protect themselves. They learn that it is never good to keep a secret about uncomfortable touch and that it is always right to talk about it so that adults who respect children's rights can help. For ages 3-10.

Books for Preadolescents and Adolescents

Adams, Caren, Jennifer Fay, and Jan Loreen-Martin. *No Is Not Enough.* Impact Publishers, P.O. Box 1094, San Luis Obispo, CA 93406, 1984.

Designed to help teenagers avoid acquaintance rape and sexual exploitation. Chapters focus on: self-esteem, myths, and messages of the media; overcoming sex-role expectations; affectionate, confusing, and exploitative touch; use and misuse of sex; avoidance of abuse in relationships; effects of family stress on teens; and recovery from assault.

Fay, Jennifer, and Billie Jo Flerchinger. *Top Secret: Sexual Assault Information for Teenagers Only.* Santa Cruz, Calif.: Network Publications, 1982.

Specially designed to capture teenagers' attention and increase their awareness of sexual assault. Includes questions and answers, quizzes, personal vignettes, and practical suggestions and advice.

Renshaw, Domeena C. *Sex Talk for a Safe Child.* Chicago, Ill.: American Medical Association, 1984.

Presents illustrated information regarding male and female sexual anatomy; healthy feelings of affection; and confusing and angry feelings related to affection, love, and sex.

Stringer, Gayle M., and Deanna Rants-Rodriguez. *So What's It to Me? Sexual Assault Information for Guys.* Renton, Wash.: King CountyRape Relief, 1987.

Provides essential information to increase awareness of and help prevent male sexual assault and harassment. This enlightened manual also tackles the problem of acquaintance rape by helping teenagers to explore ways of developing open communication and non-exploitative relationships through the use of drawings and hypothetical examples. Also available from Network Publications in Santa Cruz, California.

Terkel, Susan, and Janice Rench. *Feeling Safe Feeling Strong: How to Avoid Sexual Abuse and What to Do if It*

Happens to You. Santa Cruz, Calif.: Network Publications, 1984.

Written for preadolescents and adolescents to read for themselves, this book contains six fictionalized stories told by children and written in the first person. The stories include: an obscene phone call, attempted rape, father-daughter incest, exhibitionism, child pornography, and the right not to kiss a relative. Factual information and advice follow each story.

NATIONAL FAMILY SEXUALITY EDUCATION MONTH
Carol Cassell

National Family Sexuality Education Month, which is celebrated in October, began in 1975 under the direction of Dr. Sol Gordon at the Institute of Family Research and Education. The purpose of the month is to encourage the promotion of activities that promote family education about sexuality and support parents in their efforts to provide their children with accurate information about sexuality.

National Family Sexuality Education Month emphasizes the importance of a strong partnership between the community and the family in helping young people foster responsible and positive ideas about sexuality. It is important that celebrations be a community-wide effort, because the more positive reinforcement parents receive from the community, the more secure they will feel in sharing their knowledge with their children.

National Family Sexuality Education Month is the springboard for a multitude of activities. Over the years, communities and organizations have been: (1) sponsoring sexuality education programs, seminars, workshops, bookstore, library and shopping mall displays; (2) producing TV and radio spot announcements, talk shows, hot-line question and answer programs; (3) writing letters to newspaper editors—the list goes on and on. For example, other activities include:

An exhibit at work sites.
A series in the newspaper on NFSEM.
Special sermons in churches or synagogues.
Special parent packets for education at home.
Encouraging individuals and organizations to sign a
   proclamation officially endorsing National Family
   Sexuality Education Month.

Religious organizations, voluntary agencies, family
planning groups, and other community agencies can assume
leadership roles during NFSEM by providing information,
resources, and educational programs for parents and
children. In most communities, the agency taking the
initiative in the promotion of National Family Sexuality
Education Month forms a coalition of interested
representatives of community groups and organizations to
sponsor the month's events. The groups most often in the
coalitions include:

Teacher/parent organizations.
Churches/synagogues.
City Council health committees.
Community non-profit agencies.
County commissioners.
Board of education.
Medical associations.
Public health.
Women's clubs.
Family child services.
Mental health center groups.
Chamber of Commerce.
Civic groups.
Teen theatre groups.
Family planning agencies.
Libraries.
Youth clubs.
Pediatricians.
Hospital auxiliaries.
Labor unions/organizations.

If you are planning to spearhead activities for National Family Sexuality Education Month, try to get as many organizations as possible involved in a coalition. Each group can best identify strategies for their constituents. Successful coalitions are structured so that each member has specific responsibilities in addition to their endorsement. The coalition can involve its membership in the creation and distribution of promotional materials, posters, leaflets, flyers, buttons and bumper stickers, and other information describing NFSEM activities. Volunteers can place materials with the media, as well as do house-to-house distribution or mail campaigns. As extensions of the general publicity for National Family Sexuality Education Month, newspapers, radio, and TV stations should be advised of organizations participating in promotion of the week in order to contact them directly.

National Family Sexuality Education Month was created to encourage practical ideas and projects and is basically a grassroots effort. Therefore, each community is free to develop its own promotional activities and materials. There are so many innovative events being held each year, Planned Parenthood's Clearinghouse on Sexuality Education Programs and Materials has collected information on what communities are doing to provide guidance and inspiration on how to conduct a variety of local activities (Cassell and Auberbach, 1981).

References

"National Family Sex Education Week." *IMPACT*, The Institute for Family Research and Education, Ed-U Press, 1976.

Cassell, Carol, and Marilyn Auberbach, eds., *Guidebook for National Family Sexuality Education Week.* Planned Parenthood Federation of America, 1981.

For up-to-date guidelines and information on activities contact: Department of Education, Planned Parenthood Federation of America, 810 Seventh Avenue, New York, NY 10019.

ANNOTATED BIBLIOGRAPHY: SEXUALITY EDUCATION IN THE FAMILY

Curricula

Abbey-Harris, Nancy. *Family Life Education: Homework for Parents and Teens.* Santa Cruz, Calif.: Network Publications, 1984.

Twenty-four assignments, divided into junior and senior high age levels, cover a wide variety of issues. Each has an introduction as well as parent and teen worksheets (sometimes combined). Designed as an adjunct to classroom programs for grades 7-12.

Alter, Judith, and Pamela Wilson. *Teaching Parents to be the Primary Sexuality Educators of Their Children, Volume III: Curriculum Guide to Courses for Parents.* Edited by A.T. Cook. Washington, D.C.: U.S. Government Printing Office, 1982.

Designed for use with parent groups of various racial, ethnic, and religious backgrounds, whose children's ages range from 0-18 years. Recommends 12 hours of instruction. Emphasizes developing communication skills. Shows variety of teaching techniques, films, and activities.

Bosch, Kathryn. *Growing Up Together—Sexuality and Communication: A Curriculum Guide for Parents and*

Children. Family Planning Council of Western Massachusetts, 16 Center Street, Northampton, MA 01060, 1982.

Six units for use with parents and their children, ages 11-13, plus an introductory session for parents. Adaptable for use in a variety of time schedules. Curriculum format necessitates a minimum of two facilitators.

Bosch, Kathryn. *What Should We Tell the Children?: A Curriculum Guide for Parents.* Family Planning Council of Western Massachusetts,16 Center Street, Northampton MA 01060, 1982.

A 10-hour curriculum that provides information on myths and facts, communication skills, and peer pressures. Includes exercises and resources for parents of children of all ages.

Brown, Jean, Mary Downs, Bob Linebarger, Lynn Peterson, Carol Simpson, Judith Alter, and Douglas Kirby. *Sexuality Education: A Curriculum for Parent/Child Programs.* Santa Cruz, Calif.: Network Publications, 1984.

Developed from Jean Brown's successful parent/child program in St. Joseph, Missouri. Consists of several suggested course outlines and 9 separate units covering a wide variety of topics.

Cote, Barb, and Jan Lunquist. *Putting the Birds and Bees in Perspective: A Parent Education Manual.* Grand Rapids, Mich.: Planned Parenthood Centers of West Michigan, 1982.

Covers strategies for developing a parent education project. Includes program designs for parents of preschoolers, school-age children, and preteens/teens. Full of ideas, activities, and resources.

Dorman, Gayle, Dick Geldorf, and Bill Scarborough. *Living With 10 to 15-Year-Olds.* Center for Early Adolescence, Carr Mill Mall, Suite 223, Carrboro, NC 27510, 1982.

A parent education curriculum focusing on parent-child

communication about sexuality, risk-taking behavior of young adolescents, and understanding early adolescence. Can be used to conduct full-scale community conferences or informal parent discussion/support groups. Includes workshop designs for 20 hours of group discussion.

Goldman, Phyllis. *Connections.* Statewide Family Planning Training Program, Department of OB-GYN, University of Connecticut Health Center, Farmington, CT 06032, 1983.

Designed to help professionals with human services background conduct a three-hour workshop for parents of adolescents. Packaged as a folder with two pockets of materials—one for instructors and one for parents.

Goodman, Debby. *Straight Talk.* Oklahoma City: Planned Parenthood Association of Oklahoma City, 1985.

Gives lesson plans, structured activities, and background information for parent/child sexuality education programs.

Hunter, Judith. *Human Sexuality: A Course for Parents.* Genesee Region Family Planning Program, 315 Alexander Street, Rochester, NY 14604, 1982.

Contains objectives, activities, and resource material for eight two-hour sessions. Includes information and educational experiences appropriate for any group of parents in almost any setting.

Hunter-Geboy, Carol, and Pamela Wilson. *Families Talk About Sexuality: A Parent/Child Curriculum.* Alexandria, Va.: American Association for Counseling and Development, 1987.

A four-session curriculum for parents and their children, ages 10–13. Designed for use by counselors and pilot-tested for three years throughout the U.S. Unique format encourages parent/child rather than mother/daughter or father/son participation.

Koblinsky, Sally A. *Sexuality Education for Parents of Young Children: A Facilitator's Training Manual.* Ed-U Press, P.O. Box 583, Fayetteville, NY 13066, 1983.

Begins with an overview of parent sexuality education. Also explores ways to identify and train facilitators. Includes a model for designing, implementing, and evaluating programs for parents. Final two sections include informational summaries for sexual topics covered in both the facilitator and parent training programs, plus appendices, bibliographies, and resource lists.

Memphis Association for Planned Parenthood. *Sexuality Education: A Family Life Education Curriculum for Parents and Young Adolescents.* Planned Parenthood Federation of America, 810 Seventh Avenue, New York, NY 10019, 1984.

Developed from a research program that compared and evaluated five different approaches to training parents and young adolescents to talk comfortably about sexuality. Extensive program materials included.

Books for Professionals

Alter, Judith, and Pamela Wilson. *Teaching Parents to be the Primary Sexuality Educators of Their Children. Volume II: Guide to Designing and Implementing Multi-Session courses.* Edited by A.T. Cook. Washington, D.C.: U.S. Government Printing Office, 1982.

Suggests methods for developing community support, choosing and training teachers, assessing parents' needs, designing a course, recruiting participants, and evaluating the program.

Bernstein, Anne. *The Flight of the Stork.* New York: Dell Publishing Co., 1980.

Identifies six different stages that children aged 3-12 experience as they develop their cognitive understanding of procreation. Emphasizes that parents should be aware of their child's level of understanding when discussing the different aspects of pregnancy and birth.

Center for Early Adolescence. *Early Adolescent Sexuality: Resources for Parents, Professionals, and Young People.* Carr Mill Mall, Suite 223, Carrboro, NC 27510, 1980.

An extensive bibliography of general reading materials, journals and periodicals, training materials, curricula, and films related to early adolescent sexuality.

Clark, Toni F., and Pamela M. Wilson. *Programs for Parents: Sexuality Education Strategy and Resource Guide.* Center for Population Options, 1012 14th Street, N.W., Washington, DC 20005, 1983.

Based on information and experiences that resulted from the Youth Serving Options Agencies Project conducted at the Center for Population Options. Covers research perspectives, describes successful program models, and identifies issues to consider when implementing a program.

Fox, Greer Litton. *The Family's Role in Adolescent Sexual Development.* Washington, D.C.: George Washington Institute for Educational Leadership, 1978.

Comprehensive summary and analysis of research findings on the relationship between family communication about sexuality, healthy sexual development, and teenage sexual behavior.

Goldman, Ronald, and Juliette Goldman. *Children's Sexual Thinking.* Routledge & Kegan Paul, 9 Park Street, Boston, MA 02138, 1982.

Based on interviews with hundreds of children aged 5-15 in North America, England, Sweden, and Australia. Examines how children perceive aging, parental roles, gender identity, sex roles, conception and birth, contraception, marriage, and nudity. Findings discussed in light of various developmental theories, and the implications for sex education are examined.

Napier, Augustus. *The Family Crucible.* New York: Harper & Row, 1978.

Provides good background reading about the family system and family therapy.

Roberts, Elizabeth J. *Childhood Sexual Learning: The Unwritten Curriculum.* Ballinger Publishing, 54 Church Street, Harvard Square, Cambridge, MA 02138, 1980.

Explores the many areas in which learning about sexuality takes place, including the family, school, television, social services, peers, and religion. Examines the assumptions about sexuality that form the foundation of institutional policies and practices.

Satir, Virginia. *Peoplemaking.* Palo Alto, Calif.: Science Behavior Books, 1972.

Should be a required text for all sexuality educators working with families.

Withingtin, Amelia, and Robert Hatcher, M.D. *Teenage Sexual Health.* New York: Irvington Publishers, Inc., 1983.

Includes good sections on legal rights of minors and clinic services for teens.

Books for Parents

Calderone, Mary, and Eric Johnson. *The Family Book About Sexuality.* New York: Harper & Row, 1981.

Relevant to parents of children of all ages. While stressing the importance of sexuality education within the home, the book provides an extensive glossary, a bibliography listing additional readings, and a list of agencies specializing in sexuality issues.

Calderone, Mary, and James Ramey. *Talking with Your Child About Sex: Questions and Answers for Children from Birth to Puberty.* New York: Ballantine Books, 1982.

Provides an overview of questions that may be asked by children at various stages—from childhood to puberty. Answers are provided to help parents respond to their children's concerns.

Cassell, Carol. *Straight from the Heart: How to Talk to Your Teenagers About Love and Sex.* New York: Simon and Schuster, 1987.

Gives realistic advice on how to help teenagers become sexually sane and sensible people. Addresses today's issues: sexual and emotional exploitation and manipulation, dating, unwanted pregnancy, surviving a broken heart, homosexuality, and sexually transmitted disease. Invaluable "practice sessions" give parents the opportunity to compare their responses with Dr. Cassell's to questions teens are likely to ask.

Gochros, Jean. *What to Say After You Clear Your Throat: A Parent's Guide to Sex Education.* Oahu, Hawaii: Press Pacifica, 1980.

Discusses the art of communicating about sexuality. Provides a great deal of practical information such as techniques for handling troublesome home situations. While the author is respectful of a variety of values, the book is basically liberal. Includes a special section on sexuality education of disabled people.

Gordon, Sol, and Judith Gordon. *Raising a Child Conservatively in a Sexually Permissive World.* New York: Simon and Schuster, 1983.

Includes chapters on coming to terms with your own sexuality, becoming an askable parent, self-esteem, the role of the schools, and the most frequently asked questions by parents and children, with suggested responses. Written with warmth and concern.

Lewis, Howard, and Martha Lewis. *The Parent's Guide to Teenage Sex and Pregnancy.* New York: St. Martin's Press, 1980.

Focuses on three related topics: (1) issues related to adolescent sexual activity; (2) prevention of adolescent sexual problems; and (3) resolving problems that might occur. Acknowledges conservative parental values. Describes what researchers are learning about adolescent sexual behavior. Implies that sexual activity prior to the college years is premature. Filled with statistics concerning adolescent sexuality and pregnancy. Parents who are not put off by the textbook format may appreciate the practical suggestions for initiating discussions about sexuality and handling problems that do occur.

Morris, Lois B. *Talking Sex With Your Kids.* New York: Simon and Schuster, 1984.

Serves as a handbook that provides answers for parents who wonder when they should discuss sexuality with their children and what they should say. Easy to read.

Oettinger, Katherine. *Not My Daughter—Facing Up to Adolescent Pregnancy.* Englewood Cliffs, N.J.: Prentice-Hall, 1979.

Encourages parents to discuss sexuality with their children when they are young, in order to avoid later problems such as adolescent pregnancy. Addresses the role of male teenagers in adolescent pregnancy as well as the legal aspects of the issue. Pleads with parents to acknowledge their roles as sexuality educators of their children and, in so doing to recognize the pervasiveness of the problem of adolescent pregnancy. Provides resources and is easy to read.

Pogrebin, Letty C. *Growing Up Free: Raising Your Child in the '80's.* New York: McGraw-Hill, 1980.

Covers child rearing from conception to maturity. Emphasizes non-sexist sexuality education and parenting. Highly recommended for both parents and professionals.

Ratner, Marilyn, and Susan Chamlin. *Straight Talk: Sexuality for Parents and Kids 4-7.* Westchester, Pa.: Planned Parenthood of Westchester, Inc., 1985.

A short, very practical book for parents of 4- to 7-year-olds. Layout is attractive and easy to read. Includes answers to questions that young children commonly ask about sexuality.

Rice, F.P. *Morality and Youth: A Guide for Christian Parents.* Philadelphia: Westminster Press, 1980.

A strongly religious guide written to help parents understand how Christian character and morals are formed. Discusses various methods for teaching about morality. Examines the roles of the family, peer groups, TV, movies, schools, and church in this process. Discusses ethical decision-making in choosing a career, marriage and family values, sexual attitudes and behaviors, drug abuse, and juvenile crime and delinquency. Some liberal Christian parents find this book helpful.

Sullivan, Susan K., and Matthew A. Kawiak. *Parents Talk Love: The Catholic Family Handbook About Sexuality.* Paulist Press, 545 Island Road, Ramsey, NJ 07446, 1985.

Recommended for Catholic parents to use in their homes or in discussion groups in parish settings. Includes nine chapters, each concluding with a list of questions for discussion.

Wattleton, Faye. *How to Talk with Your Child About Sexuality: A Parent's Guide.* Garden City, N.Y: Doubleday and Co., 1986.

A how-to book designed to help parents talk with their children about sexuality. Explains how children interpret sexual information. Stresses talking with sons, as well as daughters, and reviews actions parents can take in specific situations (sexual abuse, parents' sex lives after divorce, etc.).

Wilnship, Elizabeth C. *Reaching Your Teenager.* Boston: Houghton Mifflin, 1983.

Discusses the many concerns parents have about various aspects of their teenagers' emotional and social development, including physical changes in puberty, premature sexual experiences, working out rules and guidelines, choices of friends, discipline, and self-esteem.

Books for Young Children

Andry, Andrew, and Steven Schepp. *How Babies Are Made.* Boston, Mass.: Little, Brown, 1974.

Includes discussions and colorful illustrations of reproduction in plants, animals, and humans. Simply written with clear pictures. Factually accurate and up-to-date. Can be interesting to children who already understand human reproduction.

Brooks, Robert. *So That's How I Was Born.* New York: Simon and Schuster, 1983.

Relates factual information about basic reproduction using language a young child can understand. Includes watercolor drawings of racially diverse children. Deals with animal and human reproduction within a family context.

Cole, Joanna. *How You Were Born.* New York: William Morrow, 1984.

Relates the story of birth in a simple, informative manner. Designed for parents to read to their children. Includes actual photography of the developing fetus inside the womb.

Gordon, Sol. *Girls are Girls and Boys are Boys . . . So What's the Difference?* Ed-U Press, P.O. Box 583, Fayetteville, NY 13066, 1979.

Encourages boys and girls to be anything that they want to be without the limitations of traditional sex roles. Discusses male and female bodies and how they change at puberty. Although the book could be read to younger children, it is more appropriate for children aged 7-10 who can understand the subtle humor used to explain gender roles. Drawings depict children of all ethnic groups.

Gordon, Sol, and Judith Gordon. *Did the Sun Shine Before You Were Born?* Rev. Ed. Ed-U Press, P.O. Box 583, Fayetteville, NY 13066, 1982.

Intended for parents to read to their preschool or primary school-aged children. Focusing upon family living, the authors answer the classic question, "Where do babies come from?," clearly and concisely. Includes nice drawings of children and families of different races. Describes different kinds of families. Explains the birth process in terms that preschoolers can understand.

Gruenberg, Sidonie M. *The Wonderful Story of How You Were Born.* New York: Doubleday, 1973.

Describes how life begins and how a baby develops from the union of an egg and a sperm. Compares a variety of parents (animals and humans) and describes the growth and maturation of humans. Many of the descriptions are too detailed and too long for young children to comprehend. Somewhat older children should be able to digest most of the information with parental assistance.

Kaufman, J. *How We Are Born, How We Grow, How Our Bodies Work . . . and How We Learn.* New York: Golden Press, 1975.

This comprehensive book describes the bodily functions of all the important systems of the body including perspiration, bleeding, crying, yawning, and sneezing. Reproduction is presented as one of many natural functions of the body.

Levine, Milton, and Jean Seligman. *A Baby Is Born.* Rev. Ed. New York: Golden Press, 1978.

Gives information about animal and human reproduction in a simple manner. Explains basic information about reproduction, multiple births, the importance of breastfeeding, and how babies grow and develop. Drawings of families of many races add to the appeal of this book.

Mayle, Peter. *Where Did I Come From?* Secaucus, N.J.: Lyle Stuart, 1973.

Answers the question, "Where did I come from?," in a humorous style that young children will probably enjoy but may not understand. Illustrated with chubby human cartoon characters. Explains intercourse, reproductive organs, pregnancy, and birth. Uses analogies which might be confusing for young children who tend to take things literally. Imaginative but probably more appropriate for older readers than for young children. Conservative parents may not approve of this light-hearted approach to sexuality education.

Nilsson, Leonard. *How Was I Born? A Photographic Story of Reproduction and Birth for Children.* New York: Delacorte Press, 1975.

Uses extraordinary photography of fetal development and warm family scenes to tell the story of reproduction and birth. Designed for parents to read to their children.

Sheffield, Margaret, and Sheila Bewley. *Where Do Babies Come From?* New York: Alfred A. Knopf, 1973.

Offers a clear description of reproduction and birth to the younger child. Although somewhat dated, the content is still very appropriate.

Waxman, Stephanie. *Growing Up—Feeling Good: A Child's Introduction to Sexuality.* Panjandrum Books, 11321 Iowa Avenue, Suite 1, Los Angeles, CA 90025, 1979.

An excellent introduction to many important concepts about human sexuality. Presented with simplicity and dignity.

Books for Puberty-Aged Children

Comfort, Alex, and Jane Comfort. *Facts of Love: Living, Loving, and Growing Up.* New York: Crown Publishers, 1979.

Contains a vast amount of information on a wide range of topics related to human sexuality. Encourages self-respect, caring relationships, and sexual responsibility. Although the book is recommended for children aged 11 and older, the authors recognize that the child's reading level is probably the greatest determining factor of this book's appropriateness. Although the book is written from an open-minded point of view, the authors show concern for parents with more conservative values and encourage them to use this book as a vehicle for discussions in which they can make their points of view clear.

Betancourt, Jeanne. *Am I Normal? An Illustrated Guide to Your Changing Body. Dear Diary: An Illustrated Guide to Your Changing Body.* New York: Avon Books, 1983.

Based on the award-winning films of the same titles by Debra Franco and David Shepard. The first title depicts Jimmy's successful efforts to learn, from a variety of sources, the truth about boys' sexual development. The second title describes two weeks in the life of Jamie, during which she comes to understand the normalcy of her own body and internal time clock.

Gardner-Loulan, Joann, Bonnie Lopez, and Marcia Quackenbush. *Period.* Volcano Press, 330 Ellis Street, San Francisco, CA 94102, 1981.

A unique book that addresses the concerns that most young women have about menstruating and other topics such as hair and weight. Down-to-earth, readable style that is warm and appealing. Encourages readers to recognize that individual differences related to menstruation and development are natural and normal. Spanish edition, *Periodo,* also available.

Gitchel, Sam, and Lorri Foster. *Let's Talk About . . . SEX: A Read and Discuss Guide for People 9 to 12 and Their Parents.* Planned Parenthood of Central California, Education Department, Suite C, 633 North Van Ness Avenue, Fresno, CA 93728, 1985.

Introduction for parents that covers how much children need to know, good times to talk, and practical suggestions for talking to children about sex. Main text, for preteens and parents to read together. Covers facts and feelings about puberty, sexual intercourse, and reproduction. Spanish/English bilingual edition available under title, *Hablemos acerca del . . . SEXO: Un libro para toda la familia acerca de la pubertad.*

Gordon, Sol. *Facts About Sex for Today's Youth.* Rev. Ed-U Press, P.O. Box 583, Fayetteville, NY 13066, 1983.

Provides an overview of sexuality for teenagers. Briefly discusses reproduction, love, premarital sex, male and female anatomy, sex differences, and other topics. Clear and factual drawings and graphics. Discourages adolescent sexual intercourse. Well illustrated.

Johnson, Eric W. *Sex: Telling It Straight.* New York: Harper & Row, 1979.

A simple but honest treatment of sexuality for young teens. Written for slow readers, especially those in problem environments.

Johnson, Eric W. *Love and Sex in Plain Language.* Rev. New York: Harper & Row, 1985.

Discusses reproduction, heredity, fetal development, birth, sex differences, sexual intercourse, birth control, venereal disease, dating, and love in language that is easily understood by most teenagers. Available in most public libraries.

Johnson, Corinne B., and Eric Johnson. *Love and Sex and Growing Up.* New York: Bantam Books, 1979.

Provides a simple but honest treatment of those topics in human sexuality of greatest concern to adolescents. Written for teens with below average reading ability. Presents positive, but liberal, views on sexuality.

Madaras, Lynda, and Area Madaras. *What's Happening to My Body?: A Growing-Up Guide for Mothers and Daughters.* New York: Newmarket Press, 1983.

Provides a wonderful opportunity for mothers (and fathers, too) to help their daughters aged 9-13 understand and celebrate their sexuality and their individuality.

Madaras, Lynda, and Area Madaras. *Lynda Madaras' Growing-Up Guide.* New York: Newmarket Press, 1987.

An innovative workbook/journal for girls, ages 9 to 15, that combines conversational text with quizzes, exercises, checklists, illustrations, anecdotes, and personal stories.

Madaras, Lynda, and Dane Saavedra. *What's Happening to My Body Book for Boys.* New York: Newmarket Press, 1984.

For preteen boys to read on their own, or with their parents, to understand the physical and emotional changes of puberty.

Mayle, Peter. *What's Happening to Me?* Secaucus, N.J.: Lyle Stuart, 1979.

Tells the story of puberty with humorous illustrations. Emphasizes individual differences—ages for reaching puberty, breast size, and penis size. Presents information about such topics as erections, wet dreams, and menstruation in a liberal manner. Usually well received by pre- and early adolescents. Available in most book stores.

Rosenberg, Ellen. *Growing Up Feeling Good.* Rev. Ed. New York: Beausort Books, 1988.

A handbook for children ages 9-15 that deals comprehensively with basic life issues. Contains information on friendships, family, sexuality and facts about AIDS, sexual risks and decision-making, and suicide.

Books for Teens

Bell, Ruth. *Changing Bodies, Changing Lives: A Book for Teens on Sex and Relationships.* New York: Random House, 1981.

Confronts teenagers' sexual concerns. Conveys extremely liberal values. While some people might be offended by this approach, many teenagers are eager to have this type of information. Teens especially like the segments from interviews in which young people discuss their experiences, attitudes toward their bodies, relationships, sexuality, parents, etc.

Bingham, Mindy, Judy Edmondson, and Sandy Stryker. *Choices: A Teen Woman's Journal for Self-Awareness and Personal Planning.* Advocacy Press, P.O. Box 236, Santa Barbara, CA 93102, 1983.

Addresses the myths and realities the young woman will face entering adulthood and details the critical and inevitable choices she will make either deliberately or by default. Encourages teen women to plan for careers and to avoid obstacles to future success such as teenage pregnancy. Visually engaging and includes practical exercises.

Bingham, Mindy, Judy Edmondson, and Sandy Stryker. *Challenges: A Young Man's Journal for Self-Awareness and Personal Planning.* Advocacy Press, P.O. Box 236, Santa Barbara, CA 93102, 1984.

The companion piece to *Choices.* A practical guide for life planning. Encourages teen men to reject stereotypes and myths that limit their futures.

Eagan, Andrea B. *Why Am I So Miserable If These Are the Best Years of My Life?* New York: Avon Books, 1979.

Sensitively discusses many of the bothersome and embarrassing issues of female adolescence. Topics include being yourself, relationships with both boys and girls, sexual intercourse, anatomy, menstruation, pregnancy, birth control, sexually transmitted disease, relationships with parents and legal rights of teenagers. Although some of the information is dated, the book is still excellent for middle-class teens.

Gayle, Jay. *A Young Man's Guide to Sex.* New York: Holt, Rinehart and Winston, 1984.

Source book for late teens and young adult males who want to understand the pleasures and problems of their sexuality.

Kelly, Gary F. *Learning About Sex—The Contemporary Guide for Young Adults.* Rev. Ed. New York: Barron's Educational Series, 1986.

Discusses the many important issues related to human sexuality, including communicating about sexuality, relationships, and growing as a sexual person. Includes exercises that the reader can work on alone or in small groups, in and out of the classroom. Requires a fairly high reading level.

Lieberman, E.J., and Ellen Peck. *Sex and Birth Control: A Guide for the Young.* New York: Harper and Row, 1981.

Encourages sensible and responsible use of birth control by focusing upon sexual dilemmas faced by the young. Asks readers to explore, discover, and clarify for themselves values and principles by which they live their sexual lives. Also appropriate for parents.

McCoy, Kathy. *The Teenage Body Book Guide to Sexuality.* New York: Simon and Schuster, 1984.

Resources for early and middle teens that cover both factual and emotional aspects of puberty and adolescent sexuality.

McCoy, Kathy, and Charles Wibbelsman. *The Teenage Body Book.* New York: Simon and Schuster, 1984.

A comprehensive and practical guide to understanding the physical and emotional changes of adolescence. Covers anatomy, puberty, sex, parenting, birth control, sexually transmitted diseases, teenagers' concerns about being attractive (cosmetics, ear piercing, excess hair), and their changing feelings (low self-esteem), jealousy, anger, need for privacy, relationships with parents). Every chapter contains many heart warming, sometimes humorous, sometimes tragic, letters from teenagers voicing concerns about a variety of topics.

Audiovisuals for Parent Programs

Bellybuttons Are Navels. Producer/Distributor: Multi-Focus, 16 mm or Video, 12 min., 1985.

Grandma is reading a book about body parts to four-year-old Megan and three-year-old Jonathan. Body parts including sexual parts are discussed openly.

Chillysmith Farm. Producer/Distributor: Filmmakers Library, 16 mm, 55 min., 1981.

An award-winning film that captures a family's experience with a grandfather's death at home. Explores family values and communication. Although the film is extremely long, it is highly recommended by many sexuality educators. (White characters.)

Communicating with Dr. Jesse Potter. Producer/Distributor: Sterling Productions, Inc., 16 mm or Video, 28 min., 1986.

Whether people are trying to communicate as doctor and patient, husband and wife, parent and child, worker and co-worker, the result is often one of misunderstanding, confusion, and hurt feelings. Combining humor, sensitivity and facts, this excellent film effectively dramatizes common problems in communicating as well as practical solutions.

A Family Talks About Sex. Producer/Distributor: Perennial Education, Inc., 16 mm, 28 min., 1978.

Depicts open parent-child dialogue about sex-related topics in middle-class families. Presents brief dramatizations on issues such as masturbation, human reproduction, contraception, adolescent sexuality, obscenities, and privacy. Although an older film, it is particularly popular with parents.

First Things First. Producer/Distributor: Bill Wadsworth Productions, 16 mm, 30 min., 1982.

A film about teenage relationships that encourages teenagers and parents to think and talk about the responsibilities of sexual behavior.

Heroes and Strangers. Producer/Distributor: New Day films, 16 mm or Video, 29 min., 1986.

Chronicles the attempts of two young adults, a man and a woman, to break through the silence with their fathers. The process not only significantly alters their personal relationships with their fathers but reveals the complex social forces affecting the role of men in the family. Although somewhat long for use in programs, the film is very moving. (White characters.)

Home Sweet Home: Kids Talk About Joint Custody. Producer/Distributor: Filmmakers Library, 16 mm or Video, 20 min., 1983.

Mel Roman, a psychologist, creates a relaxed atmosphere in which five children, ages 8-12, share their positive feelings (very positive) about living alternatively with their mothers and fathers after their parents were divorced. Although the film's vantage point is limited by the high socioeconomic status of the families involved, the children are spontaneous and delightful.

Human Sexuality: Values and Choices. Producer/Distributor:
   Search Institute, Video, 120 min., 1985.

Developed as part of a program for 7th and 8th graders
and their parents. Focuses on puberty, dating, sexual
attraction, gender roles, pregnancy and birth, contraception,
sexually transmitted diseases, communication and
assertiveness. Conveys the value that young teens should wait
to have sexual intercourse, while promoting an objective
understanding of masturbation, sexual orientation, and the
negative impact of gender role stereotypes. Companion
materials include a teacher manual and parent book.
Expensive but worth the cost.

Kevin. Producer/Distributor: Planned Parenthood of East
   Central Georgia, 16mm, 3 min., 1976.

In this trigger film, Kevin's father awkwardly attempts
to begin a conversation about sexuality. Kevin seems to
perceive his father's discomfort and cuts the conversation
short. Because it dramatizes some of the nonverbal and
unintended messages parents may give their children, it is a
good vehicle for exploring parent-child communication about
sexuality. (White characters.)

Loving Parents. Producer/Distributor: Texture Films, 16mm,
   24 min., 1978.

Focuses on sex education in the home. Addresses the
kinds of questions that many fathers and mothers raise: How
should we project our sexuality to our children? How should
we talk with them about sex? What information do they
need? Particularly relevant for parents of adolescents.
(Racially mixed cast.)

Mother May I? Producer/Distributor: Churchill Films,
   16mm or Video, 26 min., 1981.

Presents the relationship between 11-year-old Karen and
her older sister, Michelle. Karen finds out that Michelle
might be pregnant and tries to convince her to tell their
parents. By the end of the film Michelle finds out that she is

not pregnant, but her parents realize that they have been negligent in their communication with her. Two versions are available. (White characters.)

My Mother Was Never a Kid. Producer/Distributor: Coronet/MTI Film & Video, 16mm or Video, 30 min., 1980.

Thirteen-year-old Victoria is transported to the past where she is befriended by a 15-year-old who turns out to be her mother.

New Relations. Producer/Distributor: Fanlight Productions, 16mm or Video, 34 min., 1980.

An autobiographical study of a man who becomes a full-time father in his mid-30s. As his son reaches his first birthdate, the father frankly explores the costs and rewards of becoming a parent. Sensitive and thought-provoking.

Some of the Things that Go on Out There. Producer/Distributor: Multi-Focus, 16mm or Video, 30 min., 1982.

A discussion starter that explores issues and pressures teens face as they approach adulthood.

Walk with Me. Producer/Distributor: Perennial Education, Inc., 16mm or Video, 28 min., 1983.

Designed to encourage open and frank dialogue about sexuality. Features three different middle-class family units— a traditional mother, father, and children; a black couple with biological and adopted children; and a single mother and her son.

Part II
Sexuality Education
in the
Schools

OVERVIEW: A PERSPECTIVE ON SCHOOL PROGRAMS
Mary Lee Tatum

It is entirely appropriate that discussion of human sexuality in formal, organized groups be called sexuality education. It is also appropriate that it take place in the public and private schools of this country. Schools are a creation of our society, complementing families in the socialization and education of children. Schools have opportunities to offer young people facts about themselves as sexual beings, living as they do in a cultural milieu of media stimulation and lack of serious information. They have the ability to develop age-appropriate curricula designed to enhance young people's understanding of sexuality as a natural and positive part of human life. Since all children must attend school, it is the ideal institution to complement the family in providing sexuality information.

Definitions

There are three important constructs to consider when discussing this topic: sexuality, sexual learning, and sexuality education.

Sexuality is a component of the total personality. It is everything that has to do with being male and female—how we grow and develop, our body image, how we relate to each other, how we reproduce, what we say and do to communicate our maleness or femaleness.

Sexual learning takes place for all of us over our entire lifetimes in the total environment. From birth, children begin learning about sexuality by the way they are loved, touched, and the way their bodies feel to them. Children observe the respect family members have for one another and for them. Children continue to learn whenever they listen to music, watch television, interact with adults, and develop relationships with peers. The family is the basic unit for the child and is the focus of initial sexual learning, for better or worse.

Sexuality education, on the other hand, is a specific intervention that provides information and self-assessment opportunities in an age-appropriate manner. People often state that sexuality education belongs in the home. Considerable sexual learning, both good and bad, takes place in the home and many parents also provide sexuality education. Schools can, however, provide a unique opportunity for children and adolescents to have serious peer exchange of ideas, thoughts, and feelings under the guidance of a trained facilitator. The family at its best provides love, esteem, security, and a system of values to guide children's behavior. The schools at their best complement the family by supporting those positive values and allowing objective learning in a peer setting.

Goals of Sexuality Education

Sexuality education is designed to help children be prepared for life changes—puberty, adolescence, and stages of adulthood. It helps them know that the changes are normal. It also helps them recognize their own bodies as good, beautiful, and private. The education helps young people learn to make decisions that take into account possible consequences. It also helps children understand, for themselves, the place of sexuality in human life and loving.

The nature of the debate surrounding sex education in schools has to do with a cultural tradition of privacy and silence about sexuality. Because educators generally reflect mainstream community values and traditions in the education of children, they, too, have a history of silence. On the other hand, the cultural tradition of silence about sexuality *has* been broken by the media. Sex is used to sell products of all kinds and is portrayed usually as a thing or a behavior, almost mechanical in nature. The media implies that adults (and teens) have sexual intercourse when they feel like it and without realistic consequences. Sometimes the consequences are tragic or dramatic, and therefore appealing to adolescents. Advertising, films, television, and magazines do not claim to be responsible educators. Their purposes are to entertain and to sell.

Current Efforts in Schools

Gradually, school systems are developing family life/sexuality education programs. Spectacular issues such as AIDS, teenage pregnancy, and sexual abuse are often reasons for beginning the process. However, there are not enough data to show that sex education programs actually do change specific behaviors or prevent these problems. It is important to note also that there have been no long-term evaluations of comprehensive (kindergarten through 12th grade) sexuality education programs in the United States. Educators continue to believe that knowledge for its own sake is a good thing. There is also hope that in the future, new methods for affecting adolescents' behavior will emerge.

In 179 city school districts surveyed for program content, among other things, in 1982, 94 percent listed "promoting rational and informed decision-making about sexuality" as a major goal. "To increase students' knowledge of reproduction" was second in frequency with 77 percent. The same study showed a majority of the school districts reported that they began programs because sex education was a "part of basic education." There is tremendous variance in the number of hours devoted to instruction with the average ranging from 6 to 20 hours (Sonenstein and Pittman, 1984).

Certainly, spending 20 or fewer hours studying human

sexuality cannot be expected to impress students with the importance of the topic. In addition, sexuality educators are increasingly concerned that emotional and threatening issues like AIDS will encourage "one-shot" presentations that are more likely to frighten than educate students. Because of the public health issues involved, school administrators often decide that "something is better than nothing." However, it is extremely important that we work toward placing all sex-related issues within the context of a comprehensive and positive sexuality education program. As more and more school districts begin to see sexuality education as a part of basic education, there may be increased hours devoted to it. Because of the cultural gap between responsible sexuality education and media messages about sex, it is crucial that the majority of U.S. schools offer comprehensive, positive programs. Repeated age-appropriate instruction at various age levels will offer the best opportunity for young people to reconsider important life decisions as they increase their knowledge and skills.

Community Input

When planning a program, schools systems should ask, "What do we want to convey to our children in this very important area?" School officials should base curriculum content on three important factors:

- parental and community input,
- developmental levels of children being taught, and
- children's interests, needs, and concerns.

The best way to obtain parental and community input is to convene a community and school-based advisory committee. The committee should include parents, teachers, administrators, school board members, members of the medical profession, clergy, and other community leaders when possible. The role of the committee includes:

- identifying appropriate curriculum topics,
- reviewing curriculum content,

- reviewing all audiovisuals and books or pamphlets,
- educating parents and the larger community about the program, and
- responding to concerns about the program.

Once the sexuality education program is in place, the committee should serve as an advisory group throughout the existence of the program. This keeps the teachers and school administrators in touch with the concerns and values of the community.

Curriculum Development

The sexuality education curriculum should facilitate serious discussion of important sex-related knowledge in an age-appropriate manner, building on what we know about physical, cognitive, and psychosocial development during childhood and adolescence.

Very young children have a need to know how things work, how things fit together. They think in very concrete terms. Young children are egocentric by nature but become increasingly aware of influences from sources other than the primary caretakers in their lives. Naming body parts, discovering differences between boys and girls, learning how babies are made and born, and increasing their understanding of the role of the family are all important and interesting activities for this age group. Sexual abuse issues are often initiated in elementary school curricula but must be presented in a direct, concrete way consistent with the way in which young children process information. Sexual abuse content should never be presented by itself, as it may be misunderstood by the young child as the essence of human sexuality.

In upper elementary school, the curriculum should focus on preparing students for the physical, emotional, and social changes surrounding puberty. It should include topics such as menstruation, sperm production, hormonal changes, and individual rates of development. This age group should discuss friendships, changing family relationships, decision-making, feelings in general, and sexual desire feelings, specifically.

It is important throughout curriculum development to include discussion of physiological sexual response feelings and to put them in context. If we support the honest acceptance of sexual feelings in all of us for all of our lives, children can learn to accept their feelings for what they are: natural and valid. If we are honest in school programs in this way, then we can say to students that these frequent, natural feelings are not a reason in themselves to commit oneself to any kind of sexual behavior. The curriculum can then confront the reality of conscious decision-making about sexual behavior. Unless we acknowledge the existence of normal sexual feelings, we communicate to young people that we do not understand and we lose credibility in a manner than denies us a "hearing" when we talk about the decision not to have sexual intercourse.

Early adolescent development is the beginning of finding one's "true self." Curriculum content should include activities to promote self-understanding—biological and psychological. This will complement loving, esteem-building families as well as encourage all students to value themselves as young men and young women. The curriculum should also encourage young adolescents to act independently of their peers when that is important. Students should have opportunities to identify their individual goals and to discover that they are each responsible for the consequences of their own behavior. Communication, decision-making, and assertiveness skills should be taught and practiced in the classroom.

For middle adolescents, all of these basic topics and skills should be reinforced. In addition, since many of these students will be making decisions about sexual intercourse, this dilemma should be addressed. How can adolescents express their romantic and sexual feelings without facing the physical and emotional consequences of premature sexual intercourse, sexually transmitted diseases, and parenthood? Decision-making about relationships, sexual intercourse, contraception (including abstinence), and community resources must be discussed at this age. A listening, facilitative teacher will continue to reflect the goals and objectives of sexuality education in an age-appropriate manner.

In the upper years of high school it is important to reflect on young adult life and the transition from the primary task of identity formation to the possibility of true intimacy. At this age, the curriculum can take full advantage of the students' increased capacity for abstract thinking and reasoning. Older students are often quite capable of analyzing issues, exploring their own and others' values, and planning for their futures.

The Teachers

The most important determinant of the success or failure of a sexuality education program is the teacher. In spite of a well-designed curriculum, an ill-prepared or uncomfortable teacher can ruin the program. In fact, parents worry most that the teacher will convey personal values or inappropriate information to their children. Once parents meet a well-trained, warm, and caring teacher, they are usually reassured. It is essential that classroom teachers obtain training in all aspects of sexuality education. They need information, comfort with the topic, and comfort with their own values; they also need effective communication and group facilitation skills. As sexuality education increases in importance in American schools, it will be successful only if teacher training is comprehensive and required. Sexuality education teachers must be properly trained before they are even allowed to step into the classroom. Training requires great investment on the part of a school system but with great reward!

Implementation Steps

When a school system, for whatever reasons, begins to consider what should be done about sexuality education, an advisory committee should be formed immediately. Sub-committees of this group should:

- Help obtain school board approval for the program.
- Bring in speakers to inform the committee about various aspects of sexuality education and explore answers to the question, "What do we want for our children in this community?"
- Obtain descriptions of similar programs in other schools systems.
- Survey parents, students, and teachers to identify their needs, interests, and concerns.
- Oversee development of the curriculum, adapting existing curricula to meet local needs.
- Hold public hearings to inform parents and concerned citizens of the final plan for the program and to get their input.

The final plan should include answers to these questions:

- At what grade levels will we implement the program?
- How much time will be devoted to it?
- Will it be a separate course or integrated into other disciplines such as health, home economics, science, or physical education?
- Who will teach?
- What is the plan for teacher training?
- How much will the program cost? How will it be financed?
- By what process will parents with moral or religious objections to the course be allowed to exclude their children?

After the advisory committee presents the implementation plan to the school board, the board will usually hold open hearings, then vote. Some school districts pilot programs at different grade levels and then evaluate the pilots carefully before completing the implementation plan. The advisory committee should continue to function actively as programs expand and change.

Conclusion

Schools make a loud statement when they exclude sexuality education. Communities must ask, "Is sexuality education in our schools important? Is it serious? Does it affect healthy growth and development? Will this educational institution, so valued in our society, present opportunities for young people to be educated about these issues?" As parents, community members, school administrators, and teachers, we would be well advised to answer these and many other questions and to be confident that our answers will enhance the education and welfare of our children.

Articles that follow discuss key issues related to providing sexuality education in schools, private and public, at all levels—elementary, middle, senior high, and university. The information in each provides an invaluable resource to all readers who are interested in developing and implementing quality sexuality education programs in schools.

References

Cook, Ann Thompson, Douglas Kirby, Pamela Wilson, and Judith Alter. *Sexuality Education: A Guide to Developing and Implementing Programs.* Santa Cruz, Calif.: Network Publications, 1984.

Sonenstein, Freya L., and Karen J. Pittman. "The Availability of Sex Education in Large City School Districts." *Family Planning Perspectives* 16 (1984): 19.

FAMILY LIFE EDUCATION IN A PUBLIC SCHOOL SYSTEM
L. Jean Hunter

In Alexandria, Virginia, our public school system has made
an unusual commitment to good sexuality education. In 1981
we began developing a comprehensive kindergarten through
12th grade Family Life Education (FLE) program. It was
completed in 1988. The program consists of units on human
sexuality in each of the elementary grades; brief units added
to 7th and 8th grade health and science courses; a full-year
required course for all 9th graders; and an elective, single-
semester course available to 11th and 12th graders. The
content of each unit and course is specifically suited to the age
of the students at that grade level, and teaching methods and
student learning activities are carefully gauged for age-
appropriateness.

This FLE program began with a request from our Council
of PTAs, and it was their wish that the program begin in
kindergarten and conclude in the senior high school. Our
board responded favorably to this request and we began the
curriculum writing, the pilot programs, the teacher
training, and the endless public meetings that have all been
essential to developing an FLE curriculum. Our entire
Family Life Education program is now in place, and
compared to the experiences of many other school systems,
we have had fairly smooth going. With our year-long 9th
grade course (the most ambitious element of the entire
curriculum) well into its fourth year, and all grade levels of
the elementary program successfully launched, we continue

105

to enjoy the strong support of our parents and the active backing of community agencies and leaders. And, as importantly, our students like and value the program.

Part of our success with this FLE curriculum is due to three really fortunate circumstances: (1) We are a small manageable school system of twelve elementary schools, two junior high schools, and a single senior high school; (2) the original request for FLE came from a broad-based group of parents and community leaders; and (3) that request came at a time when the school board was chaired by a strong advocate of sexuality/family life education.

Good luck alone cannot account for a program's success; a great deal of careful thought, hard work, and attention to three or four crucial components are even more important. Our smartest initial move was to hire excellent consultants. They not only guided us to develop valid course content and teaching methods but advised us as we implemented the curriculum. They helped us to devise a realistic time frame that allowed us to proceed slowly and carefully. They also urged us to focus great energy and effort on involving parents, school board members and administrators, and teachers. That advice served us well. It may be true that there are thousands of details to be attended to by anyone attempting to establish an FLE program in a public school system, and each program's developmental history will be unique, but if there are common elements among those programs that work well, they would have to include this meaningful involvement of parents, school board and administrators, and teachers.

First among these is involvement of parents. At every step along the way, parents *must* be involved. In our case, parents made up the initial study committee that requested our program, and they then became part of the Citizens' Advisory Committee that has continued to monitor its development. Parents have reviewed our FLE lessons and materials at each stage of development. When we were ready to pilot our first elementary lessons, we invited all parents to examine the draft copies of those lessons, and we made it clear to them that their suggestions would be considered when we made revisions at the conclusion of each pilot. We also set up parent meetings at each of our twelve elementary schools and made copies of the lessons available to them at those meetings and in the reading file at each public library branch in the city. Parents' questions were answered, and their concerns and suggestions were noted. We also asked each school's PTA to appoint one parent to represent that PTA on a final review panel for our kindergarten, first grade, and fourth grade lessons. (These were the first three grade levels at which elementary FLE units were introduced.) During the marathon meetings of this PTA review panel, we went line by line through each lesson. Panel members had much to suggest, and they also brought written suggestions from other parents at their schools. The end result was marvelous. Many of the FLE lessons were improved, and the parents returned to their respective PTAs confident that the lessons really were what parents wanted them to be. This parent involvement continues to be a vital asset to our program's development.

Another key element is support from the school board and from both central administrators and building administrators. We had the support of our school board from the beginning. A strong majority of that board was convinced that good sexuality education was needed, and they were willing to face whatever controversy was likely to grow out of their decision to proceed with a meaningful program. They also committed both time and money, enough money for extensive teacher training, staff salaries for curriculum research and writing, and purchase of materials for use by both students and teachers. Despite their commitment, they never "rubber-stamped" our recommendations; members continued to be actively involved and to ask us good hard questions about how and why we intended to do each segment. But once a decision was made, they never failed to support us or to make the next hard decision that had to be made. An example is the tremendous pressure, from a number of sources, for the board not to make the FLE lessons mandatory; had they gone that route, they would have effectively eviscerated our program. They stood firm in their belief that all students need good information on human sexuality, parenting, and human growth and development; and they continue to gain support for that position. They also demonstrated their commitment to a genuinely academic, rather than token, course by approving the year-long 9th grade curriculum as a requirement for graduation in our system. And they stuck to their guns on their decision to introduce sex education lessons for even our very youngest students—although most school systems still have not taken that step.

Throughout the development of this program, board members were kept well informed through periodic reports by the Citizens' Advisory Committee that is charged with overseeing the FLE program; they also received copies of each grade level's units as they were developed and revised. In turn, individual board members made themselves available to parents by attending various parent meetings and continuing to solicit and respond to parental suggestions and concerns.

Administrators, too, were supportive of the FLE program from the beginning. When teacher training began, secondary principals were directed to enroll in the courses, and the Assistant Superintendent for Instruction, the top staff person with responsibility for instructional programs, set a good example by enrolling in the first class. When the elementary teacher training began, those principals, too, took the courses. This was a plus for us on two levels. First, the information delivered and the attitudes established in those courses were needed by the principals. Even though they would not be teaching the lessons, they would be interpreting the program to the parents served by their schools. Second, it was important to teachers to know that their building principals not only had a general background in sex education but also understood fully what would be taught at each level. This helped the teachers to feel that their principals would be fully supportive as they, the teachers, ventured into these new waters.

As important as parents, board members, and administrators are to making a program possible, only teachers can make it successful. The best program in the world will succeed only to the extent that teachers are willing and able to make it work. So it is crucial to provide whatever it takes to get that willingness and ability. Good teacher training and good curriculum development can take care of the ability factor; good two-way communication with all of the teachers is essential to create the willingness and enthusiasm that must be there if the program is going to be good. Much of our time and effort have gone to ensuring both.

Our first concern was teacher training. We recognized that very few teachers had ever taken courses in human sexuality, and it seemed obvious that a quick methods workshop would not do the trick. Instead, we committed ourselves to providing each teacher with two graduate level courses, which were contracted for through the University of Virginia and paid for by our school system. This has been an expensive part of our program development but it is also an important reason for our success. Our teachers go into their FLE teaching with good information and good resources. They have been given the facts about human sexuality—and they have learned appropriate teaching skills and techniques for their grade levels. Their skills and knowledge will be extended through future teacher workshops, but all of them will begin with a good foundation.

School systems that are really serious about a quality program will invest the money and effort necessary for training. In our case, we designed our own courses. We also located and hired instructors who had both knowledge and experience in the field but who also had the ability themselves to teach effectively. Few teachers react with joy to the news that they must complete two graduate-level courses for a new curriculum that will be added to their teaching load, so we knew that our courses had not only to be good (i.e., give them the knowledge they would need) but also had to appeal to them personally. The two instructors we hired couldn't have been better, and their courses are popular with the teachers. (Shortly after we start each new session, teachers make it a point to drop by my office or to call to say how good the courses are and how much they are gaining personally from them.) Teachers value the information they receive, and they also have real respect and admiration for the two people who teach. My advice to any system starting such training would be to focus serious attention and effort on securing instructors who are tops, both in their command of the subject matter and their ability to teach.

The good training courses we offered were of great help to us in "winning the hearts and minds" of our teachers. At the secondary level, that task was easier because we were able to select those teachers who already were enthusiastic about teaching FLE. And because we had purposely kept the junior high course out of any existing academic department, we had the choice of any teacher, no matter what that person's original area of professional certification. We were able to invite the best teachers from all departments to take the training and switch to FLE. The resulting secondary FLE departments have an unusually high number of outstandingly good teachers.

However, at the elementary level, winning teacher support was more complicated. All classroom teachers would be teaching the FLE lessons in their classrooms, so we had not only the immediately enthusiastic teachers but also those who were lukewarm about the idea of sexuality education for young children and a few who were frankly opposed. We expected all teachers to complete the training and teach the lessons unless they felt they simply could not either due to personal beliefs or because the subject matter was personally too difficult for them to discuss. In that case, other provisions would be made for their classes, and there would be no negative consequences professionally for the teacher.

I think this was a good policy for us. Teachers who have objections to FLE simply will not be able to teach it well, and much less harm is done by accommodating those few teachers than by requiring their participation. We also have a procedure for exempting teachers who, in our opinion, will not teach the lessons appropriately. There haven't been many of the latter, but it is unrealistic to believe that every teacher who wants to teach FLE will do so effectively.

We began training teachers in early 1982 and completed

the bulk of the process in 1988. During this training period, we have invited teachers to express their concerns and ideas about the program in general and the lessons specifically. We have made many changes as the result of teacher input and continue to make available a written evaluation form that teachers can submit on each unit they teach. We will continue to revise lessons based on these evaluations. Additionally, we have assured teachers that board members and school administrators are firmly behind this program and that any parental complaint can be referred directly to central administrators. I think we have convinced them that they will not be out on that teaching limb alone—and their enthusiasm for the program is growing.

An extremely important issue to be decided in implementing an FLE program is that of parental consent. To inform parents carefully and to provide exemptions based on moral or religious beliefs is important to the integrity of any good FLE program. Our school system made the decision that students would be required to participate unless their parents requested that they be excused. Our 9th grade course is required for graduation unless a parental exemption, based on religious reasons, is on file; and elementary students participate in FLE lessons in their classrooms unless parents have exempted them. The result of this is a high rate of student participation; fewer than 2 percent of the elementary children, and about 3 percent of the secondary students have been exempted.

A policy such as this requires good pre-notification of the parents. This was easy for us to accomplish at the secondary level. Parents must sign their child's class schedule for the next year's classes before that schedule is final. This ensures that each parent is aware of the 9th grade required FLE course and can take action to exempt, if desired. We needed to be sure that parental rights to exemption were made equally clear at the elementary level, so we mailed an informational brochure to each elementary student's home in late August before we began the elementary program in

September. That way, parents had prior notice and sufficient
time to act if they wanted to exempt their children from the
program.

Potential Problems

I would not want to leave the impression that our
program development has been problem free. The fact is that
we have had problems. They weren't insurmountable, but a
few of them could have been avoided had we not been so
inexperienced at initiating such a highly sensitive program.
If I were to implement such a program again, in addition to
the five areas explained earlier, I would keep the following
in mind:

*As children grow and move on to higher grade levels,
there is a constant turnover in parent leaders, especially at
the lower grade levels.* When we first got board approval for
a kindergarten through 12th grade FLE program, we had a
solid group of supporters among parents of children at all
grade levels. But it took us three years to get the 9th grade
course launched and another year to write the first lessons
for the elementary grades. By the time we began our pre-
pilot orientation meetings with parents of those youngest
elementary students, the parent group had moved on and we
suddenly realized that these parents didn't even know there
was an FLE program in the offing. Because we had not
informed them as they entered our school system, we
suddenly had whole groups of parents who wanted to know
where this FLE idea had originated and why they hadn't
been aware that it was to be developed for elementary
children. We were really caught off guard, but we
immediately began some seriously intensive discussions with
parent groups. Meetings at each school and the establishment
of a curriculum review panel helped tremendously. It didn't
take long to build a good support group among these new-to-
the-system parents, but the need to inform each new wave of
parents as their children started their school careers is one
that we should have anticipated. It is much easier to inform

initially than to have to overcome suspicion and hostility and then inform.

School board membership changes over time—just as the parent population does. Just as we had overlooked the shifts in parent groups, we failed to see that the same was true with school boards. From the beginning, our board had been firmly in favor of the program. During the first few years, as we routinely sent along information regarding the program, we took it rather for granted that the board would continue to be supportive. Then, in the fall of 1983, a board member who had been appointed just the previous summer (and had not been around when the original decisions about the FLE program development were being made) suddenly discovered that we had plans to discuss sexuality in the elementary grades. His reaction was one of total outrage. It caught both the staff and the other board members completely by surprise—and for a number of weeks there was much scrambling to explain that all of this had been thoroughly discussed and properly arrived at before he joined the board. Then we began the task of explaining to him the rationale for each grade's lessons. Because his initial reaction was one of total opposition to sex education at the elementary level, we had some anxious weeks when it seemed our program might be dismantled from within. Staff people conducted briefing sessions, and fellow board members did some persuading. Cooler heads prevailed, and this particular board member has slowly moved to a position of supporting the elementary FLE program, but the whole issue could have been avoided had we simply anticipated the need to do a brief orientation as new members joined the board. You can be sure that we now have a procedure in place for doing that. Good programs take time to develop, and the school board members that approve such a program may not be the same members who oversee its completion. New members must be informed if they are to be supportive.

There is always one segment of any community that will oppose any kind of sex education in the public schools. An anti-sex education group was our biggest headache, the one that plagues so many systems that try to implement FLE programs. We thought we had avoided it because we had had almost three years of smooth sailing before they struck. However, in 1984, a group of parents calling themselves Citizens of Alexandria for Responsible Education, but using the acronym CASE, formed to focus opposition to our elementary program. (For some reason, they had raised no objection to the very extensive and sexually explicit course we had just implemented at the 9th grade level; in fact, the son of one of the most vocal opponents was enrolled in that course at the time they were attacking the elementary curriculum. Perhaps they had sensed that parents were much less comfortable with sexuality education for very young children than for adolescents. They were right; parents of younger children were much more vulnerable to their scare tactics than parents of older children seemed to be.) The goal of the group was to stop any form of sexuality education in the elementary classroom; but, failing that, they intended to weaken and cut it back as sharply as possible. This group was very well versed in the use of the media; and, while they were few in number, they were able to leave the impression that they represented hundreds of concerned parents. (In retrospect, we realize that there were probably ten to twelve people active in their group.)

These few people attended each of the parent orientation meetings that we had set up at our elementary schools. They asked the same questions and leveled the same charges during each meeting, always under the guise of being concerned parents who were considering whether or not their children should participate in our program. Our response at each meeting was to treat them like any other parent by patiently responding to each of their questions or concerns. We knew we were not going to change their minds with facts and information, but we did want to model for the other parents the idea that *their* concerns were important to us and that we didn't intend to shut anyone out. This group's primary charge was that we had developed the program secretly and that they had been unable to get the materials to review. That became a rather weak charge when other parents saw that the materials were available both in the schools and in the public reading files at local libraries. Another charge was that our materials had been drawn from Planned Parenthood programs, and thus, were really pro-abortion lessons. Our response to that was to invite them to point out in any lesson where we were pro-abortion; they couldn't, of course, since no mention was made of abortion in any of the elementary lessons. (Planned Parenthood was not part of the development of the program at any point. We were aware of the controversy they attracted because of the abortion issue, and we simply used other resources.)

For about eight months, this group very effectively made it seem that there was a raging battle in our community over whether there should be sexuality education for elementary school children. The fact was that that issue had long since been settled and we were proceeding with implementation of the program, but they were able to make it seem otherwise. They packed school board meetings with large numbers of people, many of whom turned out not to be residents of our city; they called press conferences to denounce our program and to charge us with failing to respond to their concerns; they appeared on local television news and talk shows; and they very effectively created the impression that Alexandria might well decide not to have a sexuality education program for their younger children.

We were pretty sure that a large majority of our parents would continue to back our program, but since the elementary lessons had not yet been implemented, we worried about the public perception all of this "news" might be generating. We had a number of phone calls from parents who wanted to know when the board would be deciding whether or not to have the programs; even our own teachers began to call to ask if the program was at risk.

We were never sure what to expect from this group. (I spent one day taking phone calls from very distressed elderly women who wanted to know why I wanted to corrupt innocent children; CASE had obviously been in touch with senior citizens' groups.) However, our response to them continued to be to treat them with courtesy and respect when they appeared at meetings and made charges. We did begin

to label their misrepresentations publicly and to mention
that those charges had been raised by them at earlier parent
meetings. As other parents realized what was going on with
this group, we began to get letters and calls of support. We
had also begun working with the PTAs panel of parents by
this time, and they began to respond in our support to
charges about the program's content, because they had gone
through it word for word. At school board meetings, the
chair-person announced that anyone who wished to attend
board meetings was welcome to do so, but that only citizens of
Alexandria would be allowed to address the board about the
sexuality education program. That effectively silenced outside
opposition. By the time school was out in the spring, the
CASE group had begun to use letters to the editor in the local
newspapers to keep the issue alive, since there were no more
parent meetings scheduled. Happily for us, other parents
responded with letters of their own in support of the
program, and we stayed out of it.

We continued to be concerned about what the effect of all
this negative publicity would be when school opened in the
fall and we began the first of our elementary FLE lessons in
the lower grades. By mid-September, though, it was obvious
that we needn't have worried; of the approximately 2,500
children in kindergarten, 1st, and 4th grades, fewer than
twenty families opted their children out of participation in
the lessons.

I think our success in limiting the damage done by this
group lay with our having developed the program so carefully
before they began their attack. Our lessons were age
appropriate and had an ongoing parental input. We
responded to parents' concerns and we demonstrated our
willingness to make changes in content where it made
sense to do so. The parents in our own community were with
us early in our program development, and that was our
greatest strength against the anti-sexuality education lobby.
Be we also held firm and refused to be bullied by this very
vocal group. Groups like this seem to have their greatest
success when school systems are frightened into believing

that they are representative of large numbers of parents. They rarely are.

The best program takes time; don't allow yourself to be rushed. Our curriculum development has been slow and careful. Despite some pressure from people who did not want to wait five years for their children to be included in the FLE lessons and from some people whose children would simply be out of the system before the lessons were in place, we decided early on that the actual writing, testing, and revision of lessons would require time. We worked out a format whereby curriculum writers were given a year to research and write a course for a given grade level. That material was then tested in selected pilot classes for another year. During that pilot year, teachers' and parents' reactions, suggestions, and concerns were solicited, and during the summer following the pilot year, final revisions were made in the curriculum. The revised version was then implemented system wide for that grade level. This three-year pattern of researching/writing, piloting/revising, and full implementation has worked well for us. Because we didn't rush untested materials and activities into our classrooms, we were spared problems once the units were actually under way. By the time we were ready to implement the lessons for a given grade level, there were no surprises; those lessons had been examined thoroughly and most of the glitches had been discovered and corrected. I cannot say enough for the wisdom of taking enough time to do the curriculum development well; the results are worth every minute spent.

It seems to me that we are at a point in public education where it *is* possible to develop and implement quality programs on human sexuality. The vast majority of people indicate support of such programs. If we can be careful to start with parents and include them throughout, if we can train teachers well and gain their support, if we can get school boards and school administrations to recognize the appropriateness of human sexuality education for all children, and if we can develop the programs as carefully and accurately as we would any other academic course of studies, we should be able to move our next generation to a level of knowledge about themselves, their bodies, and their relationships that one would expect of an educated society. Such education is long overdue.

ELEMENTARY SCHOOL SEXUALITY EDUCATION
Claire Scholz

Elementary sexuality education begins at birth. Parents communicate their sexual values to their children indirectly and nonverbally during daily interaction among family members. Parents believe that it is their responsibility to impart sexual information to their children, but most still feel uncomfortable discussing sexual topics. Most adults did not learn about human sexuality from their parents or their schools. Elementary sexuality education in the school is imperative if we want the next generation of parents to be able to impart information regarding facts, healthy attitudes, and responsible sexual behavior to their children.

This generation of children and parents needs all the help it can get from schools, churches, and community organizations. Today a sizeable percentage of parents with young children are working outside the home. Many more children than ever before are enrolled in preschool and kindergarten programs. Only a few of these many programs are providing formalized sexuality education. However, in reaction to media focus on child sexual abuse, many preschool programs are conducting short presentations and assertiveness activities designed to help young children protect themselves. Unfortunately, some children will be hearing references to sexual behavior for the first time in a "sex-negative" context.

Students in the first through sixth grade classes in the United States are receiving little or no formal sexuality education. Experts in the field estimate that less than 10 percent of all students, elementary and secondary, are currently receiving a comprehensive sex education program in their schools. In the summer 1987 issue of *Family Life Educator*, a journal published by ETR Associates, 73 cities and 25 states were surveyed as to the extent of an AIDS program in their schools. It can be seen that there are very few school districts, of those surveyed, who have any comprehensive, sequential elementary level sex education instruction even when one excluded AIDS information instruction. In the United States, as of 1987, only New Jersey, Maryland, and the District of Columbia had mandates that required their public schools to have a family life or sexuality education program.

The New Jersey Department of Education, in February 1981, published "Family Life Education Curriculum Guidelines, including Program Implementation and a Suggested Curriculum." The suggested curriculum content is separated into pre-kindergarten through grade 3, grades 4 to 6, grades 7 to 9, and grades 10 to 12. The focus for this article is the suggested content for pre-kindergarten through grade 6.

It is crucial to give children accurate information prior to adolescence when they are less emotional, less likely to be experimenting with sexual behavior, and still eager to learn from adults. Many educators report that they prefer this age group because children are so open to information and are very comfortable asking questions.

The New Jersey Department of Education's pre-kindergarten through grade 3 suggested curriculum content includes six major areas. They are: "The family unit"; "People you know and don't know"; "Growth and change"; "Everyone is responsible for his/her actions and feelings"; "Appreciation and awareness of individual characteristics"; and "The difference in individual characteristics and peer relationships as significant aspects in growth and development." All of these topics should be included in an early elementary sex education program. The areas above that are usually thought of as sexuality education are "Growth and change" and "People you know and don't know." The

"Growth and change" topic includes the physical process of changes in all stages of life from birth to death, body parts and their functions, development as the interrelationship of physical, emotional, and intellectual growth, and the uniqueness of individuals. The "People you know and don't know" section teaches children to protect themselves in potentially harmful situations.

The New Jersey Department of Education's grade 4 to 6 suggested curriculum content includes eight areas of study: "The family"; "Stages of human growth and development"; "Individual difference in growth patterns"; "Understanding the emotions"; "Factors of decision-making"; "Changes in peer relationships"; "The nature of sexuality"; and "Child abuse, sexual assault, and incest." Specifically, students learn about feelings, family and peer relationships, decision-making; fertilization, fetal development secondary sex characteristics, anatomy of the reproductive system, onset of menstruation, nocturnal emissions, human sexual functions, pregnancy, childbirth, family planning, sexually transmitted diseases, sources of attitudes about sexuality, and child sexual abuse. Although some school districts do not include units on family planning and sexually transmitted disease, all of these subjects are appropriate if incorporated into an ongoing, comprehensive, and community-based family life education program whose long-term goal is to foster happy, healthy sexual attitudes and the development of responsible adults. Even when certain topics are not formally included in the curriculum, it is important for teachers to be able to answer *any* questions that students ask. Inevitably, they ask about sophisticated topics, including sexual feelings, homosexuality, AIDS, birth control, and abortion.

It is important to have school, parent, and community participation in the development and the implementation of any proposed elementary sex education program. The 1981 New Jersey legislation contains a provision for parents to have their child excused from any portion of the program due to religious or moral beliefs. A recent survey of school districts in the state indicates that less than 1 percent of parents or guardians have exercised this excusal option.

Another important consideration is the training of teachers before the program is instituted in a school. Teachers are reassured that they need not change their entrenched teaching styles. At the elementary level, sexuality lessons can be taught in the same manner as history, geography, reading, or arithmetic. The vocabulary and ideas should parallel the child's psychosocial developmental level. However, it is very important for the teachers to know and become more comfortable with the subject matter. No one would ask a teacher to teach chemistry without having taken any chemistry courses. Family life education including sexuality education also has a body of factual information that must be learned. Teachers must facilitate discussions of differing opinions and teach communication and decision-making skills.

Elementary school sexuality education should become an integral part of every elementary school program. It should be taught by the regular classroom teacher throughout the school year. In order to help children develop into healthy, happy, and responsible adults, we must help them understand their feelings, communicate comfortably about sexuality, and obtain information to help sort out the questions and concerns that arise at each stage of development.

References

"Local School Districts Active in AIDS Education: 73 City and 25 State Survey "Network Report: An Overview of the NJ Mandate." *Family Life Educator* 5 (Summer 1987): 12-27.

Wilson, Susan. *Creating Family Life Education Programs in the Public School.* Alexandria, Va.: National Association of State Board of Education, 1985.

BEYOND THE FACTS: SEXUALITY EDUCATION IN JUNIOR HIGH/MIDDLE SCHOOL

Ellen Rosenberg

It is not enough merely to present information about sexuality to middle school/junior high school students, we must help them understand feelings. Only then will courses make a difference in how students feel about themselves and their physical and sexual development, how they relate to others, and how they are able to make effective, healthy decisions.

All one need do is to look at any group of students at the middle school/junior high level to be reminded of the dramatic differences in shape, size, and level of sophistication. Add other variables such as the extent of sexual experimentation, sexual interest, information discussed with parents (usually very little), exposure to sexually related movies, books, or magazines, and it becomes that much more critical to present a sexuality course that is not only factually comprehensive but sensitive to a wide range of feelings and needs.

The challenge to make courses relevant and personal is amplified by the reality that students are likely to keep many important responses and questions hidden. Reasons for this vary. Whether due to embarrassment, to worry that classmates will laugh and tease, to fear that teachers will judge they weren't paying attention, to concern that they will be the "only one" who didn't understand, or simply to not

123

knowing how to express their feelings, the result is the same. Students often hold back. It doesn't seem to matter how sincerely teachers or parents encourage them by saying, "You can ask me anything!"

Students will often share feelings and ask questions anonymously that they might otherwise not have stated aloud. This is an excellent process for getting the issues out during class discussions and can be a less threatening way to elicit questions and identify areas that students wish clarified in response to a difficult lesson.

A comfortable class atmosphere can help reduce anxiety. Setting rules for class participation that demand respect for students' rights to say or ask anything they feel important encourages sharing. At the very beginning of the course, and throughout, reinforce the fact that each student has differing values, attitudes, and feelings. Students need be taught to listen to each other without judging. Building trust takes time.

Let students know that you understand certain topics are quite sensitive. Tell your students that it is natural for them to have many different feelings about what you are presenting. Some may be comfortable, some may not. That is normal. You might say:

> If you're sitting there and saying to yourself that you wish I would just skip this whole lesson and go on to the next topic, you're probably not alone. I know that a lot of kids (adults, too) are often uncomfortable even thinking about this. Those feelings are natural. After all, some of you are probably hearing about this information for the first time. (That's normal, too.)
>
> But there's no rule that says you must be comfortable. And I think you'll find that you'll understand yourself better if you try not to let your uncomfortable feelings get in the way of listening carefully to what I'm about to explain. I know so many kids get confused about this and end up worrying needlessly.

Or, you might add the fact that many youngsters make decisions that they are sorry for because they had the wrong information.

The more you identify feelings that students have difficulty expressing, the better it is. Try to be especially aware of their non-verbal reactions, individually and as a group. Watch their faces, their eyes. If expressions are incredulous, acknowledge the reaction. If students seem as if they are about to burst while attempting to hold their laughter in, you are probably better off giving them a few moments to let it out. Laughter can be a wonderful release; humor is a terrific desensitizer. More than likely they will be able to concentrate better afterward.

There are other student reactions that might be important to note. Over the years, I have watched many girls immediately fold their arms over their chests upon my mentioning the word "breasts." Boys have often done the same when I've indicated how common it is to experience swelling in the chest area. I have watched boys and girls give each other knowing looks about sexually related pressures and decisions. Deep blushing, eyes that are seemingly glued in a downward direction, excessive fidgeting, and faces that are suddenly drained of all their color are representative of common responses that may warrant specific, immediate attention. Such signals can also be important springboards for class discussion.

I am always amazed to realize that sitting side by side in any given middle school or junior high classroom are students who might be quite naive, who are perhaps learning about such topics as sexual intercourse for the first time, and others who might actually be pregnant. It is a challenge to find the delicate balance between presenting course content in a manner that is simple enough to be understood by those who are hearing the material for the first time yet comprehensive and stimulating enough to interest the students who are more knowledgeable and possibly more sophisticated.

While it is essential for students to understand basic concepts about their physical and sexual development, genital anatomy and physiology, sexual functions, and other topics such as pregnancy, sexually transmitted diseases, birth control, rape, and sexual abuse, facts alone are not enough. We need to nurture self-confidence, offer perspectives that will help students better understand and accept themselves and be more sensitive to differences in others. We must explore choices, examine risks, and discuss specific ways that students can respond more effectively when pressured sexually.

If we are only concerned with measuring how many students earn an A on our tests, we may miss out on providing an important, very special learning experience. High grades alone will not guarantee that students will have the inner strength and resources to act upon this information in a meaningful way. High grades will not be powerful enough to counter loneliness or insure that students are capable of relating to each other in a way that feels good. In-depth factual explanations must be blended with attention to "human" development in order to provide skills to help students grow personally as well as within their relationships.

Sexuality education is a gift for people of any age, but especially for middle school or junior high school students who are experiencing such significant changes, emotionally, physically, sexually, and socially. Sexuality education offers a marvelous opportunity to provide vital information, life skills, insight, and perspectives that can make important differences in how students feel about themselves, relate to others, and approach day-to-day experiences and decisions.

SEXUALITY EDUCATION IN SENIOR HIGH SCHOOLS
Martha Roper

Rationale

The necessity for a sexuality education course at the senior high level is greater than ever because social institutions, including the family, have experienced radical changes. School courses in sexuality are seen as a necessary supplement to, and enrichment of, family sex education; they provide young people with age appropriate skills in communication, decision-making, and conflict management. Those in their early teens, 9th and 10th graders, need information about dating and relationships, while older teens, 11th and 12th graders, have more questions about sexual activity. Now, because of the AIDS epidemic, frank discussions about sexual behavior are no longer optional.

Students also have questions about their own body changes and those changes that occur in the opposite sex. They have questions about romantic relationships, negotiation with parents, and communication. Today's adolescents are bombarded with conflicted messages about sexual behavior. Mother may say, "Don't"; Father may say, "If you can't be good, be careful"; the church often says, "Even thinking about sexual intercourse is a sin"; and friends say, "If it feels good, do it." One part of society says, "Have safe sex"; another part of society says, "Safe sex is not moral sex." At their best, sexuality education courses can help students manage these conflicting messages in a mature way. Responsible programs aim to enhance human relationships, to promote communication with parents, and to inspire young people to appreciate human sexuality as a positive aspect of being a person.

Planning Process

Getting a sexuality education course started in a high school requires considerable planning. If parents choose to accelerate their own child's sexual learning, they should contact the principal of their child's high school and share their concerns. They should find out what courses dealing with sexuality are already in place. Parents may be surprised to find that the home economics department, the health and physical education departments, and even the social science departments have sex education in the curriculum. Biology and life science classes traditionally include the study of the anatomy and physiology of the reproductive systems, and sometimes these courses offer a great deal more in the area of human sexuality. Parents are the most appropriate catalyst for the development of courses where none or inadequate programs exist. However, school administrators who want to establish a program can educate and organize parents to gain their support. Parents should always be included in the planning process by serving on advisory boards to review curricula and film and print resources.

Curriculum Development

Before designing the curriculum for a course in sexuality education, basic decisions have to be made about the length of the course and the topics to be included. Although programs can take many forms, research shows that longer courses (1) have more impact, (2) allow for relationships between student and teacher to develop, and (3) permit attitudes to be affected. Length of courses ranges from a single presentation to a full semester program. One-shot presentations can be ineffective and often raise more questions than they can answer. For example, a speaker from a family planning group presents an isolated session on contraception. The resulting questions may not be about the relative safety of the diaphragm or the pill but about dating and how to start a conversation. The speaker does not know where the students are in their development and may not be able to adequately deal with their questions and will not be around to respond to later issues or concerns.

A two-week program, perhaps a half hour a day, can be beneficial. A course of this length can be used effectively to achieve one specific goal; it is not a comprehensive sexuality education course. A midwestern school system, for example, used a two-week course to solve a playground problem. Fifth grade boys were coming in from recess talking about sexual activity with certain girls and about seeing certain parts of the girls' bodies during the recess period. To address students' concerns the school developed a two-week course that included topics such as sexual responsibility and standards. The school nurse came in and talked about anatomy, and the counselor talked about feelings and respect. A longer course of six to twelve sessions is also common and can be very successful.

The semester-long, 18-week course is rare in the United States but is considered the most effective. This kind of course may be offered through the home economics department and titled "Family Life" or "Human Growth and Development." George Mason High School in Falls Church, Virginia, offers a full-semester, 9th grade biology course that fulfills a science credit for the student. A high school in suburban Philadelphia employs six full-time human sexuality teachers and has a comprehensive health education curriculum for grades 9-12. At University City High School in St. Louis, an 18-week semester course is offered in the health education department. A one-half health credit is required for graduation, but the student has two options: a basic health education course called "Stress Management" or a course in "Human Sexuality."

The advantages of a full-semester course are numerous. There is time for growing, time to cover many issues in depth, and time to get to know and trust other students as well as the teacher. This interaction between teacher and student leads to important questions being answered. The disadvantage is obvious. It takes money to make sexuality education a priority. The school district must commit the financial resources to pay each full-time teacher. Often sexuality education is not required and is not a top priority.

Once the length of the course has been established, the curriculum can be developed. A new program with a new teacher would probably require a very specific, set curriculum with everything spelled out and included: topics, daily lesson plans, materials, movies, texts, pamphlets. With this kind of curriculum guide, teachers and parents know exactly what is being taught, and a certain comfort level is thus established for a new program. For established programs and experienced teachers a skeletal, more flexible, curriculum guide is often more effective. This kind of guide would identify the topics to be studied and suggest films and a variety of activities that could be used with each topic. For an experienced teacher this kind of guide provides the flexibility and spontaneity to deal with issues as they arise. A newer teacher, however, needs established guidelines to avoid criticism of "winging it" or running a "rap session."

The topics to be included in a senior high school semester course in human sexuality are many and varied. The course should begin with a definition of "sexuality" as it is used in the course, emphasizing that sexuality is a part of the whole personality and a major force in enhancing human relationships. Teachers also need to establish ground rules to create an atmosphere conducive to comfortable discussion of sensitive issues. Ground rules often include:

1. No put downs.
2. Be sensitive to other people's feelings. No teasing.
3. Pass, if you feel uncomfortable about participating.

Since students need to learn skills for discussing issues responsibly, programs often teach communication skills in the first unit and reinforce these skills throughout the program. The first step in learning effective communication is recognizing one' s individual rights: the right to love and be loved, the right to privacy, the right to control one's own body, the right to show respect and be respected. Students learn to listen, to speak up for themselves, to use "I" messages, and to be assertive.

One reason for rampant teenage pregnancy is the inability and unwillingness of teenagers to honestly communicate their sexual values. Sexuality education provides a forum in peer settings to clarify students' individual and family values and to support universal values such as respecting others, assuming responsibility for individual behavior, and avoiding being exploited or exploiting others.

Health issues such as body care, alcohol and drug abuse, weight, and fitness are also important at the senior high level. A semester course will further deal with such topics as gender roles, biological aspects of human sexuality, teenage relationships, human sexual response and behavior, sexually transmitted diseases, family relationships, contraception, pregnancy and birth, parenting, sexual violence, addictions, and advanced conflict management.

Advisory Group

As the curriculum is being developed, an advisory group should be established. School administrators can identify a board of approximately ten advisors, which includes people from the religious, medical, and educational communities, parents, students, and school personnel. While this group should represent the diverse values held in the community, all members should support some form of sexuality education in the school program. The advisory group should look at the literature, review the curriculum, and make recommendations. When questions arise about the course content, administrators can point to the advisory group and show that the curriculum has been reviewed and approved. This process provides a safety net for the teacher dealing with controversial topics.

Involving Parents

Parents must be involved at every stage of school sexuality education, from the initial planning through course implementation and evaluation. This can be accomplished in several ways. Once a course is in place, parents of each registered student should be invited by letter to a week-night meeting at the school. The teacher should introduce the course, give a rationale for it, present the topics to be covered in the curriculum, show one of the audio-visuals, and perhaps teach a demonstration lesson. At this meeting the teacher might hand out lists of resources: books on adolescent sexuality, local telephone resources such as the abuse hot-line, and other community health agencies. It is also useful to send parents program information in school newsletters. Parents should be made to feel welcome to visit the school, to observe classes and should be used as resources for suggestions about guest speakers, movies, and other classroom aids. Homework that involves parents should be optional. Some parents have the time and desire to be involved while others do not. A typical homework assignment for parents might be to talk with their children about "How it was when I was a teen." Offering sessions to parents to support them in their role as sexuality educators is also an excellent idea.

Course Dynamics

After the course in human sexuality is planned and the curriculum developed, the most important part begins: the classroom interaction. An atmosphere of mutual trust, openness, and acceptance must be established from the beginning. In addition to being warm and accepting, the atmosphere must also communicate the idea that sexuality education is a serious subject. Handing out a comprehensive course outline on the first day of class tells students that this is a serious course covering a range of topics, not a "rap session" in which people sit around and discuss personal sexual experiences. The course outline should include attendance and class participation rules, information about how grades are determined, tests to be given, and papers to be assigned. A part of the class participation rules are ground rules for discussion such as listening to and respecting classmates and the teacher as well as maintaining confidentiality within the class. The course outline at University City High includes the "Dreadful Don'ts" of communication, such as "don't interrupt," "don't change the subject," "don't blame," "don't yell," "don't engage in name calling," and these rules are enforced.

An effective method of encouraging participation in class discussion is to award grade points for participation. The teacher might throw out a question, then ask students to raise their hands if they have a comment. If ten hands are raised, numbers are given—Susan is number one, LaTisha is number two, Tom is number three, and they are called on in order. This device can fill in five or ten minutes at the end of class. For example, "Tell me something important you have learned today. Raise your hands." This method also helps as a review, for repetition of important ideas is essential in a high school class.

As the course goes on, a high level of trust is established between teacher and student and among the students themselves. The teacher should be sensitive to questions, never ridicule a question, and respond to appropriate risk-taking with remarks like "I understand," "I am not shocked," "You are not alone." The teacher often functions as a referral source, sending a student for help to the school nurse, the counselor, a community agency, or perhaps providing a book or a pamphlet. The sexuality education teacher should have a well-stocked desk drawer with information on a variety of teenage concerns. In the case of pregnancy, the teacher should always refer students to their parents as well as the school nurse or local health agency for pregnancy testing and counseling. When the atmosphere is right in the classroom, students often approach the teacher with personal problems. They leave notes for the teacher under the door or on the desk that ask a variety of questions not covered in the curriculum. Being available after class or after school is very important because it is the most appropriate time for discussing students' personal problems. Since teachers are not often trained as counselors, it is important for them to know their own limitations and to know when to refer students to other professionals in the community. Often students need basic information or they simply need to ventilate their feelings or concerns.

Finally, within a classroom of teenagers, particularly a sexuality education class, never lose your sense of humor. Teenagers love humor, and it can smooth over many awkward situations. One teacher was displaying a variety of sanitary napkins, when a tall boy in the back said, "Could you demonstrate the use of the mini pad; I just don't understand." The teacher became extremely angry, lambasting this boy for his impertinence. Unfortunately, the boy dropped the course, and the teacher lost some of the students' respect. If she had remembered her sense of humor, put the pad on her forehead or under her arm, the class would have laughed and she could have continued her explanation.

Evaluation

Rigorous evaluation of a sexuality education program is extremely complex and difficult. Past attempts have revealed mixed results because of limited generalizability and the absence of longitudinal research focusing on the continued impact of programs. In addition, there has been a lack of consensus as to what a sexuality education program should accomplish.

With clear and realistic goals in mind, programs should attempt to determine whether or not these goals are being achieved. At the very least, teachers should administer course evaluations at the end of the program to find out what students found useful or not useful in the course. Teachers should use student and parent input to improve the course. Probably the best evaluations of sexuality education programs are yet to come—when current students become the parents of the next generation.

SEXUALITY EDUCATION IN THE INDEPENDENT SCHOOL SETTING

Deborah M. Roffman

Independent schools are an exciting and ideal medium for the development of superior quality sexuality education programs. In both underlying philosophy and day-to-day practicalities, they are places where sexuality programs of all kinds, even while embattled and endangered elsewhere (Scales, 1984), can not only survive but flourish.

A combination of factors makes independent schools natural and unique settings for sexuality education. School boards and trustees, generally responsive to student needs and sensitive to faculty and administrative concerns, are most often supportive. Parents, relatively well educated and having carefully selected a school based on individual philosophy and program, will largely be in favor. Administrators, usually attuned to developmental issues and their crucial interface with curriculum, are cognizant of the need. Teachers, with the luxury of small class sizes and typically adopting a guidance versus authoritarian approach to teaching and classroom management, are ideally suited to implement the student-centered approaches to sexuality education currently in practice.

Structurally, independent schools afford many exciting possibilities as well. First, they most often incorporate some combination of pre-kindergarten, lower, middle, and upper-level students. As such, they are veritable laboratories for the evolution of developmentally based programs where sexuality education can be meaningfully integrated and sequenced throughout a child's total school career. Second, the virtual absence of large, complex bureaucracy makes independent schools uniquely amenable to swift changes in curriculum. Potentially, a new program can be planned, implemented, evaluated, and institutionalized in as brief a time as quality assurance and available resources will allow. Finally, independent schools are enormously flexible and creative in the day-to-day scheduling of curricular and extracurricular events. End-of-day activity times, "mini-week" sessions, breaks and assembly periods, seminar days, and other types of options are almost always available for scheduling special programs, even in schools where there is "no time" in the "regular" curriculum for more formal, extensive courses.

Given all of these ingredients for successful programming, it is paradoxical that comprehensive sexuality education does not appear to be widespread throughout the independent school network. No large study of barriers to sex education in independent schools has been undertaken in recent years (Miller and Schiller, 1977), but informal observations can be offered. As in the public sector, independent school boards and administrators struggle constantly with conflicting priorities, limited resources, and hard fiscal realities. They are also influenced and sometimes made overly cautious by the very small, but very loud, anti-sex education minority. They are influenced, too, by a cultural bias which mistakenly defines health education in general as a basically "non-intellectual" pursuit and perhaps unnecessary and inappropriate in a college-bound, relatively affluent population. And, certainly, there are independent schools and personnel who find the whole issue of sexuality, particularly adolescent sexuality, too threatening and anxiety provoking to confront.

These important issues notwithstanding, independent schools are more likely to be held back by pondering not whether they should provide sexuality education but how. Committed practically as well as philosophically to the concept of teaching "the whole child," independent school educators have a clear sense that they want to do "more than plumbing." They understand that developmentally "the whole child" needs to talk as well about relationships and responsibility, sex roles and communication, dating and pressures, values and feelings, parents and peers. They also understand that accomplishing that kind of meaningful dialogue in a classroom setting is a complex and sensitive process. As a result, they often remain immobilized, sometimes indefinitely, by the conflict of wanting badly to do it "right," but not having the methodology, they fear, to do it well.

Getting Started

With a generally willing, if hesitant, staff and an unusually conducive environment, program implementation is primarily a straightforward matter of matching needs with available resources. First, key staff must be acquainted with the field itself; books, texts, films, curriculum guides, pamphlets, journals, and newsletters can provide an overview and needed reassurance that proven methodologies for the classroom, based on an impressive body of literature, are available. The best procedure is to arrange for one or more staff members to attend an overview workshop on sexuality education techniques offered locally or regionally to teachers or youth workers.

Another critical step is to delegate direct, ongoing responsibility for program or curriculum development to one, or at most two, staff members. Since channels of responsibility and communication are often informal in independent school settings, an interested teacher, counselor, administrator, parent, or even someone as far removed from the classroom as the development officer can fill this role; dedication to the program and an understanding of the basic goals of sexuality education are the most important qualifications. At this point, a "committee" of interested board members, staff, and/or parents can be useful in an advisory capacity but is not usually a necessity in an independent school setting for policy making or curriculum approval. In fact, giving ultimate authority to such a diverse group can prolong implementation unnecessarily and may even result in the committee process becoming an avoidance mechanism. Of course, in a school where sex education has been or is anticipated to be highly controversial, a committee process that actively cultivates strong board and parent allies may be the most appropriate strategy.

Program Planning

There is no blueprint for a successful sexuality education program. As developmental needs become clearer, as confidence grows, as priorities, resources, and schedules shift, as other school divisions take on more or less responsibility, as community issues or controversies surface, as experience and errors teach, programs are shaped and reshaped. In true and best independent school tradition, decisions are made and remade about staffing, scheduling, content, age groupings, and sequencing. At each phase, key issues need to be considered:

Staffing. The first critical question is who will do the teaching. Many schools have the option of using in-house or outside personnel, each with distinct advantages and disadvantages. Utilizing in-house staff builds strength into the institution, directly integrates the sexuality component into the total program, and facilitates consistent follow-up. Moreover, an integrated staff member will likely be well acquainted with the students as individuals, knowledgeable about the school's policies, politics, and pressure points, and immediately accessible to students, staff, and parents. Outside consultants, on the other hand, bring proven and comforting expertise to a very delicate subject area as well as the ability to initiate programs quickly without the lead time required for in-depth preparation or training. Their relative anonymity with the students may also be a plus in some situations, and the problem of accessibility can be softened by arranging for communication and follow-up mechanisms.

Should in-house staff be decided upon, willingness to teach, relative comfort with the subject matter, and effective interpersonal skills should be the decisive criteria for selection, with background or discipline a secondary consideration. Administrative support and financial outlays will also be necessary for audiovisual and other learning materials and for training; preparation should include not only sexuality content material but skill development in health education, curriculum writing, and group work.

A third option is to utilize a combination of in-house and consultant staff. Consultants can be hired to handle pieces of program development or implementation. For example, they are usually equipped to train staff, teach, or co-teach a pilot, provide special programs on a particular topic or to a particular age group, observe or evaluate teaching, offer a seminar for parents, or write, evaluate, or recommend curricula or materials. Qualified consultants can be located through organizations such as the National Association of Independent Schools, the Association of Sex Educators, Counselors, and Therapists, local Planned Parenthood affiliates, nearby schools of social work or health education, and even among the parent body of the school itself.

Scheduling. Next is the issue of how to place sexuality education within the overall curriculum. A central question is whether it will take the form of a "course" or "program," with each alternative, once again, involving distinct trade-offs. Courses, with required readings, homework, and exams, insure more systematic and in-depth teaching, but the informality and potential high impact of a short, attention-getting seminar or program are decided plusses. Probably for younger students, the more structured approach is the preferred one.

Regardless of the choice, enough sections will need to be created to allow for small class size (ideally, 15-20) and teaching methods that promote personal exploration and interpersonal sharing. A sufficient number of class periods will need to be allotted for trust to develop and in-depth discussion to occur, but fine programs can be offered in as few as eight to ten class periods. These can be spread out over several weeks or held on consecutive days; for older students especially, double class periods are highly preferable. As described earlier, the potential variations are limitless, presumably making scheduling a manageable issue wherever a program is desired.

Content. Probably the best sexuality programs are those that evolve as they proceed, as students gradually open up to the teacher and each other and reveal their inner thoughts, feelings, questions, and concerns. Here independent schools have a real advantage, since rarely do they require curricula to be outlined in total in advance. Nor do they generally proscribe controversial subjects from classroom discussion. Thus programs ultimately can be shaped by emerging student needs and interests rather than preconceived adult notions or inhibitions.

Sex educators, especially "beginners," do need concrete places to start, however, as well as a working understanding of age appropriate learning needs. They also need to be able to teach the "basics"—about normal sexual development, reproductive facts, and preventive health information—and also the basics of personal values clarification and effective communication and decision-making skills. Fortunately many fine developmentally based and comprehensive curricula are available for guidance.

Age Groupings and Sequencing. Inter-division cooperation varies significantly in schools that are multi-level in structure. Divisions should work together from the outset to plan for an integrated program; however, what usually happens is that one school initiates an isolated program, and if it is successful or points to clear developmental needs of younger or older students, cooperative planning ensues. Such coordination is crucial in order to avoid gaps and duplications, to provide for continuous re-evaluation of program goals and outcomes, and to determine appropriate sequencing of content, format, and methods. This last purpose is particularly important; students will quickly "turn off" to a sequenced program if they've "had that before" and don't understand the developmental context for reintroducing similar material.

The normal developmental life cycle (as well as the traditional academic curriculum) provides many logical contexts for sexuality education. During the early school years, studies of science and nature, the animal kingdom, the human body and body differences, stages of growth, family life, relationships, safety, friendship, and preventive health practices are only some of the possible vehicles. For middle schoolers, a separate course or program on the topic of human sexuality itself should be offered, focused on the physical, social, emotional, and intellectual changes of adolescence. Sexual issues can also be raised in the study of current events, science, history, culture, religion, ethics, and literature. And older students, even those who have "had it before," almost universally respond well to a program that focuses on preparation for healthy adult sexuality, best provided through a required seminar series or an elective course on sexual health.

Implementation Issues

A sensible timetable is central to the successful implementation of a sexuality education program. Schools do not need to appoint committees to study the issue ad nauseam, nor do they need to jump with both feet into designing an extensive K-12 program. They also do not need to expend precious time and resources reinventing the wheel; one of the negatives of being "independent" is too few opportunities for useful dialogue with other schools. Coordination with other schools is, in fact, an excellent strategy. Not only is it a time-saver, but it can lead to exciting cooperative ventures, such as bringing together boys and girls from single sex schools for discussion, purchasing and sharing expensive audiovisual resources, and funding joint training programs and outside speakers.

Often, the best way for a school to begin is with a short, well-planned and executed program geared to the age group everyone involved feels most comfortable with. A follow-up evaluation, enlisting the help of the students, will likely yield positive support and lots of helpful ideas. Participants will almost always recommend a longer program and one for younger students as well, data that can be used effectively to head off opposition and calm anxieties about future programs.

In an independent-school setting, parents certainly need to be informed about the sexuality component of the curriculum but generally do not need to be asked for consent. The most prudent course is to send a letter home when the program is initiated, outlining its content and goals and the qualifications of the teacher, and simply inviting comments or questions. In this way, should there be an objection, any notion of excluding a particular student will come from the parent, not the school. The school will also avoid placing itself in the contradictory and compromising position of asking for permission to teach what it knows and has stated to be educationally sound and developmentally appropriate.

Once the program is an established part of the curriculum, parents can be kept informed in the same ways as they are about other programs, through the annually published program of studies, traditional "back to school nights," PTA and board meetings, conversations with their children, report cards, and so on. This low-key approach should not be construed as implying that schools have little or no responsibility to parents, only that a matter-of-fact, totally nondefensive posture is the most logical and self-protective. Since parents are the primary sex educators of their children and since the central importance of open family communication to healthy sexual development is well documented, all schools have the responsibility to support parents in this role (Fox, 1978). This assistance is best offered, however, in the context of the school's total parent education program, not as an "add on" to the classroom sexuality program. A number of model parent/child sex education programs have been developed, many of which are adaptable to independent school settings (Brown, 1982; Dorman, Geldorf, and Scarborough, 1982).

Conclusion

Independent schools offer a unique opportunity for the field of sexuality education, just as sexuality education is a vital and exciting challenge for the independent school community. As independent schools are encouraged and helped to respond more fully to the challenge, they will benefit not only their own students but the broader cause of sexuality education as well. With unparalleled freedom and resources—to become innovators, to set examples, to develop quality programs, and to demonstrate their worth—independent schools can help to create a climate supportive of sexual education needs of children and adolescents everywhere. Ideal partners, the sexuality education field and the independent school network thus have much to gain and much to give both to each other and to the broader educational community as well.

References

Brown, Jean. *Parent/Child Sex Education: A Training Module.* St. Joseph, Mo.: Parent-Child Experience, Inc., 1982.

Dorman, Gayle, Dick Geldorf, and Bill Scarborough. *Living with 10-15 Year Olds.* Carrboro, N.C.: Center for Early Adolescence, 1982.

Fox, Greer Litton. *The Family's Role in Adolescent Sexual Development.* Washington, D.C.: George Washington Institute for Educational Leadership, 1978.

Miller, Mary, and Patricia Schiller. *Teacher's Roundtable on Sex Education.* Boston: National Association of Independent Schools, 1977.

Scales, Peter. *The Front Lines of Sexuality Education: A Guide to Building and Maintaining Community Support.* Santa Cruz, Calif.: Network Publications, 1984.

HUMAN SEXUALITY
IN HIGHER EDUCATION
Michael Hammes

Introduction

College life is a critical transitional phase in the maturation process. More importantly, it is a significant time in the crystallization of many life values, specifically, values related to love, love of self, and love of others. The freedom students experience in the college environment provides many opportunities for experimentation pertaining to these dimensions of sexuality. Subsequently, college is often experienced by many students as a time of intense anxiety, uncertainty, and confusion.

Accordingly, students must come to understand the factors associated with the psychological confusion experienced during this transitional phase of maturity. For instance, they need to understand the biological and psychological instincts for intimacy with a significant other, the search for a marriage partner, career options, and possible life-styles. Educational strategies that assist students in comprehending such needs can help them cope with intense psychological difficulties and develop a sense of having control over their lives.

University Structure

Presently, most universities and colleges in the United States provide a specific course in sexuality education that is offered for the entire semester for three credit hours. However, an alternative means of delivery is through a personal health course that will cover sexuality for a short period of time. These courses are most always offered through the Health Education Program in the College of Education. Generally, the sex education course is part of a teacher preparation track and most students who enroll are education majors.

Course Content

EDUCATIONAL GOALS FOR A HUMAN SEXUALITY COURSE

Students in the human sexuality class will:

1. Improve their comprehension of sexual behavior by discussing the motivations of sexual behavior, particularly of college students.
2. Have an understanding of their sexuality as it relates to the biological, psychological, sociological, spiritual, and cultural aspects.
3. Increase their knowledge of effective use of contraception and the transmission and treatment of sexually transmitted diseases.
4. Increase skills needed to develop and maintain successful interpersonal relationships.

COMPONENTS OF A SEXUALITY CURRICULUM

Anatomy and Physiology

A critical dimension of an individual's sexuality is anatomy and physiology, including the functions of the endocrine system. Most university courses give information on the hypothalamus, the pituitary gland, and the production of hormones and their effects. Discussions also focus on sexual response patterns for males and females (i.e., the stages of excitement, plateau, orgasm and resolution).

Investigating the Dynamics of Traditional and Contemporary Relationships

Marriage is an indicator of the pulse of society. As reflected by divorce statistics, the traditional expected commitment of marriage has eroded in the past decade. Accordingly, young people need to examine the meaning of marriage from a traditional and contemporary sense, specifically, the changes that occurred after the 1960s to the present. This includes dating, courtship, premarital sex, and living together. In addition, a university course needs to focus on developing, maintaining, and enhancing successful intimate and interpersonal relationships. This includes communication skills, the ability to resolve conflict and issues surrounding respect, autonomy, and roles. The course must define love, the purpose of having children, and the means of fostering the development of a healthy personality during the childrearing process. Furthermore, the course needs to acquaint students not only with the responsibilities of childrearing, but with the psychological development adults must achieve if they are to raise children effectively. Most college courses also deal with relationships other than heterosexual marriage: dating, living together arrangements, and a variety of homosexual relationships.

Sexually Transmitted Diseases

The incidence of sexually transmitted diseases such as gonorrhea, herpes, and AIDS has spread to epidemic proportions in our society. Other sexual diseases are also very common in our society—vaginal infections, syphilis, pubic lice, genital warts, and chlamydia. This evidence indicates that young people have difficulty in taking preventive measures because they don't believe they are susceptible and/or they believe the disease will not be very severe and/or they lack sufficient knowledge of preventive measures. Subsequently, educational programs need to include the etiology of the sexually transmitted disease, treatment procedures, and steps of prevention to refine students' decision-making processes and, one hopes, reduce the incidence of these diseases.

The Nature and Origins of Sexual Difficulties and Sexual Satisfaction

Social scientific research pertaining to the various dimensions of sexuality has revealed that a large proportion of individuals experience fears that inhibit them from experiencing a joyful and fulfilling sex life. Such sexual difficulties include inability to reach orgasm, difficulty in maintaining an erection, and many other difficulties associated with sexual intercourse. These fears can often be traced to negative childhood experiences, religious and family endoctrination, and also include personal factors such as lack of self-confidence as a result of negative sexual experiences, lack of knowledge, fear of pregnancy, fear of disease, and the double standard of female and male sexuality. Subsequently, programs need to address these causative factors and to inform the students of existing counseling services.

Methods of Birth Control

Although contraceptive technology has expanded with the inception of oral contraceptives, and improvements in such conventional methods as diaphragms, spermicides, and condoms, unwanted pregnancy remains a major problem among young adults. Furthermore, the financial burdens and severe emotional distress of unwanted pregnancies usually become burdens on society in general. Therefore, a human sexuality course needs to provide accurate information on contraception, including such considerations as proper usage, convenience, effectiveness, cost, and possible side effects to health. Also discussed are the advantages and disadvantages of male and female sterilization as well as the moral and legal issues of abortion. The objectives here are to improve students' decision-making ability and reduce the incidence of unwanted pregnancy.

Course Format

Class enrollment can range anywhere between 10 and 100 students. However, a class size of about twenty students is most manageable. The greatest amount of learning occurs in small classes because the instructor can give more personal attention to each student and students are more willing to share their views. This size class also allows the instructor to effectively use creative teaching methods. Teaching methods most often utilized are lecture-discussion, films, small-group discussion, and role-playing. Requirements usually include class attendance and participation, exams, quizzes, and a term paper. Courses are usually evaluated using a form recommended by the university or department. In their evaluations students usually report that the course is very interesting, informative, and helpful in clarifying sexuality issues. Generally, a sexuality course not only enhances knowledge but has some influence on values, beliefs, and behavior.

Summary

College life is a very significant period in the development of an individual's sexuality. College students need assistance in exploring their sexuality and in coping with the intense confusion associated with this process. Furthermore, many sexual problems (i.e., unwanted pregnancy, sexual dissatisfaction, sexually transmitted disease) are often the result of having insufficient knowledge. Accordingly, human sexuality courses are indeed imperative.

Textbooks Used in Many College Courses Throughout the Country

Allgeier, Elizabeth, and Albert Allgeier. *Sexual Interactions.* Lexington, Mass.: D.C. Health and Co., 1984.

Crooks, Robert, and Karla Bauer. *Our Sexuality.* Second Ed. Menlo Park, Calif.: Benjamin/Cummings Publishing Co., 1983.

Delora, Joann S., Carol A.B. Warren, and Carol Rinkleib Ellison. *Understanding Sexual Interaction.* Second Ed. Boston, Mass.: Houghton Mifflin, 1981.

Francocur, Robert T. *Becoming a Sexual Person.* New York: John Wiley, 1984.

Gotwald, William, and Gale Golden. *Sexuality: The Human Experience.* New York: Macmillan, 1981.

Hyde, Janet Shibley. *Understanding Human Sexuality.* Second Ed. New York: McGraw-Hill, 1982.

Mahoney, E.R. *Human Sexuality.* New York: McGraw-Hill Co., 1983.

McCary, James L. and Stephen P. McCary. *Human Sexuality.* Fourth Ed. Florence, Ky.: Wadsworth Publishing Co., 1982.

Meeks, Linda Bower, and Phililp Heit. *Human Sexuality: Making Responsible Decisions.* New York: Saunders College Publishing Co., 1982.

Rosenfeld, Jeffrey. *Relationships: The Marriage and Family Reader.* Glenview, Ill.: Scott, Foresman, 1982.

References

Landis, Sandra. "Human Sexuality Services: A Holistic Approach to Sex Education and Counseling in a University Setting." *Health Values: Achieving High Level Wellness* (September-October 1980): 229-233.

Paz, Rose, and Dwight Kirkpatrick. "Two Times for Teaching Human Sexuality." *Teaching of Psychology* (April 1983): 84-88.

Taylor, Mary. "A Discriminant Analysis Approach to Exploring Changes in Human Sexuality Attitudes Among University Students." *Journal of American College Health* (December 1982): 124-129.

Wanlass, Richard, Peter Kilmann, Bonnie Bella, and Ken Tarnowski. "Effects of Sex Education on Sexual Guilt, Anxiety and Attitudes: A Comparison of Instruction Formats." *Archives of Sexual Behavior* (December 1983): 487-502.

Wiechmann, Gerald, and Altis Ellis. "A Study of the Effects of Sex Education on Premarital Petting and Coital Behavior." *The Family Coordinator* (July 1969): 231-234.

Zucherman, Marvin, Richard Tushup, and Steven Finner. "Sexual Attitudes and Experience: Attitude and Personality Correlates and Changes Produced by a Course in Sexuality." *Journal of Consulting and Clinical Psychology* 44 (1976): 7-19.

SEXUALITY EDUCATION WITHIN THE HEALTH EDUCATION CURRICULA
Sue Steed

In 1979 a legislative mandate requiring that health education be taught at every grade level was passed in the state of New Mexico. There were no specific guidelines for what or how much health education should be taught. The 1976 edition of Minimum Education standards for New Mexico Schools contains a section that states:

4.4.5 The following shall be integrated into the curriculum:

f. Health Education: (All schools shall implement a comprehensive health program by the 1980-81 school year. The program shall include concepts appropriate to the student's physical, social, and mental development and which are necessary for decision-making in nutrition, human growth, family health, health maintenance, consumerhealth, environmental, and community health.)

The Albuquerque Public Schools (APS) surpassed this mandate by adopting two curricula for the elementary grades and a locally developed curriculum for middle and high school. The elementary curricula components are part of Growing Healthy, formally the School Health Project, which is based in the Bureau of Health, Education, and Welfare and is distributed and periodically revised by the Centers for Disease Control. The programs are nicknamed after their place of origin. The Seattle curriculum was designed for grades kindergarten through third grade and the Berkeley curriculum is used for grades four and five. Both of these programs are well-written and include information on all body systems.

The APS comprehensive school health education goals are clearly stated and are congruent with other programs in the nation. These goals define the nature and character of the curriculum and instruction. They provide the foundation upon which educational planning and evaluation is based.

Both middle and high school APS health education curricula are comprehensive programs. As defined by the national professional school health organizations, a comprehensive school health program is designed to meet the specific health needs and interests of all students as they progress through various grade levels.

The content of a comprehensive program is balanced so as to provide adequate coverage for each topic area. Included in each topic area as the basis for study are four dimensions: physical, mental, emotional, and social health.

The following topic areas are listed in alphabetical order. One does not have precedence over the others.

Community health
Consumer health
Environmental health
Family life
Growth and development
Nutritional health
Personal health
Prevention and control of disease and disorders
Safety and accident prevention
Substance use and abuse.

Elementary School Sexuality Education

The APS elementary health education program approaches sex education by building on the affective domain. The primary grades (K, 1, and 2) stress the uniqueness of being human, differences between acceptable and unacceptable behavior, and the meaning of friendship.

In the 3rd grade, students identify unique social and physical characteristics of girls and boys and describe different kinds of friendships. The 4th and 5th grade programs locate, identify, and describe the functions of the major body systems, including the reproductive system. The life cycle from birth through death is presented in the fifth grade. Reducing the effects of peer pressure in making decisions also becomes a prime objective in the fifth grade health education curriculum.

Information about adolescent growth and development with a special focus on menstruation is given to many fifth grade classes. The decision to include this topic depends on administrative and community support. Permission letters are sent home to parents and returned with their signatures, if parents approve of their child participating. The parents are also invited to the schools to screen any materials used in the presentations.

Middle School Sexuality Education

The middle school sexuality unit is taught in a two-week period within the required one-semester health education course at the seventh grade. The following statement forms the rationale for the unit: human sexuality is related to growth and development patterns and family experiences and continues to be influenced by family, peers, and life experience. The student objectives are:

1. to describe adolescent growth patterns.
2. to identify physical changes that occur during adolescence.
3. to distinguish several types of love.
4. to describe social customs relating to dating and marriage.

In many instances the objectives are accomplished through the use of films. However, parent permission letters are sent home before students view any films. These films have been previously screened and approved by the health education advisory council. In the middle school program peer pressure, self-concept, and responsible decision-making are explored in great detail.

High School Sexuality Education

The high school sexuality education unit is taught for a minimum of two weeks in the required 9th grade, one-semester health education course. The stated rationale for this unit is: "Human sexuality, which involves growth and development as well as the complex drive associated with love, is the basis for many facets of behavior." The students study in detail the male and female reproductive systems, conception, alternatives to pregnancy, childbirth, the social implications involved in teenage pregnancy, and community agencies that offer help. Dating, marriage, parenting, and divorce are also discussed.

Before taking the one-semester health education course, all students must have parent permission letters signed and returned to school. The guest speakers and materials used in class have been screened and approved by the Health Education Advisory Council. Students may be exempted from any health unit covered. If exempted, the student completes alternative assignments. However, exemption is rarely requested.

Health Education Program Evaluation

The Albuquerque public schools have recently completed the health education program evaluation. Parents were asked if sex education should be included in the health education program at the various levels and, if so, what topics should be included in sex education. When asked if sex education should be included in the health education program curriculum, nearly three-fourths (73%) of the APS parents agreed that it should be taught at the elementary school. Nearly all APS parents agreed that sex education should be taught at the middle (91%) and high school (94%) levels.

Parental Rating of Topics to Be Taught

There are notable differences between what parents believe should be taught in the elementary school and what they believe to be appropriate topics for the middle and high school. The table below reveals that, of the four topics being considered, biology of reproduction was the only topic that most parents felt to be appropriate for all three grade levels.

Topics Respondents Think Should Be Included in Sex Education*

	Elementary APS	Middle APS	High APS
Venereal Disease	14%	72%	85%
Birth Control	11	65	80
Biology of Reproduction	60	79	74
Abortion	7	47	73

*All results are expressed in percent of respondents. Columns will not total 100% since questions were asked separately.

Conclusion

Currently, Acquired Immune Deficiency Syndrome (AIDS) prevention education has been included in the middle and high school health education curriculum. It is part of the communicable disease unit that includes other sexually transmitted diseases. It is interesting to note that we have had no parental objections to the teaching of AIDS prevention education. Overall, very few parents choose to have their students exempted from sexuality education.

Careful planning and implementation steps must be followed to introduce sexuality education in the schools. It takes the support of the school administration and the community to make sexuality education acceptable and successful.

FAMILY LIFE EDUCATION
TEACHER TRAINING
Ellen Wagman

The Need for Teacher Training

Since the mid-1970s, the increasing acceptance of the importance of school-based family life education programs has proceeded hand in hand with the growing recognition of the need for comprehensive training to prepare teachers for the role of family life educator. This role requires the teacher to meet student learning needs in the controversial, value-laden, difficult-to-discuss, and constantly expanding field of human sexuality. In addition, family life teachers must support parents as the primary educators of their own children and use materials and methods that are both effective with students and acceptable to the adult community.

Competent family life educators are expected to be knowledgeable about the physical, psychological, social, and moral dimensions of human sexuality and to possess positive attitudes that promote the goals of family life education. Such attitudes include being comfortable with one's own sexuality, respectful of the diversity of backgrounds, values, beliefs, and behaviors of others, committed to the importance of family life education, and supportive of parents' roles as primary sexuality educators. Family life educators also must be skilled in communicating and teaching about human sexuality and must be respected by parents, students, and school administrators (Cooper, 1982; Kirby and Alter, 1980).

161

Given these high expectations, it is no wonder that a primary concern of parents and school administrators is the qualifications and preparation of prospective teachers, and that a major reason for educators' resistance to teaching family life education classes is their inadequate preparation for the assignment (Clawar, 1977). Teacher training is, therefore, critical to the success of any attempts to initiate school-based family life education programs. In order for such training to be effective, however, it must provide teachers with the prerequisite knowledge, attitudes, and skills of competent family life educators. These lofty expectations are translated into ambitious objectives for teacher training.

Objectives of Teacher Training

Cognitive Objectives. Teacher training should inform educators about the goals, rationale, principles, and impact of family life education. It should clarify state law and, in the case of in-service training, acquaint teachers with specific school or district policies and procedures, including teachers' rights and responsibilities in helping students with sexually related problems (e.g., sexual abuse, sexually transmissible diseases, unplanned pregnancy).

Training should also provide accurate information about human sexuality, an emerging discipline that includes but is not limited to information about gender role development, body image and self-concept, families, interpersonal relationships, reproduction, childbirth, erotic behavior, and associated health issues (adapted from Simpson et al., 1978). Training should provide information about the wealth of resource materials, organizations, and local "experts" that may be integrated into classroom presentations. Finally, training should provide guidelines for selecting and using these resources.

Affective Objectives. Training should increase teachers' awareness of and comfort with their own values regarding controversial human sexuality issues. This will, in turn, improve their ability to accept and validate diversity in their students. This should not, however, be interpreted as an endorsement of value-free family life education. In fact training should help teachers clarify their responsibility in regard to the teaching of values.

Within the last few years, a distinction has been made in the field of family life education between two groups of values: values regarding controversial issues about which there is no societal agreement (for example, homosexuality, abortion, contraception, and masturbation) and universal values about which society in general would agree (for example, it is wrong to exploit or force someone into an unwanted sexual experience and to knowingly spread venereal disease) (Scales, 1983).

Training should prepare educators to deal with both types of values. Teachers must be able to lead objective discussions about controversial issues in which the diversity of beliefs among their students are acknowledged and supported, to work with representative advisory comittees to identify the universal values upon which to build their local family life education courses, and in both cases to refer students to their parents in order to stimulate intrafamily communication about these issues.

Toward these ends, training should provide ample opportunity for teachers to discuss their feelings about controversial issues with colleagues. Such discussions allow teachers to clarify their own beliefs and expose them to the similarities and differences that exist even within their own peer group. For the same reasons, training should include guest speakers (e.g., clergy) and panels (e.g., multicultural, pregnancy alternatives) to present and affirm both the similarities in universal values as well as the differences in beliefs about controversial issues that exist in our greater society.

A second important affective objective for family life training is to enhance teachers' ability to support parents as the primary sexuality educators of their own children. Training should explain common parental concerns: Who is the teacher? What will be taught? Will it undermine my values? How can I educate my child if I've never been educated myself? It should present ways in which teachers can provide information about and secure parental involvement in their curriculum development process. These might include parent advisory committees, presentations at parent groups, information in school newsletters, preclass information letters or packets, and parent feedback forms. Training should advise teachers as to ways they can facilitate parent-child communication about sexuality content and values (including referring students to parents for discussions about family values, use of parent-child homework assignments, and the development of parent/child sexuality classes).

Training should point out how teacher defensiveness and fear may exacerbate parental concerns and then provide practice sessions in which teachers can rehearse communication skills for preventing and responding to these concerns. Better yet, training should include parents as participants so as to bridge the communication gap that all too often exists between parents and educators.

Skill Objectives. Family life education training should increase teachers' skill in leading classroom discussions about human sexuality. This can be accomplished by presenting and modeling facilitation techniques throughout the training. Active listening, taking responsibility for one's feelings and thoughts, open-ended questions, positive body language, establishment of classroom ground rules are examples. Teachers should then be given ample opportunities to practice talking and answering questions about sexual issues using sexual vocabulary.

From the educator's perspective, perhaps the most important objective of training is to enhance teachers' ability to use effective teaching approaches and methods (Cooper, 1981). This can be accomplished by discussing criteria for selecting learning activities, by demonstrating the variety of teaching techniques commonly used in family life education classes, and by discussing their classroom applications. These activities should reflect a teaching approach that actively involves students in their own learning, e.g., information sharing (students collectively supply information about a particular subject), information processing (students develop specific questions they wish addressed in a particular presentation), classroom research (students gather facts and opinions from others in the class), brainstorming, case studies, and role playing. Training methods considered inappropriate for use with young people should be avoided since enthusiastic new teachers may forget disclaimers and use learning activities that are intended for adults in the classroom with children. Teacher preparation programs may also include opportunities for teachers to practice and receive feedback on their facilitation skills and their ability to conduct structured learning activities.

Problems in Teacher Training. There are at least three major problems inherent in accomplishing the objectives just described. First and foremost is time. In continuing education programs and in-service classes where time constraints severely limit the scope of material that can be covered, priority should be assigned to information that reflects: (1) the perceived needs of teachers; (2) the developmental level and interests of the age group(s) they will be teaching; (3) the concerns of the adults (parents, community members, school administrators) who will be affected by the course; and (4) where appropriate, the topics included in approved curricula.

Even using these guidelines, those who develop training programs will be forced to make difficult decisions about what content is essential for new teachers and what can be saved for teacher self-instruction, follow-up, or ongoing training. They must also develop training designs that accomplish their objectives as efficiently as possible while taking into account the time needed for new teachers to process this highly sensitive material.

One approach used successfully with approximately 2000 teachers (grades 6-12) is the training design pictured in Figure 1 (Wagman et al., 1981). Due to the increasing difficulty in releasing teachers to attend training, the length of this design has shrunk from 35 to 25 hours. Nonetheless, it addresses all the objectives discussed in this chapter by covering only the most important and/or controversial content areas and the most essential characteristics and skills of family life educators and by using each session to accomplish multiple objectives.

During content sessions, knowledge is provided, attitudes and values discussed, communication skills practiced, and resources shared, usually through the process of modelling classroom activities. At the conclusion of each content section comes a "teaching about" discussion that highlights key points related to goals, approach, values, education code, district policy, and/or parent concerns specific to content area. (During teacher skill sessions activities that are demonstrated can also be used to teach similar behaviors with students, e.g., communication skills.)

A second major problem in teacher training is the difficulty of accomplishing attitudinal objectives. Although teacher preparation may have some impact on attitudes and beliefs,

Figure 1

FAMILY LIFE EDUCATION TEACHER TRAINING

	Day 1 (3 1/2 Hours)	Day 2 (8 1/2 Hours)	Day 3 (6 1/2 Hours)	Day 4 (6 1/2 Hours)
Morning		Enhancing Student Self-Esteem	Teaching About Sensitive Issues: •Abstinence •Birth Control •Pregnancy Alternatives •STDs	Helping Students With Personal Problems Involving and Supporting Parents Teaching FLE in a Culturally Sensitive Manner
Afternoon	Orientation to Training Teacher Facilitation Skills	Teaching About Relationships Part I: Family and Friends	Answering Questions About Sexual Behavior	Religious Views Planning for Implementation
Evening		Part II: Dating Relationships		

expecting training to cause significant personality changes is unrealistic. Persons who express deep resentment about having to teach family life education, view parents negatively, are hypercritical of young people, hold strong views about controversial (especially sex-related) issues and try to push them on others, inappropriately discuss highly personal information about themselves, and/or have unclear professional boundaries about relationships with students are questionable candidates for the role of family life educator (Cook et al., 1984).

Herein lies a selection and not a training problem that must be addressed by a screening process involving principals and teachers themselves. Teachers who are selected for family life educator training should be willing to teach this sensitive subject and willing to invest the time necessary to become familiar and stay current with its content, issues, and approaches. They must also have established good rapport with students, parents, and administrators.

One final problem that should be acknowledged is the inability of even the best and most comprehensive of such training, in and of itself, to result in school-based family life education classes. In order for such classes to be implemented, training must take place not as an isolated event but as part of a comprehensive program development process. Ideally, this process would include the securing of parent, student, community, administrative, and board involvement and support; the writing and approval of effective curriculum materials; the official endorsement of the curriculum; the scheduling of family life education units or classes; and finally the selection of appropriate instructors. Teacher preparation classes occurring in such an environment can then equip these motivated individuals to go back to their classrooms and transfer to young people what they have learned in training.

References

Clawar, S.S. "Resistance to Sex Education: Constituency Perspective." *Journal of Sex Education and Therapy* (Spring/Summer, 1977): 31-35.

Cook, Ann, Doug Kirby, Pamela Wilson, and Judith Alter. *Sexuality Education: A Guide to Developing and Implementing Programs.* Santa Cruz, Calif.: Network Publications, 1984.

Cooper, Lynne. "Results of the Evaluation of the Five-day Teacher Training." Unpublished data. Santa Cruz, Calif.: ETR Associates, 1981.

Cooper, Lynne. *Selection and Preparation of Family Life Educators: A Review of the Literature.* Santa Cruz, Calif.: Network Publications, 1982.

Family Life Education and Training Program. "Family Life Education Teacher Training Design." Unpublished. Santa Cruz, Calif.: ETR Associates, 1986.

Kirby, Douglas, and Judith Alter. "The Experts Rate Important Features and Outcomes of Sex Education Programs." *The Journal of School Health* (November 1980): 497-502.

Scales, Peter. "Sexuality Education: The Value of Values." New York: Emphasis Subscriber Service, Planned Parenthood Federation of America, Inc., 1983.

Simpson, Judith, Lucille Aptelsar-Litton, and Elizabeth J. Roberts. *Harmonizing Sexual Conventions: Service Providers and Learning.* Cleveland, Ohio: Cleveland Program for Sexual Learning, Inc., 1978.

Wagman, Ellen, Lynne Cooper, and Kay Rodenberg Todd. *Family Life Education Teacher Training Manual.* Santa Cruz, Calif.: Network Publications, 1981.

SCHOOL-BASED HEALTH CLINICS: IMPROVING ADOLESCENT HEALTH AND REDUCING TEENAGE PREGNANCY

Douglas Kirby
Sharon Lovick

In recent years, sexuality educators and health professionals have become increasingly interested in a new program model, school-based clinics. These clinics respond to the wide range of physical and psychosocial needs of adolescents by providing comprehensive primary care in a school setting. Of course, among the important health needs of adolescents are those related to sexuality. Consequently, an increasing number of clinics provide counseling about sexual issues; education, referrals, and/or prescriptions for contraceptives; and education, laboratory tests, and treatment for sexually transmitted diseases. Many professionals believe this approach is effective because it is a holistic approach, dealing with a wide range of adolescents' health needs and integrating both health education and health services in a school setting.

Adolescents' Need for Health Care

Although most adolescents in this country are quite healthy, many adolescents have serious health problems and need medical attention. Adolescents not only experience some of the same health problems as the general population, they also experience other problems that characterize puberty and adolescence—menstrual problems, growth disorders, and acne, to name a few. They also have psychological problems, and many teenagers take risks with drugs, driving, and sex.

However, in many communities, adolescents are not receiving the health care they need. According to Dr. Mark Raifman at Long Beach Memorial Hospital, adolescents are the most medically underserved group in the United States. Throughout the nation, about 15 percent of adolescents aged sixteen to seventeen report no regular source of medical care, in comparison with 7 percent for children under the age of six (Green and Horton, 1982). In economically deprived areas, the percentage of underserved adolescents is much greater.

The Development of School-Based Clinics

In response to those clear needs, numerous communities have opened school-based clinics. The first opened in Dallas in 1970; three years later additional clinics opened in St. Paul. These are the first known clinics to provide comprehensive health care, including family planning services on high school campuses.

Since those clinics opened, the number of school-based clinics has doubled about every two years. This is clearly a very rapid increase. By the end of 1988, at least 120 schools had opened clinics, and many more communities were planning clinics. Many of these clinics have developed quite independently of one another—they represent a grassroots movement across the country.

Clinic Goals and Service

Most of the clinics adopt a holistic approach. They try to:

- Improve adolescent knowledge and decision-making and thereby promote healthy life-styles.
- Teach adolescents how to use the health care system.

- Provide earlier detection of acute, chronic, and psychosocial problems.
- Treat both physical and emotional problems.
- Facilitate use of birth control and prevent pregnancy.
- Improve prenatal care.
- Enhance interagency cooperation and facilitate continuing comprehensive care for the students.

Although school-based clinics differ considerably from one another, most of them provide a wide variety of services, including athletic physicals, general health assessments, laboratory and diagnostic screenings (e.g., sickle cell anemia and sexually transmitted disease screenings), immunizations, first aid and hygiene, early periodic screening, diagnosis, and treatment (EPSDT), family planning counseling and services, prenatal and postpartum care, drug and alcohol abuse programs, and family counseling. A few clinics also provide dental care and day care. These numerous services clearly demonstrate the clinics' commitment to general health care.

In order to be considered pregnancy prevention efforts, the clinics must facilitate family planning. At a minimum, they all do counseling about sexual activity and birth control, make referrals, and do a follow-up after the referral. About half of them also conduct pelvic exams and write prescriptions for birth control. More than a fourth of them actually dispense birth control methods.

The clinics' policies about birth control are often consistent with their policies about other treatments: if the clinics write prescriptions for other medications, they also write prescriptions for contraceptives, if they fill other prescriptions, they also fill prescriptions for contraceptives. Thus, family planning is an integrated part of this adolescent health care delivery system.

Even though these clinics facilitate family planning, it is not appropriate to view them as family planning clinics. Typically, about 85 percent of the visits are for other health problems, while only 15 percent of the visits are for family planning.

None of the clinics perform abortions. Although a few clinics may discuss with pregnant teenagers all their legal options, few, if any, of them make referrals to abortion clinics. At these clinics, most of the teenagers receiving positive pregnancy tests do go to term.

Clinic Administration and Staffing

Although the existing clinics by definition are located on school grounds, with only one exception the direct day-to-day management of these programs is provided by non-school agencies that more traditionally provide medical care (e.g., departments of public health, community clinics, hospitals, and medical schools).

Most clinics rely heavily upon nurse practitioners and either social workers or counselors. The smallest clinics with the most limited funding commonly employ a nurse practitioner and a social worker or counselor about half the time. If funds permit, they also have a medical assistant. The nurse practitioners work under written medical protocols established by the physicians associated with established medical institutions. Those doctors also visit the clinic for specific appointments, review and cosign charts, and perform other quality assurance measures.

The larger clinics tend to have full-time nurse practitioners, counselors, and medical assistants. They also employ part-time or full-time physicians, health educators or nutritionists, counselors specializing in drug and alcohol abuse, clinic receptionists, and occasionally dentists and dental assistants. They may also have directors or administrators who coordinate a variety of administrative, budgetary, and public relations functions.

As much as possible, the clinics select staff that both enjoy working with adolescents and are trained to do so. For example, the nurse practitioners and physicians are typically trained in pediatrics or obstetrics and gynecology, and nearly all the counselors are either trained or experienced in working with adolescents. Training is a continuous process for the staff as they learn more about the needs of the specific adolescents they are serving.

Interaction with the Schools

Many school-based clinics operate within the regular school building. They have converted a variety of rooms—classrooms, locker rooms, storage rooms, former nurse's or counselors' offices, and others—into examination rooms, counseling or educational areas, and reception areas.

Because of school restrictions, these clinics commonly cannot serve teenagers who have dropped out of school or teenagers from other schools. Consequently, some clinics operate on the school grounds but in separate buildings so that they can serve dropouts and other students.

Clinics make a considerable effort to become well integrated into the schools. The staff often try to get to know the administration as well as the teachers and counselors and, of course, the students. In many schools, the clinic staff give guest lectures or teach entire units in the health or sexuality education classes.

Students go to the school clinic just as they would go to the nurse's office. Whenever possible, the clinic staff try to schedule appointments during the students' study hall or during other classes that can be more easily missed.

However, the efforts of the clinic to become integrated into the school do not extend to clinic records. All clinic records are strictly confidential, and no school personnel are allowed to see them. This requirement assures the protection of the students.

Parental Involvement

Most, if not all, of the clinics obtain written consent from the parents of each student before that student can receive their medical services. Each fall when the students come back to school, most of the clinics send the parents a written description of the clinic and all of the health services it offers. At some sites, the parents have the option of consenting to some services but denying specific ones. In practice, the vast majority of parents request that their children be given all needed care.

This procedure provides parental consent but at the same time maintains the anonymity of students' use of the clinics. For example, parents do not know when or if the students use the clinic for family planning. However, if any student has a serious medical problem, then the parents would definitely be notified. More generally, clinics make a major effort to involve parents in their children's health care.

Why Clinics Work

Schools are, after all, where the young people are. And according to the providers, being there does offer a number of obvious advantages:

- The clinic is extremely accessible—adolescents don't have to take a bus or drive to another part of town, nor do their parents have to come and pick them up.
- It is familiar—students are in the school daily during the school year.
- Many students are in the clinic for a variety of health and educational reasons and become familiar with the clinic's other services and procedures.
- Many clinic services are consolidated—for many health problems students do not have to go elsewhere for care.
- Service is continually available—students do not have to make an appointment for many services.
- Students know that their friends use the clinic, and thus peers indicate that it is an "OK" place.
- Clinic visits are either free or have a minimal annual cost.
- Obtaining services is confidential. Because students visit the clinic for wide variety of reasons, no one automatically assumes that an appointment at the clinic is for any particular reason.
- Because it is strictly for adolescents, the clinic can hire staff that are fully accustomed to and skilled at working with the adolescent population.

- The clinic staff can better integrate classroom health and sexuality education with health care in the clinic.
- If a student needs care not provided by the clinic, the clinic can make the appropriate referrals to other agencies and then do appropriate follow-up afterward.

Evidence of Success

Various types of evidence prove that clinics work. First, the rapid growth of clinics means that, at a minimum, clinics have gained the acceptance and support of many communities. Moreover, where they have opened, the vast majority of parents sign the consent forms and encourage their children to use the clinics when needed.

A second type of evidence is provided by the clinic statistics on usage. The clinics do prove themselves with the students and do provide needed care. When a clinic opened in the South Side of Chicago, it provided more than 2,000 medical encounters in the first two months. In Kansas City about 70 percent of the students use the clinic each year, in St. Paul about 75 percent, in Dallas about 85 percent. Last year, the Dallas clinic served more than 3,200 students during 11,000 clinic visits. These are high usage rates, especially when many of the remaining students may not need to use the clinic. Some of the small clinics have lower usage rates, but typically, this is because limited funding prevents the clinics from being open a greater number of hours.

Third, during many of the visits, the clinics find previously undetected chronic health problems that deserve further attention or care. For example, some of them have detected vision problems, hearing problems, diabetes, heart murmurs, severe psychological problems, and other problems. The detection and treatment of these problems are important in themselves, but in addition, they eliminate important obstacles to improved school performance.

Finally, there is some evidence that the clinics reduce unintended pregnancy and its effects. None of the clinics serves the entire student population or even a majority of the students for any specific health problem, including family planning. Thus, most clinics probably do not have a measurable impact upon the entire student population on any specific health outcome. However, a few clinics do report success in improving the reproductive health outcomes of the entire school. For example, the data from the four St. Paul clinics indicate that about 35 percent of all the female students in those schools use the clinics for family planning, that they have high contraceptive continuation rates, and that known birth rates for all the students in the four schools have declined since the clinics opened. Those clinics have also reported considerable success in keeping teen mothers in school and preventing repeat pregnancies. Similarly, the Dallas clinic has reported a decline in repeat pregnancies and low-birth weight rates among its patients. The Kansas City school clinics have also reported lower low-birth weight rates among their patients.

In sum, these data indicate that clinics are increasingly being viewed by communities as effective approaches to providing needed health care, that students do use them and obtain needed health care, and that some clinics may reduce teenage pregnancy and its consequences.

Clinic Costs and Funding

The costs of the clinics vary greatly, depending upon their physical size, their staffing, the services they offer, and the types of costs included. The range seems to be from about $25,000 to $400,000 per clinic annually. A more descriptive figure is $125 to $150 per student per year for reasonably comprehensive care.

Most clinics have combined funding from federal, state, and local public and private monies. These sources include maternal and child health grants, Medicaid (especially EPSDT), Title X (family planning funds), Title XX (The Adolescent Family Life Act), Title XX (the Social Services Block Grant), the National Health Service Corps, state and city public health department funds, private foundations, and in-kind support. Most obtain in-kind support in the form of space and utilities, while some clinics also receive some time and support from the staff of certain organizations, e.g., the schools' registered nurses and other departments' social workers, counselors, or administrators.

Clinic Limitations

Although the school-based clinic model appears to have a number of important advantages over other health delivery models for adolescents, the model does have some limitations. A major limitation is, of course, that clinics do not currently have a stable source of funding as do some other health delivery systems. And there are other limitations: clinics located in the school building often cannot serve non-students; some teenagers might prefer a non-school setting; some clinics cannot prescribe or dispense prescriptions (e.g., birth control); clinics have limited hours and cannot provide service during non-clinic hours; coordinating referrals and other arrangements with other agencies can be cumbersome and time consuming; some state or school requirements thwart the provision of some kinds of needed health care. All these limitations clearly indicate that school-based clinics can only partially fill the health and family planning needs of teenagers, and that other programs should be maintained and enhanced.

Summary

School-based clinics represent a grass-roots movement and are now providing effective health care to thousands of adolescents who need care. Some clinics may also reduce unintended teenage pregnancy. Thus, the available evidence indicates that this model is a promising one that should be expanded.

References

Ahartz, et al. *The St. Paul Story: A Working Manual on the Pioneer School-Based Clinics in St. Paul, Minnesota.* St. Paul: Healthstart, 1986.

Green, L., and D. Horton. "Adolescent Health: Issues and Challenges." In *Promoting Adolescent Health: A Dialog on Research and Practice.* Edited by T. Coates, A. Petersen, and C. Perry. New York: Academic Press, 1982.

Hadley, E., D. Kirby, and S. Lovick. *School-Based Clinics: A Guide to Implementing Programs.* Washington, D.C.: Center for Population Options, 1986.

Kirby, D. *School-Based Health Clinics: An Emerging Approach to Improving Adolescent Health and Addressing Teenage Pregnancy.* Washington, D.C.: Center for Population Options, 1985.

Lovick, S., and W. Wilson. *School-Based Clinics: Update.* Washington, D.C.: Center for Population Options, 1986.

Rickets, A. Unpublished data obtained from Ann Rickets, Program Director, St. Paul Adolescent Health Services Project, St. Paul, 1985.

ANNOTATED BIBLIOGRAPHY: SEXUALITY EDUCATION IN THE SCHOOLS

Curricula

Benesch, Joan, Jean Kapp, and Louise Peloquin. *Implementation of Family Life Education Curriculum: Teaching Materials and Strategies.* Rev. Ed. Washington, D.C.: Sex Education Coalition, 1985.

Designed for junior and senior high family life education teachers in Washington, D.C. Offers clear instructions for conducting learning activities on a variety of topics: anatomy and physiology, self-esteem and decision-making, sex roles, relationships, contraception, sexually transmitted diseases (STD), sexual assault, pregnancy, and parenting. Compact, inexpensive, and easy to follow. Intended for urban populations, but would be helpful to any educator.

Bignell, Steven. *Sex Education: Teacher's Guide and Resource Manual.* Santa Cruz, Calif.: Network Publications, 1982.

Provides background information and teaching techniques for the following topics: reproduction, anatomy and physiology, pregnancy and birth, homosexuality, pregnancy alternatives, and sexually transmitted diseases. Section on teaching techniques includes activities such as films, discussion, incomplete sentences, brainstorming, advantages vs. disadvantages, question cards, and others. Also includes film guides and bibliographies. Considered an excellent resource by sexuality educators.

Bignell, Steven, ed. *Family Life Education: Curriculum Guide.* Santa Cruz, Calif.: Network Publications, 1982.

Designed to serve as a model for teachers setting up programs at the secondary level. It presents specific 10-session models for programs at both the junior and senior high school levels. Presents excellent teaching techniques and activities.

Bosch, Kathryn. *Changes and Choices: Human Growth and Development for Classroom Use.* Northampton, Mass.: Family Planning Council of Western Massachusetts, 1982.

Outlines 14 family life education sessions for fifth and sixth grade students. Includes suggestions for journal assignments and for homework with parents.

Burt, John, and Linda B. Meeks. *Education for Sexuality: Concepts and Programs for Teaching.* Third Ed. New York: CBS College Publishing, 1985.

Originally considered the sex educators' handbook. The first half of the book provides knowledge of the biological aspects of human sexuality. Provides a scope and sequence for grades kindergarten through twelve. Also includes factual information and an actual curriculum that follows the scope and sequence. Includes a "Glossary of Terms" and an "Atlas of Teaching Illustrations."

Cavanaugh, Michelle. *When I Grow Up: Structured Experiences for Expanding Male and Female Roles.* Humanics, Ltd., P.O. Box 7447, Atlanta, GA 30309, 1979.

A guide to helping children and adolescents eliminate sex-role stereotyping. Volume I deals with grades pre-K through 8; Volume II focuses on grades 9-12. Incorporates topics such as family life, career education, and science. Each activity includes a list of objectives, appropriate grade level, materials needed, time required, and an extensive procedural description.

Cooperman, Carolyn, and Chuck Rhoades. *New Methods for Puberty Education: Grades 4-9*. Morristown, N.J.: Planned Parenthood of Northwest New Jersey, 1983.

Outlines lesson plans for the following topics: physical and emotional changes of puberty, body image and self esteem, and relationships. Includes a plan for an evening program for parents.

DeSpelder, Lynne A., and Albert Strickland. *Family Life Education: Resources for the Elementary Classroom: Grades 4, 5, and 6*. Santa Cruz, Calif.: Network Publications, 1982.

A comprehensive collection of family education activities pertaining to five topic areas: self, family, friends, body, and decisions. Includes many new kinds of activities for elementary school-aged children.

Dodds, Jane M. *Human Sexuality: A Curriculum for Pre-Teens*. Rochester, N.Y.: Planned Parenthood of Rochester, 1980.

Designed to be used with students in grades five through eight. Contains a description of twelve suggested units on sexuality and sex roles, puberty, facts about girls, facts about boys, families, pregnancy, birth and babies, family planning, problems, decisions about relationships, sex and the law, and myths, rumors, and stories. Each unit contains an introduction, background information, activities, resources, and a test or evaluation.

Dodds, Jane M. *Human Sexuality: A Curriculum for Teens*. Rochester, N.Y.: Planned Parenthood of Rochester, 1980.

Focuses on the following topics: sexuality/roles, anatomy, pregnancy, pregnancy/birth, sexually transmitted diseases, responsibility, contraception, relationships, sexual response, parenting, unplanned pregnancy, homosexuality and sexual assault. Each unit includes an introduction, background information, activities, resources, and a test or evaluation.

Howard, Marian, Marie Mitchell, and Bette Pollard. *Postponing Sexual Involvement: An Educational Series for Young People*. Atlanta: Grady Memorial Hospital, 1983.

Designed to teach young teenagers how to say "no" to sexual behavior. Presents information regarding the general nature of relationships and sources of societal pressure influencing sexual behavior. Teaches assertive responses that teens can use in peer pressure situations. Consists of four 90-minute sessions.

Planned Parenthood Center of Memphis. *Family Life Education: A Problem-Solving Curriculum for Adolescents (Ages 15-19)*, 1980.

Designed specifically for use with five trigger films also developed by Planned Parenthood of Memphis. Contains a variety of activities that involve the use of the films. Includes other exercises that explore relationships with parents and peers, sexual identity, marriage and parenthood, and other health issues.

Planned Parenthood Center of Memphis. *In Between: A Family life Education Curriculum for Early Adolescents (Ages 10-14)*, 1980.

A collection of curriculum activities for young adolescents. Emphasizes a decision-making approach to helping preadolescents deal with the new privileges and problems associated with reaching puberty. Designed especially for use with a trigger film package also entitled *In Between.*

Schniedwind, Nancy, and Ellen Davidson. *Open Minds to Equality: A Sourcebook of Learning Activities to Promote Race, Sex, Class, and Age Equality.* Englewood Cliffs, N.J.: Prentice-Hall, 1983.

An innovative curriculum for educators who are interested in creating and maintaining an egalitarian program or classroom.

Stanford, B., and G. Stanford. *Roles and Relationships: A Practical Guide to Teaching About Masculinity and Femininity.* New York: Bantam Books, 1976.

Describes ideas for incorporating units on sex roles and sexuality into courses such as language arts, social studies, science, and family living and sexuality education. Special attention is given to how black men and women are depicted in literature and the effects of discrimination on gender role identity and relationships.

Thompson, Doug. *As Boys Become Men: Learning New Male Roles.* New York: Irvington Publishers, 1985.

Activities for junior and senior high school students that attempt to expand students' attitudes about male roles and masculinity.

Wilson, Pamela, and Douglas Kirby. *Sexuality Education: A Curriculum for Adolescents.* Santa Cruz, Calif.: Network Publications, 1984.

A comprehensive curriculum based on the semester-long nationally acclaimed programs at Council Rock High School in Newtown, Pennsylvania; University City High School in St. Louis, Missouri; and George Mason High School in Falls Church, Virginia. Consists of 11 units, each of which has a statement of goals and objectives, and an overview of the unit's contents, activity descriptions, lecture notes, and handouts.

Books for Professionals

American Library Association Order Department. *Sex Education for Adolescents: A Bibliography of Low-Cost Materials.* 50 East Huron Street, Chicago, IL 60611, 1980.

A bibliography of materials that meet the following criteria: easy to read; cost of $6.00 or less; and not likely to be labeled as liberal or conservative.

Bruess, Clint E., and Jerrold S. Greenberg. *Sex Education: Theory and Practice.* Wadsworth Publishing, 7625 Empire Drive, Florence, KY 41042, 1981.

A textbook on sex education. Includes sections on instituting and expanding sex education programs; biological, psychological, and sociological aspects of sex education; sexual decision-making; conducting sex education; and evaluation and research.

Constantine, Larry L., and Floyd M. Martinson, eds. *Children and Sex: New Findings, New Perspectives.* Boston: Little, Brown, 1981.

Deals seriously with sex and sexuality as essential components of childhood. Looks at sexuality throughout the life cycle. Coverage takes into account the full spectrum of disciplines, including anthropology, sociology, psychology, social work, psychiatry, and psychoanalysis.

Cook, Ann Thompson, Douglas Kirby, Pamela M. Wilson, and Judith S. Alter. *Sexuality Education: A Guide to Developing and Implementing Programs.* Santa Cruz, Calif.: Network Publications, 1984.

Covers building support for a program, establishing goals and objectives, designing the course, selecting and training leaders, implementing programs, linking young people with medical services, and evaluating the program. Also included are fact sheets on such topics as sexual knowledge and behavior of adolescents, parent/child communication about sexuality, and effects of sexuality education programs.

Dickman, Irving R. *Winning the Battle for Sex Education.* New York: SIECUS, 1982.

Designed to help parents, teachers, administrators, and other members of a community effectively organize support for a public school sex education program. Includes answers to the 20 questions most often asked about such programs.

Dumont, Jacqueline Pappalardo. *A Guide to Values Clarification in Sex Education.* Preterm Cleveland, University-Cedar Medical Building, 10900 Carnegie Avenue, Cleveland, OH 44106, 1979.

Exercises designed to increase students' awareness of values, to clarify how these values were developed or inherited, and to evaluate their effectiveness, importance, and relevance to the students' lives. Section One contains 33 exercises which, when used progressively, will build trust and risk levels. Section Two contains specific resource materials on a variety of human sexuality topics.

ETR Associates Training Staff. *Beyond Reproduction: Tips and Techniques for Teaching Sensitive Family Life Education Issues.* Santa Cruz, Calif.: Network Publications, 1983.

Includes tips for dealing with the following sensitive issues: decision-making, contraception, and pregnancy alternatives. Offers guidelines for selecting learning activities and a discussion of facilitation skills in the classroom.

Gordon, Sol, and Irving R. Dickman. *Schools and Parents: Partners in Sex Education.* Public Affairs Committee, 3381 Park Avenue South, New York, NY 10016, 1980.

Stresses the importance of including parents as partners in sex education. Includes an outline of a model curriculum. Booklet format.

Nelson, Mary, ed. *Family Life Educator.* Santa Cruz, Calif.: Network Publications.

Provides, in a quarterly magazine format, up-to-date information, resources, and techniques for teachers, parents, clergy, health care professionals, and community agency personnel involved in family life education. Includes abstracts of journal articles, reviews of current materials, copies of tested teaching activities, and descriptions of new programs, research, laws, and public policies.

Scales, Peter. *The Front Lines of Sexuality Education: A Guide to Building and Maintaining Community Support.* Santa Cruz, Calif.: Network Publications, 1983.

Presents results of ten years of study in a wide variety of communities across the nation. Focuses on influence of opponent and proponent groups and media. Provides guidelines for program operation, dealing with controversy, evaluation, public relations, curriculum development, and staff training.

Teacher Training Resources

Beresford, Terry. *How to Be a Trainer.* Baltimore: Planned Parenthood of Maryland, 1980.

Gives specific tips to facilitators on training techniques, group dynamics, and effective communication.

Boyer, Maggi, with Sally McCormick. *Helping People Learn . . . About Sexuality.* Bristol, Pa.: Planned Parenthood of Bucks County, 1986.

Includes training tips, designs, and actual training activities.

Knowles, Malcolm. *The Adult Learner: A Neglected Species.* Houston, Tex.: Gulf Publishing Company, 1978.

Reviews traditional theories about learning and teaching and describes and contrasts emerging theories about adult learning. Provides theoretical basis for principles of training design.

Margolis, Frederick H., and Chip R. Bell. *Managing the Learning Process.* Minneapolis, Minn.: Training Books, Lakewood Publications, 1984.

Focuses on the "delivery" aspect of training, including trainer role and style, setting and maintaining a learning climate, making presentations, monitoring group and individual tasks, facilitating the reporting process, managing learning activities. Also covers training management and evaluation tasks.

Parcel, Guy, and Sol Gordon, eds. "Sex Education in the Public School." *Journal of School Health* (April 1981).

Reviews state of the art of school-based sex education programs. Addresses the following issues: definition and history of sex education, community organization, teacher preparation and political concerns. Includes four papers documenting evaluations of four programs and implications for planning new programs.

Wagman, Ellen, Lynne Cooper, with Kay Rodenberg Todd. *Family Life Education Teacher Training Manual.* Santa Cruz, Calif.: Network Publications, 1981.

Covers tasks involved in designing and delivering family life education teacher training programs, including teacher selection, needs assessment, training design, training management and group leadership skills. Contains sample materials for every aspect of training: flyers, course descriptions, press releases, needs assessment and evaluation forms, and over 70 training activities.

Audiovisuals: Elementary and Middle Schools

Am I Normal? Producer/Distributor: New Day Films, 16mm or Video, 22 min., 1979.

In this humorous film, 13-year-old Jimmy tries to discover the "real story" behind the changes that his body is going through. Despite the pressures to "be cool" and "know all the answers," he finally finds some friendly adults who answer his questions about erections, wet dreams, masturbation, and other common concerns of boys. Most sexuality educators consider this film to be of excellent quality. (Ethnically mixed characters.)

Better Safe Than Sorry II. Producer/Distributor: Film Fair Communications. 16mm or Video, 15 min., 1984.

Television personality Stephanie Edwards talks to a group of young children about the prevention of child sexual abuse. She communicates to the children in a very simple and straightforward manner. Numerous situations are dramatized and the children are asked to decide how to react to each based on what they have just been taught. (Racially mixed characters.)

Boy Stuff. Producer/Distributor: Churchill Films, 16mm or Video, 21 min., 1985.

An inventory of afflictions suffered by boys, with engaging advice on how a little simple hygiene can avoid most of them. Deals with fungus of foot and genital area; odor of body and clothes; cleanliness of hands, nails, hair, and penis; head lice; spontaneous erections. (Some animation.)

Boy to Man. Second Rev. Producer/Distributor: Churchill Films, 16mm or Video, 15 min., 1984.

Describes the changes in boys during puberty: the growth spurt, skin changes (acne), masculine physique, endocrine glands, and secondary sex characteristics. Explains the female reproductive system. Also discusses personal health, hygiene, and emotional aspects of adolescence. One of the most widely used sex education films in the country. (Racially mixed characters.)

Dear Diary. Producer/Distributor: New Day Films, 16mm or Video, 24 min., 1981.

This humorous film focuses on the issues that concern many young adolescent girls. Three friends explore their feelings about boys, female roles, breast development, menstruation, and growing up. While the film successfully gives information through humor, some find a few of the scenes corny. The mother in the film is portrayed as a totally inadequate resource for her daughter. Widely used in many schools. (Racially mixed cast.)

Families. Producer/Distributor: Perennial Education, Inc., 16 mm, 10 min., 1970.

An animated film depicting the interdependence of all human beings and the importance and functions of the family. Describes different kinds of families in a very simple manner. (Animated.)

Feelings Grow, Too. Producer/Distributor: Sunburst Communications, 2 Filmstrips and Cassettes, 1983.

Filmstrips entitled "You and Yourself" and "You and Others" alert preadolescents to the emotional ups and downs that arrive along with puberty.

Fertilization and Birth. Producer/Distributor: Perennial Education, Inc., 16mm, 10 min., 1967.

Provides realistic and frank discussion of fertilization and birth in a simple manner. Shows live animal births. Uses animation to depict human birth. This film is a companion to *Human and Animal Beginnings*. Old but still useful in elementary school classrooms.

Free to Be . . . You and Me. Producer: Marlo Thomas and Carole Hart for Ms. Foundation. Distributor: McGraw-Hill Films, 16mm, 42 min., 1974.

Produced for television, this film encourages young people to develop their personalities free of sex-role stereotypes and to aim for self-actualization. The following people appear in the film: Alan Alda, Harry Belafonte, Mel Brooks, Rita Coolidge, Roberta Flack, Roosevelt Grier, Michael Jackson, Kris Kristofferson, Bobby Morse, The New Seekers, Tommy Smothers, Marlo Thomas, and Cicely Tyson. Dated, but still good.

Girl Stuff. Producer/Distributor: Churchill Films, 16mm or Video, 21 min., 1985.

Presents information about female puberty and feminine health and hygiene. Includes a lot of good information that is often left out of films on puberty. (Racially mixed characters.)

Girl to Woman. Second Rev. Producer/Distributor: Churchill Films, 16mm or Video, 17 min., 1984.

Presents the changes of puberty in girls: the growth spurt, skin changes (acne), endocrine glands, and secondary sex characteristics. Explains the male reproductive system, personal health, hygiene, and emotional aspects of adolescence. Emphasizes the normality of individual differences. One of the most widely used sex education films in the country. (Racially mixed characters.)

Growing Up Female. Producer/Distributor: Film Fair Communications, 16mm, 12 min., 1980.

Three preadolescent girls at different stages of physical and emotional growth learn about puberty from an older sister. Uses narration and animation to give factual information about anatomy, menstruation, and reproduction. (Racially mixed characters.)

Happy Little Hamsters. Rev. Producer/Distributor: Perennial
    Education, Inc., 16mm or Video, 13 min., 1984.

This is the third film edition of the story of two hamsters Naomi and Abdullah, and their litter of eight babies. Describes the complete life cycle of hamsters. Intended to be nonsexist.

Happy to Be Me. Producer/Distributor: Arthur Mokin Productions,
    16mm, 25 min., 1979.

Based on a survey of more than 600 New York City public school children, this film provides an objective view of young people's attitudes toward male and female gender roles. Students of different ages and different races voice a variety of attitudes ranging from traditional to nonsexist. The range of attitudes that are expressed and the spontaneity of the interviews stimulate discussion among older children and adolescents.

Human and Animal Beginnings II. Producer/Distributor: Perennial
    Education Inc., 16mm, 15 min., 1979.

Presents basic information about human reproduction and family life. Includes natural science film clips of baby monkeys, mice, guinea pigs, and rabbits. Uses time-lapse photography to show chicken and fish eggs hatching. These pictures clearly show the live embryos. On the human side, it shows babies in the hospital nursery and at home. Animated and still photography sequences show prenatal growth, development and birth. Dated but still very good.

In Between. Producer: Viscount Productions. Distributor: Planned
    Parenthood Center of Memphis, 16mm, 10 min., 1981.

Dramatizes the changing feelings and concerns of pre- and early adolescents. In three segments, the key characters interact with family and friends in situations where they are required to make important decisions. The story takes place on a summer day in a small suburban, racially mixed community. May work best with middle-class 5th and 6th graders. (Southern accents.)

It Must Be Love Cause I Feel So Dumb. Producer/Distributor: Coronet/MTI Film & Video, 16mm or Video, 29 min., 1976.

This humorous and touching love story captures the awkwardness of adolescent first love. It points out the sometimes painful process of deciding personal values and learning to judge relationships with other people. The language and dress of the characters in this recommended film are representative of suburban, white preteenagers. Dated, but still good.

It's a Thought. Producer/Distributor: Centron Films, 16mm, 22 min., 1980.

In this film, Debbie fails in her attempts to make friends with the popular girls in her junior high school. She naturally feels insecure and rejected. Her older sister, Missy, gives Debbie some positive advice about friendship based on her own experiences in junior high school. Although their mother in the film is not a believable character, both Debbie and Missy are extremely realistic. They yell and scream at each other but they also demonstrate their concern for one another. The film would probably appeal most to suburban junior high school audiences. (White characters.)

Julie's Story. Producer/Distributor: Kimberly-Clark Audio-Visual Library, 16mm or Video, 1986.

Eleven-year-old Julie starts her period during tryouts for the school musical. She gets information and support from the teacher, her mother, and her friend's older sister.

Learning to Say No. Producer/Distributor: Sunburst Communications, 2 Filmstrips and Cassettes, 1984.

Teaches assertiveness techniques, emphasizes a sense of accomplishment and the admiration and self-respect for others that result. Involves students in typical problem situations that require assertiveness. Provides opportunities for role playing and classroom discussion.

Looking Great, Feeling Great. Producer/Distributor: Sunburst Communications, 2 Filmstrips and Cassettes, 1983.

Makes preadolescents aware of the new personal hygiene needs that accompany puberty. Urges viewers to take responsibility for keeping their bodies clean and healthy.

My Mom Is Having a Baby. Producer/Distributor: Time-Life, Inc. 16 mm or Video, 47 min., 1976.

Presents the facts about pregnancy and birth in a simple manner appropriate for elementary school aged children. Petey Evans's mother is pregnant and he is confused, anxious, and a bit jealous about the impending arrival. Includes footage of an actual birth.

The New Me: Accepting Body Changes. Producer/ Distributor: Sunburst Communications, 2 Filmstrips and Cassettes, 1983.

Filmstrips entitled "Boy to Man"and "Girl to Woman" describe the physical and emotional changes of puberty for boys and girls.

Nicholas and the Baby. Producer/Distributor: Centre Productions, 16mm, 23 min., 1981.

Addresses sibling participation in a prepared childbirth. Nicholas's parents include him in many aspects of their preparation for a new baby. When Nicholas accompanies his mother to the doctor's office, he learns how the baby is developing. When his mother begins labor, Nicholas is picked up from school and taken to the hospital. Although he is not present during the actual delivery, he does get to visit his mother during labor and meets "his baby" shortly after birth. The child's perspective is portrayed with warmth and humor. (White characters.)

Oh, Boy! Babies. Producer/Distributor: Coronet/MTI Film & Video, 16mm or Video, 30 min., 1983.

Based on a true story and originally shown on television, this moving film follows a group of 6th-grade boys at a private school in New York City through their school's elective course on infant care. Useful resource for encouraging nurturing behavior in boys and men.

The Same Inside. Producer/Distributor: March of Dimes, 16mm or Video, 13 min., 1984.

Explores the feelings of four children who are physically handicapped. In their own words they discuss their feelings and explain how they wish to be treated. Sensitive and moving. Evokes an understanding of disabled individuals' wishes to be considered as individuals.

Seeing Through Commercials. Producer/Distributor: Barr Films, 16mm, 15 min., 1976.

Explores how a toy commerical is made, showing children how producers of the ads try to persuade viewers to buy their products. Shows how, through the use of special lighting, sound, and background, the toy is made to look much larger than it really is and to be so appealing that the children think they must have it. A wonderful beginning tool for teaching children to be media critics.

Then One Year. Producer/Distributor: Churchill Films, 16mm or Video, 19 min., 1984.

Describes physical and emotional aspects of puberty. Covers both the male and female reproductive systems and emphasizes the wide variation in normal growth and maturation rates. Widely used in coeducational classes instead of *Boy to Man* and *Girl to Woman.* (Racially mixed characters.)

Where Did I Come From? Sex Education Can Be Fun. Producer: Coronet/MTI Film & Video. Distributor: Network Publications, Video Format, 1985.

Based upon a popular book by Peter Mayle and Arthur Robins. Deals openly with reproductive anatomy and physiology. Presents nudity tastefully. Explains human beginnings in a multicultural setting with well done birthing sequences. Analogies used to describe conception, orgasm, and other reproductive functions are likely to be confusing to young children. Must be shown by a responsible adult who can review the content and give simpler explanations. Very inexpensive and available in many video stores.

Who Am I Now? Producer/Distributor: Tambrands, Inc., Video, 21 min., 1988.

Colorful graphics and several unexpected fantasies provide young girls and boys with information about the physical, emotional, and social changes of puberty. Gives information on both the female and male reproductive systems but is weak on males. Promotes Tambrands sanitary products.

Who Do You Tell. Producer/Distributor: Coronet/MTI Film & Video, 16mm or Video, 11 min., 1978.

Utilizes animation and live action to address the question of whom to tell in several problem situations: when you're lost, if your house catches fire, if someone touches you in a way that you don't understand. (Racially mixed characters.)

Audiovisuals: Secondary Level

Acquaintance Rape Prevention Materials. Producer/ Distributor: ODN Productions, 16mm, 1978.

A collection of four films with accompanying teachers' guides , student materials, and discussion posters.

The Party Game (9 min.): Kathy, a white teenage girl who has just broken up with her boyfriend, meets Mark at a party. What she fails to communicate after Mark's advances leads to sexual assault. (White characters.)

The Date (7 min.): A black couple, Raymond, 20, and Charlotte, 16, have just come in from a date to celebrate her 16th birthday. Their different expectations of how a "perfect evening" should end demonstrate how sex-role stereotyping can lead to rape. (Black characters.)

Just One of the Boys (8 min.): After a big game, Mike, who is sexually naive, is pressured into joining his teammates on a date with Josie, a girl with a "bad reputation." Mike is placed in a tough situation when his friends insist that he join their sexual attack upon Josie. (White characters.)

End of the Road (10 min.): Jenny's car breaks down on a deserted road and Dan, a familiar face from summer school, stops to help her. Jenny's assertiveness prevents an attack. (White characters.)

AIDS in Your School. Producer/Distributor: Peregrine Productions, 16mm or Video, 17 min., 1986.

An engaging, informative film with some very clear, important messages. Stresses that AIDS is everyone's problem, that it is caused by very specific behaviors, and that it can be avoided. Presenters, including a junior high student with AIDS, are appealing. High quality graphics are used to explain the immune system.

The AIDS Movie. Producer/Distributor: New Day Films, 16mm or Video, 26 min., 1986.

In this film, aimed at teenagers, the focus switches back and forth between an AIDS educator speaking to a mostly white middle-class group of high school students, and three AIDS patients who talk one at a time about how they contracted the AIDS virus and what the experience of having AIDS has been like.

AIDS: Questions and Answers. Producer/Distributor: Community TV Network, 16mm or Video, 14 min., 1986.

Uses clear vocabulary and excellent explanations to provide basic AIDS information. Presenters are primarily people of color. Emphasizes risk behaviors rather than risk groups. Strong language may make this film unacceptable for school programs, although it would work well with clinic or community programs.

AIDS: What Everyone Needs to Know. Producer/Distributor: Churchill Films, 16mm or Video, 18 min., 1986.

Surveys the facts and dispels the myths about AIDS. Woven throughout the factual material are clips of an interview with an PWA (person with AIDS), who is a former drug abuser, and his wife.

Anatomy and Attitudes: Understanding Sexuality. Producer/Distributor: Sunburst Communications, 3 Filmstrips and Cassettes, 1983.

Focuses primarily on male and female sexual anatomy and physiology. Emphasizes the need for teenagers to be accurately informed about sexuality. Demonstrates with unusual sensitivity how early interaction with parents conditions attitudes about the body and the role of sex in life.

Another Half. Producer/Distributor: Bill Wadsworth Productions, 16mm or Video, 27 min., 1985.

Depicts a friendship between two boys who both feel the pressure to conform to sex-role stereotypes. Shows the negative consequences of giving into this pressure. Excellent discussion stimulant. (White characters.)

Babies are People, Too. Producer/Distributor: Churchill Films, 16mm or Video, 27 min., 1985.

Designed to give teenage parents a better understanding of infant development during the first two years. Shows how a baby's behavior indicates its basic needs.

The Birth Control Movie. Producer: ETR Associates. Distributor: Perennial Education, Inc., 16mm or Video, 24 min., 1982.

Using a very innovative format, this film explores issues surrounding teenage sexuality and gives information on birth control. A group of teenagers in a drama class produce a film about birth control. Thus, the audience sees two different story lines: the interaction between the teens who are making the film and the birth control film that they produce. (Racially mixed characters.)

Choices: The Mating Game. Producer/Distributor: The Ounce of Prevention Fund, Video, 58 min., 1984.

An emcee asks two teenagers various questions about growing up, making sexual decisions, sexually transmitted diseases, marriage and parenting responsibilities. When they do not answer correctly, they watch clever skits by the Twelfth Night Repertory Company that are the highlight of this video. Younger teens would probably be particularly responsive to the valuable information and messages about sexuality presented here in a highly entertaining format.

Condom Sense. Producer/Distributor: Perennial Education, Inc., 16mm, 25 min., 1981.

Designed especially for male audiences. Promotes condoms as a practical, inexpensive method of preventing pregnancy and sexually transmitted disease. Although effective in parts, the film tries to accomplish too much. (Racially mixed characters.)

Dating: Coping With the Pressures. Producer/Distributor: Sunburst Communications, 3 Filmstrips and Cassettes, 1981.

Examines the pressures today's teenagers face in dating. Focuses on role stereotyping, the double standard, sexual activity, drug use, and parental attitudes.

Daughters of Time. Producer/Distributor: New Day Films, 16mm, 29 min., 1981.

Promotes the use of midwives as an alternative to obstetricians in childbirth. Documents the professional lives of three midwives in different parts of the United States. Encourages expectant mothers to participate more actively in their own health care and to have the kind of childbirth experience that they truly desire. Although long, the film is quite fascinating, especially for professionals. (Ethnically mixed characters.)

Do I Want to Be a Parent? Now? Ever? Producer/Distributor: Sunburst Communication, 2 Filmstrips and Cassettes, 1980.

Examines the emotional and intellectual advantages and disadvantages of becoming a parent in today's society. Part one shows how changing life-styles, family patterns, and financial considerations have encouraged many people to view parenthood as a personal choice rather than a cultural necessity. Part two uses interviews to dramatize the diverse viewpoints about the decision to have or not have children.

Everyday Miracle: Childbirth. Producer/Distributor: Films Incorporated, 16mm, 27 min., 1980.

A film about prenatal development and childbirth. Shows actual photography of fertilization and fetal development in the uterus. Follows a woman through her pregnancy and delivery. Amazing photography. (White characters with British accents.)

Fathers. Producer/Distributor: Churchill Films, 16mm or Video, 23 min, 1980.

Portrays three different fathering styles and perceptions of the father's role in parenting. A black man discusses his lifestyle as a single parent. The other two fathers, one Hispanic and one white, demonstrate two different approaches to fathering in two-parent homes. Shows the fathers in typical interactions with their children and wives. Slightly tedious format.

Feeling Good About Yourself: How to Build Self-Confidence. Producer/Distributor: Guidance Associates, 4 Filmstrips and Cassettes, 1978.

Uses scenarios to address sensitive problems related to adolescent fears and confusions. Each vignette touches upon issues that sometimes undermine self-confidence in teenagers, such as changing needs and desires, peer pressure, and close parental supervision.

First Things First. Producer/Distributor: Bill Wadsworth Productions, 16mm or Video, 30 min., 1982.

A white middle-class couple grapple with the decision to have sex. The film does a good job of identifying common differences in the way males and females approach this important decision. Shows a parent as a positive role model—she discusses sexuality comfortably with her son. Focuses on the importance of communication in a romantic relationship. Validates a teenager's right to say "no" to sex. May be a little too intellectual for some audiences. Highly recommended.

Four Pregnant Teenagers: Four Different Decisions. Producer/Distributor: Sunburst Communications, 3 Filmstrips and Cassettes or Live-action Video, 1983.

Poignant vignettes dramatize the difficult decisions that pregnant teenagers face. Encourages adolescents to weigh the emotional, ethical, and financial consequences involved in each of the four options available to the pregnant teenager: adoption, marriage, single parenthood, and abortion.

The Gentle Art of Saying No: Principles of Assertiveness. Producer/Distributor: Sunburst Communications, 3 Filmstrips and Cassettes or Video, 1979.

Outlines three basic rules and practical techniques that will help young people become more assertive. A series of role playing exercises encourages the student to apply these principles to practical situations. A classic.

Getting Through the Bad Times: Teenage Crisis. Producer/Distributor: Sunburst Communications, 3 Filmstrips and Cassettes, 1980.

Presents a step-by-step self-help technique for coping with emotional crises. Through the use of unresolved dilemmas, viewers can be assisted in practicing the "crisis technique" as well as exploring possible solutions to crises.

Girl on the Edge of Town. Producer/Distributor: Paulist Productions, 16mm, 25 min., 1980.

A value-laden film about a teenage girl who gets pregnant. Supports the option of having the baby and putting it up for adoption. Shows a very positive father/daughter relationship, but gives an inaccurate and distorted picture of pregnancy counseling in a family planning clinic. (White characters.)

The Great Chastity Experiment. Producer/Distributor: Paulist Productions, 16mm, 27 min., 1985.

Theme of physical vs. emotional intimacy. Deeply in love, two high school students who are very affectionate with each other want to consummate their relationship. Fearing the consequences of sexual involvement at this point in their lives, the couple decides to try chastity and, as a result, discover new things about each other. (White characters.)

Growing Up Young. Producer Distributor: Perennial Education,
   Inc., 16mm or Video, 22 min., 1980.

Explores the special problems of adolescent sexuality and the
need for friendship and approval in making decisions about sex.
Four teenage women, all seemingly well educated and from
middle-class homes, make different decisions about their
relationships with their boyfriends, ranging from deciding not to
have sex, to having sex, to getting pregnant and consequently
deciding to get married. (Racially mixed characters.)

Hard Climb. Producer/Distributor: Perennial Education, Inc.,
   16mm, 27 min., 1983.

Encourages teenage boys to feel good about themselves
without having to prove their sexual prowess to their friends.
Shows that caring, sensitivity, and emotional bonds are more
important and satisfying than casual sex. Somewhat sterile.
(Racially mixed characters.)

Have a Healthy Baby: Labor and Delivery. Producer/ Distributor:
   Churchill Films, 1984, 29 min.

A superb, tender birthing film focusing on a black couple
having their first child in a hospital with all of the trappings of
modern medicine and a Caucasian/Hispanic couple having their
fourth child at a birthing center. Animation effectively depicts the
various stages of the birth process.

Herpes Simplex II. Producer/Distributor: Milner-Fenwick, Inc.,
   16mm or Video, 19 min., 1983.

Gives not only factual information about genital herpes, but
also insight into the life experience and feelings of people who
have contracted the disease. A sane and rational approach to the
topic. (Racially mixed characters.)

His Baby, Too: Problems of Teenage Pregnancy. Producer/Distributor:
   Sunburst Communications, 3 Filmstrips and Cassettes, 1980.

Focuses on the rights and responsibilities as well as the legal
and moral obligations of the young father-to-be. The case studies
presented are an effective vehicle for exploring the options

available to teenage couples facing an unplanned pregnancy. Poses open-ended questions that successfully involve the viewer in making difficult decisions. Also explores the legal rights of fathers regarding adoption, marriage, child support, and visitation. Well done.

Hope Is Not a Method III. Producer/Distributor: Perennial Education, Inc., 16mm or Video, 22 min., 1984.

An update of the 1977 version, this film provides objective information about contraception. Diagrams are clear and easy to understand. Includes information on abortion.

How to Make Good Decisions. Producer/Distributor: Sunburst Communications, 3 Filmstrips and Cassettes or Video, 1983.

Helps teenagers develop the decision-making skills to help them take control of their lives. Depicts several typical situations that call for the decision-making process.

Human Growth IV. Producer/Distributor: Perennial Education, Inc., 16mm or Video, 20 min., 1986.

An update of an old classic. Describes the changes in the human body from birth to physical maturity. Also explores common feelings as children approach puberty and later stages of adolescence. Tries to cover too much information in one film. (Racially mixed characters.)

Human Sexuality: The Lifelong Experience. Producer/ Distributor: Sunburst Communications, 2 Filmstrips and Cassettes, 1982.

Offers a broad definition of human sexuality. Stresses the central role that sexuality plays in everyone's life from birth to death.

If You Want to Dance. Producer/Distributor: New Dimension Films, 16mm or Video, 14 min., 1981.

A white teenage couple faces the consequences of an unplanned pregnancy. Impresses upon boys that pregnancy is not just a girl's problem. Despite peer pressure to be sexually active, a young man learns that it is not cool to get a girl pregnant.

Includes a great quote, "If you really care about a girl, you don't get her pregnant in the first place."

In Due Time. Producer/Distributor: ODN Productions, 16mm, 13 min., 1985.

Meet Pat Bradley, a young black woman with a plan. Learn why she decided not to become a teenage pregnancy statistic. Hear her views on sex, birth control, relationships, and work. Excellent.

Is That What You Want for Yourself? Producer/Distributor: Coronet/MTI Film & Video, 16mm or Video, 13 min., 1980.

Explores the reaction of a working class family when the teenage daughter suspects that she is pregnant. While communication between the teenage couple seems good, communication within the girl's family is poor. The stilted acting does not reduce the emotional power of the film. (White characters.)

I Think I'm Having a Baby. Producer/Distributor: Coronet/MTI Film & Video, 16mm or Video, 29 min., 1981.

Highlights the naivete and intensity of a young adolescent girl's feelings for an older teenage boy. She has a sexual encounter with him and fears that she is pregnant. When she tells him, he barely remembers her and wants no part of the situation. Originated as an ABC after-school special on television. (White characters.)

It's OK to Say No Way. Producer/Distributor: YWCA of the USA, Video, 7 min., 1985.

Conveys the message that teens can say "no" to sex, using a popular adolescent medium, rapping. Very entertaining—the rhythm and message stay with you after the video is over. Music video format. Break dancing somewhat dates this video.

Journey to Birth. Producer/Distributor: March of Dimes, Birth Defects Foundation, 16mm or Video, 20 min., 1985.

Examines how a mother's personal choices can foster or harm the health of her child. Fetal growth is shown inside the uterus at 2, 6, 8, 12, and 18 weeks, emphasizing the message that mother and baby share everything. Includes interviews with pregnant mothers and doctors. Explains the ultrasound examination.

Kids Who Have Kids Are Kidding Themselves. Producer/ Distributor: Educational Activities, Inc., Filmstrip and Cassette, 1979.

Includes statistics about teenage pregnancy designed to help students see this event in its true light. Dr. Sol Gordon has found that teen audiences are not turned off when he says, "The best oral contraceptive is 'no!'" Includes the illustrated book, "You Would if You Loved Me."

Let's Do Something Different. Producer: Education Development Corporation. Distributor: Planned Parenthood Federation of America, Video, 16 min., 1986.

In soap opera format, a young adult couple who have just recovered from STD discuss the use of condoms. Conveys the message that condoms may enhance lovemaking, can be fun to use, and are essential for preventing disease. (Black characters.)

Linkletter on Love, Sex, and Values. Producer/Distributor: Marshfilm, 4 Filmstrips and Cassettes, 1983.
1. "Choices: An Individual Responsibility"
2. "Love: Real or Romance"
3. "Chastity: It's Okay to Say No"
4. "Pregnancy: It's Easy to have a Baby, But Hard to Raise a Child"

Art Linkletter narrates these four filmstrips on decision-making, love, and adolescent sexuality. Very well done.

Looking for Love. Producer/Distributor: Educational Consortium for Cable, 16mm or Video, 30 min., 1982.

A poignant documentary about the effect of a teenage pregnancy on the lives of all involved. Very realistic. (Ethnically mixed characters.)

Making Decisions About Sex. Producer/Distributor: Churchill Films,
   16mm or Video, 25 min., 1981.

Shows eight California teenagers discussing their views about
having sexual intercourse at their age. While the teenagers express
realistic points of view, the voice-over format is boring for many
viewers. (Racially mixed characters.)

A Matter of Respect. Producer/Distributor: National Audiovisual
   Center, 16mm, 18 min., 1980.

Designed to emphasize the male role in sexual responsibility.
However, the film includes few examples of teenage men being
responsible for their own sexual behavior. On the other hand,
there are some excellent documentary sequences interspersed
throughout the film: rap sessions with teenage mothers and with a
group of young men, interviews with teenage men, and excerpts
from a speech on sexual responsibility by Jesse Jackson. Dated but
still useful. (Racially mixed characters.)

Me, A Teen Father. Producer/Distributor: Centron Films, 16mm or
   Video, 13 min., 1981.

Presents a teenage pregnancy from the point of view of the
young male. Uses a voice-over format which many viewers find
boring. (White characters.)

Me Power: Building Self-Confidence. Producer/Distributor: Sunburst
   Communications, 2 Filmstrips and Cassettes or Video, 1980.

Traces the development of self-confidence. Outlines steps that
teenagers can take to build their self-confidence.

A Million Teenagers. Fourth Ed. Producer/Distributor: Churchill
   Films, 16mm and Video, 23 min., 1985.

A new edition of a classic film. Added are new sequences on
herpes, and chlamydia with its sequellae of pelvic inflammatory
diesease and nongonococcal urethritis. AIDS is discussed briefly.
Explains the physiology of the diseases, their transmission,
symptoms, treatment, and dangers, and contains an appeal to
good sense. (Racially mixed characters.)

No Time Soon. Producer/Distributor: ODN Productions, 16mm or Video, 16 min., 1986.

Male companion piece to the film *In Due Time.* Vincent and Arty are different in background and age. Although they have different views on many issues, they agree that teenage parenthood is not for them. Viewers are introduced to positive male role models who have found alternatives to the pressures of teenage parenthood. Excellent.

OK to Say No: The Case for Waiting. Producer/Distributor: Sunburst Communications, 3 Filmstrips and Cassettes or Video, 1980.

Uses the stories of three teenagers to present the case for abstinence as a valid sexual option. Points out that "everybody" is not doing it, thus providing support to teenagers who are not yet having sexual intercourse and are interested in waiting. Well done.

Personal Decisions. Producer/Distributor: Planned Parenthood Federation of America, 16mm or Video, 28 min., 1986.

Seven women share their reasons for choosing to abort. Reasons include such things as rape, teenage pregnancy, mental retardation diagnosed by amniocentesis, birth control failure, and single parenting. Discusses reasons why abortion should remain the personal decision of the woman. (Racially mixed characters.)

Pregnant Teens: Taking Care. Producer/Distributor: Perennial Education, Inc., 16mm or Video, 22 min., 1983.

Offers complete prenatal care information to pregnant teenagers. Covers nutrition, fetal development, effects of drug and alcohol use, "telling your parents," and other topics. Includes microphotography showing an actual fetus in the womb. (Racially mixed characters.)

Prisoners of Chance (Teenage Parents). Producer/ Distributor: Filmfair Communications, 23 min., 1979.

Based on real characters, this film dramatizes the life-styles of several parenting teens. The first, Maureen, is an articulate young woman who had many problems and thought having a baby would improve her life. The second, Lynn, no longer sees the baby's father and lives with her mother with whom she struggles over parenting responsibilities. The last couple, Rick and Anna, married during her pregnancy and opted to separate two years later due to emotional and financial strain. (Racially mixed characters.)

Rape: Escape without Violence. Producer/Distributor: Perennial Education, Inc., 16mm, 18 min., 1979.

Discusses nonviolent techniques for stopping a rapist. Narrated by a rape victim who encourages women to have a realistic awareness of rape. Stresses that many rapists are intimidated by a woman with assertive body language. Dispels many of the myths about rape. (White characters.)

Reaching Out. Producer/Distributor: Coronet/MTI Film & Video, 16mm or Video, 32 min. 1980.

A love story about two teenagers with extraordinary needs. One is physically disabled; the other is emotionally troubled. Raises questions about sexuality and the disabled as well as the needs of "forgotten" youngsters who are shunted off to group homes. (Racially mixed characters.)

Reflections: Josie. Producer/Distributor: Paulist Productions, 16mm, 25 min., 1981.

Designed to explore self-concept in relation to sexuality. Presented by adolescents who explain the decision-making process and emphasize the importance of making mature decisions.

Running My Way. Producer/Distributor: Children's Home Society of California, 16mm or Video, 28 min., 1981.

Focuses on the many sensitive issues, dilemmas, peer pressures, and decisions confronting 15-year-old Lisa and her boyfriend, Tony. A realistic example of today's adolescent scene in middle-class communities. Identifies negative emotional consequences of adolescent sexual activity that can occur even when pregnancy and sexually transmitted disease are avoided. Portrays the intensity of a first love. Considered an excellent film for exploring decision-making about sexuality. (Racially mixed.)

Saying No: A Few Words to Young Women about Sex. Producer/Distributor: Perennial Education, Inc., 16mm or Video, 17 min., 1982.

Young women talk about their personal decisions to abstain from sexual intercourse. Selected vignettes demonstrate how girls can be pressured to have sex. Later, the film returns to the same situations but the girls use assertiveness skills to say "no." Sexist, in that it gives the message that only girls should say "no." (Racially mixed.)

Schoolboy Father. Producer/Distributor: Coronet/MTI Film & Video, 16mm or Video, 30 min., 1982.

Tells the story about a very concerned and responsible teenage father (Rob Lowe) who wants to get custody of his baby boy. He arranges to take care of his son one week, during which he realizes that the responsibility of taking care of an infant is more than he can handle. Although hairstyles and clothing are dated, it is a real tear jerker. (White characters.)

Setting Limits. Producer/Distributor: ODN Productions, Video, Captioned and in Sign Language, 1982.

A collection of three films on assertiveness with accompanying comprehensive study guides. (White deaf characters.)

Sex and Decisions: Remember Tomorrow. Producer/ Distributor: Perennial Education, 16mm and Video, 29 min., 1985.

Deals with the decision to have sexual intercourse. A young couple who have a good relationship weigh the options of both sides of the question and decide to abstain. Soap opera format— the young man in the film comes from a wealthy family and drives a Mercedes convertible. If this fact is explained to the audience before they view the film, it does not cause as big a distraction. (White characters.)

Sex, Drugs, and AIDS. Producer/Distributor: ODN Productions, Video, 17 min., 1986.

Begins with the idea that AIDS is hard to get. Includes the following segments: young women talking about protecting themselves against sexually transmitted diseases and pregnancy, five people who have AIDS telling how they got it, and a man who was previously homophobic talking about how his attitudes changed when he watched his gay brother die of AIDS.

Sexual Myths and Facts. Producer/Distributor: Sunburst Communications, Filmstrip and Cassette, 1980.

Dispels many popular sexual myths. Via realistic vignettes, portrays teenagers discussing their beliefs, concerns, and attitudes concerning sexuality. A clinic counselor clarifies information about sexually transmitted disease.

Shelley and Pete . . . (and Carol). Producer/Distributor: National Audiovisual Center, 16mm, 22 min., 1980.

Depicts the story of Pete and Shelley, two working-class high school students who become teenage parents. The story line is compelling and realistic. Dramatic ending adds to the appeal for junior and senior high school students. (Racially mixed characters.)

Stale Roles and Tight Buns. Producer: O.A.S.I.S., Inc., Distributor: Multi-Focus, 23 min., 140 slides and Cassette, 1984.

Produced by a Boston-based group of men who are organized against sexism and institutional stereotypes. Educates viewers about sex-role socialization that limits men's opportunity for open and healthy relationships with other men, women, and children. Focuses on the destructive images of men in advertising. Excellent.

Still Killing Us Softly. Producer: Jean Kilbourne. Distributor: Cambridge Documentary Films, 16mm and Video, 30 min., 1987.

An update of *Killing Us Softly*. Again, Jean Kilbourne uses advertising clips to illustrate the impact of the media on our perceptions of male and female roles. With an interesting mixture of insight, humor, and outrage, she shows the audience that seemingly harmless ads are a powerful form of cultural conditioning. Explores the relationship of media images to actual problems in the society, such as the channeling of men and women into traditional roles and occupations, economic discrimination against women, teenage pregnancy, and sexual exploitation. Highly recommended.

The Subject is AIDS. Producer/Distributor: ODN Productions, Video, 18 min., 1987.

An adaptation of *Sex, Drugs and AIDS.* Intended to be more appropriate for a younger (junior high) audience. Emphasizes abstinence as the key form of AIDS prevention. Includes an introduction by Surgeon General Everett Koop on the importance of AIDS education.

Taking Charge: Teens Speak Out About Sex and Birth Control. Producer/Distributor: Fanlight Productions, 16mm and video. 1984.

Looks at the myths and misconceptions that many teens hold, and the complex realities they confront in seeking to deal with this new and confusing aspect of their lives. Stresses that accurate information about birth control is the first step toward making responsible decisions. Interweaves the intimate conversations of five teenagers and comments from a woman physician concerning sexuality and birth control. Shows part of a pelvic exam. (Ethnically mixed characters.)

Teenage Birth Control: Why Doesn't It Work? Producer/ Distributor: Sunburst Communications, 2 Filmstrips and Cassettes or Live-Action Video, 1980.

Clarifies the emotional and psychological reasons why many teenagers take chances with unprotected sexual intercourse. In part one, Janie suspects that she is pregnant. She regrets not having used birth control and remembers some of the reasons for her irresponsible behavior. Janie considers six of the most common reasons teenagers cite for failing to use birth control, pointing out the inherent fallacies of each. When Janie finds out that she is not pregnant, she and her boyfriend seek information about contraception from a counselor. Well done.

Teenage Father. Producer/Distributor: Children's Home Society of
California, 16mm, 28 min., 1978.

Explores the thoughts and feelings of a 17-year-old who has
become a teenage father. Shows the young couple talking with
their parents and debating their options with a social worker. Only
the credits at the film's end reveal that the cast members are
professionals and that the story is a dramatization. Academy Award
winner. (Racially mixed characters.)

Teenage Sex: How to Say "No." Producer/Distributor: Sunburst
Communications, 3 Filmstrips and Cassettes or Video, 1982.

Designed to help adolescents resist pressure to have sexual
intercourse. Adapts principles of assertiveness training to general
and specific sexual situations.

Teen Mother: A Story of Coping. Producer/Distributor: Churchill
Films, 16mm or Video, 24 min., 1981.

Nineteen-year-old Rosie is surviving as a teenager mother.
Portrays the realities of parenting in the teenage years. Attempts
to show the brighter side of this situation with a teenager who is
"making it."

Teens Having Babies. Producer/Distributor: Polymorph Films,
16mm, 20 min., 1983.

Gives information on prenatal care and childbirth to pregnant
teenagers. Shows teens giving a medical history, getting a pelvic,
exam, attending childbirth classes, and delivering their babies.

The Touch Film. Producer/Distributor: Sterling Productions,
16mm, 22 min., 1983.

Through dramatizations and true-to-life scenes, Dr. Jesse
Potter gives insight into the emotional and physical benefits of
touch. Dr. Potter's warmth and sensitivity make this film an
excellent choice for teenagers and adults.

Understanding Human Reproduction. Producer/Distributor:
Sunburst Communications, 2 Filmstrips and Cassettes or
Video, 1985.

Gives a detailed presentation of the male and female reproductive system. Also discusses conception, the stages of pregnancy, and alternatives, including Caesarean section.

A Very Delicate Matter. Producer/Distributor: Coronet/MTI Film & Video, 16mm and Video, 30 min., 1983.

A few months after a single encounter with a fellow counselor at summer camp, Kristin learns she has contracted a sexually transmitted disease. She seeks medical treatment but is afraid to warn her steady boyfriend that he may also be infected. He makes the discovery himself, but because Kristin has failed to warn him, their relationship is irrevocably damaged.

Wayne's Decision. Producer: Viscount Productions. Distributor: Planned Parenthood Center of Memphis, 16mm, 4 min., 1979.

Seventeen-year-old Wayne confronts his parents with the fact that his girlfriend, Donna, is pregnant. He wants to marry her but his distraught parents violently oppose his decision. Intended to stimulate discussion of decision-making around an unplanned pregnancy. May have special appeal to fathers. Trigger film. (White characters with heavy Memphis accents.)

What Can a Guy Do? Producer/Distributor: Serious Business Company, 16mm or Video, 15 min., 1980.

Rather than giving factual information about birth control methods, this film focuses on teenage boys' attitudes and opinions about contraceptive use. Three couples deal with the possibility of pregnancy. In other segments, Angel Martinez leads a discussion group with a diverse group of teenage boys. One episode shows a boy purchasing condoms in the drug store for the first time. (Ethnically mixed characters.)

What Guys Want. Producer/Distributor: Polymorph Films, 16mm, 16 min., 1983.

Teenage boys discuss their attitudes and feelings about maleness and sexual behavior. Gives teen girls convincing reasons

for delaying sexual activity. Very realistic. (Ethnically mixed
characters.)

What's to Understand? Producer: Viscount Productions. Distributor:
   Planned Parenthood Center of Memphis, 16mm, 4 min.,
   1979.

A black teenage couple, Floyd and Laura, are alone in his
family's apartment. Floyd pushes Laura to have sex, but she resists.
Their off-camera voices let the viewer know how they really feel
about having sex together. Trigger film.

When Sex Means Trouble. Producer/Distributor: Sunburst
   Communications, 3 Filmstrips and Cassettes or Video, 1986.

Introduces the sensitive subject of sexual exploitation. Deals
with three aspects—peer and media pressure to have sex,
acquaintance rape, and sexual abuse. Help teens understand their
own rights, learn to recognize abuse and develop strategies for
protecting themselves.

When Teens Get Pregnant. Producer/Distributor: Polymorph Films,
   16mm, 19 min., 1982.

Five pregnant adolescents discuss how they got pregnant and
their feelings about being pregnant. The girls give advice to other
teenagers who might be considering having sexual intercourse or
having a baby. Very realistic. (Ethnically mixed characters.)

You Would If You Loved Me. Producer/Distributor: Guidance
   Associates, 4 Filmstrips and cassettes, 1981.

Addresses critical questions about sexuality that young people
often encounter. Differentiates between love and infatuation.
Discusses common lines that teenagers use on each other.

Part III
Sexuality Education in the Community

OVERVIEW:
CURRENT ISSUES, FUTURE DIRECTIONS

Joe Fay

Like democracy itself, sexuality education flourishes where individuals on the grass-roots level take an active part in its occurrence. For this reason, community sexuality education programs are the foundation of the sexuality education movement. Those of us who conduct sexuality education programs in our communities find ourselves in the front lines of the movement. Our work in the trenches allows us to see first hand the opportunities as well as the impediments to our progress. This article will discuss the meaning, scope, and current status of community sexuality education, briefly exploring some of the different types of programs. It will then examine some of the unresolved issues in the field, which may point the way to future directions.

Sexuality educators have made tremendous progress throughout the nation. To a large extent, mainstream America has come to realize the importance of sexuality education. For example, public opinion polls consistently show that over 80 percent of Americans support sexuality education in the schools (Mathtech, Inc., 1979). In addition, sexuality educators have made great strides in adapting their goals and programs to the needs of those they serve. Part of this accommodation was simply the free market at work, with suppliers and consumers reaching an accord on what the product should be. Another ingredient was society's growing willingness to bring sexuality out of the closet. But the most important factor was the increasing maturity of the sexuality education movement. Over the last decade, we have done a much better job of defining what we mean by sexuality and sexuality education. Some of our most basic tenets—that sexuality is a positive part of being human, that we are sexual throughout life, and that sexuality education is not an event but a life-long process—are becoming an accepted part of the American consciousness. We are also escaping the stigma of "value-free" sexuality by clearly articulating the basic values of our programs (Scales, 1982).

Community sexuality education takes many forms. Generally, it strives to promote healthy attitudes about sexuality by providing factual information, enabling people to clarify their personal values and attitudes about sexuality, and increasing people's self-esteem. In addition to helping people on a personal level, these programs hope to play a role in reducing the incidence of society's sex-related problems: teenage pregnancy, sexually transmitted disease, sexual abuse and exploitation, domestic violence, and discrimination against women.

The main advantages of community sexuality education are that programs can be made available to anyone, are voluntary, and allow the educator to be as creative as possible in determining target groups and program content. Unlike school programs, which can require years of preparation including coalition building, curriculum development, and teacher training, community programs can usually be implemented more quickly. The bureaucratic inertia that often plagues school systems is usually not a factor when working with community groups.

Many different community organizations are now offering sexuality education programs, for example, schools (addressed in the previous section, "Sexuality Education in the Schools"), health agencies, youth-serving agencies, religious institutions, social service agencies, including those that serve the disabled, colleges, and college organizations such as fraternities and sororities. While these and many more groups are participating in the movement, the unchallenged leaders in the field have been the family planning organizations, especially Planned Parenthood. In fact, it is often the family planning agency that acts as the community's catalyst, providing resources, offering encouragement and assistance, or even organizing and conducting the programs for other groups.

Community programs are occurring with all age groups on a variety of topics. For example, with the increasing agreement among a wide range of groups that parents should be the primary sexuality educators of their children, parent education programs have been initiated throughout the country. Many programs combine parents and children in an effort to foster effective communication about sexual issues. Programs for children of varying ages are being offered, from the basic "Where did I come from?" to the difficult issue of sexual abuse prevention. It is a tribute to the progress of our field that issues such as sexual abuse, taboo a short time ago even in the adult community, are now openly discussed with children as young as preschool age.

Adult groups also have a variety of programs to choose from. With the increasing percentage of young singles in our society, programs exploring sex roles, relationships, and intimacy have proven to be popular. As society begins to increase its recognition that people are sexual throughout life, programs for the elderly become more prevalent.

While community sexuality education programs now span the life cycle, programs for adolescents remain the most common. However, where ten years ago most teen programs focused narrowly on prevention of unwanted pregnancy or STD, the scope of today's programs are usually much more comprehensive, discussing values, self-esteem, decision-making, relationships, life planning, sexual exploitation, peer pressure, sexual orientation, sex roles and other issues designed to promote healthy sexuality.

While the popularity of community sexuality education has increased dramatically in the past decade, opposition still exists. Educators need to be sensitive to the reasons for the opposition. Sex is a potent political issue. Sexuality educators learn very early in their careers that acceptance or rejection of their program by a school or community group often has very little to do with the program's educational merits but has a great deal to do with politics. Therefore, if sexuality educators are to increase their effectiveness, they must become more politically astute.

Part of this process entails keeping up with current events and legislation. It also involves public relations—making the community, the press, local opinion leaders and legislators more aware of the importance of sexuality education. Forming coalitions with local supporters is also valuable. In a larger sense, being political means becoming more aware of how our personal attitudes about sexuality are influenced by cultural problems such as sexism, racism, violence, poverty, and religious intolerance.

While understanding the politics of sexuality and becoming proficient at community organization is an important part of the job of any community sexuality educator, it is beyond the scope of this article to discuss these issues in detail. However, for those who want very helpful and practical suggestions for building community support for sexuality education, three sources are mentioned in the references (Dickman, 1982; Fay, 1985; and Scales, 1984).

The articles that follow illustrate the great diversity of settings in which sexuality education occurs. During the 1980s, the pendulum of sexual mores has swung more rapidly than ever, creating confusion among people of all ages. This confusion makes decisions about sexual behavior, relationships, intimacy, and gender roles increasingly difficult. There are also new challenges because people have more options than in the past. With more options come more opportunities for growth. Today's social atmosphere provides fertile ground for community sexuality educators. Demand for our programs should continue to rise. While the improvement and breadth of our programs is bound to continue, we need to maintain a sense of our own fallibility. Because the times are so confusing, people have a great desire for simple answers to their sexual concerns. Once our communities bestow upon us the title of sexuality "expert," it is tempting to play the role and pretend we have the final answers.

A brief look at our own history should warn us of the dangers of infallibility. One decade ago, sexuality educators generally believed that birth control "methods talks" would reduce the teenage pregnancy rate. We were trained to refrain from imposing values and to encourage teens to make their own decisions about sexual activity. We thought we were doing the right thing. Today, guided by a different set of assumptions, many of us take a more conservative position. We feel it's best to tell young teens that they're too immature to be having intercourse. Once again, we think we're doing the right thing. Part of our problem is that we lack a solid research base to guide our assumptions. More disturbing is that the data we do have generally give way to political considerations in the formation of public policy. All too often, we do what we think will sell rather than what we think is right.

The "saying no" programs are a current example of this trend. While learning to say "no" is an important component of any comprehensive program, it is not, by itself, sexuality education. Moreover, the assumption guiding some of these programs is that young teens do not possess the cognitive capabilities to consider the consequences of their actions and, therefore, cannot be good contraceptors (Howard, Mitchell, and Pollard, 1983). This assumption overlooks cross-cultural research showing that young teens can be responsible contraceptors if birth control and teen sexual behavior are accepted parts of the culture (Jones et al., 1985). As long as we live in a culture with an anti-sex bias, our efforts to deliver sex-positive messages will be met with confusion and resistance. Even now, many programs are guided by the desire to control children rather than educate them.

Given the fact that teenagers are sexual beings with sexual feelings who often develop relationships based on sincere affection, how can we help them manage those feelings? How can we teach them that sexuality is natural and wonderful, that feelings are healthy and normal, without enticing them to have sexual intercourse at early ages? Some educators feel that we should encourage adolescents to express themselves through behaviors other than intercourse such as masturbation, manual stimulation, and other forms of "outercourse." Obviously, there are other educators who feel that this would be inappropriate; that it would be more like sex instruction vs. sexuality education. But our lack of certainty is no reason to remain silent. Throughout history, the greatest educators were not those with the best answers, but those who asked the best questions. We need to continue to raise the unpleasant issues, both within our own movement and in society at large. We can ask the questions that will help people find their way through the morass of sexual confusion. We can also continue to explore the social forces that perpetuate the anti-sex bias of our culture.

The greatest challenge for community sexuality educators is to remain on the cutting edge of the movement; to allow ourselves no complacency about the great progress we've made, to derive no comfort from the status quo. A social movement always faces the danger of losing its special vitality and uniqueness once it reaches a certain level of popular acceptance. When this happens, its central message can become watered down or even trivialized. The best way for us to keep our movement vital is to remain vigilant about our key issues and goals. The roots of the American sexuality education movement are firmly embedded in the women's movement and clearly consistent with the goals of a democratic society: freedom of choice, equality, opportunity, social justice, and the search for a better way of life, including that peculiarly American value of the "pursuit of happiness." Community educators are in a unique position to make a contribution because our work in the trenches allows us to see that this American dream is still unavailable to many.

References

Dickman, Irving R. *Winning the Battle for Sex Education.* New York: Siecus, 1982.

Fay, Joe. "Ten Keys to Success in a Conservative Community." *Impact 85.* Syracuse, N.Y.: Institute for Family Research and Education, 1985, pp. 1, 5, 8.

Howard, Marion, Marie Mitchell, and Bette Pollard. *Postponing Sexual Involvement: An Educational Series for Young People.* Atlanta: Grady Memorial Hospital, 1983, p. 1.

Jones, Elise, Jacqueline Forrest, Noreen Goldman, Stanley K. Henshaw, Richard Lincoln, Jeannie Rosoff, Charles Westoff, and Deirdre Wulf. "Teenage Pregnancy in Developed Countries: Determinants and Policy Implications." *Family Planning Perspectives,* 17, No. 2 (March/April 1985): 53-63.

Kirby, Douglas, Judy Alter, and Peter Scales. *An Evaluation of U.S. Sex Education Programs and Evaluation Methods.* Bethesda, Md.: Mathtech, Inc., 1979.

Scales, Peter. *The Front Lines of Sexuality Education: A Guide to Building and Maintaining Community Support.* Santa Cruz, Calif.: Network Publications, 1984.

Scales, Peter. "Value's Role in Sexuality Education." *Planned Parenthood Review,* 11, No. 3 (Fall, 1982): 6-7.

YOUTH ORGANIZATIONS:
A VALUABLE SEX EDUCATION RESOURCE
Jane Quinn

Introduction

Youth-serving agencies in the United States rank second only to the public school system in the number of young participants they serve. Collectively such organizations as Girls Clubs, Boys Clubs, Girl Scouts, Boy Scouts, Camp Fire, 4-H, the YWCA and the YMCA reach an estimated 25 million young people per year. Most American youth organizations consider health education to be an important part of their repertoire of program offerings, and an increasing number are including—and even emphasizing—sexuality information in their programming.

This trend has not occurred accidentally. Twenty of the nation's major youth organizations have, since 1977, voluntarily participated in a Program to Expand Sexuality Education in Cooperation with Youth Serving Agencies, initiated and sponsored by the Center for Population Options. This project has provided individual consultation, technical assistance, training, and resource materials to members of the national staffs (and, in some cases, boards of directors) of these organizations in an effort to harness their potential as sexuality education providers.

Other more general factors also contribute to this positive trend. Most youth organizations stay abreast of research studies related to a variety of issues. The burgeoning professional literature on adolescent sexuality (particularly the Guttmacher,

Zelnik and Kantner, and Mathtech studies) has helped to spur several organizations into action. The findings of this body of work have been corroborated by studies initiated by individual agencies. For example, membership surveys conducted by the YWCA and 4-H during the 1970s revealed that sex education was a major unmet need among respondents. Youths' perceptions of their needs have had an influence on both the programs and policies of several agencies. In November of 1981, the Congress of Camp Fire, Inc. (a body of voting delegates from the 320 Camp Fire councils) gave near-unanimous approval to a resolution that delineated Camp Fire's role in supplementing the family's responsibility to provide sex education. Adding to the drama—and the broad base of support—at the time of adoption was a position statement prepared by a caucus of youth that pointed to the urgency and importance of the statement. "We feel Camp Fire has a responsibility to the concerns of youth and since we, the youth, are confronted with a constantly changing society, Camp Fire's implementation of sexuality education will help us toward finding our own self-identity," wrote the Youth Caucus.

The relationship between organizational policy and program development, or between research and program, is a complex but important factor in moving organizations from a position of reticence or inertia to one of commitment and action. This chapter will offer a case study of how one national organization, Girls Clubs of America, implemented an agency wide focus on sexuality education. This analysis will be followed by an update on the current sex education efforts of several other national youth-serving agencies. The chapter will conclude with a summary of the characteristics of these groups that make them current and future resources in addressing the sexual information needs of young people.

How One Organization Did It

Girls Clubs of America (GCA) is considered a leader among national youth organizations in its commitment to providing family life and sexuality education to its members. GCA's most recent (1984) survey date indicates that 83 percent of its affiliates provide programming in this area. These heartening statistics show a marked increase from previous years, largely as a result of the national organization's multi-step efforts over the past ten years. These efforts follow a logical progression that can be characterized by general, then specific, descriptions:

1. *The Organization Educates Itself About the Issue.* GCA began responding to research information (most notably, the 1976 Guttmacher study, *11 Million Teenagers: What Can Be Done About the Epidemic of Adolescent Pregnancies?*) and consulting the outside experts in 1976 and 1977, when staff and board members began planning a 1978 Wingspread Conference entitled "Today's Girls: Tomorrow's Women." This conference explored three issues facing girls: adolescent sexuality; career awareness/youth employment; and juvenile justice. The several speakers who addressed the issue of adolescent sexuality included: Mary Calderone, M.D., then President of the Sex Information and Education Council of the United States; Frederick S. Jaffe, then President of The Alan Guttmacher Institute; and Elizabeth Jerome, M.D., Medical Director, Teen Age Medical Services, Minneapolis Children's Health Center and Hospital. While one outcome of the conference was to focus national attention on the unmet needs of girls in these three subject areas, another outcome was to increase GCA's internal commitment to conduct specific activities around these themes.

2. *The Organization Adopts Specific Goals.* In 1980, GCA's Board of Directors and Council (its highest governing body) established three program priorities as part of its five-year long range plan. Not surprisingly these priority areas paralleled the three issues addressed by the "Today's Girls: Tomorrow's Women" panelists. These program goals committed GCA's organizational resources to the implementation of national-level program activities in the three priority areas.

3. *The Organization Develops a Positive Policy Statement.* In 1981, GCA's board and council adopted the following policy statement, designed to spell out the organization's beliefs about its role in providing sexuality education to its members:

Girls Clubs of America, as a national direct service and advocacy organization, affirms its belief in the right of girls and young women to age-appropriate, comprehensive and accurate sexuality information.

Recognizing that the primary source of such information should be the family, GCA believes that social agencies and schools should provide girls and their families with assistance by offering sexuality education that will support the development of responsible personal values. Sensitive, responsible, age-appropriate programming, developed with girls and parents and drawing upon appropriate community resources and services, can provide a solid framework for responsible, confident decision making. We believe that such a positive approach to sexuality education by schools and social agencies will reinforce parental guidance and lead to responsible behavior.

4. *The Organization Develops, Implements, and Evaluates a National-Level Program.* In 1981, GCA received federal funding to support its Family Life Education for Adolescents Program. This program was designed to provide training and technical assistance to local Girls Clubs to enable them to initiate or expand programming in family life and sexuality education. During each of the program's two years of operation, national staff provided three-day training workshops in each of GCA's seven regions, reaching a total of more than 350 Girls Club professionals with comprehensive program training. An evaluation conducted by the Center for Informative Evaluation concluded that GCA "performed an exemplary family life education training program for its

local staff. From the trainees' perspective, this program has given them the tools and knowledge necessary to design and implement effective family life education programs for the adolescents in their Girls Clubs." Even more compelling is the fact that, during the two years of the project, the number of clubs offering sexuality education rose from 68 to 83 percent.

5. *The Organization Continues to Build Its Research Base.* While the Family Life Education for Adolescents Program was being conducted under the auspices of GCA's Department of Program Services, staff at its National Resource Center (GCA's research arm) continued to review and assess pertinent research, making the results available to clubs on an ongoing basis. In 1982, GCA published *Facts and Reflections on Female Adolescent Sexuality,* a major research compendium designed to help practitioners assess the program implications of current research findings.

6. *The Organization Develops, Implements, and Evaluates a Second National-Level Program.* In March of 1985, GCA launched a second national-level adolescent sexuality program, this one targeted specifically at pregnancy prevention. The three-year "Preventing Adolescent Pregnancy Project" applies the findings of the *Facts and Reflections* study and builds on member clubs' program activities in the areas of family life and sexuality education. This action-research program combines four program models into a comprehensive approach to pregnancy prevention.

7. *The Organization Maintains Its Advocacy Efforts.* Throughout this several-year period, GCA has been an active participant in various national-level coalitions organized to promote sexuality education and to maintain adolescent access to clinical services. This participation, carried out largely by GCA's Washington office, is consistent with the organization's mission of service and advocacy.

8. *The Organization Institutionalizes Its Commitment and Program Activities.* An agency-wide task force recently recommended that sexuality education be included as a part of GCA's new Core Program. Such inclusion ensures the continuing commitment to program delivery in this subject area.

What Other Organizations Have Done

Several of the country's other national youth-serving agencies have taken similar steps to address the sexuality education needs of their members. While an exhaustive listing of their activities is not possible in the confines of a single book chapter, the following programmatic highlights of some of the agencies are offered in the hope that they will round out the very positive picture that currently exists:

American Red Cross. This organization received a Federal grant to develop an "Adolescent Life and Family Communication" curriculum for young people in grades 5-7 and their parents. This demonstration will develop and implement an educational program designed to increase youth's knowledge in adolescent life-skills and emotional and physical changes during puberty and to promote positive adult-youth communication.

Boys Clubs of America. This agency integrated sexuality education into its popular "Body Works" health promotion program that was developed several years ago. More recently, Boys Clubs of America received federal funding for a multi-issue prevention program that includes pregnancy prevention as one focus.

Camp Fire, Inc. This organization's 1981 policy statement delineates Camp Fire's role in supplementing the family's responsibility to provide sexuality education. On a program level, Camp Fire's new handbook for early adolescents, *A Rainbow of Discovery*, features a unit on physical, social, and emotional changes of puberty for girls and boys.

Girl Scouts. The largest national girl-serving organization has a policy statement that emphasizes the importance of human sexuality education and authorizes its local councils to address the issue, based on a determination of local need. In 1983 the National Board of Directors of Girl Scouts reaffirmed its commitment to provide human sexuality education within the Girl Scouts program. Several councils have developed comprehensive programs dealing with preparation for puberty and menarche, and with broader aspects of sex education. GSUSA's national office has a series of booklets on contemporary issues for local councils and leaders. Some of these booklets focus on issues related to human sexuality and provide a framework for developing programs related to human sexuality. These booklets contain factual information about girls' development, planning guidelines, training information, advice for leaders, and recommended program activities and resources. In addition, the new program handbook for junior Girl Scouts (grades 4-6) contains a section on preparation for menarche and puberty.

Salvation Army. With over 1,600 community centers nationwide, this organization reaches large numbers of young people on a regular (often daily) basis. Several years ago, the Salvation Army received federal funding for development of "Bridging the Gap Between Youth and Community Services," a life-skills education program that teaches adolescents to know and utilize a variety of community resources. Sexuality education and decision-making are integrated into this popular, value-based program.

Young Women's Christian Association. The YWCA's commitment to sexuality education dates back to the early 1900s when the organization both advocated for and provided programs in this area. In the 1960s and 1970s, community YWCA's pioneered in providing educational programs for young women who were released from school because of pregnancy. In 1983, the YWCA's national office published a *Program Guide for Teen Sexuality Education,* with federal (Title X) funding. Subsequently, a national network of YWCA's local associations was formed around the issue of adolescent sexuality, and a "National Adolescent Sexuality Brief" newsletter continues to be distributed to all YWCAs and to other organizations on a regular basis. The YWCA is also currently engaged in national-level efforts to replicate two sexuality education programs created by local affiliates—one, an extensive peer education program and the other, a life options program utilizing a game format. In addition, its national office has recently developed an innovative educational rock music video, entitled "It's OK to Say No Way."

What Youth Organizations Can Offer as Sex Education Providers

Youth membership organizations such as those described in this chapter offer a unique set of characteristics that make them an excellent resource as sex education providers. They provide an already-existing network for reaching large numbers of young people on a regular basis. Because their members choose to belong to these groups, they are willing participants in program activities. The adults who work with youths in such settings usually have established a high level of trust and possess good communication skills, enabling members to feel comfortable exploring sexual issues with these leaders. And because secular and religious youth groups are respected by parents and the larger community, they tend to be viewed as credible, safe sources of sexual information for young people.

Other characteristics that enhance the usefulness of youth agencies as sex education providers are the following: parents are often involved in the programs as group leaders or program planners, and this factor can assist in discouraging opposition to proposed programs and in encouraging dialogue about sexuality within families; and youth organizations serve significant numbers of preadolescents and males, groups that tend to be underserved by traditional sex education sources.

Conclusion

Youth-serving organizations are an incredibly rich resource as providers of a variety of educational programs, including sex education. The expansion of their activities in this area during the past decade provides a strong base on which to build future efforts. School- and clinic-based sex educators may want to consider broadening their view of potential allies and forming new partnerships with their youthwork colleagues.

References

11 Million Teenagers: What Can Be Done About the Epidemic of Adolescent Pregnancies in the United States. New York: The Alan Guttmacher Institute, 1976.

Evaluation of the Girls Clubs of America's Family Life Education Program: Year 1 Report. Tuscon, Ariz.: Center for Informative Evaluation, 1982.

Facts and Reflections on Female Adolescent Sexuality. New York: Girls Clubs of America, Inc., 1982.

Kantner, John F., and Melvin Zelnik. "Sexual and Contraceptive Experience of Young Unmarried Women in the United States, 1976 and 1977." *Family Planning Perspectives* 9 (October 1977).

Kirby, Douglas. *Sexuality Education: An Evaluation of Programs and Their Effects.* Santa Cruz, Calif.: Network Publications, 1984.

Shah, F., Melvin Zelnik, and John F. Kantner. "Unprotected Intercourse Among Unwed Teenagers." *Family Planning Perspectives* (January-February 1975): 39-44..

Teenage Pregnancy: The Problem That Hasn't Gone Away. New York: The Alan Guttmacher Institute, 1981.

RESOURCES AVAILABLE FROM YOUTH ORGANIZATIONS

BOYS CLUBS OF AMERICA

Title: *Body Works*
Format: Program Kit
Available From: Supply Service, Boys Clubs of America, 771 First Avenue, New York, NY 10017
Description: This activity-based program guide offers a wealth of excellent ideas about how to integrate health information into a youth agency's core program. Sexuality education is one of the several issues covered by the *Body Works* program.

THE CENTER FOR POPULATION OPTIONS

Title: *Sexuality Education Resource Guides*
Format: Six Program Booklets on the Following Topics: Peer Education Programs, Programs for Parents, Programs for Pre-adolescents, Small Group Workshops, Programs in Religious Settings, and Programs for Young Men
Available From: The Center for Population Options, 1012 14th Street, N.W. Washington, DC 20036

Description: These volumes are the result of CPO's collaboration with 20 national organizations in the multi-year Program to Expand Sexuality Education in Cooperation with Youth-Serving Agencies. The guides contain basic information on the selected topics, program models based on real-life agency experiences, and resource bibliographies.

Title: *Life Planning Education*
Format: Printed Curriculum Guide
Available From: The Center for Population Options, 1012 14th Street, N.W., Washington, DC 20036

Description: This innovative curriculum, designed for use with junior and senior high school age youth, integrates sexuality education with employment planning in an effort to help teenagers make decisions about their future.

Title: *Preventing Adolescent Pregnancy: The Role of the Youth Servicing Agency*
Format: Program Report
Available From: The Center for Population Options, 1012 14th Street, N.W. Washington, DC 20036

Description: This report of a 1982 conference emphasizes the important role that youth-serving agencies can play in teenage pregnancy prevention. The report contains practical suggestions from youth organizations across the country on developing sexuality education and pregnancy prevention programs.

Title: *Involving Parents in Sexuality Education: The Role of Agencies Serving Youth*
Format: Program Report
Available From: The Center for Population Options, 1012 14th Street, N.W. Washington, DC 20036

Description: This report outlines the crucial role that parents play in sexuality education, based on discussions at a 1983 Wingspread conference. The report includes a summary of research, descriptions of model programs, creative uses of the media, and strategies for overcoming problems in program implementation.

GIRLS CLUBS OF AMERICA

Title: *Choices: A Teen Woman's Journal for Self-Awareness and Personal Planning*
Format: Workbook/Journal
Available From: Girls Clubs of America National Resource Center, 441 West Michigan Street, Indianapolis, IN 46202

Description: This journal for young women, ages 14-20, contains thought-provoking exercises designed to help them develop and realize personal goals in the areas of education, careers and family life.

Title: *Challenges: A Young Man's Journal for Self-Awareness and Personal Planning*
Format: Workbook/Journal
Available From: GCA National Resource Center, 441 West Michigan Street, Indianapolis, IN 46202
Description: This journal assists young men in the 14-20 age range to consider education, career and family decisions that are part of the shift from adolescence to adulthood.

Title: *Individual Choices/ Challenges Workbook*
Format: Workbook/Journal
Available From: GCA National Resource Center, 441 West Michigan Street, Indianapolis, IN 46202

Description: This money-saving exercise book allows individual teens to complete and keep their worksheets when the main *Choices/Challenges* texts are shared by groups.

Title: *Women Helping Girls with Choices*
Format: Program Guide
Available From: GCA National Resource Center, 441 West Michigan Street, Indianapolis, IN 46202

Description: This guide was written for community volunteers who want to help girls make informed decisions about their futures. The guide describes a program model developed by GCA in conjunction with the New Hampshire Chapter of the Federation of Business and Professional Women's Clubs.

Title: *Facts and Reflections on Female Adolescent Sexuality*
Format: Research Report
Available From: GCA National Resource Center, 441 West Michigan Street, Indianapolis, IN 46202

Description: This well-organized survey of current research promotes an understanding of the way girls develop and provides important facts on adolescent sexual activity, pregnancy and parenthood. The publication can be used for program development, as a supplementary text, and as a resource guide to contemporary findings in this field.

Title: *Growing Together: A Sexuality Education Program for Girls Ages 9-11*

Format: Printed Curriculum Guide

Available From: GCA National Resource Center, 441 West Michigan Street, Indianapolis, IN 46202

Description: This series of four workshops was designed to increase positive communication between parents and daughters (ages 9-11) about sexual information and values. The guide is one component of the Preventing Adolescent Pregnancy Program.

Title: *Will Power/Won't Power: A Sexuality Education Program for Girls Ages 12-14*

Format: Printed Curriculum Guide

Available From: GCA National Resource Center, 441 West Michigan Street, Indianapolis, IN 46202

Description: This eight-session curriculum describes an assertiveness training program with the specific goal of encouraging early adolescent girls to delay engaging in sexual intercourse. The guide is the second component of GCA's Preventing Adolescent Pregnancy Program.

SALVATION ARMY

Title: *Bridging the Gap Between Youth and Community Services: A Life Skills Education Program*

Format: Printed Curriculum Guide

Available From: Salvation Army Social Service Department, 120 West 14th Street, New York, NY 10011

Description: This curriculum outlines a comprehensive program designed to assist teens in identifying and using a variety of useful community resources. "Supplementary Notes for Leaders in Religious Settings" are also available.

YOUNG WOMEN'S CHRISTIAN ASSOCIATION
(YWCA OF THE U.S.A.)

Title: *It's OK to Say No Way!*

Format: 63/4 min., 1/2" video cassette tape and leader's guide

Available From: Program Services Division, YWCA of the U.S.A.,
    National Board, 726 Broadway, New York, NY 10003

Description: This dynamic music video, designed for an early
adolescent (ages 11-16) audience, provides a clear message about
the appropriateness of postponing sexual involvement. The
accompanying leader's guide offers background information,
recommended discussion questions, role-playing ideas, resources
for leaders, and suggestions for the video's use.

THE ROLE OF FAMILY PLANNING/HEALTH AGENCIES
Janet Alyn

The family planning agency is an ideal community sexuality education resource for information, materials, advocacy, programs, and knowledgeable people. Family planners choose their profession because of a commitment to preventing unwanted pregnancy and the belief that education is an integral part of that prevention. This attitude, plus easy access to materials on human sexuality and reproductive health, gives the family planning agency and its educators the basic elements to work with the community.

While family planning agencies vary in operational styles and services offered, they are sufficiently similar to allow using the experiences of Planned Parenthood of San Antonio (PPSA) as an example of the role played by family planning agencies in sexuality education.

Since the early 1970s, PPSA has been teaching sexuality education in the local public schools and in the community. From the first one-hour presentation on contraception given to a single high school class, PPSA's primary education program has grown into a six-hour program based on a decision-making model presented by a seven-person professional staff to 11,000 students annually.

Evaluations of the in-school program have shown that students increase their knowledge of sexuality and retain this knowledge (Kirby, 1984). More difficult to document but equally important are informally reported attitude and behavior changes from an education program. A school nurse describes her experience.

> My 8th grade students and I spent one week together being educated on sexual decision-making, and a special trust . . . a bonding . . . was built between us. I am pleased to give credit to your program.

Student comments also reflect positive learning experiences. These comments range from the flip, "I'd better get some condoms for my date tonight," to the thoughtful, "I think I'd be better off postponing sex" and "You gave me a lot to think about." PPSA also includes teacher training, peer counselor training, and adult education in its programs for the community.

In addition to having committed and knowledgeable staff members, family planning agencies have access to proven curricula through the family planning network of agencies. A curriculum, however, is only a guide, and training is needed to create an effective teacher. At PPSA the training plan for new educators consists of preparation, observation, participation, and evaluation. New educators are first given an extensive reading list and a copy of the PPSA curriculum. They then observe the program as it is given by experienced educators and are instructed to note not only program content but the personal style of all speakers. Content must meet the standards of the curriculum guide, and information must be accurate and relevant for the particular audience. While individual style of delivery will vary, all speakers must demonstrate confidence, sincerity, appropriate use of humor, and respect for the audience.

To ease the transition from observer to speaker, new educators team-teach with experienced educators before tackling a solo teaching assignment. While knowledge and teaching skills increase with experience, continuing education is essential for all educators. Through their professional affiliations, family planning agencies have access to current information and to seminars with recognized experts in the sexuality education field.

This extensive training is essential for sexuality educators from a family planning agency who are in a unique position in the community. They provide a needed and wanted service but are guests in the classroom. This guest status carries both rewards and challenges.

Family planning educators gain instant credibility with an audience because of their familiarity with the operation of a family planning clinic and their first-hand knowledge of pregnancy testing, contraception, and pelvic exams. This credibility hastens the educator's acceptance by the group and is a key to successfully dispelling the fears and misconceptions most teenagers have about reproductive health care. When a student who is contemplating a visit to a family planning clinic considers the educator to be warm, caring, and knowledgeable, that student will assume all family planning personnel are warm, caring, and knowledgeable and will be more likely to seek family planning services when they are needed.

Unlike regular classroom teachers who have students with them for many months and can expand and compress planned lessons during that time, guest educators have a limited amount of time with each group and must be prepared to revise a teaching plan without notice. An unscheduled fire drill or pep rally can wreak havoc with a lesson plan. To be effective, the family planning educator must be flexible and innovative.

While guest status has its imperfections, they are outweighed by its benefits. Guest educators are not required to discipline students, administer and grade tests, or monitor the lunchroom. Removing these responsibilities leaves only the most positive aspects of teaching. Also, many classroom teachers recognize their own discomfort with the topic of human sexuality and are delighted to have a family planning educator who is comfortable with the language of sexuality come into the classroom to provide this education. Students react positively to guest speakers, often viewing them as experts, and accept information presented by a guest more readily than the same material given by the regular classroom teacher. Students also approach the family planning educator with personal problems they hesitate to share with even the most supportive classroom teacher. These problems range from boy/girlfriend situations to sexual abuse. Family planning educators' familiarity with other community resources allows them to make appropriate referrals, thus providing help when it is most needed. The family planning educator's responsibility is to preserve this image of expert and confidant by being responsive, factual, and nonjudgmental.

Once the education curriculum is prepared and speakers are trained, the family planning agency must make itself known in the marketplace. PPSA sends flyers describing its educational services to a list of public school personnel, youth service agencies, and to other community groups. For those who may be unfamiliar with the agency's community education program, telephone calls and personal contacts follow the flyer. A ten-minute meeting between a school principal and a family planning educator can develop into a professional relationship and the realization that the goal of preventing student problems is one shared by the agency and the school. When it has been established that the tenets of sexuality education are positive and that sexuality educators are responsible adults, two barriers to initiating a sexuality education program have been overcome.

While written program and speaker evaluations are always helpful, they are critical when a program is being initiated. Classroom teachers often are able to see weaknesses and strengths that can be corrected or expanded to further the effectiveness of both the speaker and the program. A file of evaluations is priceless documentation of the quality of sexuality education being provided and is particularly important to have when problems arise.

Several possible problem areas exist for the family planning agency teaching in the community. The first is money. While it is possible to charge for-profit groups for programs, most sexuality education is taught to teenagers in schools and other non-profit agencies. Overall, education is not a money-making process. It is the family planning agency's philosophical and financial commitment to community education that allows the program to survive and progress.

A second problem facing the family planning agency is satisfying the concerns of those who may be uninformed or misinformed about the agency and its goals and may be unaware that the sexuality education program encourages responsible decision-making, assertiveness skills, and improved family communication. Inviting concerned individuals to observe the entire program will usually alleviate their anxieties.

It is important to differentiate between the objections of the sincerely concerned person and the rabid anti-family planning, anti-sexuality education person. When informed, the concerned person becomes a potential advocate. The small but extremely vocal "anti" groups are different and present a third problem for family planning agencies. This vocal minority objects to sexuality education, particularly contraceptive education, and objects vehemently to the presence of a family planning agency representative on a school campus. Because they disrupt, distort, and persist, the "anti" groups occasionally overwhelm a school administrator who will abandon a quality education program rather than contend with the time-consuming tactics. Careful program planning and coordination with school administrators and supportive parents prior to implementing a sexuality education program is essential for diffusing the effects of such groups.

When the family planning agency and the community unite to produce a sexuality education program, both groups benefit. Several years ago such a merger occurred between PPSA and a local school district. It began with a school nurse's request to "do something for our students," progressed through several levels of the school system, and culminated in an open meeting attended by school nurses, teachers, administrators, school board members, interested parents, and a PPSA representative. Following a lengthy discussion of what was to be taught by whom and how, a decision was made to incorporate the PPSA sexuality education program into the school district's health curriculum. Since that meeting, PPSA has presented its program annually to more than thirty high school and middle school classes in this district. Recently, an anti-sexuality education group asked the school administration to eliminate PPSA's participation in teaching activities on their campuses. The school administration reviewed the record and decided to continue the program based on the strength of the original decision and the perceived—and documented—benefits to their students.

The family planning agency is an educational resource with much to offer the community. Its commitment to prevention, its knowledgeable, trained staff, and the wealth of available materials and information allow the family planning agency to fulfill an important role in making sexuality education an integral part of the community learning experience.

References

Kirby, Douglas. *Sexuality Education: An Evaluation of Programs and Their Effects. An Executive Summary.* Santa Cruz, Calif.: Network Publications, 1984, p. 36.

Planned Parenthood of San Antonio. *Speaker's Manual.*

THE ROLE OF CHURCHES
Esther Walter

This essay is addressed to people who work in denominations that base their teaching on a combination of Bible, tradition, and reason, that are willing to examine the Bible in the light of history, and that believe God continues to provide us with new revelation. While this is drawn primarily from the experience of a large segment of the Christian religious community, much also applies to parts of the Jewish community.

Introduction

Most people assume that churches give their members religious education about sexual behavior; the fact is that many congregations avoid the subject as much as possible. A college student summarized a discussion of what the members of his group had learned about sexuality from the various churches in which they grew up by drawing a large "0" to show what had been explicitly taught about sexual behavior, and then a large "NO" to show what was implied about the "standing divine answer to questions about sex. So you don't even ask."

People will not automatically apply religious principles to their sexual attitudes and actions or feel comfortable about taking their sexual questions into their religious life. They need help in making these connections, in learning to love responsibly, especially in the context of the powerful messages about sex-as-exploitation presented by our culture.

It is also important to help church members recognize and overcome the harmful residues of past religious ideas about sex-as-evil that some of us still unconsciously associate with "religion." No major church today believes that our sexual nature is inherently evil, or that God loves virgins best, or that "woman" caused us to be evicted from paradise. Yet people in past centuries interpreted human behavior and sought the cause of illness with minds conditioned by these beliefs.

The results of sex-as-evil thinking can be seen in the view of women and children as objects to be used rather than as people to be respected. It can be seen when sexual *acts* are rated in relative degrees of sinfulness without attention to the more profound issues of the attitudes, motives, and consequences surrounding those acts. It shows in the guilt we associate with sexual emotions, physical responses, and even dreams. If we are to avoid being trapped by such unexamined assumptions, we need to see them in the light of our religious heritage of sexuality as we understand it today: Sexuality as God's good gift.

Method

Fortunately, the most effective process of teaching applies both to religion and sexuality. It consists of reflecting on experience in the light of new knowledge. Thomas Groome, in *Christian Religious Education*, describes it this way (Groome, 1980). "We share our opinions in dialogue rather than in debate. The Christian Story is presented in a form appropriate to the age and development of the group. We are given a chance to explore the way in which that Story changes or affirms our perspective. The final goal is an active Christian faith, and since each of us is in a different place in our faith journeys, each of us must be given a private way in which to reflect on our learning and to grow."

Content

There is no area of sexuality that is inappropriate for Christian religious education. Many educators begin by asking the group what questions are important to them or by surveying a congregation to see where the concerns lie. This can help the educator decide both whom to teach, and what to teach, given the practical limits of time and resources.

The basic need for the educator working in the church is to identify the appropriate Christian or Jewish story about sexuality and its many aspects. The underlying story is that our sexuality, our maleness and femaleness, is a good gift of our Creator, to be understood, affirmed, and celebrated. For specific questions one can seek out denominational positions or explore the way in which churches are actively rethinking their sexual theology. The following examples are taken from lesson plans. They give a piece of the story and the faith goal that goes with it. The actual lessons, addressing embarrassment or fertility or sexual prejudice or inappropriate guilt, parallel those that would be used in other settings.

1. God created us as sexual people, able to love and care for one another. Therefore, my maleness/femaleness is mine without embarrassment or shame, to be used as responsibly as I would use any of God's good gifts.

2. God created us as women and men who can have children and care for them. Therefore, when I become a fertile person at puberty, I become responsible for the outcome of that fertility.

3. God created men and women and blessed us both, giving each of us equal dignity. Therefore, my attitudes and my actions should show both men and women that dignity that God has given us.

4. My sexual orientation is a part of my created human nature. Therefore, my sexual behavior should be judged on the way in which it honors or dishonors God's image in other people, not by my orientation alone.

5. God gave us the freedom to choose what to believe and how to act. God loves us, will guide us when we ask, and forgives us when we stumble. Therefore, I can bring my sexual attitudes and actions into my religious life without fear.

Models

Churches teach about sexuality in every action from the Sunday sermon to the coffee hour conversation. (Few people today would find racist remarks accepted in a church setting, but what about sexual jokes or put-downs?) Some suggestions:

Formal teaching can be done with any age group, and many lesson plans exist for children, teenagers, and parents. It is easy to neglect the needs of less traditional groups such as single adults or people with disabilities because lesson plans are not as evident in the publishers' catalogs, but their needs are just as great. Even if an instructor cannot find or design a specifically "religious" curriculum, the act of teaching honestly in a church setting about the sexual issues that really concern people tells them that their sexuality is good, and that their church is willing to help them struggle with the question of responsible love.

Information for personal or home use in the form of books, pamphlets, and audio- or videocassettes can be used alone or to enhance formal teaching. Parents welcome books to use with their children, and videocassettes can focus a family discussion. Sensitive issues like sexual orientation, in one's self or in a child, are often explored first in print before someone risks embarrassment by talking it over with another person.

Teachable moments can evolve out of many everyday situations in the church. Adults mingling at the social hour can refuse to laugh at inappropriate jokes. Name-calling by young adolescents can be dealt with by the youth group leader as it occurs. Teachers using the Bible with young students can be alert to the sexual implications of the stories. For instance, there is the example of Christ forgiving the woman who was taken in adultery. To adults, this story is about the sins of the spirit being worse than the sins of the flesh. But what do younger listeners think? This woman committed a sexual sin that called for the death penalty—pretty serious in our culture. And she alone bore the burden of guilt; her partner does not appear in the story. The teacher needs to place such a story in the context of its times with the issues of sexism and sexual sin made clear to children, or else avoid stories such as this one that are subject to misinterpretation (Roberts, 1980).

Weekend retreats or church camps have the advantage of isolating a group in an environment where sustained learning can take place, but such events need careful planning so that a group of peers does not simply reinforce shared prejudices.

Community activity takes many forms. Churches join with other groups to provide sexuality education, comment publicly about issues related to sexuality, or provide space to outside groups working with sexual problems. (Examples are Rape Centers, Parents and Friends of Lesbians and Gays, Community Crisis Lines, etc.) Churches can also face the social/sexual issues like the "feminization of poverty" that stem in part from the attitudes about the relative worth of women and men that were enshrined for centuries in Western religious teaching.

Action against pornography appeals to those concerned about the exposure of children to the vivid connections between sex and violence seen on television and in magazines. Yet the subject needs clearer definition. Is the essence of pornography the depiction of genitals or love-making, or is it the exploitation of people for the sexual gratification of others? People who have explored the religious meaning of sexuality are more thoughtful in assessing the harmfulness of erotic materials. Children who have had their questions answered and who have had a chance to develop a healthy attitude toward sexuality that is free of inappropriate guilt are less likely to be influenced by exploitative images of sexual behavior.

Television provides a chance to discuss a wide range of issues and values in the light of the religious story; there is almost no sexual issue left untouched on prime time TV. Discussing these issues helps ensure that anti-religious values will not be mindlessly absorbed by the viewers.

Sermons and newsletters are one-directional communications that can give consistent messages about sexuality or can raise questions for people to consider.

Counseling, as a two-way process, permits some exploration of sexual attitudes and knowledge as these affect the problems being considered.

Laying the Groundwork for Sexuality Education in Your Church

Careful preparation prevents many problems that could result from anxiety or from a misunderstanding of the program's purpose. The instructor can show the same concern for the feelings of church members at large that he or she would show for the people in the classroom. A congregational survey that helps target initial age groups and study topics can give church members a sense of ownership of the project. Touch all the organizational bases: boards, committees, and church school staff. And don't forget that informal groups can be just as powerful to help or harm. In one church the base of support for sexuality education came from the senior citizens who gathered weekly for lunch, a group that might have been forgotten in an organization chart.

State clear program goals in a positive manner, using simple English. The fuzzy language that can turn up in official statements about sexuality can cause confusion and misunderstanding. Focus the goals on positive outcomes; programs that aim only at preventing out-of-wedlock pregnancy or STD give the impression that God really does disapprove of sex. Look for the hidden meanings in the words you choose. For many people, "sex" implies "doing it," and "sex education" thus becomes "teaching them how to do it." Use "sexuality" instead.

Line up your supporting arguments that answer the questions many people have about this kind of education. *Why teach about sex in the church?*/So people will apply their Christian faith to their sexual behavior. *Won't telling children about sex only encourage them to experiment?*/ The world tells them plenty about sex that is harmful; we want to arm children with the protection of sound values. *Doesn't this belong in the home?*/ Of course it does, but sexuality education takes place, as well, in the child's whole environment. Parents need all the helpful friends they can find to help in the nurture of their children. *Why not just have rules about sexual behavior and penalties for breaking those rules?*/ Fear of God-the-policeman is not a healthy way to help us be loving and responsible about sexual behavior. A grateful response to a loving God helps us adopt the *internal* controls that are far more effective.

References

Groome, Thomas. *Christian Religious Education: Sharing Our Story and Vision.* New York: Harper and Row, 1980.

Roberts, Elizabeth J., ed. *Childhood Sexual Learning: The Unwritten Curriculum.* Cambridge, Mass.: Ballinger Publishing Co., 1980.

SEXUALITY EDUCATION:
WORKING WITH A COMMUNITY
Susan J. Hart

Community-based programs are probably most effective and successful when they acknowledge and accept the diversity of opinions of community members. This concept, however, is both the basis for, and the nemesis of, community-based sexuality/family life education programs. A primary goal of sexuality education is to foster in young people an appreciation of self. Unless individuals feel good about themselves as people, the additional goals of sexuality education are difficult, if not impossible, to attain. Ideally, sexuality education will lead to an increased knowledge of, and comfort with, masculine and feminine development and then, ultimately, to a positive, responsible attitude and approach toward the individual's own sexuality and sexual behavior. Accomplishing this educational task becomes extremely difficult when implementing programs on a community wide basis.

In most programs, basic questions lead to much debate. When should the education begin? Any particular grade level may be considered too early by some, too late by others. To what extent should information be provided? Many will want to impart as little information as is possible; others will want to "tell all." Nearly all will determine that there is only one way and one message to impart to all program participants–their way and their message. After all, what is a "responsible" attitude and approach? The definitions are endless. As opinions reflect the value systems present in the community, it becomes important to work with community values rather than against them. Community-based programs can be successful only when they attempt to enhance the values established in the home and church and when they seek to improve communication skills in these settings.

In addition, health agencies involved in sexuality/family life education are committed to having a positive impact on (1) the reduction of teenage and/or unplanned pregnancies; (2) the reduction of the incidence of sexually transmitted diseases; (3) increasing general knowledge about reproductive health; and (4) improving the general quality of human life (an abstract concept, but important, nonetheless). For these goals to be accomplished, intervention/education must be consistent and sequential. It must begin while individuals are in their early, formative years.

When initiating a community-based program, the health agency must help participants (or potential participants and parents) to define sex/sexuality. For most people the word sex has an immediate definition—intercourse. This is a troublesome definition for sexuality education programs because it leads many, especially the more concrete thinkers, to believe that sexuality education teaches young people how to do "it" (sexual intercourse) and how not to get pregnant (contraception). The community members need to be encouraged to recognize that these two topics only begin to address the whole of sexuality education and its goals. By encouraging those who are concerned about "sex education" to recognize that sex/sexuality refers not only to sexual intercourse but also to gender, gender roles, relationships, and the individual's thoughts, attitudes, and feelings, we enhance their opportunity to grasp the full focus of sexuality education—the whole person.

The Health Education Services Project

South Texas Family Planning and Health Corporation, a Corpus Christi-based program, offers a unique method of helping the community to distinguish between sexuality education and the dispensing of birth control information alone. In 1978 the agency expanded its education efforts beyond the clinic setting by developing the Health Education Service Project. Four community education sites were established throughout a 26-county service area (no clinics were used to house these offices). Educators were hired to provide sexuality education on a full-time basis to interested schools, churches, or community organizations. Topics covered include self-esteem, puberty, dating and relationships, sex roles, sexual decision-making, teenage pregnancy, prenatal care, birth, contraception, reproductive anatomy and physiology, sexually transmitted diseases, reproductive health, etc. On an average, any one person receives approximately three hours of instruction (generally in one hour segments). Age-appropriateness is a key determinant in the selection of topics and materials for inclusion in a program. The community-based education aids individuals in making appropriate choices (self-determined) regarding their sexuality and sexual behavior. The clinics provide counseling and services related to reproductive health and family planning.

Both the clinic and community education efforts rely on guidance from local advisory councils. These councils enable the agency to use the community members' opinions in assessing appropriate content and resources for the programs. They also often serve as a link to community resources and other health and youth-serving agencies. Advisory council members are, for the most part, individuals who actually use the education services. The advisory councils tend to be stronger when they include members from diverse religious, civic, and socioeconomic backgrounds.

Essentially, three services are provided by the Education Project. These include: (1) furnishing education materials to instructors teaching or preparing to teach sexuality education; (2) providing in-service training for instructors to help prepare them with lesson plans and techniques for dealing with sensitive subject matters; and (3) providing consultants to do presentations for instructors who may not feel adequately prepared in this particular area or who wish to supplement their own program with a resource person. Agencies and individuals who are developing or enhancing a sexuality education program are also asked to consider providing programs, or at the very least, information for parents.

It is virtually impossible to provide sexuality education for an entire community. The task becomes more manageable when accomplished by one school, one church, or one organization at a time. Rather than marketing the program via a huge media blitz, a direct-mail approach was implemented for the project. Schools, churches, and community organizations which, conceivably, would be interested in having the program were targeted for these mailings. As support and enthusiasm are generated in any one setting, demand for additional services in that community increases.

In large part, however, the success of a program like the Education Project relies on having a well-thought-out approach to sexuality education and its component topics, a strong library of quality resource materials (especially learning activities), and the flexibility to use these resources to create a program that meets specific educational needs. Ensuring that sponsors have input as to program content, setting, instructors, etc., is a critical first step in gaining program acceptance. Encouraging parent participation as well as offering specific programs for parents is also important.

Procedures

Before actually delivering an education program, the sexuality educator documents the specific request for services (who, what, when, and why). This is done during an initial meeting with key representatives from the community organization. Once agency needs are established, the educator prepares a lesson plan that includes discussion topics, learning activities, and/or audio-visuals. During the introduction of a program, the educator ensures that each individual is participating voluntarily through use of consent forms and rosters of attendance. A program is complete when a final contact report is filed documenting that the planned education sessions took place and that the services were received by identifiable individuals (referencing the rosters). The educator notes any suggested changes or planned expansions for the program, so follow-up in that specific setting may be handled effectively.

Evaluation

Are community-based programs meeting with success? There are several different techniques to assess this. Program funders will generally be interested in the answers to two questions. First, how many people are being served by the program and how many hours of instruction is each of the individuals receiving? Second, what is the program's impact on the reduction of teenage pregnancies and sexually transmitted diseases in the community served? The latter question is difficult to answer because community-based sexuality education programs are only one small piece of the intervention efforts necessary to reduce these problems. A direct documentation of the impact of the program alone is nearly impossible to attain. (These are two good reasons for making sure that programs are not funded on these goals alone.) Socioeconomic factors, the home environment in particular, have such a real effect on teen pregnancy and STD rates that education efforts would have to be incredibly intense over a prolonged period of time to make a significant impact. Community education programs, on a wide-scale basis, can only attempt to be a catalyst for coordinating community efforts in the battle against these two social problems.

Success, on the health agencies' part, can be measured through more subjective means. By administering evaluation forms before and after a program, the agency can determine if there has been an increase in knowledge related to the specific aspect of sexuality education examined and/or increased parent-child communication. Comments received by the Health Education Services Project have clearly stated that community education programs can have a positive impact: "The program really gets you to think about what's going on because a lot of times you can't see the forest because of all the trees, and these presentations help a *lot* in decision making and relationships." "I think it's great because a lot of us wouldn't go anywhere else for this information. It's a lot easier to be given information than it is to ask for it." "The most important thing I learned is about the pressures that are put on teenagers and how to deal with them. Also I learned a lot about V.D. Some of the stuff I knew was a little bit wrong, and this program helped me personally." "The most important thing I learned was how hard it really is to raise a child when you're a teenager." "I learned that it is right to respect each others' decisions if you want to be together." "I feel confident to talk to my parents now." A sample of comments from parents: "I loved this class because it makes me realize how important it is to talk to your kids. I learned a lot and will take the information and talk to my kids. Thank you!"

In summary, support and success for sexuality education come, not only in dollar form, but from enthusiastic participant response to a well-planned and delivered program.

THE AIDS EPIDEMIC AND
SEXUALITY EDUCATION
Debra W. Haffner

The AIDS epidemic poses numerous challenges for sexuality education. More schools and community organizations are calling for sexuality education than ever before. Indeed the Surgeon General of the United States, C. Everett Koop, has written, "Education about AIDS should start in early elementary school and at home so that children can grow up knowing the behaviors to avoid to protect themselves from exposure to the AIDS virus" (Koop, 1986). Yet many of the programs that have been developed do little more than teach people about the biomedical aspects of the disease and ignore behavioral messages. In fact, many programs warn young people about the "dangers of sex" and advise abstinence from all sexual activities. Sexuality educators must help design AIDS prevention programs to assure that AIDS is placed in the context of healthy, positive sexuality.

Existing school-based AIDS education programs are, by-and-large, inadequate. According to a survey conducted by the U.S. Conference of Mayors in December 1986, just over half of the country's largest local school districts and state school agencies were beginning to provide some type of AIDS education. However, only a small number have developed and implemented comprehensive programs that include teacher training, curriculum guides, and student materials. Almost all education is focused at the junior and senior high levels (U.S. Conference of Mayors, 1987).

A CDC (Centers for Disease Control) review of 18 AIDS curricula found that two-thirds of the curricula advocated programs that were very brief—no longer than one hour or class session; only one in 10 provided more than three hours of programming on AIDS. One-quarter of the curricula did not address abstinence or condom use. Fewer than one third mentioned that (1) sex between uninfected partners could not spread the disease, (2) individuals should seek counseling if they had personal concerns, or (3) condoms and spermicides should be used together to provide maximum protection against AIDS. Only 22 percent of the curricula emphasized that it is behavior that places a person at risk, and over half inappropriately emphasized high risk groups. Although 61 percent of the curricula used the term "anal intercourse" and 50 percent mentioned "oral intercourse," only 39 percent mentioned "vaginal intercourse" (personal communication with Andrea Lawrence, 1987).

Why Educate Teens About AIDS

There are many reasons why teenagers need AIDS education:

- Some teenagers are at risk of contracting the Human Immunodeficiency Virus (HIV) that causes AIDS because of their involvement with risky sexual behaviors or with I-V drugs.
- Because teenagers are forming lifetime health habits, they need guidance in their development of adult sexual behaviors.
- Teenagers are exposed to a barrage of misinformation about sexuality and AIDS, and education is urgently needed to counter this misinformation and reduce the panic surrounding the disease.
- Teenagers are the major source of health-related information for their peers and can also educate their siblings and parents.
- Many young people have already been affected personally by AIDS. They have parents, other family members, teachers, or friends who are ill or have been infected with the virus.

Although it is true that all young people need education about AIDS, certain groups of teenagers must be targets for special education efforts. Teens who use I-V drugs, gay teens, homeless teens, and teens involved in solicitation and prostitution are at greatest risk if they practice behaviors that can transmit the virus that causes AIDS. Education programs for these groups must help teens develop the skills to practice safe behavior. Minority teenagers need to have culturally sensitive materials developed. Teenagers from certain areas with high prevalence rates of AIDS, such as New York, New Jersey, Washington D.C., Miami, Houston, and San Francisco, are at greater risk because of the prevalence of the virus in the community.

It is also important to reduce the stigma of AIDS. Young people need to understand that there is nothing about being gay, or Black, or Hispanic, that makes people biologically susceptible to AIDS. They need to understand that it is behavior that poses risks, not being a member of a "risk group," and that individuals can reduce or eliminate the risk by practicing different behaviors.

Teenagers lack basic knowledge regarding transmission of and protection against HIV. In a 1985 study of teens in San Francisco, one-third did not know that AIDS could not be spread by using someone's personal belongings, and 40 percent did not know that using condoms lowers the risk of the disease (DiClemente, 1986).

A 1986 survey of Massachusetts teenagers found that many teenagers believe that AIDS can be transmitted by kissing, sharing eating utensils, sitting on toilet seats, and donating blood; 96 percent of these teens had heard about AIDS, but only 15 percent of the sexually active teens were taking appropriate steps to avoid its transmission. Only one-third were concerned about contracting the disease (Strunin, 1987).

Still the survey had some hopeful results. Half of the teens surveyed said that a teacher had talked with them about AIDS and 45 percent had discussed AIDS with a parent. Only 7 percent thought AIDS could be spread by shaking hands, compared with 25 percent in a survey of San Francisco teens the previous year. Nevertheless, the need for more information remains painfully clear (Strunin, 1987).

Goals of AIDS Education

AIDS prevention programs for teenagers should have four primary goals:

1. To reduce the panic and misinformation about the disease and its transmission and to increase understanding of risk behaviors.
2. To help teenagers delay the initiation of sexual intercourse.
3. To ensure that teenagers who are having any type of intercourse use condoms consistently and effectively.
4. To reduce experimentation with drugs and prevent I-V drug use.

Teenagers lack knowledge about AIDS and its transmission. Many incorrectly belive that they can get AIDS from food handlers, toilet seats, or being in a room with gay people. The AIDS epidemic has led to a rise in incidences of violence against homosexuals and has the very real potential of increasing homophobia (fear of homosexuals) among teens. Teenagers need to understand that homosexuals did not cause AIDS, that they are not at risk of contracting AIDS from gay people they know socially or casually, that some of their classmates may be gay and deserve respect and support, and that they should demonstrate compassion for people who have the disease.

Second, teenagers must be assisted to delay premature sexual intercourse. The average age of first coitus is now 16 years in the United States (Zelnick, 1980); in some communities, the average age for boys is about twelve (Clark, 1984). Teenagers are becoming sexually active at earlier ages, and most have neither the cognitive nor emotional capacity to handle the implications of sexual relationships. Educators need to help teenagers understand that intercourse is not necessary to give or receive sexual pleasure. Young people need to be educated about "alternatives to intercourse." This means kissing, petting, "outercourse," and mutual masturbation. Teens need to understand that "anybody who cares about you won't ask you to have unsafe sex." Further, young people should be encouraged to express affection through non-sexual avenues.

Promising strategies have been developed to help young teenagers postpone sexual involvement. Unlike the simplistic "Just Say No" programs, these programs are designed to help teens identify and resist the social and peer pressures that encourage early sexual involvement. The emphasis is on developing skills and changing behaviors.

Third, sexually active teenagers must use condoms each and every time they have intercourse. Condom use is quite low among sexually active American teenagers—fewer than one in four uses condoms regularly (National Center for Health Statistics, 1984). Education about condoms should focus on behavior. Both male and female teenagers should be encouraged to purchase them and help distribute them to sexually active friends. Boys who are sexually active, or thinking of becoming so, should practice putting condoms on in private. Indeed, in a Swedish government public service campaign, boys are encouraged to practice masturbating with condoms in place!

Teenagers also need help in talking with one another about condoms. Girls should have ready answers for boys who say, "But it's like taking a shower with a raincoat on." Boys should have ready answers for girls who say, "But I'm on the pill," or "Do you have a disease or something?" This education will also help teenagers prevent pregnancies and other sexually transmitted diseases.

Fourth, all AIDS education programs need to warn teenagers about the dangers of drug use, especially intravenous drugs. Teenagers need to understand that the use of alcohol or drugs may impair their ability to make good decisions in sexual situations, that some drugs, such as marijuana, may be involved with suppressing the immune system, and that sharing any kind of needle puts a person at risk of becoming infected through blood products. Programs working with drug abusing youth must teach them to use sterile equipment.

Lessons to Learn from Sexuality and Health Education

The majority of existing AIDS education programs have ignored many of the lessons to be learned from other health education programs for teenagers. Like teenage pregnancy, AIDS is a social problem that will not be eliminated by simply providing young people with facts. Teenagers need the opportunity to clarify their values, to practice decision-making and communication skills, and to learn to resist peer pressure related to sex and drug use.

It would be naive to think that school-based AIDS education programs will dramatically change young people's behaviors. Evaluations of sexuality education programs have found that they are quite effective in increasing knowledge, but significantly less effective in changing behaviors or attitudes. Existing attitudes can be reinforced and communication between parents and children can be increased. However, unless sexuality education is combined with family planning services, there is little likelihood that sexual behaviors will be affected (Kirby, 1984).

Numerous studies have shown that teenagers take risks even when they are well informed about the consequences. Providing facts is not enough. The majority of teenage pregnancies are unintended, even though most teenagers know how pregnancies occur and how they can be prevented.

Health education efforts that target individual behavioral change have often been unsuccessful. The most promising health education interventions with teenagers have been those that are coordinated by the teenagers themselves and deal with changing teenage behavioral norms. Peer mediated approaches to resisting cigarette and marijuana smoking and "students against drinking and driving" campaigns have all contributed to behavior change, while other interventions, such as contraceptive lectures, typically have not.

Programs need to focus on changing the normative school environment. Classrooms that teach "just say no" offer advice that conflicts with the talk in the halls and locker rooms where students learn that "everybody is doing it." Faced with this contradiction, teens practice "cognitive repression"—they accept only one message and do what makes them most socially acceptable. Thus, AIDS programs that are designed to alter the peer culture and the school norms concerning sex and drugs are likely to be more successful than classroom programs alone.

Content of AIDS Education Programs

AIDS education would ideally be part of a comprehensive health or sexuality education program. These programs would place the discussion of the disease in the broader context of health behaviors and human sexuality. AIDS prevention information would be discussed after units on self-esteem, drug prevention, and peer pressure. Further, programs would include ample opportunity for behavioral skill development, ranging from how to say "no" to peer pressure, to talking about the decision to have sex with a partner, to accessing a family planning clinic.

It is also clear, however, that the immediacy of the AIDS emergency requires the acceptance of programs that are less than comprehensive. Schools cannot afford to wait to introduce AIDS education until all school boards have the will to approve sexuality education programs.

AIDS education programs need to emphasize certain information. "One-shot programs" that involve a single class on AIDS are likely to have little behavioral impact, but may slightly increase teens' knowledge. If these less-than-comprehensive programs are conducted, they should at least include information on:

1. *How AIDS is transmitted*, including sexual transmission, parenteral transmission through the exchange of blood products, including drug use, and perinatal transmission.
2. *How AIDS is not transmitted*, including clear information about the overwhelming evidence that AIDS is not transmitted through casual contact.
3. *How to protect oneself from the AIDS virus*, including abstinence from intercourse and I-V drug use, and the practice of safer sex.

The National Coalition of Advocates for Students (NCAS) suggests that all curricula follow five basic principles. According to NCAS, programs should:

1. Offer information in words students can understand;
2. Emphasize safe sex behavior—including abstinence and the use of condoms—over biomedical aspects of AIDS;
3. Discuss the dangers of I-V drug use;
4. Focus on high-risk behaviors rather than risk groups; and
5. Provide an ample number of sessions to give students multiple opportunities to assimilate the information (National Coalition of Advocates for Students, 1987).

AIDS Education Can Be Sex-Positive

Many of the AIDS education programs that have been developed have focused on giving young people two messages about sexuality—abstain from sex or engage in long-term monogamous sexual relationships. One young person recently asked me whether a two-month relationship was long enough. Clearly, teenagers need more specific guidance about sexual behaviors.

AIDS education must be sex-positive. Programs should not be designed to give young people negative and scary impressions of sexuality. Just as good sexual abuse prevention programs include information about the importance of appropriate touching, AIDS education programs must be careful to present sexuality as a positive aspect of life, rather than as a single behavior that kills. Courses should emphasize that genital activity is only one aspect of sexuality. All education programs should include a variety of activities designed to increase knowledge, explore attitudes, and facilitate desired behavioral outcomes.

It is important for teachers to acknowledge the wide range of sexual experiences represented in a classroom or group of young people. Some teens will have already had heterosexual experiences; some teens will have had homosexual experiences. Some teenagers will have had intercourse; others may have no interest in sex yet. Some teens may have good reasons to believe that they have been exposed to HIV; others may believe they have contacted it from a drinking fountain. Individual students may have friends or relatives with AIDS; others will live with single parents who are involved in heterosexual or homosexual relationships.

It is important for the teacher to address all of the young people in a classroom. One could begin by saying something like, "Today we are going to be discussing AIDS. AIDS is a national emergency. All of us need to know more about this disease and how it is transmitted. We will be talking later about prevention. You may not need this information now or ever, but it is important for all of you to listen so that you can help a friend, a family member, or even yourself in the future." Leaders should anticipate homophobic responses and be prepared to support the gay students who will be in the program (whether or not they are identified to the group).

Teens need to be given a personal view of AIDS. They need to understand that AIDS is a fatal disease with no known cure. People with AIDS have a role to play in the classroom. They can dramatically portray the reality of living with AIDS and help break through teenagers' wall of invincibility. Movies, such as "The AIDS Movie," that include such people can be very powerful teaching tools. In that movie, the three people with AIDS have each died since the movie was produced.

AIDS Education Must Be Explicit

It is important to use the correct language when presenting AIDS information. Programs should not talk about "body fluids" or "private parts." As in all sexuality education programs, teachers should use correct language but should acknowledge students' use of slang. A helpful exercise for new groups is for leaders to ask teens what words they use for such terminology as "penis," "vagina," "oral sex," "masturbation," etc. Teachers also need to refer to persons who have the disease as "people with AIDS" rather than AIDS "victims."

Teenagers need to receive information about the sexual behaviors that place them at risk of HIV infection. Because most teenagers experiment with some type of sexual behavior, educators should help teens understand which ones are safe and which ones are risky.

There are some sexual activities that are truly safe, i.e., they cannot transmit the virus that causes AIDS. These include touching, hugging, and masturbation. Abstinence from any type of sexual intercourse—oral, vaginal, rectal—is safe.

Any type of sex between two uninfected partners is safe sex. The difficulty is that most people, whether teenagers or adults, do not know their HIV antibody status. "Knowing someone well" or "asking your partner about AIDS" is an unrealistic way to assess potential risk, especially for teenagers. Teenagers need to understand that it is impossible to tell whether someone is infected by looking or through intuitive powers.

Most sexual activities, however, can only be called "safer sex," as there are few guarantees. Having intercourse with an infected partner can only be considered "safer." While condoms have been proven to be an effective barrier to HIV in the laboratory, there is a small chance of breakage or leakage, especially when condoms are not used correctly. Although condoms are not 100 percent effective against the spread of HIV or preventing pregnancy, they offer the best protection available for people who are going to have intercourse with a partner with an unknown antibody status.

A Call to Action

Sexuality educators have a major role to play in reducing the impact of the AIDS epidemic on the nation's young people. It is important that we become involved in designing and offering education programs to assure that effective programs are implemented. We must educate ourselves about the disease, and challenge ourselves to develop strategies that will help change young people's behaviors. We must work to prevent the further spread of the disease while maintaining a positive approach to sexuality education. We must help to develop an understanding of homosexuality and bisexuality and work to reduce homophobia.

We must remember that, in spite of AIDS, our teenagers need to continue to learn to celebrate their sexuality while practicing responsible behaviors.

References

Clark, S.D., L.S. Zabin, and J.B. Hardy. "Sex, Contraception, and Parenthood: Experiences and Attitudes Among Urban Black Young Men." *Family Planning Perspectives* 16 (March/April 1984): 40-45.

DiClemente, R.J., J. Zorn, and L. Temoshok. "Adolescents and AIDS." *American Journal of Public Health* 76 (November 1986).

Kirby, D. *Sexuality Education: An Evaluation of Programs and Their Effects.* Santa Cruz, Calif.: Network Publications, 1984.

Koop, C. Everett. *Surgeon General's Report on Acquired Immune Deficiency Syndrome.* Washington, D.C.: U.S. Public Health Service, 1986.

Lawrence, Andrea. Centers for Disease Control, Personal Communication, June 1987.

National Center for Health Statistics. *NCHS Advance data* (December 1984).

National Coalition of Advocates for Students. *Criteria for Evaluating an AIDS Curriculum.* Boston: NCAS, 1987.

Strunin, L., and R. Hingson. "Acquired Immune Deficiency Syndrome: Knowledge, Beliefs, Attitudes, and Behaviors." *Pediatrics* 79 (May 1987).

U.S. Conference of Mayors. "Local School Districts Active in AIDS Education." *AIDS Information Exchange* (January 1987).

Zelnick, M., and J.F. Kantner. "Sexual Activity, Contraceptive Use, and Pregnancy Among Metropolitan Teenagers: 1981-1979." *Family Planning Perspectives* 12 (September/October 1980): 230-238.

HOW TO TALK ABOUT EVALUATION OF SEX EDUCATON PROGRAMS WITHOUT BLUSHING OR STAMMERING

Jesse Blatt

Back in the "good old days" when everybody thought that sex education was a good idea, no one gave much thought to what, exactly, sex education programs ought to accomplish. The field of sex education was a "child," and programs were allowed to experiment, to learn, to grow. The field now appears to be emerging from a rather turbulent adolescence: a complicated and emotional period filled with idealism and one that was severely misunderstood (and criticized) by a sober public. Now sex education is almost grown up, and like grown-ups everywhere, it is expected to support itself.

For a variety of reasons (not the least of which are political), sex education programs must now convincingly demonstrate that they are doing good in some areas and not doing harm in others. Program administrators are facing the need to move beyond endorsements ("The students all said that they *loved* the course!") to more rigorous assessments of program accomplishments.

The tool kit designed for this purpose is called "program evaluation." Program evaluation has, rightly or wrongly, acquired a reputation for being somewhat mystical, probably statistical, and certainly mathematical. Consequently, many educators and administrators (who can talk about menstruation or wet dreams without missing a beat) freeze completely when required to discuss such topics as evaluation design or the significance of results. This chapter will *not* teach you how to perform a program evaluation (although a thorough study of the resources cited at the end of the chapter could have that effect). Rather, its purpose is to introduce you to the terms and procedures of program evaluation in a manner to permit you to engage in intelligent conversation with program evaluators and sponsors alike.

What Is Program Evaluation?

Program evaluation is the process of finding out the extent to which a program actually accomplished what it was designed to do. The main purpose of program evaluation is to provide program sponsors with vital information to enable them to decide on some future action.

In its strictest form, evaluation research compares the program's accomplishments with previously defined standards. This comparison provides the basis for determining if the results were worth the effort put into obtaining them, for specifying parts of the program that need further refinement, or for justifying further expenditures or expansion of the program.

Process evaluation (sometimes called administrative evaluation) focuses on how the program is implemented or conducted; outcome (or impact) evaluation focuses on what the program accomplishes.

Process evaluations may involve keeping simple objective records, such as who signs up, who attends, who drops out, and so on. However, they frequently deal with people's subjective responses to the program: what they liked or disliked, what they would change or leave unchanged, how they reacted to or felt about various parts of the program, or where they ran into difficulty understanding or accepting program content. Collecting such qualitative data usually involves interviewing people, asking open-ended questions on a questionnaire, or having people keep "diaries" of their reactions or "logs" of *ad hoc* changes in the program. Process variables are generally more qualitative than quantitative.

Outcome evaluations examine the things that the program is intended to affect, either directly or indirectly, such as pregnancy rates, or students' knowledge, attitudes, and practices. Outcome evaluations frequently involve a variety of tests, questionnaires, and inventories that permit quanitification of changes in knowledge, attitudes, or behaviors.

Program evaluation involves four separate activities:

1. Setting objectives for the program's conduct and accomplishments.
2. Designing systematic methods for ruling out ambiguities in the interpretation of program effects.
3. Measuring how the program worked and what it accomplished.
4. Finding out if the results were significant.

Both the process and outcome evaluations follow the same basic steps. The following sections provide a brief description of the logic behind each of the steps, concentrating on outcome evaluation.

Setting Objectives for the Program's Conduct and Accomplishments

You cannot evaluate a program's outcomes unless you have in mind what you expected it to achieve. You cannot evaluate the conduct of a program unless you know how the program was supposed to function. Statements of your expectations for your program are called "objectives." Objectives are the standards against which your program's performance will be measured.

Objectives should be stated as clearly and specifically as possible, so that the program can be evaluated unequivocally. A well-constructed objective states an anticipated level of effect and implies the kind of data required for its evaluation. You can establish an approximate level of effect on the basis of how much benefit is required to offset the cost of the program.

Above all, objectives must be realistic. It is naive, for example, to expect a three-hour one-shot seminar to change participants' beliefs and attitudes. There is even some question about the ability of a semester-long sex education class to influence students' sexual behavior. Dare we dream that we might decrease pregnancy rates by offering one or two courses? An objective that specifies an idealistic or politically "saleable" level of effect will, at the least, create an embarrassing situation and may result in cancellation of the program.

Typically, a program will have more than one objective. For example, a teen education program might set as its outcome objectives: (1) to increase teenagers' knowledge about human sexuality, (2) to decrease the number of sexually active teenagers (usually by delaying the initiation of sexual activity), and (3) to increase the effective use of contraceptives by sexually active teenagers. The program's process objectives might include, (1) providing the program to at least 100 individuals between the ages of 12 and 15 during the year, (2) maintaining an equal split between boys and girls, and (3) defining the content of the program on the basis of participants' questions.

By considering program objectives early in program development, the educator helps to focus attention on the program's desired outcomes and processes. With clearly stated objectives in hand, the program designer can more effectively limit the program's content to relevant issues. Without the intrusion of material unrelated to program objectives, the course is free to cover essential content in greater depth.

Designing Systematic Methods for Ruling out Ambiguities in the Interpretation of Program Effects

In order to claim that the program was responsible for changes in the outcome measures, we must rule out alternative explanations for those changes. We design a system of checks and balances, called "controls," to anticipate as many problems as possible with interpretation of the data. A weak design allows so many possible alternative explanations that we cannot draw any firm conclusions. A strong design ensures that data will be collected in a logical manner so that interpretation of the results is unambiguous.

There are two kinds of information on which to base program evaluations: new information that you gather during the conduct of the program being evaluated and information collected by existing recordkeeping systems of public agencies. Each of these requires a different evaluation approach.

Evaluations Based on Gathering New Information

To find out if teenaged girls attending a rap session learned how to use contraceptive foam correctly, we give them a test at the end of the session (a post-test). High test scores could mean that the rap session was effective in conveying information. We cannot rule out, however, the possibility that the girls already knew the information before they participated.

We could "control" for this possibility by also giving a test at the beginning of the session (a pre-test). If the post-test scores were about the same as the pre-test scores, then clearly the girls' knowledge levels had not changed.

If the post-test scores were higher than the pre-test scores, the participants might have remembered information from the pre-test when they took the post-test. To rule out this alternative, we could give the pre-test and post-test to a second group of people (a control group or comparison group) that doesn't participate in the rap session (although they should be involved in some other activity that takes about the same amount of time). If the control group's test scores increase as much as the scores of the group that attended the rap session (the treatment group), then the rap cannot have caused the change.

Even if the treatment group had higher scores than the control group, this research design does not rule out the possibility that the members of the control group were not as smart or as motivated as members of the treatment group. The only way to rule out *this* alternative is to arrange for the two groups to be as nearly equivalent as possible.

The most effective method for equating treatment and control groups is to use "random assignment." Random assignment simply means that chance alone determines whether a person was in one group or the other.

For example, we could make an alphabetical list of girls' names, number them from one to however-many, and place the odd-numbered names in one group and the even-numbered names in the other. This method is random because there is no systematic relationship between a person's name and their previous knowledge or motivation.

Even using a pre-test and a post-test, a treatment group and a control group, and random assignment of participants to the two groups, interpretation of the results is *still* ambiguous! In this design, the post-test measures the knowledge of the participants after they have *both* taken the pre-test *and* participated in the rap session. We cannot determine how much of the change in knowledge was due to the program alone. Participants may have paid more careful attention to those parts of the program that were covered by the pre-test. (This is not a problem if you never give the program by itself, i.e., if the pre-test becomes a permanent part of the curriculum.)

We could, of course, develop a more complicated design using more groups, some of which have the pre-test and others not, but we could do away with the pre-test entirely if we could form our two groups using strict random assignment and if each group contained 30 or more individuals. Since random assignment creates equivalent groups, the difference between the post-test scores of the group that participates in the rap session and the control group must be due to the program.

Of course, things are rarely simple. You may not have enough people to form the groups you need at the same time. It is possible to combine several smaller groups into one larger one if the time span is short and if you segment both treatment and control groups in the same way. However, if you test one group now and another later, you will need to find a logical way to rule out differences between groups related to the time-lag between the two groups (e.g., increased sexual information or experience in the later, and therefore older, group).

If you cannot legally or ethically withhold certain information from anyone, you can still evaluate your program by having some people participate now and the others later (e.g., give a course in the fall and then again in the spring), assuming that group membership is determined by random assignment. You would use the current participants as the experimental group, using the "later" group as the control group while the first group participates in the program.

If you can't use random assignment, you must use extensive matching procedures to be able to show convincing evidence that your groups were equivalent to start with. Matching is far less preferable to random assignment and not very practical in most situations.

Strong evaluation designs almost always require setting up pre-tests and forming treatment and control groups in advance of course implementation. Evaluations planned after a course has already begun must, by necessity, employ weaker evaluation designs.

Evaluations Based on Existing Record-Keeping Systems

Now look at another kind of evaluation problem. Suppose that our program is intended to decrease pregnancy rates among teenagers. Evaluation of the program's effects would require comparing the "after program" rate with the "before program" rate. ("Rate" implies that we know the number of all teenaged girls in the group we are interested in as well as how many of them get pregnant.) If the "after" rate was lower than the "before' rate, we would like to celebrate our success.

However, without looking at the rates for several years both before and after the implementation of our programs, we cannot logically eliminate other interpretations of the results. What if the rate had already been decreasing over a period of years before our program started? Was this year's decrease a result of the program or just a continuation of an ongoing trend? Perhaps the pregnancy rates normally just go up and down from one year to the next, varying about a rather stable average. Was the decrease we saw due to our program or just another wiggle on the graph?

Looking at a series of measurements over a period of time is called, logically enough, "time series analysis." Typically, time-series data come from examining records kept by agencies such as schools, hospitals, clinics, health departments, and so on. Like other designs, interpretation of time-series data can be improved by use of a comparison group—an equivalent agency that has shown rates similar to the treatment group rates over a long period of time prior to the implementation of the program. If we plot the data from the two groups on the same graph, and they are relatively parallel up to the time of the program, after which they diverge, we can make a strong case for the program having an effect.

As one might imagine, researchers keep coming up against the same design problems. Since research situations present more or less "standard" problems, researchers have developed more or less "standard" solutions to deal with them. This section has only touched on some of the problems. If you have other problems, including not being able to use random assignment, the book by Campbell and Stanley listed in the References provides one of the more informative and simply stated collections of design information.

Measuring How the Program Worked and What It Accomplished

The primary purpose of data collection for program evaluation is to measure certain features of the program as specified in its objectives. Accordingly, tests, questionnaires, inventories, and interview protocols should be firmly rooted in those objectives. Each item should contribute directly to determining whether the program met its objectives. If not, the item is extraneous and irrelevant and should be discarded.

Whenever one prepares a data-collection instrument, repeat the cardinal rule of instrument design: If an item does not directly address a specific program objective, don't use it. Probably the least acceptable reason for including an item in an evaluation is that "it would be nice to know." Collecting unnecessary data will increase the cost of the evaluation and decrease the quality of the data you get. Educators spend a lot of time and energy devising tests to assess students' performance. However, the focus of evaluation is somewhat different: We give a knowledge test to program participants in order to grade the program's ability to convey knowledge, not to grade the participants' ability to absorb it. These different purposes lead to quite different instruments. A knowledge test for grading participants should be designed to produce a wide distribution of scores to distinguish students who learned a lot from those who didn't. For program evaluation, however, the test should be constructed so that if the program successfully meets its objectives, all participants would obtain high scores, indicating that they learned what the program intended to teach. A grading instrument requires considerably more items than an evaluation instrument, thus increasing cost and potentially decreasing reliability. (This is not to say than an evaluation instrument should not be presented in a "test" atmosphere. Some evaluators of high school programs feel that the students would not respond seriously if they felt they were not being tested.)

An evaluation of a program's effects on behavior should assess minimally acceptable performance. A driver's license exam is a good example of this kind of test. It cannot distinguish really outstanding drivers from barely competent one; it measures only what is absolutely essential to demonstrate minimum competence. Course evaluation is not the appropriate time for developing detailed behavioral (or attitudinal) profiles of participants however desirable such profiles might be.

Before beginning to develop tests and instruments, consider the possibility of drawing from those that someone else has already gone to the expense of developing and validating. The test items included in the publications by Kirby et al. (see References) are probably the most thoroughly validated in the field of sex education. If you must develop your own, pay careful attention to the issues of validity and reliability. Unless an instrument truly measures what it claims to address (validity) and provides comparable results each time it is used (reliability), an evaluation will be meaningless.

Finding Out if the Results Were Significant

One of the most common questions asked of an evaluation is: "Are the results significant?" There are two ways to interpret this question:

- Are the results statistically significant (i.e., not due to chance)?
- Are the results programmatically significant (i.e., meaningful)?

The first can be answered by using appropriate statistical methods, but the second can only be answered relative to the monetary, social, and political costs of the program.

Statistical Significance

The ultimate conclusion an evaluator wishes to draw about a program is that changes in knowledge, attitude, behavior, or any other measure following the implementation of the program are not due to some factor or event other than the program. Some specific factors can be ruled out by careful attention to the design of the evaluation but it is still possible that the difference between control groups and treatment groups occurred simply by random chance.

Statistical tests permit you to estimate the probability of obtaining the observed results on the basis of chance. A program's effects are statistically significant if the probability of their being the result of chance is reasonably small, usually less than 5 out of 100.

Generally speaking, statistical significance is affected by the size of the difference between the average scores of the treatment and control groups, the range of scores within each group, and the number of people in each group. Given enough participants in a study, it is possible to show that even very small differences between control groups and treatment groups are statistically significant. For example, a program might, on the average, increase people's knowledge by one point on a 100-point test. Based on tests of thousands of people, this difference would probably be "statistically significant."

Programmatic Significance

Is a 1 percent increase in knowledge-test scores a meaningful program effect? The degree to which an effect is meaningful depends to some extend on how much it costs to bring about, relative to the costs of not achieving the change. For example, an increase of 1 percent on a knowledge test is probably not worth achieving if the program costs $500 per participant. However, a decrease of 1 percent in teenage pregnancies would probably be worth achieving even if it costs five times as much. Each evaluator will have to decide what constitutes a meaningful effect in terms of his or her own program objectives.

If you feel that a given outcome would be found to be statistically significant if only the measures were more refined, if only more students were tested, if only random assignment could be used, if only this, if only that; then that outcome is probably not programmatically significant.

Statistically significant results are not necessarily meaningful. Conversely, however, if an effect is large enough to be meaningful, it will usually be large enough to be statistically significant. *Provided that the research design is a valid one to begin with,* this relationship does away with many of the concerns people have about interpreting the results of statistical tests. Issues such as sample size, sensitivity of measurement, inter-judge agreement—even the appropriateness of the statistical test, itself—are only relevant when attempting to "tease out" small differences between groups. When differences are large enough to be programmatically significant, these issues are of little or no concern.

In Conclusion

Properly executed, program evaluation is a risky business. You may find that your program reaches an entirely different audience than you originally intended. You may discover that it doesn't do all the things that you had hoped for and perhaps even claimed in order to persuade sponsors to provide funding.

If the results of an evaluation show that a program does not meet its objectives, we are challenged to change something. For example, if participants made low scores on a knowledge test, either the test was too difficult for the objective, the objective was too ambitious for the program, or the program was ineffective for the participants. (In evaluation, low scores are not attributed to the participants' lack of ability, motivation, or other characteristics.)

In this case, we must examine the test, the program's content, its methods, and our objectives for possible improvements. Based on this review and considering the costs and consequences, we may choose to alter any one or all of these factors and subject the new program to the evaluation process. If, however, we find little room for improvement, we might conclude that the best course of action would be to terminate the program.

The threat of program termination is, of course, the "bottom line" of evaluation. Program evaluation is, after all, the process of finding out the extent to which a program actually accomplishes what it was designed to do. A program that does not meet its objectives cannot long survive. When evaluation shows that the program was successful, good things happen: funding may be increased, the program may be expanded.

As programs compete for fewer dollars, those that most convincingly demonstrate the achievement of practical objectives have the best chance to survive and grow strong. And if the programs' administrators are not intimidated by talking about evaluation issues, so much the better.

References

Campbell, D.T., and J.C. Stanley. *Experimental and Quasi-Experimental Designs for Research.* Chicago: Rand McNally, 1966.

Cook, T.D., and D.T. Campbell. *Quasi-Experimentation: Design and Analysis Issues for Field Settings.* Chicago: Rand McNally, 1979.

Kirby, D. *Sexuality Education: A Handbook for Evaluating Programs.* Santa Cruz, Calif.: Network Publications, 1984.

Patton, M.Q. *Qualitative Evaluation Methods.* Beverly Hills: Sage
    Publications, 1980.
Siegel, S. *Nonparametric Statistics for the Behavioral Sciences.* New
    York: McGraw-Hill, 1956.

ANNOTATED BIBLIOGRAPHY: SEXUALITY EDUCATION IN THE COMMUNITY

Curricula

Barr, Linda, and Catherine Monserrat. *Working with Childbearing Adolescents.* New Futures, Inc., 2120 Louisiana, N.E., Albuquerque, NM 87110, 1980.

Presents guidelines for working effectively with pregnant teenagers and teenage parents. Includes lesson plans for an accompanying textbook for pregnant adolescents.

Calderwood, Deryck. *About Your Sexuality.* Boston, Mass.: Unitarian Universalist Association, 1983.

This clear, explicit and thorough curriculum for young adolescents includes filmstrips and audiotapes that are often useful with adult learners as well as with younger students. Because it is explicit, the program is best used by an educator with experience. Users often find that its honesty and directness meet the needs of their students.

Calnek, Jeannette M., and Steven G. Levine. *Human Sexuality: A Training Manual for Job Corps Centers.* Genesee Region Family Planning Program, 315 Alexander Street, Rochester, NY 14604, 1981.

Begins with an outline of a 14-16 hour training program for counselors, instructors, medical and recreational personnel, and dormitory staff. Also includes a description of a two-day sexuality education program for job corps members aged 16-21; program assumes correctly that many corps members may already be sexually active.

Cook, Ann T., and Pamela M. Wilson. *Practical Approaches to Sexuality Education Programs: Preadolescents, Adolescents, Parents, and Mentally Retarded Persons.* Sex Education Coalition, 2001 O Street, N.W., Washington, DC 20036, 1982.

Offers very practical mini-guides to conducting family life education programs with four different populations. Each section gives a program rationale, basic lesson plan, special considerations, and selected resources.

Gussin, Gilda, Ann Buxhaum, and Nicholas Danforth. *Self Discovery—Caring, Loving, and Sexuality: Using Skills to Make Tough Choices.* Santa Cruz, Calif.: Network Publications, 1984.

Reviews basic facts about reproduction, teen pregnancy, and birth control. Helps teenagers help themselves through the complexities of adolescence. Students learn to use self-discovery skills to meet needs for loving and caring without necessarily relying on sexual activity.

Hartman, Carl, Jane Quinn, and Brenda Young. *Sexual Expression: A Manual for Trainers.* New York: Human Sciences Press, 1980.

Overall emphasis is on developing comfort, both with one's own sexuality and with sexual issues presented by clients and students. Includes individual, one-to-one, and small group exercises.

Hunter-Geboy, Carol, Lynn Peterson, Sean Casey, Leslie Hardy, and Sarah Renner. *Life Planning Education: A Youth Development Program.* Washington, D.C.: Center for Population Options, 1985.

In Unit I, "Who Am I?," there are chapters on self-esteem, personal and family values, and sex-role stereotypes. Unit II, "Where Am I Going?," covers goal-setting, decision-making, and parenthood. The final unit, "How Do I Get There?," includes chapters on sexuality, employment, and communication. Designed for middle adolescents.

McDermott, Bob, and Barbara Petrich. *Intimacy Is for Everyone: Sex Educator's Guide to Teaching Intimacy Skills.* Santa Barbara, Calif.: Planned Parenthood of Santa Barbara, 1983.

Based on a program conducted with institutionalized adolescents. Promotes the value that sexuality is more than intercourse in that it incorporates love, relationships, and our expression of ourselves as men and women. Includes special sections on heartache, hopelessness, and overcoming fear.

National Alliance for Optional Parenthood. *Exploring the Parenthood Choice: An Activities Guide for Educators.* Santa Cruz, Calif.: Network Publications, 1981.

Promotes the notion that parenthood is optional. Describes techniques for getting youth to think about parenthood and to be aware of alternatives to consider when making responsible choices. Suggests 20 different activities grouped in six sections.

Peloquin, Louise, Jinny Sewell, and Ginny Levin. *Peer Education in Human Sexuality.* Washington, D.C.: Planned Parenthood of Metropolitan Washington, 1981.

Designed to give an understanding of the peer education model. A step-by-step guide to initiating and continuing a peer education program. Includes ideas for using peer educators after training.

Planned Parenthood of Monterey County. *Peer Education: An Adolescent Sex Education Program.* Monterey, Calif.: Planned Parenthood of Monterey, 1981.

Covers methods for starting a peer education program, recruiting students to be peer educators, training them for 30 hours over a 10-day period, and having them present a one-week sexuality education program.

Planned Parenthood of Southeastern Pennsylvania. *We're Not Just Talking Sex . . . A Leader's Guide for Teen Sex Education.* Philadelphia, Pa., 1983.

Outlines three programs that can be conducted independently or together. Topics include health care for teens, values, decision-making and sexuality, and relationships. Gives excellent information on group facilitation, teaching methods, and resources.

Sadker, David. *Being a Man: A Unit of Instructional Activities on Male Role Stereotyping.* Washington, D.C.: Superintendent of Documents, U.S. Government Printing Office, 1980.

For use with junior high students. First section provides background information about the issue; second section contains strategies and lesson plans intended to help youth identify, analyze, and evaluate male sex-role stereotypes in particular, and sex-role stereotyping in general.

Schultz, Jerelyn B. *Sexuality and the Adolescent: A Teaching Guide.* Ames, Iowa: Iowa State University Press, 1981.

Focuses on three major subject areas: self-esteem, relationships, and pregnancy. Each of the units deals with many other topics and skills, such as effective communication and decision-making.

Segal, Judith. *A Training Manual for Working with Adolescents as Peer Counselors.* Pasadena, Calif.: Pasadena Planned Parenthood, 1979.

Includes an overview of the peer counseling program from which this manual evolved. Also includes many examples of techniques for team building, trust development, information giving, and skill development. Suggests ways to keep in touch with participants and discusses administrative considerations.

Sofferin, Pam, L. Elder, J. Overton, B. Towns, and L. Desonier. *Lifestyles Education and Counseling Program.* Lifestyles Center, 1221 West Lakeview Avenue, Pensacola, FL 32501, 1984.

For each of 16 units, the program outlines goals and objectives, optional exercises, overhead transparencies, suggested discussion questions, and pre- and post-tests. Also includes brief fact sheets for most topics and film sheets that include suggestions for discussion, as well as purchasing information.

Teen Advisory Committee and Education Department. *To Be a Leader: Skills in Group Leadership for Teenagers.* Philadelphia, Pa.: Planned Parenthood of Southeastern Pennsylvania, 1983.

Offers advice on becoming an effective group leader, understanding group dynamics, preparing for a group, co-facilitating a group, opening and closing sessions, and handling difficult situations. Suggests "icebreakers" and program activities and discusses special concerns in peer education group leadership.

Van Putten, Juliette. *Peer Education: A Family Health Education Program.* Office of Health Education, San Bernardino County Department of Public Health, 351 North Mountain View Avenue, San Bernardino, CA 92415, 1982.

Consists of fifteen 90-minute sessions. Teaching methods include lectures, role playing, films, group discussions, and values clarification strategies.

Watson, Andre, and Debra Haffner. *Implementing a Young Men's Sexuality Education Program: A How-To Guide.* Washington, D.C.: Planned Parenthood of Metropolitan Washington, 1982.

Provides suggestions, ideas, and activities for developing innovative sexuality education programs for young men. Based on a curriculum initially developed for Big Brothers of the National Capital Area.

Books for Professionals

Bell, Alan P., Martin S. Weinberg, and Sue Kiefer Hammersmith. *Sexual Preference: Its Development in Men and Women.* Bloomington, Ind.: Indiana University Press, 1981.

Based on data from interviews with approximately 1,500 individuals. Charts the development of both homosexuality and heterosexuality among males and females. Statistically tests popular notions about the causes of homosexuality. Presents actual questions and quotes typical answers. Complete sets of diagrams and tables presented in Statistical Appendix.

Benson, Peter, Dorothy Williams, and Arthur Johnson. *The Quicksilver Years: The Hopes and Fears of Early Adolescence.* New York: Harper and Row, 1987.

A thorough study of young American adolescents' values, behaviors, worries, and enthusiasms. With data gathered from 8,000 students and 11,000 parents nationwide, this survey is alive with important facts and figures on teenage sexuality, drug use, attitudes, and religious beliefs. Also available from Network Publications, Santa Cruz, California.

Chilman, Catherine S. *Adolescent Sexuality in a Changing American Society: Social and Psychological Perspectives for the Human Services Professions.* Rev. New York: John Wiley and Sons, 1983.

Includes an analytic overview and summary of available research, as well as chapters on sex education and counseling of adolescents, the development of family planning programs and programs for adolescent parents and their children, and suggestions for further policy and program development.

Durden-Smith, Jo, and Diane de Simone. *Sex and the Brain.* New York: Warner Books, 1983.

Argues that women and men differ irrevocably in behavior and in mental life because of brain differences. Presents most recent research findings on brain science as substantiation.

Golub, Sharon, ed. *Lifting the Curse of Menstruation: A Feminist Appraisal of the Influence of Menstruation on Women's Lives.* Binghamton, N.Y.: Haworth Press, 1983.

Explores the menstrual cycle from menarche to menopause. Discusses such current issues as premenstrual syndrome (PMS), toxic shock syndrome, and clinical treatment of dysmenorrhea.

Johnson, Warren, and Winifred Kempton. *Sex Education and Counseling of Special Groups: The Mentally and Physically Disabled, Ill, and Elderly.* Charles C. Thomas, 2600 South First Street, Springfield, IL 62717, 1981.

Deals with the problem areas of sex education and counseling of disabled persons. Points out danger of losing the individual behind group labels. Offers suggestions for dealing with sex-related topics from masturbation to abortion.

Klein, Fred. *The Bisexual Option: A Concept of One-Hundred Percent Intimacy.* New York: Arbor House, 1978.

Myth-shattering close-up of who bisexuals are, what bisexuality means, and how it may be a far more significant alternative in American life than most experts have heretofore been willing to acknowledge.

Luker, Kristin. *Abortion and the Politics of Motherhood.* Berkeley, Calif.: University of California Press, 1984.

Divided into two major sections—one providing historical background and the other setting forth the present situation regarding abortion. Concludes that the present round of controversy has become a debate among women with different values, experiences, and resources.

Money, John, and Patricia Tucker. *Sexual Signatures: On Being a Man or a Woman.* Boston: Little, Brown , 1975.

An interpretation of the more technical *Man and Woman, Boy and Girl* (Johns Hopkins University Press, 1973). Summarizes research on the process of gender identity differentiation in individuals, and the possible genetic, hormonal, or psychosocial influences that result in the taking of different pathways toward sexual identity. Provides a detailed account of how we respond to the variety of forces influencing us from conception onward.

Sarrel, Lorna, and Phillip Sarrel. *Sexual Unfolding: Sexual Development and Sex Therapies in Late Adolescence.* Boston: Little, Brown, 1979.

Presents the stages that humans typically experience as they develop and affirm their own sexuality. Written for professionals interested in dealing positively with the sexual mores and sexual adjustment of young adults.

Smith, Peggy, and David Mumford. *Adolescent Reproductive Health: Handbook for the Health Professional.* New York: Gardner Press, 1985.

An invaluable resource book for counselors, educators, clinicians, and others involved in the health care of adolescent populations. Openly and realistically treats issues of teenage contraception, fertility, pregnancy, abortion, and venereal disease. Specialists from a variety of medical, psychological, political, economic, and ethical perspectives present their materials in an informative, readable fashion. Also available from Network Publications, of Santa Cruz, California.

Starr, Bernard D., and Marcella Bakur Weiner. *The Starr-Weiner Report on Sex and Sexuality in the Mature Years.* New York: McGraw-Hill, 1981.

Based on responses from more than 800 individuals over the age of 60, the majority of whom are sexually active. Includes information on attitudes toward oral sex, masturbation, living together outside of marriage, and nudity.

Evaluation Resources

Campbell, D.T., and J.C. Stanley. *Experimental and Quasi-Experimental Designs for Research.* Chicago: Rand McNally, 1966.

Describes 16 basic designs for educational and social research in handbook form. Covers designs for situations in which random assignment to groups is possible (experimental designs) and for those in which it is *not* possible (quasi-experimental designs). Discusses the strengths and weaknesses of each design in terms of features of the design that render results difficult or impossible to interpret. Concentrates on the logic of choosing among rival interpretations, making only passing reference to statistical analyses of results. Originally a chapter in a handbook on educational research, now a stand-alone classic.

Cook, T.D., and D.T. Campbell. *Quasi-Experimentation: Design & Analysis Issues for Field Setting.* Chicago: Rand McNally, 1979. More theoretical and analytical than Campbell and Stanley, taking on such topics as the nature of causality and types of validity. Presents mathematically sophisticated methods for statistical analyses of results obtained using quasi-experimental methods. Lists and discusses both obstacles to conducting true experiments in field settings and situations conducive to true experiments.

Kirby, D. *Sexuality Education: A Handbook for Evaluating Programs.* Santa Cruz: Network Publications, 1984.

Provides a step-by-step guide to designing, conducting, and analyzing evaluations of sexuality education programs. Introduces technical terms in practical contexts, thus making otherwise difficult concepts understandable to novice evaluators. Describes several alternative approaches to a variety of evaluation problems, explaining reasons why one method might be preferred over another. Provides sample questionnaires containing validated items for assessing knowledge, attitudes, and behaviors related to human sexuality. Volume 5 of a six-volume "encyclopedia" of evaluation of sexuality education programs in the United States.

Patton, M.Q. *Qualitative Evaluation Methods.* Beverly Hills: Sage Publications, 1980.

Places qualitative evaluation in the context of evaluation in general through parable and pedagogy. Discusses research strategies and designs for use with qualitative methods. Describes collection of qualitative data using observation and interviewing, illustrating "how to" and "how not to" using extensive examples and quotations (exceptionally good advice on interviewing). Suggests several methods for organizing, analyzing, and presenting qualitative data (but not as clearly or as extensively as might be desired).

Siegel, S. *Nonparametric Statistics for the Behavioral Sciences.* New York: McGraw-Hill, 1956.

Presents useful statistical tests in extremely usable, almost "cookbook" form. Describes the limits on the kinds of arithmetic that can be used on the types of data that are likely to result from social science research and outlines procedures for conducting valid statistical analyses of data that are thus limited. Demonstrates the use of each statistical test and correlational measure through clear examples and step-by-step instructions. Unequalled by newer books in clarity and ease of use for the non-mathematically inclined.

Books For Adults: General

Andrews, Laurie. *New Conceptions: A Consumer's Guide to the Newest Fertility Treatments.* New York: Ballantine, 1984.

Expands on the many causes of infertility, the practical and psychological aspects of male and female fertility tests, the technical and personal sides of genetic screening and counseling, and the emotional effects of infertility. Describes remedies available or soon to be available, including in vitro fertilization, surrogate motherhood, artificial insemination, embryo transfer, and so on.

Benedict, Helen. *Recovery: How to Survive Sexual Assault for Women, Men, Teenagers, Their Friends and Families.* New York: Doubleday, 1985.

Offers information about the mythology surrounding sexual assault, both short- and long-term traumatic effects, reporting, medical care, finding and giving support, and self-defense. Includes sections written for men, teens, homosexual people, and older adults.

Bing, Elizabeth, and Libby Colman. *Making Love During Pregnancy.* New York: Bantam Books, 1982.

Frank, firsthand descriptions of pregnancy experiences. Discusses fears and misconceptions of future parents.

Bingham, Mindy, and Sandy Stryker. *More Choices: Strategic Planning Guide for Mixing Career and Family.* Santa Barbara, Calif.: Advocacy Press, 1987.

Shows that it is possible to support a family and find time to enjoy it. Offers practical ideas for women 18 and older who are contemplating a career and a family. The exercises and suggestions will also help working parents in search of new answers. Workbook format. Also available from Network Publications in Santa Cruz, California.

Bingham, Mindy, Sandy Stryker, and Judy Edmonson. *Changes: A Women's Journal for Self-Awareness and Personal Planning.* Santa Barbara, Calif.: Advocacy Press, 1987.

Includes thought-provoking and practical information about finances, careers, marriage and children, and assertiveness. Developed for adult women. Workbook format. Also available from Network Publications in Santa Cruz, California.

Briggs, Anne. *Circumcision: What Every Parent Should Know.* Birth and Parenting Publications. Order from International Childbirth Education Association, P.O. Box 20048, Minneapolis, MN 55420, 1984.

Presents arguments against routine circumcision, which author views as unnecessary and potentially harmful surgery.

Butler, Robert N., and Myrna Lewis. *Love and Sex After Forty: A Guide for Men and Women for Their Mid and Later Years.* New York: Harper and Row, 1986.

Deals with the psychology of aging and sexuality. Discusses medical issues such as new diagnostic and surgical procedures relevant to this age group.

Carrera, Michael. *Sex: The Facts, The Acts and Your Feelings.* New York: Crown Publishers, 1981.

Comprehensive, accurate, and easy-to-understand information about sexuality, presented in a nonjudgmental manner. Imparts positive values for understanding people and relationships. Also used as a text in some colleges.

Comfort, Alex. *The Joy of Sex: A Cordon Bleu Guide to Lovemaking. More Joy: A Lovemaking Companion to the Joy of Sex.* New York: Simon and Schuster, 1st title 1974, 2nd title 1975.

Finely illustrated, explicit guides to lovemaking. Sections on sex and aging, sex and disability, and, in second title, on less conventional sexual behaviors, such as group sex.

Dodson, Betty. *Sex for One: The Joy of Self-loving.* New York: Harmony Books, 1987.

Confronts one of our last and most deeply rooted sexual taboos—masturbation. Demonstrates how anyone can learn to make love alone without guilt or feelings of loneliness. Also recommends sharing masturbation with a partner (same or opposite sex) as a form of safe sex, as well as an erotic treat. Illustrated.

Haeberle, Erwin J. *The Sex Atlas.* Rev. New York: Continuum Publishing, 1982.

A comprehensive sourcebook of basic textual information on human sexuality in a popular reference edition.

Hallingby, Leigh. *Acquired Immune Deficiency Syndrome: An Annotated Bibliography of Print and Audio-Visual Materials for Sale.* SIECUS, New York University, 32 Washington Place, New York, NY 10003, 1986.

Lists 60 books, pamphlets, bibliographies, and audiovisuals available to consumers and professionals on the topic of AIDS.

Harkness, Carla. *The Infertility Book: A Comprehensive Medical and Emotional Guide.* San Francisco, Calif.: Volcano Press, 1987.

A detailed sourcebook that presents comprehensible, compassionate information for persons challenging their infertility. Written with the input of over 70 individuals personally or professionally touched by infertility. Also available from Network Publications in Santa Cruz, California.

Institute for the Advanced Study of Human Sexuality. *Safe Sex in the Age of AIDS.* Citadel Press, 120 Enterprise Avenue, Secaucus, NJ 07094, 1986.

Aimed at both adolescents and adults, men and women. Covers what is safe and unsafe in sexual contact, what can be done to prevent transmission of AIDS while maintaining a healthy, pleasurable sex life, how to negotiate safe sex with a partner, and what products can help prevent exposure to the AIDS virus.

Kolodny, Robert C., William H. Masters, and Virginia E. Johnson. *Masters and Johnson on Sex and Human Loving.* Boston: Little, Brown, 1986.

Revised and reformatted edition of college text by the same authors. Provides information on all aspects of human sexuality.

O'Connor, Dagmar. *How to Make Love to the Same Person for the Rest of Your Life (And Still Love It).* New York: Doubleday, 1985.

Offers couples many practical suggestions for avoiding sexual boredom and exploring a variety of sexual options such as sensate focus exercises. Stresses idea of responsibility for one's own sexual pleasure.

Olds, Sally Wendkos. *The Eternal Garden: Seasons of Our Sexuality.* Westminster, Md.: Random House, 1985.

Covers stages of adult sexual development, decade by decade, from young adulthood to old age. Focuses on major life events such as marriage, divorce, menopause, and aging, as well as the impact of the different stages of life on sexuality.

Sarrel, Lorna, and Philip Sarrel. *Sexual Turning Points: The Seven Stages of Adult Sexuality.* New York: Macmillan, 1984.

Enlightened discussion of the adult sexual life cycle. Includes such biological turning points as puberty, pregnancy, menopause, illness, and aging as well as interpersonal and social transitions, such as first love, marriage, parenting, breaking up and widowhood.

Witkin, Mildred Hope, and Burton Lehrenbaum. *45—And Single Again.* New York: Debner Books, 1985.

Provides a wealth of information on sex, love, and relationships. Useful not only to single people over 45, but also to those in long-term marriages.

Books for Adults: Especially for Men

Castleman, Michael. *Sexual Solutions—An Informative Guide.* New York: Simon and Schuster, 1980.

A sensitive and sensible guide to sexuality and self-care for today's man. Discusses birth control, sensuality, rape, sexual dysfunctions, and other sexual issues. Illustrated with a few tasteful line drawings.

Goldberg, Herb. *The Hazards of Being Male: Surviving the Myth of Masculine Privilege.* New York: Signet Books, 1976.

Explains how men's lives are limited by society's narrow definition of masculinity. A very readable guide to personal growth for men.

Goldberg, Herb. *The New Male: From Self-Destruction to Self-Care.* New York: William Morrow, 1979.

Explores the psychological and social price of the male stereotype and offers advice on ways to survive these consequences.

Hite, Shere. *The Hite Report on Male Sexuality.* New York: Ballantine, 1981.

Depicts the enormous variety and diversity of male sexual expressions and attitudes and presents provocative ideas about the nature of sexual intercourse and other forms of sexual behavior.

Julty, Sam. *Men's Bodies, Men's Selves: The Complete Guide to the Health and the Well-Being of Men's Bodies, Minds and Spirits.* New York: Dial Press, 1979.

A man's version of *Our Bodies Our Selves* that includes useful information from numerous sources. Concise without being simplistic. The author defines health broadly to include mental, physical, emotional, social, and spiritual realms.

Kelly, Gary. *Good Sex: A Healthy Man's Guide to Sexual Fulfillment.* New York: Harcourt Brace Jovanovich, 1979.

Insightful and sensitive self-help book for men who want more total sexual fulfillment.

Man's Body: An Owner's Manual. Rev. New York: Simon and Schuster, 1981.

Diagrams the male body. Describes bodily functions beginning in infancy and continuing through old age.

Zilbergeld, Bernie, with John Ullman. *Male Sexuality.* New York: Bantam, 1978.

For the man who wants to get more in touch with his own sexuality or any woman who wants to understand male sexuality more fully.

Books for Adults: Especially for Women

Barbach, Lonnie. *For Each Other: Sharing Sexual Intimacy.* New York: Anchor Press/Doubleday, 1982.

Gives women a complete program for dealing with the physical and psychological aspects of sexuality within a relationship. Over 50 easy-to-follow exercises showing women how to reduce anger, enhance communication, increase vaginal sensitivity, and break unfulfilling love patterns.

Barbach, Lonnie Garfield. *For Yourself: The Fulfillment of Female Sexuality.* New York: Signet (New American Library), 1975.

A classic in the field, written primarily for women having difficulty achieving orgasm. Discusses sources of confusion about female sexuality, describes female sexual physiology, and suggests specific exercises to do at home.

Boston Women's Health Book Collective. *The New Our Bodies, Our Selves: A Book by and for Women.* New York: Simon and Schuster, 1984.

Written to help women know themselves and their bodies better. Covers sexuality, contraception, relationships, health care, sexual physiology and reproduction.

Cassell, Carol. *Swept Away.* New York: Bantam, 1984.

Focuses on why women confuse love and sex and how they can have both. Cites material from psychotherapists, literature, magazines, and newspapers. Sprinkled liberally with quotes from interviews with women.

Federation of Feminist Women's Health Centers. *A New View of a Woman's Body: A Fully Illustrated Guide.* New York: Simon and Schuster, 1981.

A feminist perspective on female sexuality written by pioneers in the women's self-help movement. Discussion and drawings of the clitoris are particularly notable.

Fromer, Margot Joan. *Menopause: What It Is, Why It Happens, How You Can Deal With It.* New York: Pinnacle, 1985.

Written in chatty style and enlivened by a number of case histories. Much good information provided to educate women to be responsible about their own health care. Based on medical model.

Greenwood, Sadie. *Menopause, Naturally: Preparing for the Second Half of Life.* Volcano Press, 330 Ellis Street, San Francisco, CA 94102, 1984.

Grounded in the belief that good nutrition and regular exercise can make all the difference in the physical and psychological changes menopause can bring. Combines prevention and medical treatment models of health care.

Hite, Shere. *The Hite Report.* New York: Dell, 1976.

Based on responses to in-depth questionnaires returned by some 3,000 women. A provocative and revealing study that examines the subject of female sexuality from the inside. Makes extensive use of direct quotes.

Kitzinger, Shiela. *Women's Experience of Sex.* New York: G.P. Putnam's Sons, 1983.

A comprehensive, sensitively written source book on women's sexuality. Beautifully illustrated. Feminist perspective.

Loulan, JoAnn. *Lesbian Sex.* Spinsters/Aunt Lute, P.O. Box 410687, San Francisco, CA 94141, 1984.

Written primarily for lesbians, but can definitely contribute to any woman's understanding of herself and her sexuality. Workbook format. Includes tasteful graphics and diagrams.

Madaras, Linda, and Jane Patterson. *Woman Care: A Gynecological Guide to Our Body.* New York: Avon Books, 1984.

A moving, compassionate book that contributes to a positive recognition of the right of post-menopause women to a full sexual life. Includes self-study exercises.

Martin, Del, and Phyllis Lyon. *Lesbian/Woman.* New York: Bantam, 1983.

Written by a couple who have been together over 25 years. Depicts what it is like to grow up gay, to be a lesbian mother, and to face living, loving, and surviving as a lesbian in a male-dominated world. Provides a review of the gains and setbacks in lesbian culture over the past 10 years.

Books for Older Adults

Berger, Raymond, M. *Gay and Gray: The Older Homosexual Man.* Champaign, Ill.: University of Illinois Press, 1982.

Report on a study of 112 men between the ages of 44 and 72. A sensitively written account of how these men adapted to the aging process and to society's discrimination against them.

Brecher, Edward, M., and the editors of Consumer Reports Books. *Love, Sex and Aging.* Boston, Mass.: Little, Brown, 1984.

Reports the findings of a 1978-79 Consumers Union study of love and sex, conducted with over 4,000 volunteer male and female respondents, aged 50 to 93. Includes both statistics and direct quotations from questionnaires returned.

Butler, Robert N., and Myrna I. Lewis. *Love and Sex After Sixty: A Guide for Men and Women for Their Later Years.* New York: Harper and Row, 1977.

Gives guidance to older people for enjoying—to whatever degree and in whatever way they wish—the satisfactions of physical sex and pleasurable sensuality.

Schover, Leslie R. *Prime Time: Sexual Health for Men over Fifty.* New York: Holt, Rinehart & Winston, 1984.

A sensitive, reassuring self-help book that provides straightforward advice and information about sexuality for middle-aged and older men and their partners.

Witkin, Ruth K., and Robert J. Nissen. *Good Sex After Fifty.* Regency Press, 32 Ridge Drive, Port Washington, NY 11050, 1980.

Compact, well-written booklet designed to encourage middle-aged and older people to maintain their sexual lives.

Religion and Sexuality

Batchelor, Edward, ed. *Homosexuality and Ethics.* New York: Pilgrim Press, 1982.

Well-chosen, comprehensive selection of essays covering the wide spectrum of Jewish, Protestant, and Roman Catholic views on homosexuality. Useful for reaching a greater understanding of today's issues and debates involving homosexuality.

Boswell, John. *Christianity, Social Tolerance, and Homosexuality: Gay People in Western Europe from the Beginning of the Christian Era to the Fourteenth Century.* Chicago, Ill.: University of Chicago Press, 1980.

Scholarly analysis of the changes in early Christian attitudes toward homosexuality. Presents historical background on the issue as well as alternatives to Christian mainstream homophobia.

Brandt, Allan M. *No Magic Bullet: A Social History of Venereal Disease in the United States since 1880.* New York: Oxford University Press, 1985.

Explores the interaction of religion, American culture, and attitudes about sex and sin.

Donnelly, Dody H. *Radical Love: An Approach to Sexual Spirituality.* Minneapolis, Minn.: Winston Press, 1984.

Argues that spirituality must be sexual and sexuality must be spiritual to avoid dualisms that split mind from body, God from world, male from female, and heterosexual from homosexual. Lively, readable book.

Fox, Matthew. *A Spirituality Named Compassion.* Minneapolis: Winston Press, 1979.

Examines creation-centered spirituality and its effect on religious attitudes regarding sexuality and behavior.

Gardella, Peter. *Innocent Ecstasy: How Christianity Gave America an Ethic of Sexual Pleasure.* New York: Oxford University Press, 1985.

Of interest to anyone who wants to have a better understanding of the religious and sexual heritage that marks American culture.

Gittelsohn, Roland B. *Love, Sex and Marriage: A Jewish View.* Union of American Hebrew Congregations, 838 Fifth Avenue, New York, NY 10021, 1980.

A textbook for high school students and young adults, with a Jewish viewpoint on all aspects of male/female relationships.

Kosnik, Anthony, et al. *Human Sexuality: New Directions in American Catholic Thought.* Ramsey, N.J.: Paulist Press, 1977.

Prepared by a study group of the Catholic Theological Society of America. Broadens the traditional view of sexuality from "procreative and unitive" to "creative and integrative." Of interest to non-Catholics as well.

McNaught, Brian. *On Being Gay: Thoughts on Family, Faith and Love.* New York: St. Martin's Press, 1988.

Includes essays on such topics as growing up gay, friends and lovers, and the Catholic Church. Clearly lays out the issues surrounding Catholic teachings and homosexuality. Written with honesty and insight.

Money, John. *The Destroying Angel, Sex, Fitness and Food in the Legacy of Degeneracy Theory, Graham Crackers, Kellogg's Corn Flakes and American Health History.* Buffalo, N.Y.: Prometheus Books, 1985.

Examines the impact of religion and socialization on attitudes toward sex and morality.

Nelson, James B. *Between Two Gardens: Reflections on Sexuality and Religious Experience.* New York: Pilgrim Press, 1983.

Essays attempting to integrate religious and sexual experiences in the face of the western cultural split between the two. Written in non-technical language.

Nelson, James B. *Embodiment: An Approach to Sexuality and Christian Thinking.* Augsburg Publishing, 426 South Fifth Street, Minneapolis, MN 55415, 1979.

Encourages ongoing dialogue in the Christian community on the theological meaning of human sexuality.

Parrinder, Geoffrey. *Sex in the World's Religions.* New York: Oxford University Press, 1980.

Numerous citations from author's sources, stories from his own experiences, along with a number of resources. Suggestions for further study and an excellent index. Helpful guide to a complicated subject.

Reuther, Rosemary Radford. *Sexism and God-Talk: Toward a Feminist Theology.* Boston: Beacon Press, 1983.

Presents the case for confronting the habit of presenting religion only in male terms.

Sawicki, Marianne. *Faith and Sexism: Guidelines for Religious Educators.* New York: Seabury Press, 1979.

Offers guidelines for conducting nonsexist religious education.

Part IV
Model Programs

FAMILY CENTERED SEXUALITY EDUCATION

Helen Patricia Mudd
Elizabeth Nixon West

In 1982, Catholic Charities of the Diocese of Arlington, Inc., a multi-service family agency, began offering courses in Family Centered Sexuality Education for adolescents and their parents. The courses, partly funded for the first three years by the Office of Adolescent Pregnancy Programs of the U.S. Department of Health and Human Services, have had some 1800 participants.

Rationale

Sexuality education is a service we felt impelled to offer. During the years since our agency was begun in 1948, we have counseled thousands of pregnant adolescents, the fathers of their babies, and the families of each. We help young people back difficult and life-changing decisions and help them attempt to put their lives back together after a pregnancy. Although they come from all segments of the community, the young people have many things in common. They are young and unmarried. Most are living at home with a parent or parents. The majority are still in school. They have incomplete and inaccurate information about sex and for the most part do not communicate about sexual matters with parents or sexual partners. Our teen clients tend to make decisions impulsively rather than logically, and have little knowledge of the possible emotional, medical, legal, and financial consequences of sexual activity. Like many other parents, our clients' parents lack important information and skills needed to educate their children about sexuality.

We believe that an educational approach can address all these issues, provided it combines factual information, exploration of values, and opportunities to learn skills required to use the new knowledge. Both parents and adolescents need to become conscious of their values and able to articulate these to each other. With these things in mind, we designed our courses.

In keeping with our strong pro-family agency policy, we chose a family-centered approach to implement sexuality education. The family-centered approach brings parents and their adolescent children together to learn new information, to hear each other's points of view, and to go home each week with new ideas for communicating honestly about the sensitive issue of sexuality. We believe that this approach best supports the family, the primary source for learning about sexuality.

Agency Preparation

Having clarified our basic philosophy regarding sexuality education, we then needed to prepare to implement such a program. While social workers within the agency were experienced counselors of pregnant teenagers, they had limited experience leading educational groups. Also, many workers felt uncomfortable with the prospect of talking to parents and adolescents about sexuality. How would parents respond? What were the best teaching techniques? Did the staff know enough about anatomy, physiology, and reproduction? Could they get parents and teenagers to open up to one another? How would they handle controversial issues in the group? What if planned activities failed to stimulate productive discussion? Given all these legitimate concerns, we decided to hire a consultant to help us develop our curriculum and train our staff.

Before developing any curriculum materials our consultant, an experienced sexuality educator, conducted a five-day workshop with agency staff. By the end of the workshop, our social workers were noticeably more comfortable with the task ahead. They had gained a lot of information, were more aware of their own values, and had a clearer sense of teaching techniques to use in the program.

Course Design and Format

Now that staff were feeling more prepared, we began the difficult task of developing curricula. In an attempt to address developmental differences, we designed two curricula—one for high school students and their parents, and one for seventh and eight graders and their parents. The goals for both programs are the same: to increase sexual knowledge, to increase self-esteem, and to improve communication about sexuality between parents and teens. Each program, however, highlights the developmental issues crucial to the ages of the young people participating. The small group method, featuring a combination of parent groups, teen groups, and joint parent and teen groups, is utilized in both programs. Groups range in size from 15 to 22 people, with the parent groups generally being slightly larger than teen groups. Both programs begin with group-building activities designed to establish an atmosphere of warmth, trust, and open communication. Finding the right balance and flow of activities took tremendous effort. We revised the curriculum many times as a result of our early experiences. Copies of our curriculum and manual are available from the agency at cost.

The high school program addresses the following possible topics: anatomy and physiology, adolescent growth and development, values, peer relationships, decision-making, sexually transmitted diseases, contraception, peer pressure, the case for abstinence, consequences of teen sexual relations, the influence of the media, communication skills, adoption, and sexual assault.

The seventh- and eighth-grade program addresses the topics of puberty, peer relationships, decision-making, adolescent growth and development, peer pressure, values, sexually transmitted diseases, contraception (if requested by the advisory committee), advantages of abstinence, and communication between parents and teens.

Both courses utilize a variety of teaching methods: films, a talk by a doctor and/or family life educator, question-and-answer period, mini-lectures, group discussions, role playing, and various experiential group activities. Our primary focus in this program is to reinforce the role of parents as sources of sexual information, guidance, and counsel for their adolescent sons and daughters. Throughout the program parents practice ways to share their values with their teens. Homework assigned after each session helps to promote a discussion of relevant sexual issues at home.

Sponsors

In an attempt to find sponsors for family centered sexuality education, we contacted a variety of community groups concerned with youth, with special emphasis on churches. Since our program was federally funded and required strict observance of the separation of church and state, we developed the program to be suitable for any religious denomination or for groups of mixed religions. Our agency has a natural linkage with Catholic churches in northern Virginia. As a result, the course has been sponsored by many Catholic churches in northern Virginia.

As it turns out, we greatly reduced the task of recruiting families by targeting parishes as our primary sponsors. In fact, churches have proven to be ideal sponsors for sexuality education. There is already a sense of mutual trust and sharing in church groups. Participants tend to feel that their values will be respected in a religious setting, thus they have come to our sexuality education programs in large numbers. Also, church staff have been very helpful with (1) planning the program, (2) recruiting families, and (3) making the implementation process as smooth as possible.

Planning the Program

The first step of the planning process is to meet with the pastor of the church or his delegate, often a minister of religious education or a school principal. Usually the pastor chooses other key individuals to attend the first meeting, during which we outline the philosophy of our work in sexuality education, the history of our involvement, and the proposed content of the course. If this group expresses an interest in sponsoring a course, we ask them to form an advisory committee of approximately twelve people, including community leaders, parents, and teens to review our films and literature. The advisory group also suggests topics and/or activities to be included or excluded from the course, based on the particular needs of their group. Advisory groups meet two or three times to complete the planning process. Because the advisory group tailors the content of the program to the particular needs and values of their parish, the church community feels a sense of ownership of the sexuality education program.

Advisory groups are invaluable in "marketing" sexuality education courses. They take responsibility for publicizing the course and for gaining the community acceptance needed for the success of the program. Advisory groups have encouraged participation by (1) having the pastor send a special letter of invitation to all parents and teens of appropriate ages, (2) placing announcements in Sunday bulletins and/or parish newsletters, (3) arranging for the pastor to make announcements from the pulpit, (4) recommending the program to friends, and (5) placing notices and articles in local newspapers.

Opposition to sexuality education has surfaced in advisory group meetings in several churches that were considering sponsorship of the program. Although this is not what we hope for, we realize that opposition is a fact of life in sexuality education. In most cases the group has been able to handle the objections of individuals, and we have been able to offer the program successfully. In a few cases, however, it became clear that we were not going to have the community support needed for a successful program. In these cases, we have withdrawn, thankful not to be presiding over a fiasco. In all churches, we found a substantial number of persons prepared to encourage and support a responsible sexuality education program.

In the presentation of any sexuality education program, there are certain sensitive issues that need to be addressed. The issues of contraception and abortion are two of the most sensitive, especially for Catholic Church sponsors. The Catholic Church's stand on respect for human life and opposition to abortion is well known. Contraception is an equally sensitive subject. Each of our advisory committees spends a great deal of time discussing these issues and deciding how such information will be presented to the particular group, i.e., by lecture, distribution of pamphlets, and/or question-and-answer period. These discussions sometimes become heated and emotional debates. We believe that parents and teens participating in a sexuality education program have a right to expect that any questions they ask, regardless of the topic, will be answered. This is a principle that we discuss carefully with each advisory committee. We also believe the advisory committee should know and support our intention to answer any question raised. To date, every sponsoring agency has agreed to have us answer all participant questions, including those that ask about contraception and abortion.

All of the advisory groups have chosen to present basic information about contraception. They know that teens can get information from peers, from drug store shelves, and from clinics or doctors, but believe it is better that teens receive this information in a setting where parents can share their values about this subject. In order to present basic information on contraception that did not appear to "promote" the idea, we developed a pamphlet that has been used by some of our sponsors. Other groups have chosen to write their own pamphlets on the subject. Some of these pamphlets contain information only while others contain Catholic Church teachings and have been distributed during a follow-up program after the conclusion of the Catholic Charities program.

Because we had federal funding in the early years of the program, we were not allowed to teach religion. However, participants often bring up religious issues related to sexuality. In order to address the religious issues, sponsors have conducted a follow-up program, so participants' discussion during the Catholic Charities program sessions would not be inhibited. Deferring discussion of religious teachings until after the program has allowed participants to discuss their family and personal values freely.

One unique feature of the Family Centered Sexuality Education Program has been the large numbers who attend. Approximately 40 to 180 parents and teens participate in each program.

Conducting the Program

Participants pre-register about 10 days prior to the first session. We charge a fee of $20.00 per family. However, we waive the fee for families who cannot afford to pay. Parents are required to register with their teens. When planning for large numbers of people, it is important to have parent and teen group assignments made before the program begins. Small group space should be assigned, clearly marked and set up with chairs in a circle before participants arrive. A well-organized approach, coupled with light refreshments, helps put participants at ease. Our advisory groups assume responsibility for reserving space, handling pre-registration, setting up chairs, and providing refreshments at each session.

We find that parents are eager for the training and sometimes pressure their teens to come. Usually the resentment that some teens initially feel fades as they begin to participate in and enjoy the program. Facilitators' efforts to be warm and friendly help to ease participants' initial nervousness. It is important to remember that it seems new and strange to many participants to discuss sexuality, especially in a small group setting where there are others whom they may not know very well or, indeed, may not even have seen before.

The actual program consists of five two-hour sessions. We usually begin at 7:30 P.M. and end at 9:30 P.M. During the program, groups of teens and parents meet both separately and together to express and share their concerns, questions, and values. To keep the course dynamic, we utilize a variety of teaching methods and activities including many visual aids.

Throughout the program, we encourage parents to share their values with their teens. This is particularly important in discussions of sensitive topics, as we remind parents that they are the primary sexuality educators of their sons and daughters. Some parents are disturbed by the question-and-answer period during which controversial questions such as the following are answered.

1. Should a parent discuss masturbation openly or just leave the child alone?
2. What is a wet dream?
3. Why is it important to have a moral value system in regard to dating and sex?
4. What is menstruation?
5. What should you say to a boy/girl on your first date?
6. What should you say to your child if she were to say she was pregnant?
7. How do you have sex when you are in bed?
8. What age should you be before you have sex?
9. My concern is: Where do we draw the line in communicating on sex, so that it does not appear that we are condoning permissive sex?
10. Exactly when can a girl get pregnant?
11. Explain venereal disease.
12. Do rubbers and birth control pills "always" protect you from getting pregnant?
13. How does a boy know know when he has gotten to his puberty stage?
14. How long do you have to have sex to get a girl pregnant?
15. If a lady is pregnant with twins, how many umbilical cords are there?

We answer, giving only facts and enforcing fairly universal values, such as:

- It is wrong to exploit another person (sexually or otherwise).
- Sexuality is a natural and positive aspect of being human.
- Teenagers should postpone having sexual intercourse and becoming parents.
- All human beings have worth and dignity, regardless of age, race, religion, and sexual orientation.
- We should treat others with justice and compassion.

Still, some parents want us to take a stronger stand on issues such as abortion, contraception, premarital sex, and homosexuality. We tell the families at the beginning of the question-and-answer period that we are there to give information and to encourage them to discuss their positions on these controversial topics with their children. When is it right to have sex? Is homosexuality a sin? Is abortion ever acceptable? It is important for teenagers to know what their parents believe and why. It is also important for parents to know how their teenagers feel about these issues.

Evaluation

According to the evaluation of the first three years conducted by Dr. Gerald J. Stahler, National Center for Family Studies, Catholic University, Washington, D.C., the program has been successful to a statistically significant degree in improving sexual knowledge, self-esteem, and communication between parents and teens. In addition, participants evaluated the program in the following manner: 90 percent of the teens were "very pleased" or "somewhat pleased" with the program, while 97 percent of the parents were "very pleased" or "somewhat pleased." 99 percent of the parents rated the program as "very useful" or "useful," while 84 percent of the teens gave it the same rating. There appears to be a high degree of satisfaction with the program among participants, with parents being slightly more enthusiastic than teens.

We receive many requests for detailed information about our program. As a result, we have made our curriculum containing activities and hand-out materials available to other groups for a small fee. In addition, we have conducted training for adults in our sponsoring agencies so that they can offer family centered sexuality education programs independently of Catholic Charities.

There is today a widespread recognition of the importance of sexuality education. The demand for our course has kept us scheduled a year in advance. When the community learned that family-centered courses were available, requests came to us in larger numbers than we could handle.

Following each course, parents tell us that their family relationships have been enriched. Teens have told us of the bonds of mutual understanding formed with friends and classmates who attended the course together. The following are some comments from participants:

9th Grade Boy: The friends I met at this program last year are friends I have kept in high school. We spend a lot of time together. It's nice to know kids who believe the same things as you.

10th Grade Boy: The facilitator helped me share my worries that I was gay with my parents.

10th Grade Boy: After the film, *Teenage Father*, whew! I'm glad I'm not in that boy's shoes!

Mother: After taking this course, a whole new level of communication with my daughter opened up. Our relationship is much deeper as a result.

Mother: As a result of the support I got in group discussions, I feel much more confident about dealing with my teenagers

Father: As a physician, I have had to deal with sexual issues with many patients. Until I took this course, I felt uncomfortable discussing the same things with my son. The course really opened up communication with my children.

8th Grade Girl: After seeing last week's film on parent-teen relationships, I went home and cooked dinner for my mother. She works hard and needs some help.

9th Grade Girl: I'd like to take another course, now that I'm in high school.

Sponsoring Educator: The format is excellent because it presents information and gives people an opportunity to reflect on and discuss their values. It encourages in-depth communication between parents and teens.

7th Grade Girl: I didn't want to come at first, but my mother made me. I really have enjoyed it and I've learned a lot.

Clergyman: This has been an invaluable program for us. Many parents have told me how it's improved communication in their families.

Parents and teens alike report that they have achieved a sense of enhanced competency in dealing with the issues of sexuality.

Family Centered Sexuality Education Associates

In October 1985 the federal funds for this program were not renewed. The program is not presently offered under Catholic Charities auspices. However, the professional staff involved has formed an association called Family Centered Sexuality Associates. This group is continuing to offer the program on a contract basis to schools, churches, and youth groups.

References

Alter, Judith, and Pamela Wilson. *Teaching Parents to Be the Primary Sexuality Educators of Their Children,* Volumes II & III. U.S. Government Printing Office, 1982.

Brown, Downs, Peterson, Simpson, Alter, and Kirby. *Sexuality Education: A Curriculum for Parent-Child Programs.* Santa Cruz, Calif.: Network Publications, 1984.

Feibelman, Barbara, and Michael Hamrick. *Family Life Education: A Problem Solving Curriculum* (Ages 15-19). U.S. Department of Health, Education and Welfare, 1980.

U.S. Department of Health and Human Services. *In Between: A Family Life Education Curriculum for Early Adolescents* (Ages 10-14), 1980.

West, Elizabeth N., Patricia H. Mudd, et al. *Family Centered Sexuality Education; Curriculum and Manual.* Catholic Charities of the Diocese of Arlington, Inc., 1985.

Wilson, Pamela. *Sexuality Education: An Annotated Guide for Resource Materials.* Santa Cruz, Calif.: Network Publications, 1984.

THE MOTHER-DAUGHTER EXPERIENCE

Kathy Hazelwood
Gwen Killmer

Introduction

The relationship between a mother and daughter differs from any alliance either will have with another person and therefore there is a distinct need for programs designed specifically for mothers and daughters. For example, as Signe Hammer in *Daughters and Mothers/Mothers and Daughters* writes:

> For any daughter, the relationship with her mother is the first relationship in her life and may also be the most important she will ever have. In the context of her relationship with her mother, a daughter first learns what it means to be a person or finds that she is not encouraged to develop a sense of her own separate identity. Through her mother's response to and initiatives toward her body and its needs, a daughter begins to form her own relationship to her body, laying the groundwork for her developing sense of sexual identity. And through her mother, a daughter first begins to learn about the cultural expectations of feminine role behavior.

Our agency, Panhandle Planned Parenthood, has been conducting sexuality education programs since 1979. Programs that we offered for mothers alone or daughters alone were not well attended. In contrast, mother-daughter programs have been very well attended. By billing the event as a time for mothers and daughters to share, gain knowledge and insight, we found that both parties were less threatened and more willing to attend. Adolescence is a time of always being on the run between school and social life. Slowing down long enough to talk things through with parents is often at the bottom of a long list of priorities for young people. In this regard, providing a structured opportunity for communication in a quiet setting seems to attract participants.

Goals of Mother-Daughter Workshops

The overall goal of the program is to provide an atmosphere for mothers and daughters to enhance their communication skills, particularly on the subject of sexuality. The program also strives to present contemporary and accurate information to replace myths and inaccuracies that characterize the education process most parents have experienced. In addition, participants explore pertinent issues within their own families and possible methods of handling them.

Program content is designed to be appropriate for the age of the child and can be adapted to any age range from six to eighteen. Content is also geared specifically to the needs of the group. Many groups indicate, at first contact, some very precise material or topics they wish to have covered. For instance, a group of mothers and young daughters may show an interest in learning more about themselves and enhancing self-esteem. In most cases, when group members have similar needs, the content is directed toward building on these commonalties. For example, single mothers and their daughters have some very unique concerns. Therefore, the content of a workshop for this group needs to highlight issues particular to single parenting.

The teaching techniques are specifically designed to help participants: (1) become more comfortable with their own sexuality, (2) acquire more accurate information, and (3) encourage dialogue between mother and daughter. Exercises such as value clarification, role-playing, and attitude sharing encourage group discussion. At the very beginning of the program, group leaders establish an atmosphere of trust and rapport that leads to open discussion.

Our specific intent when selecting and implementing activities is to create a physical closeness between mother and daughter. We have asked daughters of all ages to sit on their mothers' laps or be seated face to face with knees touching. By bringing mother and daughter this close, the physical act of touching creates a bond that encourages sharing and closer attention to what each is saying to the other. Especially with adolescents, it may have been some time since they held their mothers' hands or were close enough to read the expression on their mothers' faces.

No activity is ever included or conducted in a way that would threaten or embarrass any participant in front of the group. Most sessions begin with an exercise or a series of exercises deigned to establish group cohesiveness. As time progresses, the activities become more personal as participants are asked to share their own thoughts and feelings. This leads to an increased understanding between mothers and daughters. As the risk of exposing personal feelings increases, the activities are more restricted to sharing between individual mothers and daughters. Participants, at all times, retain control over what they share with the group.

We conclude each session by encouraging ongoing communication and sharing beyond the workshop itself—in the hours, days, weeks, and even years to come. Many times, exercises are incorporated that deal with difficult issues common to all mothers and daughters. This is done in the hope that, on neutral ground and in the company of others, participants realize they are not alone in struggling with certain issues. There is no attempt made to "solve" problems or reach concrete conclusions but rather to gain new insight and initiate dialogue that for some families may have reached an impasse.

In nearly every program, pamphlets and other materials are made available to participants to share in their own home. See the list of annotated resources for ideas.

Public Relations

Efforts to publicize workshops vary depending on the composition of the group. If the group existed prior to the program, such as Camp Fire or Girl Scouts, most of the publicity would be focused within the membership. If the workshop is offered to the general public, an extensive media campaign is conducted. This campaign includes newspaper, television, and radio coverage, and announcements in various community publications.

Miscellaneous Considerations

In order to accomplish the intended objectives of the workshop, a small-group approach is recommended. A limit of 10 mother-daughter couples is ideal. The dynamics of small groups—for instance the ability to get to know one another, establishing trust, and being comfortable with each other—are crucial advantages of a small-group format.

A preferable and effective setting for this workshop is the home of a participant. The comfortable relaxed atmosphere of a home lends a more personal effect and establishes the groundwork for sharing. Other settings have been classrooms, churches, and YWCOs.

The workshop time frame must allow for flexibility in scheduling although the most successful thus far has been two sessions, each lasting two to three hours. When planning a workshop it is always important to consider the needs and convenience of each individual group.

Refreshments always contribute to a comfortable and relaxed atmosphere. Sometimes, parents or a representative of the sponsoring agency bring refreshments. This arrangement gives the participants a feeling of cooperation as they are contributing as well as benefiting from the effort.

Evaluation

Success or failure can be evaluated from several perspectives. For facilitators, the number of participants is often an important indicator of success or failure. If the attendance is below what was originally anticipated, one could easily presume the venture was a failure. Numbers should not, however, be the only consideration. A program could be poorly attended but still be considered successful if those participating felt they had benefited.

Evaluation forms, administered at the end of the program, measure the participants' perception of the benefits of the workshop. By completing the survey, a participant can critique the workshop and indicate whether her needs were met.

In some instances, highly cohesive groups have requested follow-up programs. These groups are usually quite motivated to attend further sessions as a level of trust has been established between the facilitator and group as well as between participants.

Conclusion

Daughters inherit a different world than their mothers. Their lives are accelerating at a more rapid pace. They are faced with many more complicated social pressures, more complicated dilemmas, and simply more information to cope with than at any other time in history.

If workshops do nothing more than evoke a first-time, honest-to-goodness discussion between mothers and daughters in which both parties find out "where each one stands," a positive impact has been made on the relationship.

STRAIGHT TALK: A PROGRAM TO INCREASE FAMILY COMMUNICATION ABOUT SEXUALITY
Debby Goodman

Over a two year period the "Straight Talk" program was developed at Planned Parenthood of Oklahoma City. Persistence has been a key word. Feedback has frequently included comments like: "A special thank you for your fabulous 'Straight Talk' presentation. Becky and I really benefited from your approach and are continuing to open doors regarding our sexuality . . ."

Some key ingredients that help to make programs like "Straight Talk" effective for families are the following:

1. The goals are positive.
2. The family systems concept is key.
3. There is ample communication practice time.
4. Activities bring unconscious beliefs into awareness.
5. The format allows flexibility.

There are other considerations in good programs, but let us elaborate on these five because they are important and frequently overlooked.

The Goals Are Positive

In programs where the goals are positive, plenty of time and energy are spent on learning constructive behaviors, and there is

325

not an emphasis on problems. Time is spent defining, describing, and picturing positive, desired outcomes such as (1) being sexually responsible, (2) increasing family communication about sexuality, (3) having accurate sexuality information, and (4) making good sexual decisions. Group activities become focused on ways to attain these positive goals. There are brainstorming activities that list the characteristics of a sexually responsible person. Interviewing and large group discussions increase communication. Films, structured activities, and written materials provide accurate information. Skill-building activities help increase effective decision-making.

In contrast, programs where the goals are problem oriented (e.g., preventing teen pregnancy, stopping sexual abuse, or saying "no" to premature sexual activity) focus on what is *wrong* about sexuality. In those programs time is spent defining the problems, analyzing the problems, and coming up with solutions to the problems. Too much time is spent on what is wrong, and not enough is spent on how to make it right.

By spending time understanding appropriate sexual behavior, participants also learn about inappropriate sexual behavior. By teaching effective decision-making, they understand how mistakes are made. And by discussing the importance of accurate information, they become aware of the consequences of ignorance. Rather than ignoring the problems related to sexuality, we focus more on the positives.

The Family Systems Concept Is Key

In sex education programs where the family systems concept is key, the curriculum is developed with all of the family members in mind. It is important to understand the family as a "system" in order to recognize the influence individuals in a family have on one another. If we look at the family as a "system," we see the way the family is organized . . . the way its members communicate . . . the way they work out their daily interactions. Each individual is influenced by the family process. Virginia Satir (in her book *Peoplemaking*) compares the family system to a mobile: ". . . all the pieces can be grouped together in balance by shortening or lengthening the strings attached, or rearranging the distance between the pieces . . . you can't arrange one without thinking of the other." Family members are at different levels of growth at different times, and that growth affects other family members. The sexuality of the adults affects the children, and vice versa.

For example, it is important to understand the physical, emotional, and social changes of adolescence and how that affects the family. It is equally important to understand the physical, emotional, and social changes of mid-life and how that affects the family. When asking questions and stimulating discussion about important sexuality topics such as peer pressure and body image, the adults and the children can be asked, "How do you handle peer pressure? Do you like your body and the way you look?" In other words, the sexual growth of all members of the group is addressed and, one hopes, the interrelatedness of all family members is recognized.

There Is Ample Communication Practice Time

Actual communication is an integral part of a family program because it may open the door for more communication later. Too often sexuality educators talk about the importance of quality communication about sexuality but do not allow enough "practice" time for the group to actually talk and share.

In "Straight Talk" we allow plenty of time for people to talk because we know they they've seldom had the opportunity to share their sexual concerns. We also know that the more the participants talk, the better the chance they will continue communicating at home. It helps to encourage discussion in groups through brainstorming, film discussions, and question-and-answer times. But structured private conversations just between parent and child help facilitate conversation for those who don't feel comfortable in front of the whole group.

The differences in the way people communicate are important to discuss, too. Children usually want detailed information, and they ask very specific questions. Adults usually give vague, generalized answers. It is helpful to identify ways those differences can be overcome to improve communication.

Thus, if enough practice time is allowed, communication about sexuality already will be increased and enhanced within the family by the end of the group.

Bring Unconscious Messages into Awareness

We are often unaware of some of the values, beliefs, and messages we have received that affect our sexual behavior. We have received messages about our bodies, love, and relationships that influence us greatly. In family sexuality education programs it is helpful to facilitate increased awareness of those messages in order to consider making some changes. As George Eliot said: "Keep what's worth keeping and with a breath of kindness, blow the rest away."

Society also gives us many messages through the media and peers that can be hidden and unhealthy influences on our sexual behavior. Becoming aware of these subtle messages helps us recognize their powerful influence.

Modified sexual learning histories (questionnaires about what we believe, what we heard our parents say, what society says about love, sex, men, and women) facilitate awareness and stimulate discussion. Forced choice activities (a structured exercise where people are given specific choices to help them understand what they believe) are effective, also. Large-group discussion about sexual myths (e.g., "The woman should be responsible for contraception") can help point out unhealthy beliefs that may cause males and females to be sexually irresponsible.

With new awareness, some of the outdated, erroneous, and irresponsible beliefs may be replaced with new, accurate, and healthier ones. After all, clear values and beliefs are the first steps toward responsible behavior.

The Format Allows Flexibility

Over the last two years, "Straight Talk" programs have been successful in all communities regardless of race or socioeconomics. Flexibility is the key ingredient for this success.

For example, in some groups a two-hour program instead of the usual six is all that is possible. In other communities we have advertised "Straight Talk" as a "program" or "meeting" instead of a "workshop." To some targeted groups "workshop" sounds too boring and intellectual. So, the publicity in some communities is different than in others. We also find we accomplish some of the goals of the program whether the group is made up of parents only, children only, or parents and children together. Even the fees we charge vary from group to group based on families' ability to pay. We usually charge a fee, but in some cases it is waived or reduced.

Obviously, the flexibility in the programming dictates the need for well-trained group leaders. They must be able to vary the content according to the group's needs and abilities. They must be able to plan the activities around time constraints, ethnic variations, and age differences.

In order to vary the approach, there has been an increase in work in some areas, especially training, publicity, and marketing. But all in all, we have found the extra effort profitable. We are beginning to reach ethnic and economic groups we haven't reached in the past.

Conclusion

I am convinced that quality sexuality education programs for families will make America a more sexually responsible society. The ideas presented in this article will help make a program effective, even though there are many other considerations, variations and possibilities. I hope you are challenged by my thoughts and motivated to develop your own successful program. You are bound to profit personally from the experience—and you could make a positive difference in the lives of many, many people.

FEELING GOOD WORKSHOPS
Gloria Blum

People who are slow learners grow up, and as they do, they can become more independent and responsible. Like all of us, they need to develop a positive sense of themselves that can support their advance into the world of adulthood. They need to learn how to communicate effectively with nondisabled adults. They need particular attention in order to learn appropriate social behavior. Growing up in a sheltered environment, they often lack the experiences required for independent decision-making. Our experience has shown that when slow learners are provided with the necessary training in these living skills, not only are their lives enriched but also those around them soon notice the appropriate behavioral changes associated with responsible adulthood.

The Feeling Good Program was the basis for a three-year model program, developed and tested in several school settings in San Francisco from 1979 to 1981. It was called the M.E.N.C.H. Project (Meaningful Education Now for Citizens with Handicaps). Funding was provided by the Office of Special Education Handicapped Children's Program from the Department of Health Education and Welfare, grant #G007903012. Feeling Good Associates is now located at 507 Palm Way, Mill Valley, CA 94941 (415-383-5439). Using the *Feeling Good About Yourself* curriculum guide, the Feeling Good Model Program presents a variety of useful verbal and nonverbal activities and techniques to assist in preventing victimization by promoting self-esteem, social skills, and sex information. The primary emphasis is on self-esteem. As sexuality educator Sol Gordon says, "People who feel good about themselves are less available for sexual exploitation and they are less interested in exploiting others."

The Feeling Good program is based on two self-esteem principles. First, each of us is unique and special, and we are also like other people. Second, the on-going success of the participant is more important than predetermined goals, objectives, or expectations. Both principles are important. Together they keep a balance between goal-oriented activity and individual or process-oriented activity. We keep our goals in mind but they are not more important than our students or clients. The result is a rapid development of trust and eagerness to participate on the part of both the clients and the staff.

The self-esteem activities address the first half of the self-esteem principle, "Each of us is unique and special." The sexual information addresses the second half of the self-esteem principle, "We are also like other people." Our clients/students need to know about normal physical and emotional changes taking place into adulthood so that they don't get the wrong idea about themselves. They need to know that they are experiencing normal changes as they enter adulthood.

Parts of the workshop may be co-led by someone who was labelled a slow learner but who is now living independently and has had leadership training with the Feeling Good Curriculum. His/her participation as a leader is an inspiration for the clients, parents, and staff. The program is designed to train teachers, nurses, social workers, parents, relatives, home-care staff, physicians, therapists, and other professionals *along* with the clients or residents of institutions. Everyone is included. There is opportunity for everyone to learn from each other.

Part I:

How to Create a Safe, Supportive Environment
Techniques for Teaching Self-Esteem
Guidelines for Teaching Slow-Learners
Teaching About Private/Public Places and Private/Public
    Body Parts

Learning How to Say No; The Yes-No Process, Preparation
for Decision Making
How to Teach What Is Appropriate and Inappropriate
Behavior
Whom Can You Tell?
How to Get Help If You Are Being Abused.

Part II:

How to Teach Sexual Information (Including How to
Deal with Discomfort)
Feeling, Recognizing, and Knowing Emotions
Getting to Know One's Body
Relating to Others
Sex Roles
How to Teach How Babies Are Made
How to Teach Responsibilities of Sexual Behavior
Birth Control
Sexually Transmitted Diseases

Part III:

How to Develop Leadership Skills
Addressing Specific Needs
Role Playing to Rehearse Social Situations
Assertiveness Training
The Use of Video for Improving Self-Image
Demonstration of Resource Materials

Initially, we want to create a safe, supportive environment by
improving our communication skills and becoming less critical of
ourselves and each other. One way we playfully promote self-
esteem is by using noncompetitive, nonjudgemental, success-
oriented games such as the "Feeling Good Cards."

The "Feeling Good Cards" each have a different question.
Some questions are playful or even silly. Some make you think a
little about your priorities in life. None is threatening. There are

no wrong answers and there is no way to fail. The cards stimulate conversation and feedback with all age and ability groups. We use the cards to practice appropriate affective behavior, for risk taking, for social conversation practice, as well as to develop techniques for active listening.

"The Clapping Warm-Up Activity," which is taught and used within the first hour of the program, teaches everyone that we are here to appreciate and support each other. We are taught to applaud whenever someone takes the risk to participate. This drastically reduces the fear associated with risk-taking and gives people a sense of success and confidence. It also raises the general level of energy and participation in the room. It is interesting to note that many professionals do not actively volunteer in activities, often because they are fearful of appearing foolish in front of the group. This is a good demonstration of how our students or clients are our teachers. The so-called "disabled" clients are often less fearful of appearing foolish. They may have real strengths that can serve as positive role-models for the professionals, to encourage us to take more risks in a group and feel good about ourselves. We utilize energetic music and circle activities to balance sitting time with movement. Everyone has a chance to take risks and succeed.

To learn about appropriate social and sexual behavior, the participants are taught early in the program the concepts of *private* and *public* body parts and *private* and *public* places. If someone is exposing or touching his private parts in public, we can address the behavior without lowering the person's self-esteem by simply reminding, "Private parts are for private places. This is a public place. People can see you." Even the more profoundly retarded individual understands this simple public/private rule. The rule applies to other behaviors concerning social appropriateness, even including nose picking, reading adult magazines, swearing, talking about private matters, and many other issues. The Feeling Good Program prevents further victimization by teaching participants the consequences in society for touching other people on their private parts without permission. One special student was doing well until he touched a young girl's chest while he was lonely on the bus. The bus driver was the girl's father. The young man was sent to prison, and he was forever labeled a "sex offender." This young man was a victim of the rule of society because he was not informed about the consequences of such actions.

Seattle Rape Relief research indicates that up to 97 percent of the mentally disabled population in their region have been sexually abused; many were unaware of what was happening to them. Our participants spend time discussing whom they could go to for help if they are sexually abused. They are assured that it is not their fault and that they will not be blamed if they seek help.

Parents and care-providers are included in the program and kept informed regularly. They attend a special workshop and learn how to reinforce the program objectives at home. Clear and frequent review is essential.

RESOURCES ON SEXUALITY AND DISABILITY

Curricula

Bednarczyk, Angela M. *Growing Up Sexually.* Washington, D.C.:
   Gallaudet College, Kendall Demonstration Elementary
   School, 1982.

   Organizes student chapters according to comfort level criteria.
   Each chapter includes an introduction, discussion questions, and
   activities.

Blum, Gloria, and Barry Blum. *Feeling Good About Yourself.* Third
   Edition. Feeling Good Associates, 507 Palm Way, Mill Valley,
   CA 94941.

   Curriculum guide for the Feeling Good Model Program.
   Covers socialization, decision-making skills and a wide variety of
   sexual topics.

Cooksey, Phyllis, and Pamela Brown. *A Guide for Teaching Human
   Sexuality to the Mentally Handicapped.* Third Ed. St. Paul, Minn.:
   Planned Parenthood of Minnesota, 1981.

   Covers nine topics, including contraception and interpersonal
   relations. Gives a simple but very practical approach to teaching
   people who are mentally handicapped about sexuality.

Greenbaum, Madeline, and Sandra Noll. *Education for Adulthood.*
   Staten Island Mental Health Society, 657 Castleton Avenue,
   Staten Island, NY 10301, 1982.

   Designed to help mentally retarded adolescents and adults
   reach an understanding of being sexual. Also deals with aging,
   death and dying, being disabled, expressing feelings, developing
   relationships, and keeping fit. Includes a training program for
   those who will teach this curriculum.

Edwards, Jean, et al. *Feeling Free: A Social/Sexual Training Guide for
   Those Who Work with the Hearing and Visually Impaired.* Ednick
   Communications, Inc., P.O. Box 3612 , Portland, OR 97208,
   1982.

Teaches responsible decision-making to people of all ages; focuses on increasing appropriate social and sexual behavior. Includes lesson plans and resources.

Howes, Nancy. *Fully Human.* Box 2107, Hanover, MA 02339, 1986. In lesson plan format this comprehensive curriculum covers twelve sequential topics from sexual identity through parenting at four progressive levels of ability. Includes teacher training information, activity pages and drawings, and specific teaching techniques for each lesson.

Throckmorton, Teresa. *Becoming Me: A Personal Adjustment Guide for Secondary Students.* Grand Rapids Public Schools, 143 Bostwick, N.E., Grand Rapids, MI 49503, 1980.

Includes units on personal and social development, health and self-care, and human growth and development, all focuses on nurturing the practical skills needed for everyday life. For each topic, a content outline, behavioral objectives, learning activities, and suggested resources are presented.

Audiovisuals

All Women Have Periods. Producer/Distributor: Perennial Education, Inc., 16mm, 11 min., 1978.

A real family, mother, father, older sister, and Jill, who is retarded, discuss menstruation. All family members participate in repeating the basic information many times. Jill's older sister takes her into the bathroom and explicitly shows her how to change a sanitary napkin, step by step, and then allows her to practice changing a napkin herself. Although the characters portraying family members appear nervous and over-rehearsed, the film is effective with developmentally disabled youth and their parents. (White characters.)

And Contact Is Made. Producer/Distributor: John P. Armour, 16mm, 13 min., 1982.

A film about self-image, communication, and relationships. Offers new insights about people who are physically handicapped and often viewed as "different." Helps the viewer realize that any of us can become handicapped at some point in our lives.

Board and Care. Producer/Distributor: Pyramid Films, 16mm, 27 min., 1980.

Two adolescents with Down's Syndrome meet in an activities center and fall in love. They are later separated because of different educational settings. Emphasizes the fact that developmentally disabled adolescents have the same emotional needs and feelings as other teenagers. Very moving. (White characters.)

Circles: A Multi-Media Package to Aid in the Development of Appropriate Social/Sexual Behavior in the Developmentally Disabled Individual. Producer/Distributor: Stanfield Film Associates, Curriculum, Slides and Photos, 1983.

Teaches appropriate social distancing, acceptable and nonacceptable touch, as well as many other sexuality topics.

Essential Adult Sex Education for the Mentally Retarded. Producer/ Distributor: Stanfield Film Associates, Curriculum, 2 Cassettes, Filmstrip, 1979.

Sequenced set of objectives, procedures, and materials grouped into four instructional units: biological data, sexual behavior, health, and relationships. Also includes a menstruation and birth control kit.

Feeling Good About Yourself. Producer/Distributor: Multi-Focus, 16mm or Video, 22 min., 1980.

Therapist Gloria Blum models techniques for helping developmentally disabled students enhance their self-esteem, learn social skills, and practice assertiveness skills. (White characters.)

I Can Say No! Producer: Gloria and Barry Blum. Distributor: Feeling Good Associates, Filmstrip and Cassette, 1984.

Teens of differing abilities learn how to say "no" to peer pressure without giving mixed messages.

Learning to Talk About Sex When You'd Rather Not. Producer/Distributor: Special Purpose Films, 16mm, 29 min., 1976.

Dramatizes the fact that persons with mental retardation have the same emotional needs as other people. Advocates sexuality education for people with mental retardation. Models appropriate teaching and group techniques with groups of young men and women.

Like Other People. Producer: Kastrel Films, Distributor: Perennial Education, Inc., 16mm, 37 min., 1973.

A moving film dealing with the sexual, emotional, and social needs of people who are physically handicapped. Main characters are two cerebral palsy patients who, in their own words, make a plea to humanity to understand that they are "real" people. Dialogue is difficult to understand in parts because of speech problems of the people involved, but the film is well worth the effort. (White characters.)

Charts, Models, Dolls

Effie Dolls. Producer/Distributor: Mrs. Judith Franing, 4812 48th Avenue, Moline, Il. 61265, 2 dolls.

Two rag dolls (male and female) complete with genitalia. The female doll is pregnant. The birth process can be shown as the doll is complete with umbilical cord and placenta attachment. Includes a sanitary napkin to use for instruction on how to wear and change a sanitary napkin.

Feeling Good Card Game. Producer: Gloria Blum. Distributor: Feeling Good Associates, 507 Palma Way, Mill Valley CA 94941, 1976.

Contains over 75 different question cards and a game instruction booklet.

Jim Jackson Reproductive Anatomy Models. Producer/Distributor: Jim Jackson, 33 Richdale Avenue, Cambridge, MA 02140.

Male and female genital models in black and white skin tones. Also, female and male reproductive systems in cross-section. Gender dolls are also available.

Life Size Instructional Charts Kit. Producer/Distributor: Planned Parenthood of Minnesota, Inc., 2 charts with inserts and carrying case.

Contains a chart of a male figure and one of a female; includes four overlays for the male and six for the female demonstrating various aspects of sexual physiology.

Teach-A-Bodies. Producer/Distributor: June Harnest, 2544 Boyd Street, Fort Worth, TX 76109, dolls.

Anatomically correct soft rag dolls available in male, female, Black, Caucasian, adult, child, and toddler versions. Can be used for teaching about puberty, birth control, childbirth, sexual abuse, and other sexuality topics.

Bibliographies and Resource Guides

Hallingby, Leigh. *Sexuality and Disability: A Bibliography of Resources Available for Purchase.* SIECUS, 32 Washington Place, New York, NY 10003, March 1986.

Includes thoughtful annotations for books and pamphlets on the following disabilities: hearing and visual impairment, kidney disease, mental handicaps, multiple sclerosis, ostomy, cancer, spinal cord injured, and alcoholism.

Jacobson, Denise Sherer. *Sex and Disability Resource Manual.* United Cerebral Palsy of San Francisco, Golden Gate Theater Building, 25 Taylor Street, Fifth Floor, San Francisco, CA 94012, 1983.

Includes national and international listings of sex and disability educators, counselors, and consultants. Reviews methods for updating resource information and includes information on speakers bureaus.

Sex and Disability Project. *Who Cares? A Handbook on Sex Education and Counseling Services for Disabled People.* PRO-ED, 5341 Industrial Oaks Boulevard, Austin, TX 78735, 1982.

A comprehensive handbook describing sexuality services for disabled persons. Unique, outstanding, and highly recommended.

POSTPONING SEXUAL INVOLVEMENT: AN EDUCATIONAL SERIES FOR YOUNG PEOPLE

Marie E. Mitchell

"Postponing Sexual Involvement: An Educational Series for Young People" was developed to help younger adolescents resist social and peer pressures toward early sexual involvement. The power of peer influences and pressure to conform among early adolescents is well known (Sherif and Sherif, 1964). The need to be part of the "in" group, to be popular, to feel important, makes it extremely difficult for teens to resist pressures from their peer group. Educational programs in the past have not had as an expressed goal helping young people to resist social and peer influences leading to early sexual involvement. Indeed, it has only been in recent years that programs have had as a stated goal "to encourage abstinence until young people are older and better prepared for sexual activity . . ." (Kirby, 1984).

Traditionally, the goals of sex, "education programs have been to provide factual information, to assist young people in clarifying their values, to increase young people's decision-making skills, and to encourage responsible sexual behavior. The desired behavioral outcomes hoped for from these programs were for young people to either abstain from sexual activity or protect themselves against unintended pregnancies. Kirby (1984) in his evaluation of sexuality education programs and their effects stated, "Educators initially tried to change behavior by replacing ignorance with correct information. However, they soon realized that young

343

people not only needed correct information, they also needed clearer insight into themselves, their beliefs, and their values. Educators also recognized that many of the behavior goals of programs also required many skills that many young people lacked." Thus, providing skills, in addition to imparting knowledge and changing behaviors and attitudes, became a part of the goals of sexuality education.

Goals of the Series

The "Postponing Sexual Involvement Series" provides young adolescents with information on the sources of societal and peer pressures influencing sexual behavior, the general nature of relationships, and some ways of expressing feelings within a relationship other than through sexual intercourse. The goals of the series are:

1. To increase young teens' understanding of the pressures in our society which influence their sexual behavior.
2. To increase young teens' knowledge of one's rights in a social relationship.
3. To increase young teens' ability to use assertive skills in situations where they feel pressured to do things they don't want to do.

Rationale for the Series

Schinke et al. (1979) affirmed that adolescents need accurate information to make informed choices, but simply exposing teenagers to the consequences of certain behaviors does not have long-lasting effects. This Series is designed to provide young people with skills to help them bridge the gap between their early physical maturation and their later cognitive development. These skills help teens handle the physical and emotional needs that occur during this developmental stage. The assumptions and underlying rationales that guided the development of this series to help early adolescents postpone sexual intercourse include the following:

Assumption: Young adolescents should not be having sexual intercourse.

Rationale: Adolescents under the age of sixteen lack the cognitive skills to deal responsibly with their sexual behavior. Piaget (1969) says early adolescents are in transition developmentally from concrete to formal operations thinking. This means they lack those adult-level cognitive skills of problem-solving, planning, and decision-making described by Gilchrist (1981) as necessary for coping responsibly with sexual behavior.

Assumption: For adolescents sixteen and younger, the negative consequences of early sexual intercourse outweigh the positive gains.

Rationale: The possible negative health consequences of early sexual intercourse such as premature pregnancy, sexually transmitted diseases, increased risks of cervical cancer, or future infertility far outweigh the positive short-term gains younger teens may derive from sexual intercourse. Furthermore, the gains often stated by adolescents (i.e., pleasure, popularity, holding onto a relationship, or feeling grown-up) could more appropriately be attained through social relationships not requiring sexual intercourse.

Assumption: Adolescents are often pressured into engaging in behaviors they really do not want to be involved in.

Rationale: "Teens are telling us that it is pressure from their friends that influences them most" (De Armond, 1983). Girls most often receive this pressure from their male partners and boys most often receive it from their male peers, though girls do pressure boys to have sex. Along with these pressures and others encountered in our sexually permissive society, adolescents are also attempting to accomplish the tasks of adolescence: to establish independence from parents, to develop their own value systems, to establish their sexual identity, and to make a career/vocational choice. Adolescents sometimes resort to sexual experimentation as a way to relieve some of these pressures and achieve some of these tasks.

Assumption: Adolescents do not naturally know how to resist the social and peer pressure toward early sexual involvement.

They need to be taught the skills to enable them to resist these pressures.

Rationale: "A significant number of fifteen- to seventeen-year-olds in a national survey reported becoming sexually involved because it seemed expected of them and didn't know how to refuse" (Cvetkovich and Grote, 1976). Helping adolescents develop assertive skills will enable them to deal with pressure situations, to protect their rights within relationships, and to defend their values.

Theoretical Concepts of the Series

The basic concept of the "Postponing Sexual Involvement Series" was taken from materials published by Alfred McAlister (1980) on studies of the Stanford-based smoking prevention project. McAlister proposed a procedure of "psychological inoculation" as a particularly appropriate way of countering the social influences that tend to lead toward smoking in young teens. He described the procedure in these terms:

> The concept of psychological inoculation is almost perfectly analogous to the equally important concept of inoculation in traditional preventive medicine. The idea is that if we expect the individual to encounter the cultural analog of "germs" (i.e., social pressures toward adoption of a behavior detrimental to health), then we can prevent "infection" if we expose the person to a weak dose of those "germs" in a way that facilitates the development of "anti-bodies" (i.e., skills for resisting pressures toward adoption of unhealthy behaviors).

The series was also influenced by Lewayne D. Gilchrist's (1981) report on"Group Procedures for Helping Adolescents Cope with Sex." Gilchrist feels this skills training approach avoids some of the shortcomings of information-only programs, especially with younger adolescents who may not yet possess the cognitive skills necessary for processing information and applying it to their behavior. The basic concepts of the group skills training approach (information input, skills training, and practice applying skills) were used in structuring the format of the leader's guide. Information input, according to Gilchrist, is taking young people through a "personalization process" by which abstract information becomes a part of their everyday reality. This process can be accomplished by actively involving teens in gathering and assimilating information and by engaging them in direct discussions of illusions and faulty thinking patterns.

The "Postponing Sexual Involvement Series" takes teens through this process in a group activity in which they are asked to critically analyze the reasons why teens have sex and why teens should postpone early sexual involvement. Experiential exercises requiring teens to write or verbalize their personal responses to such pressure lines as: "If you love me, you'll have sex with me"; "Everybody's doing it"; or "If you don't, someone else will" are included throughout the series.

Another, and perhaps the most important, of Gilchrist's group skills training techniques is allowing adolescents to practice applying skills in a variety of situations. In the "Postponing Series" young teens are asked to act out skits in which pressure is being exerted from a variety of sources, i.e., partners, peers, the media. The teens are instructed to make sure that the individual being pressured uses the assertive techniques taught to say "no" or to resist the pressure. These practice situations are crucial to helping young teens feel confident they can say "no" and have "no" accepted. When young people are able to successfully resist pressure, they are left with increased feelings of self-respect and a feeling of control over their behavior.

Implementation of the Series

Intended Audience

The series is designed for younger adolescents (males and females) and the parents of these adolescents. These young people and their parents may be reached in a variety of settings: school, churches, or youth-serving agencies.

Leader Knowledge and Skills

1. *Good Facilitation Skills.* As with any group, the effectiveness of the "Postponing Sexual Involvement Series" rests heavily on the group leaders' facilitation skills. The abilities to encourage discussion, establish a positive group atmosphere, and keep the group on track are essential to the success of the series.

2. *Knowledge of Adolescent Development.* In group discussion with young people, it is important to remember their developmental level. Many teens have had little experience, generally, in discussing their feelings or comparing their values with those of their peers. Group discussion should be concrete and focused; all examples cited should be relevant to the teen's everyday experiences. Episodes from TV or from school often seem most real to young teens. If the hypothetical moral dilemmas presented are beyond the young teen's experience, they generally will not be effective.

3. *Knowledge of the Principles of Assertiveness.* Assertiveness is an interpersonal skill that employs a set of specific techniques for responding to pressure. Viewing assertiveness as a learnable, practical way for teens to protect their options and defend their values will increase the facilitator's effectiveness in teaching the skills to young teens.

4. *Comfort with the Philosophical Approach of the Series.* The "Postponing Sexual Involvement Series" starts with the given value judgment: Younger adolescents should not be having sexual intercourse. Unless the group leader is comfortable with this premise, imparting the contents of this series to young teens in a believable and effective manner will be very difficult.

Structure and Content

This educational series contains a detailed leader's guide, slides, and tape which enable either adult leaders or teen leaders, accompanied by an adult leader, to conduct *four* sessions of instruction to young teens. The first three sessions are designed to be given in close sequence, either on three consecutive days or once a week for three consecutive weeks. The fourth session is given as a reinforcement session anywhere from one month to six months later. When using the complete series in a classroom setting, at least five classroom periods are needed. Session I usually takes two periods; the rest, one period each.

Session I: Information and Exercises Relating to Social Pressure. Through a brainstorming activity, all participants are given an opportunity to explore their feelings regarding young teens having sexual intercourse. Next, a case study involving a young teen who made the decision to have sex is discussed. During the discussion, participants are asked to think through and feel vicariously some of the problems young teens can encounter if they decide to have sex. This session also explores with young teens some of the societal pressures of today's world. For example, a presentation is given on how commercial advertising uses sex to sell products ranging from perfume to cars. Leaders help participants understand the subliminal effect of advertising on behavior.

Session II: Information and Exercises Relating to Peer Pressure. This session presents the concept that teens have the right to say "no." This right can be exerted in both groups and one-to-one situations in which someone asks them to do something they do not want to do. Most importantly, during this session it should be stressed that the majority of young teens are not having sexual intercourse; so when participants hear that "everybody's doing it," they recognize that this really is not the case, and that if they say "no," they will actually be part of the majority rather than the minority.

Session III: Information and Exercises Related to Assertiveness. During this session, the group leader explains that many teens often experience ambivalent feelings about sexual involvement and that these feelings are normal. In addition, the leader stresses that handling ambivalence is a normal part of setting limits in a relationship. Teens also have the opportunity to practice some basic assertiveness skills to enable them to feel confident they can say "no" and have that "no" accepted.

Session IV: Additional Practice Exercises. Youths participate in more activities designed to reinforce the assertiveness skills they learned earlier in the program.

Participants' Reaction to Series

Youth Reaction

In the field test of the "Postponing Sexual Involvement Series," 86 percent of the young teens rated the series as being helpful to them. The 14 percent who felt it was not helpful stated that (1) they had not needed such a program or (2) the series had not met their needs. Of those who found the series helpful, two-thirds found it extremely helpful or very helpful, with the majority indicating it was extremely helpful. About a third found it somewhat helpful.

Adult Reaction

The goals of the parent series are to help parents understand the pressures in our society that influence young people's sexual behavior and to give parents tools to help young teens postpone sexual involvement. Ninety-three percent of the adults who filled out the parent survey during the field test indicated they found the series helpful. Of those who found it helpful, three-quarters found it extremely helpful or very helpful. One-quarter found it somewhat helpful.

The evaluation of the long-term effects of the "Postponing Sexual Involvement Series" is still in progress. However, the immediate feedback of participants has been very positive. Parents are very supportive of the series as it reinforces the values they would like shared with their young teens. Young people appear to find the series informative and refreshing for it differs from traditional approaches in several ways.

Teens are not given detailed information about reproduction, family planning, or sexually transmitted diseases (hence this series does not replace sexuality education, but is another component).

The series focuses on social and peer pressures that lead young people into early sexual involvement and ways to resist such pressures.

The series focuses on why young people are having sex rather than the consequences of such behavior. Peers are the primary communicators of the messages of the series. When peer leaders are not used, the audio tapes of teens' voices accompany the curriculum guide and slides, impart information, model attitudes and response, and ask for teens' active participation in the series.

The series starts with a given value: "You ought not to be having sex at a young age." All activities in the series are designed to promote reinforce this value for younger adolescents in a way that avoids giving teens conflicting messages.

References

Blamey, Judith, Marion Howard, and William Pollard. "Postponing Sexual Involvement: Progress Report on the Education Series." Emory University/Grady Teen Services Program, Grady Memorial Hospital, 80 Butler Street, S.E., Atlanta, GA 30335-3801, January 1985.

Cvetkovich, G., and B. Grote. "Psychosocial Development and the Social Problems of Teenage Illegitimacy." Paper presented at the conference on Determinants of Adolescent Pregnancy and Childbearing, Elkridge, Maryland, May 1976.

DeArmond, Charlotte. "Let's Listen to What the Kids Are Saying." *SIECUS Report* XI, No. 4 (March 1983): 3-4.

Farel, Anita M. "Early Adolescence: What Parents Need to Know." Center for Early Adolescence, Suite 223, Carr Mill Mall, Carrboro, North Carolina, 1982.

The Gentle Art of Saying No: Principles of Assertiveness. Sunburst Communications, Department AV, 39 Washington Avenue, Peasantville, NY 10570.

Gilchrist, Lewayne D. "Group Procedures for Helping Adolescents Cope with Sex." *Behavior Group Therapy* 3, 2 (1981): 3-8.

Hill, John P. *Understanding Early Adolescence: A Framework.* Center for Early Adolescence, Suite 223, Carr Mill Mall, Carrboro, North Carolina, 1980.

Kirby, Douglas. *Sexuality Education: An Evaluation of Programs and Their Effects. An Executive Summary.* Santa Cruz: Network Publications, 1984.

McAlister, Alfred. *Adolescent Smoking: Onset and Prevention.* Creative Curricula, Box 371 Wellesley Hills, MA 02181, 1980.

Schinke, S.P., L.D. Gilchrist, and R.W. Small. "Preventing Unwanted Adolescent Pregnancy: A Cognitive-Behavioral Approach." *American Journal of Orthopsychiatry* 49 (1979): 81-88.

Sherif, M., and C.W. Sherif. *Reference Groups: Exploration into Conformity and Deviation of Adolescents.* New York: Harper and Row, 1964.

CHALLENGING YOUTH WITH CHOICES: THE LIFE OPTIONS STRATEGY FOR SEXUALITY EDUCATION
Carol Hunter-Geboy

In 1976, many of us working in the field of sexuality education with an emphasis on adolescent pregnancy prevention heralded the Alan Guttmacher Institute's (AGI) publication, "Eleven Million Teenagers: The Problem of Teenage Pregnancy," as an essential component of the public education campaign necessary to rally local, state, and federal support behind our efforts. In 1981, however, when AGI titled its five-year update on teenage pregnancy "The Problem That Hasn't Gone Away," we began to scrutinize our efforts and evaluate our strategies in the hope that 1986 would not necessitate a third publication from AGI rhetorically asking us, "What Are You People *Doing* Out There?"

The answer, should the question surface, is that for several years sex educators have been conceptualizing, developing, implementing, and evaluating a new and innovative approach to the prevention of unintended adolescent pregnancy. The "life options" approach is a comprehensive educational strategy that, put very simply, (a) tells young people what their reproductive as well as educational/vocational options are, (b) provides them with the necessary information, skills, and attitudes to make good choices concerning their family and vocational futures, and (c) challenges them to avoid future health, social, and especially, *economic* pitfalls (e.g., interrupted education, unemployment or underemployment, and welfare dependency) associated with early

353

pregnancy and parenting. The assumption is that youth armed with options will be more likely to realize their life goals and experience productive, satisfying futures.

An interesting phenomenon is that model programs employing a similar strategy have developed simultaneously in several geographic areas under the sponsorship of distinctively different organizations such as the Center for Population Options (CPO) in Washington, D.C.; the Girls Clubs of Santa Barbara, California; the Salvation Army in New York City; the Northwest Regional Laboratory in Seattle; and Public/Private Ventures in Philadelphia. These programs have emerged under a variety of names like "Life Planning Education," "Life Skills and Opportunities," "Nontraditional Careers," "Choices," or "Challenges," and others. Various programs embodying the "life options" strategy have focussed on young women, on young men, on both men and women; they have targeted middle school, secondary, and post-secondary youth; and they have emphasized seemingly divergent topics, including contraception, employability skills, gender roles and stereotypes, nontraditional career choices, delaying sexual intercourse, and experience in the world of work. But across a rich diversity of sponsoring agencies and target populations, there has existed an underlying thread of continuity in these programs: the goal of preventing adolescent pregnancy by helping young people to become aware of the interrelatedness of their sexual/reproductive decisions and their vocational decisions. The expected and hoped for outcome in each program is that youth will ultimately make decisions that maximize rather than diminish their life options.

How Did the Life Options Strategy Come About?

The impetus behind recently developed life options programs seems to have come from several sources. One important factor in the decision to design a program focusing on the dual issues of family planning and job planning was the substantial body of evidence relating teens' reproductive behavior to their vocational and economic futures. A review of the research on the economic consequences of adolescent pregnancy revealed the following information:

- Teenage mothers earn about 50 percent of the income of those who first give birth in their twenties (AGI, 1981).
- Women who have their first baby as a teenager work in lower-status occupations, accumulate less work experience, receive lower hourly wages, and earn less annually (Moore and Burt, 1981).
- About 50 percent of women in families receiving Aid to Families with Dependent Children (AFDC) have given birth as teenagers, compared to about 33 percent of women in families not receiving such payments (AGI, 1981).
- In 1985, $16.65 billion in federal funds went to families in which women had first given birth as teenagers (CPO, 1986).

Life options programs are intended to help teens avoid the diminished economic status that accompanies early parenthood.

A second influencing factor was the changing status of women in the work force today as well as the economic realities that will face young women as they become part of tomorrow's labor force. Very few teens seem aware of the following facts:

1. Over 50 million women work outside their homes today, most in full-time employment.
2. Almost 70 percent of women in their peak childbearing years (ages 25 to 34) are working.
3. Married women living *with* a husband comprise the largest group of women in the labor force (56 percent).
4. Of the 10 million women who head families, 66 percent have pre- or school-age children and 60 percent of those are working.
5. Seventy-five percent of divorced women work. (Waldman, 1985)

Life options programs were developed in the past to help teen women realize the importance of preparing themselves for economic self-sufficiency. At the same time, they were designed to help young men recognize that their future role will differ from the traditional one of sole provider—men of tomorrow will need to share work and family responsibilities with their partners.

Another significant factor leading to the development of the life options model appears to have been the previous experience of leading youth organizations in the area of youth employment/employability. In recent years various organizations concerned about the well-being of young people (e.g., Girls Clubs of America, Boy Scouts of America, Camp Fire, the YMCA, and the American Red Cross) have explored program strategies that address the problems of youth seeking to enter the labor force. These problems often include inadequate education (because of school failure and/or school termination), lack of job access skills (e.g., interviewing, completing an application), lack of clear vocational goals, and poor social skills (e.g., communication and assertiveness) necessary in the workplace. Several statistics suggested that educational inadequacies plaguing many unemployed youth could be related to teenage pregnancy, as well:

- Forty-four percent of female dropouts in the U.S. indicate pregnancy/marriage as their primary reason for dropping out (Fine, 1985).
- Only 50 percent of teenage women who give birth before age eighteen ever complete high school, compared to 96 percent of those who do not have children before age twenty (Card and Wise, 1978).
- Seventy percent of teenage men who become parents complete high school, compared to 95 percent of those who do not become parents (Card and Wise, 1978).

What seemed to be necessary was a program that could motivate youth to stay in school and obtain an education while at the same time enabling them to avoid pregnancy and parenthood and preparing them for the world of work. Youth organizations that recognized this need were instrumental in the subsequent "wedding" of family planning with employment preparation that comprises a life options program.

A final incentive came from the accumulated wisdom of several key researchers and analysts who had worked for years on the issue of teenage pregnancy and were arriving at similar conclusions:

- Teens who have positive attitudes toward education, higher levels of educational achievement, and clear educational goals are less likely to have premarital intercourse and more likely to use contraceptives if they do (Chilman, 1980). Thus, strong educational ambition seems of central importance in preventing early out-of-wedlock pregnancy.
- Prior to parenthood, teens who subsequently become young parents have notably different post-secondary plans, career goals, and attitudes than their classmates who do not become parents. They do not rank as high on scholastic performance or on educational expectations, and they do not share the aims and criteria for success of many of their classmates (Haggstrom, Blaschke, Kanouse, et al., 1981).
- If (disadvantaged) children can be assisted to stay in school, learn to read and write, develop vocational goals, learn employable skills, perhaps they will enjoy higher self-esteem, higher aspirations, and greater achievement . . . a sense of future (will be) engendered, (and) the option of childbearing will seem less acceptable (Dryfoos, 1984).

From these findings and remarks, it seems reasonable to conclude that life options may be a major key to pregnancy prevention.

What Are the Advantages of the Life Options Approach?

There are four clear advantages to the selection of a life options approach to sexuality education that have been evidenced in the experience of current program providers.

First, a life options program is efficient and cost effective because it addresses two serious problems confronting any youth agency or community—teenage pregnancy and youth unemployment—at the same time and in an integrated way. Such integration of issues makes possible the dual application of limited resources including staff, training materials, and time allocated for programs. It also brings agencies and professionals from two issue areas into an alliance with one another. Youth employment program staff and sex educators can work hand in hand to combat a dual threat to any young person's future.

Second, such a program may be more readily funded than either a traditional sexuality education program or a youth employment program alone. It is seen as a more comprehensive and, therefore, more successful approach, and it will attract the interest and the dollars of the corporate world. Foundations and philanthropists are more eager to fund a program that employs a novel approach; furthermore, funds can be garnered from sources that might not have supported one issue (for example, sexuality education) but will support this program because of their commitment to the other issue (youth employment). In addition, the business community cannot argue with the fact that keeping youths in school and preparing them for the world of work is advantageous to employers who seek capable entry-level employees for the future. Nor can they argue that prevention of early pregnancy and childbearing is not important to school completion for most young women and many young men.

Third, and perhaps herein lies the greatest appeal of "life options," these programs focus on the economic cost of early childbearing borne by individuals, families, future generations, and all taxpayers. Unfortunately, people seem to hear more clearly when the discussion includes their dollars. As a community is made increasingly aware of the dollars it must spend because of unintended adolescent pregnancies coupled with dollars it loses when potentially competent, contributing young members of society drop out of school and/or fail to enter the work force, that community becomes more willing to listen to the advice and counsel of sexuality educators who propose preventive strategies.

What Can Such a Program Do for Youth?

A life options program focuses on two of the most critical developmental tasks confronting young people: (1) managing their sexual/reproductive development and behavior and (2) preparing for the world of work. Sex educators are most familiar with the first of those and readily recognize the tools youth need to make responsible sexual decisions. Life options program objectives related to sexuality include:

1. Increasing knowledge about the reproductive process and contraceptive options.
2. Reducing gender role stereotypes that lead to premature intercourse, teenage pregnancy, and parenthood.
3. Increasing acceptance of one's body, its appearance and functioning.
4. Increasing awareness of family, personal, and societal values related to sexuality and reproduction and how these may affect decision-making and goal-setting.
5. Increasing responsible sexual decision-making that includes abstinence or consistent use of contraception if sexually active.
6. Enforcing the belief that adolescent parenthood is difficult and that parenthood should be postponed until adulthood.
7. Increasing communication skills necessary for healthy interpersonal relationships, including assertiveness, expressing feelings, and negotiating when there is a conflict.

A second developmental task facing youths preparing for the world of work is one that may be less familiar to sexuality educators but nevertheless necessitates many similar skills along with access to new areas of information. Life option program objectives related to preparation for the world of work include:

1. Increasing knowledge of vocational options that exist today, with emphasis on nontraditional jobs for women as well as men.
2. Encouraging values that support employment, education, economic gain, social status, and other positive aspects of work.

3. Increasing knowledge of the required education, necessary skills, economic and other benefits, and availability of jobs associated with different vocations.
4. Increasing goal-setting skills.
5. Increasing skills for vocational decision-making that incorporate options and consider consequences.
6. Increasing job-related communication skills including interviewing, asking for assistance, expressing needs and emotions, resolving conflicts, and being assertive.
7. Increasing job entry skills necessary to access the world of work, including resume-writing, completing an application and interviewing.

What makes the life options approach so innovative is the dual relevance of so many skills to both primary youth issues: sexuality and employment. For example, in a life options program youths learn a decision-making model they can apply to sexual and reproductive decisions (e.g., "Should I have sex?"; "Do I want a baby now?") as well as educational/vocational decisions ("Should I drop out of school and get a job?" "Do I want to work with people or on my own?"). They practice communication skills they will need in dating relationships (e.g., "I feel angry when you don't meet me on time") as well as in the world of work (e.g., "I would like to cover for you but I won't lie to the boss"). And most essential, adolescents learn to clarify their values and set goals for themselves that take into consideration what they want for their personal and family futures as well as for their vocational futures.

What Do We Know About the Impact of Life Options Programs?

At this writing, evaluation results exist for only two of the life options programs discussed in this article. "Life Planning Education," implemented and evaluated in El Paso, Texas, by the Center for Population Options, was found to be a successful strategy for introducing sexuality education in a conservative community. In a report on the project, CPO noted that "prior to the Life Planning Project there were virtually no teenage pregnancy prevention programs and only minimal sexuality education in the El Paso community." At present, over 150 professionals in El Paso are now teaching life planning, and over 24,000 teens participated in programs between March 1984 and November 1985. In addition, the report indicated that life planning programs varied in terms of their impact on participating youth. Some programs increased knowledge, while others positively affected attitudes related to women in nontraditional careers, and still others increased the motivation of youth to achieve a certain measure of success before they become parents.

A second educational program, "Life Skills and Opportunities," conducted by Public/Private Ventures as part of the Summer Youth Employment Program in five U.S. cities, has demonstrated similar results. A positive change in attitudes about women working in nontraditional careers was found among *boys* only, while an increase in knowledge related to pregnancy prevention (contraception and its availability) was found among all participating youth. One behavior finding unique to the Public/Private Ventures experience was that boys who participated in the Life Skills and Opportunities program were less likely than nonparticipating boys to have been sexually active during the summer. These reported findings, while indicating only slight gains, are reassuring to program planners who may seek to implement an educational program employing the life options strategy.

Conclusion

The basic premise of the life options model seems to be this: young people face an uncertain future filled with choices, and while we can't tell teens what choices they must make, we can tell them what their options are, give them honest information about probable consequences, and then challenge them—with hope, with education, and with basic skills, with whatever we have that might kindle their motivation to strive and to succeed in this world. So many youth today arrive at their adolescence with very little in the way of life skills and life opportunities. Programs that promote life options can open doors never before imagined. Most importantly, such programs can help youth to avoid closing the door to their futures with early and unintended pregnancies.

References

The Alan Guttmacher Institute. *Teenage Pregnancy: The Problem That Hasn't Gone Away.* New York, 1981.

Card, J., and L. Wise. "Teenage Mothers and Teenage Fathers: The Impact of Early Childbearing on the Parents' Personal and Professional Lives." *Family Planning Perspectives* (July/August, 1978).

The Center for Population Options. *Estimates of Public Cost for Teenage Childbearing.* Washington, D.C., 1986.

Chilman, C.S. *Adolescent Sexuality in a Changing American Society: Social and Psychological Perspectives.* NIH Publication #80-1426, Bethesda, Md., 1980.

Dryfoos, J.C. "Strategies for Prevention of Adolescent Pregnancy: A Personal Quest." *Impact,* Institute for Family Research and Education, Syracuse University, No. 6, 1983-1984 edition.

Fine, M. "Why Adolescents Drop into and out of Public High School." Unpublished Manuscript, Columbia Teachers College. New York, 1985.

Haggstrom, G., T.J. Blaschke, D. Kanouse, W. Lesowsky, and P. Morrison. *Teenage Parents: Their Ambitions and Attainments.* Santa Monica, Calif.: Rand, 1981.

Moore, K., and M. Burt. "Teenage Childbearing and Welfare: Policy Perspectives on Sexual Activity, Pregnancy, and Public Dependency." The Urban Institute, Washington, D.C., September 1981.

Waldman, E. "Today's Girls in Tomorrow's Labor Force: Projecting Their Participation and Occupations." *Youth and Society* 16, 3 (March 1985).

BRIDGING THE GAP
Robert A. Hatcher
Monica M. Oakley

Introduction

During the 1970s the Emory University Family Planning Program at Grady Memorial Hospital in Atlanta, Georgia, produced several editions of a magazine for teenagers entitled *What's Happening*. This publication was designed to provide reproductive health information. Approximately 700,000 copies were distributed to schools, health departments, and Planned Parenthood affiliates. In June of 1978 Emory University sponsored a national conference in Atlanta's Omni International for 3000 teenagers from 32 states utilizing the "What's Happening" title. The most important goal of the conference was to assist participants as they made decisions about their health. We sought to underscore the concept that each individual is the captain of his or her own health team and that each individual may decide what his or her habits will be. Speakers included Mary Calderone, Jesse Jackson, and many others. In addition to the plenary sessions, small group sessions were led by 100 facilitators. Over 50 educational exhibits were reviewed by participants. Topics ranged from sickle cell disease, hypertension, and contraception to the prevention of rape, use of seat belts, and good nutrition. While a number of teenagers attending the conference outside the state of Georgia did come with their parents, the program was primarily planned for teen participation.

The conference was covered by "Good Morning America," "The Today Show," several national news programs, and local radio and television stations. Although the conference successfully met the objectives, those who coordinated this program felt it could not be readily reproduced without monumental effort.

Objectives of the Initial "Bridging the Gap" Planning Committee

In 1982 a broad-based group of individuals in Atlanta met over a number of months to discuss the establishment of a series of conferences for teenagers and their parents. The title the group decided upon was "Bridging the Gap." Early in the planning stages for the Bridging the Gap conferences, the following four objectives were established:

1. To hold a national conference for 500 parents and teenagers to present information and improve communication about the health challenges of the adolescent years.

2. To include discussions on how a person's self-esteem (self-respect, self-image, and self-confidence) determines how he or she makes decisions regarding parenting, drugs, alcohol, smoking, violence, driving, nutrition, sexuality, and other health issues.

3. To develop a conference, the content and objectives and success of which are reproducible.

4. To have a national impact through the production of a one-hour television segment on this conference and to make available the format materials of this initial conference to other communities in the hope that they will conduct similar Bridging the Gap conferences in their cities and towns.

Making the Format Adaptable to Other Communities

The planning committee for the first four conferences made a number of decisions related to its objective of producing a conference format that could be readily adapted for use by many organizations throughout the country. Reference was repeatedly made to a medium-sized hypothetical Methodist church in the heartland of the country, Des Moines, Iowa. If a technique could not be carried out by this imaginary church, then the idea was not incorporated into the initial Atlanta conferences. The planning committee decided that three products should come out of the initial year of work:

1. A brief, interesting movie.
2. A magazine that teenagers and their parents could enjoy reading.
3. A "How To" manual for groups considering carrying out a Bridging the Gap parent-teen conference.

THE MAGAZINE

In contrast to the more narrow focus of the original *What's Happening* magazine designed to provide reproductive health information, *Bridging the Gap* focuses on the more holistic and comprehensive concepts of self-knowledge, communication, self-control (decision-making), and contracts and commitment. The emphasis on communication skills is divided into the areas of Looking, Listening, Leveling, and Loving—the four L's as they are called in *Bridging the Gap*. The comprehensive content includes information and strategies to assist in making decisions about drinking, drugs, driving, peer pressure, and reproductive health concerns. Although the design, writing style, and graphics appeal to teens, the content areas readily "open up" topics for discussion by families as well.

Bridging the Gap sets forth the structure and content of the Bridging the Gap conference. It is utilized as a "workbook" by conference participants and facilitators. The magazine has also been used as a study guide or as a textbook by school health education classes, church groups, Girl Scout troops, and drug rehabilitation programs. This 52-page magazine was designed primarily for teenagers, with the knowledge that it would be used extensively by parents as well. Single copies of the magazine are available for $3.00 through Ms. Donna Armstrong, Printed Matter, Inc., P.O. Box 15246, Atlanta, GA 30333 (404-875-5306). Most conferences make bulk purchases of the magazine for $1.00 to $2.00 each, depending on the number of copies purchased. Printed Matter, Inc., is willing to revise the magazine, place into it local names, addresses, and phone numbers of teen-serving agencies, and add photographs of teenagers from a given locale if a state or region wishes to produce an area-specific edition.

THE MOVIE

This 20-minute film, produced for Emory University by WTBS, Channel 17 in Atlanta, was designed to highlight the central issues of parent-teen communication. A group of parents and a group of teens alternately discuss common concerns, such as peer and parental pressure, substance use and abuse, adolescent sexuality, as well as the struggle to communicate effectively and with love.

The film is an excellent adjunct to the Bridging the Gap conferences, truly setting the stage for the small-group workshops. It may be used to recruit parents and teenagers to the conference, at conferences, and at school programs for parent or teenage groups. The sensitivity and sincerity evident in the parent and teen discussions give conference participants permission to comfortably discuss similar concerns, thus functioning as an effective ice-breaker.

In most Bridging the Gap conferences a panel of parents and teenagers is chosen and for 30-45 minutes following the showing of the film, the panel discusses the concepts raised. The film also serves to facilitate any introductory discussion of parent-teen relationships in civic, parent, or church groups. The movie is available in three formats from Printed Matter, Inc.: 16mm, VHS, and 1/4" video.

THE CONFERENCE

The following excerpt from a promotional flyer reflects the positive features of the Bridging the Gap conference model:

Would you like to . . .

- be able to *talk* with your *parent/teen* and feel like they're really *listening?*
- *handle pressure* from the people in your life?
- feel good about yourself and your family?

More formally stated, the goals of the conference are to:

1. Present information to parents and teenagers to improve family communication.
2. Focus on how a person's self-esteem determines decision-making regarding drugs, alcohol, smoking, driving, nutrition, sexuality, and other health issues.

In order to successfully meet the stated objectives, Bridging the Gap conferences should include the following four components, regardless of the format option chosen:

1. *Plenary session* with keynote speaker addressing the theme of "The Four Tasks of Adolescence."
2. *Bridging the Gap* film with discussion after viewing.
3. Use of the *magazine* as a "workbook" by all participants, including parents, teens, and facilitators.
4. *Parent-teen small group workshops* (approximately 20 persons) including:
   A. Communication skills
      - Looking

- Listening
- Leveling
- Loving

B. Decision-making and self-control
- Peer pressure issues for teens
- Stress management issues for parents

C. Contracts and commitment
- Personal life plans
- Setting *measurable* objectives through the use of contracts

Conference developers also recommend the inclusion of health fairs with participatory exhibits, including health risk appraisals, stress testing, respiratory and cardiac functioning as well as informational exhibits, i.e., American Cancer Society, substance abuse projects, highway safety programs, March of Dimes, sickle cell disease programs, mental health programs, Planned Parenthood clinics, books and pamphlets that participants may purchase. While exhibits are optional, they are generally appreciated by conference participants.

Criteria all conference planners should consider:

1. *Location*: Space is needed for the total group as well as adequate "break-out" rooms for small groups, food service, and exhibits. Ideal locations: schools or colleges, churches, community centers. Appropriate space for viewing the film is also needed.

2. *Target Groups*: Church youth groups, girls and boys clubs, schools (through guidance departments or Parent-Teacher Organization initiatives), other civic organizations, community parenting task forces, health maintenance organizations.

3. *Timing*: Carefully check school and community calendars for conflicts, consider local community factors (e.g. weather, sporting and entertainment events, school vacation and holiday schedules). Begin planning at least 6 months to 1 year prior to the conference.

4. *Format:* Recommended "conference" schedules.

A. Friday night and all day Saturday.
B. All day Saturday.
C. All day Saturday and Sunday afternoon.
5. *Facilitators*: They should be (1) skilled in group dynamics, (2) comfortable with parent or teen groups, and (3) able to create a non-threatening environment for discussion. It is ideal to have two facilitators per group, one male, one female. Training of facilitators should be done well in advance of conference date, ensuring adequate preparation time.
6. *Marketing*: Send direct mail letters to target group (parents and teens) and use posters, flyers, public service announcements, newspaper ads, press releases, editorials, talk shows, and newsletters.
7. *Financial considerations* (donated or solicited) may include: printing, mailing, rental of facility, magazines, film, T-shirts, entertainment, food, packets, nametags, security and/or custodial, door prizes (if given), telephone charges, facilitator honoraria, reception for keynote speaker and facilitators, travel, lodging and honorarium for keynote speaker.
8. *Supplies* include: Magazines for each participant, *Bridging the Gap* (film), workshop training modules for facilitators, personal life plans, contracts, T-shirts, nametags, participant packets, directional signs, exhibit tables, extension cords, pencils, food/beverages/snacks, and public address system.

Acknowledgments

Printed Matter, Inc.
The Georgia State Department of Health & Human Services
The Emory University Family Planning Program

The Jesse Smith Noyes Foundation
The Oppenheimer Family Foundation

Evaluation

Schools, Churches, HMOs, health departments, and Planned Parenthood affiliates have sponsored Bridging the Gap conferences throughout the United States. Parent and teen evaluations have been overwhelmingly positive. Typical comments include:

From Teens	*From Parents*
"I learned what questions other teens and parents have and how to cope."	"It opened my eyes to the importance of listening."
"You can learn a lot of things about yourself."	"I enjoyed the open discussion—hearing teens' and parents' views, concerns, and thoughts."
""It was great spending a whole day with my parents.	"I saw people change in a short period of time."

The most important aspect of the Bridging the Gap conference model is the measurable goal-setting completed by all participants in Workshop III—Contracts and Commitment. This workshop is designed to encourage modification of specific individual behaviors. Each participant is instructed to list 3-5 measurable objectives which they work to complete within 30 days. Examples of contract objectives developed by participants include:

- I will express my love to my boys verbally every day.
- I will communicate with my husband for 10 minutes, 4 times a week, over personal family concerns.
- I will not raise my voice once in the next 2 weeks when talking with my mom.
- I will wear my retainer all day for the next 4 weeks.

- I will do 20 sit-ups every night for the next 4 weeks.
- I will pray each night for the next 2 weeks.

Conference participants are surveyed by mail or telephone to determine the percentage of goals actually completed. Many Bridging the Gap sponsors report that 60-65 percent of the individuals goals are completed within the established time frame. In addition, families do report that the contracts have been renegotiated for a longer time span. This positive identification of behavioral change is the most significant aspect of the Bridging the Gap conference model.

In conclusion, the benefits of the Bridging the Gap parent-teen programs include the following:

1. The approach is holistic.
2. Relationship building concepts are the central theme.
3. Sexual activity is *not* the focus.
4. The family unit is strengthened.
5. Provides the basis for continued family discussion.
6. Brings about positive results for sponsoring organization in community networking.
7. Provides practice or "rehearsal" strategies for parents and teens.
8. Evaluation of behavioral change is possible due to development of contracts in which parents and teenagers commit themselves to several *measurable* objectives.

TEENAGE COMMUNICATION THEATER
Elena Love

Planned Parenthood of Greater Dallas's TeenAge Communication Theatre (TACT) is an educational vehicle that uses the dramatic process to heighten public awareness of the problems teens encounter in their process through adolescence. TACT's success, measured by enthusiastic audience response, performance demand, and critical acclaim from the health education community, is due, to a considerable extent, to the timing of the development of the TACT project in Dallas, Texas.

The education teen theater format originated in New York in 1973 in the Family Life Division of New York Medical College. However, TACT's debut in Dallas in the Fall of 1984 was the Dallas community's introduction to the innovative educational strategy.

Planned Parenthood of Greater Dallas (PPGD) decided to develop a teen theater project in the Spring of 1984 after making a thorough assessment of the other formats through which Dallas youth traditionally received instruction about problem areas endemic to adolescence. Also during the Spring of 1984, PPGD staff members participated in Mayor Starke Taylor's Task Force on Adolescent Pregnancy in Dallas County. Members of the Task Force included local teenagers who were candid in their criticism of the current methods of teaching about human sexual behavior and its consequences. These young men and women pleaded with the adult committee members for an educational vehicle that would employ local youth trained as peer health educators. They described a project that would caution, but not lecture, adolescents about the obstacles they might meet along the path to adulthood. The Task Force teenagers' request was compatible with the plans for program development already under consideration within the PPGD Education Department.

Encouraged by the Dallas mayor's convening of a task force on the local adolescent pregnancy problem and reinforced by the task force youths' recommendations, the PPGD staff took the teen theater project proposal to its board for approval. Approval was granted immediately, since the board members felt that the timing was right to harness the abundant natural energy of a group of carefully selected Dallas adolescents and, with an appropriate training program, to develop them into skillful teen peer educators.

TACT Program Design

The structure of the TACT production follows the model established by the New York troupe in 1973. The performance is divided into three sections that last a total of one and one quarter hours.

Part One consists of a series of brief skits, delivered improvisationally, which the cast members have created from their awareness of areas of concern to themselves and their peers.

In order to ensure that the subjects addressed in Part One are as informed as they are inspired, TACT members complete an educational training program during the summer that precedes the performance season. The training segment consists of approximately forty class hours offered by PPGD staff members and volunteer educators from the Dallas community.

The TACT Production

Topics presented during Part One of the TACT production range from sibling rivalry and loneliness to adolescent depression and post-divorce adjustment. Many of the skits focus on sexuality issues, such as peer pressure to have sex, unplanned pregnancy, sexual orientation, and sexually transmitted diseases. However, it is noteworthy that the decision was made to broaden the scope of subject matter considered in the TACT projection to include topics in addition to sexuality issues. This choice illustrates an awareness of the interrelatedness between adolescent sexual activity and other stresses, such as substance abuse and peer pressure. Another striking feature of Part One of a TACT performance is the effective employment of humor as a teaching tool. The TACT members recognize that many of life's most poignant experiences have their humorous moments. TACT also respects its audiences' need to laugh to relieve tension that may accumulate after the presentation of several skits on particularly sensitive issues.

In Part Two of a TACT performance, the cast members return to the stage, and while remaining in character, invite questions and comments from the audience. The skits offered in Part One have deliberately been left unresolved. For example, the pregnant teenager has considered her options but not decided how to proceed with her pregnancy. Or the teenager being pressured to take an illegal drug has weighed the pros and cons but not yet accepted or refused the pill.

Part Two of a TACT presentation gives the audience an opportunity to question the characters about their motivations for past behaviors and their plans for future actions. It also gives audience members a chance to share their feelings about what they have seen. This section of the TACT production is powerful because the audience has an opportunity for immediate involvement with the cast members and subject matter unequaled in traditional dramatic productions.

In Part Three of a TACT performance, the cast members introduce themselves, announce their ages and the schools they attend, and field questions about their participation in the TACT project.

TACT Goals

The goals of the TACT project are multiple and varied. One obvious goal is to present accurate information about issues of particular relevance to adolescents. Another goal is to provide a vehicle through which teenagers can be viewed as competent and dedicated peer educators and counselors. The objective is to encourage people to associate "adolescence" with positive behaviors.

The third goal is to help adolescents make the connection between their behavior and its consequences. In the TACT skits, while actions are purposely not labeled "good" or "bad," they *are* connected on stage with the outcomes they precipitate. This strategy helps the adolescents in the audiences reflect on their behaviors and take responsibility for the linkage between their behaviors and subsequent consequences.

Finally, if one goal takes precedence over all others, it is to model candid, appropriate communication on topics that people think and worry about a lot but are often too uncomfortable to discuss. When audience members observe a TACT character talking about the effects of the stresses in his life on his health and mood or a TACT character sharing with the audience what it feels like to be lonely in the midst of a group of peers or a TACT divorced mother and teenage daughter sharing the anxiety and excitement of Mom's first date in twenty years, they may then feel more comfortable discussing these issues should they encounter them in their own lives.

Casting TACT

The first TeenAge Communication Theatre cast consisted of eleven Dallas teenagers who ranged in age from fourteen to eighteen and who represented seven area schools, both public and private. Five of these teens had some acting experience; six did not. The latter were attracted to the project exclusively because of its potential as an educational resource and an emotional support for themselves and their peers.

Five members of the first TACT cast were male, six female. During the course of the year the cast number decreased to eight. One boy found that the time commitment (approximately three hours of rehearsal and three performance hours per week) was more than he could allocate given his other activities. One girl withdrew because her family had to move. Finally, one girl was asked to leave because she was unwilling to conform to the rehearsal attendance requirements. While the eight TACT members who completed the first season performed with amazing versatility and dedication, the project coordinators felt that the second season's cast should be expanded, both to allow for the natural attrition rate and to enable TACT to accept more performance requests.

The 1985-1986 TACT cast included eighteen members from eleven area schools. Six of the cast members were male, twelve were female. The increased troupe size was a mixed blessing. TACT was able to accept more bookings because each of the skits could be double cast. However, it was more difficult to manage rehearsals, because of the sheer number of adolescents per square foot in the rehearsal area. Troupe members appeared also to know each other less well than members of the previous year's troupe, due very possibly to the size of the cast.

Determining and achieving the ideal teen theater cast size is a problem shared by several of the Planned Parenthood-sponsored teen theater troupes throughout the country.

Community Response to TACT

TACT premiered in Dallas on October 20, 1984, at the PPGD conference at Southern Methodist University in honor of National Family Sexuality Education Month. In the first TACT season, the troupe performed before more than 5,000 people in a wide variety of settings and for audiences that represented a broad range of social, racial, and economic backgrounds.

Throughout the performance season, TACT members studied, rehearsed, and performed with an energy and intensity level that is the most enviable aspect of adolescence, and their preparation was rewarded by statements of community support such as:

- "TACT is one of the finest prevention programs ever developed for adolescents."—*Dallas Mental Health Association's Primary Prevention Committee*

- "TACT really illustrates some dilemmas that we are faced with all the time. We need TACT at our school *so bad!*"—*Dallas high school student*
- "Teenagers on stage dealing with stress, substance abuse, peer pressure, and sexuality seem to open the doors of communication for the teenage audience."— *Youth Activities' Director, Temple Emanu-El*
- "Seeing the TACT skits, I recognized for the first time how much stress my child is living with. Thanks for opening my eyes!"—*A Dallas parent*
- "TACT is one of the most innovative and unique educational projects in this community."—*Project Director, Dallas Commission on Children and Youth*

Planned Parenthood of Greater Dallas's positive experience with TACT has convinced the agency that Dallas was both ready and eager for a local teen peer educational vehicle that would encourage the recognition and acceptance of the connection between adolescent behavior and its consequences while inspiring people to communicate candidly about sensitive issues.

Planned Parenthood Affiliates Sponsoring Teen Troupes

Planned Parenthood of Central and Northern Arizona
5651 North 7th Street
Phoenix, AZ 85014
(602) 277-7526

Positive Force Players

Contact: Debra Petty, Community Health Educator (602)268-1580

Planned Parenthood of Eastern Oklahoma & Western Arkansas
1007 South Peoria
Tulsa, OK 74120
(918) 587-7674

Teens Helping Teens

Contact: Jacquie Carr, Project Director

Planned Parenthood of Greater Charlotte, Inc.
East Independence Plaza Building
951 South Independence Boulevard
Suite 430
Charlotte, NC 28202
(704) 377-0841

Focus

Contact: Paige Morrow, Director of Teen Theater

Planned Parenthood of Greater Dallas, Inc.
7515 Greenville Avenue
Suite 707
Dallas, TX 75231
(214) 363-2004

Teenage Communication Theatre (TACT)

Contact: Susan Henderson, Project Coordinator

Planned Parenthood League, Inc.
1553 Woodward
Suite 1337
Detroit, MI 48226
(313) 963-2870

Family Theater Group

Contact: Loretta Davis, Director of Education

Planned Parenthood League of Massachusetts
99 Bishop Richard Allen Drive
Cambridge, MA 02139
(617) 492-0518

Youth Expression Theater (YET)

Contact: Nancy Olin, Teen Education Coordinator

Planned Parenthood of Lehigh Valley
112 North 13th Street
Allentown, PA 18102
(215) 439-0820

Youth Are Capable and Concerned (YACC)

Contact Heidi Freemer, Project Coordinator

Planned Parenthood of Metropolitan Washington, D.C., Inc.
1108 16th Street, N.W.
Washington, DC 20036
(202) 347-8500

Washington Area Improvisational Teen Theater (WAITT)

Contact: Margaret Copemann, Project Coordinator

Planned Parenthood of Monterey County, Inc.
5 Via Joaquin
Monterey, CA 93940
(408) 373-1709

Teen Life Company

Contact: Denise Clifford, Project Coordinator (408) 758-8261

Planned Parenthood of North Central Florida, Inc.
914 Northwest 13th Street
Gainesville, FL 32601
(904) 376-9000

Gainesville Area Improvisational Teen Theater

Contact: Sharon Althouse, Education Director

Planned Parenthood of the Permian Basin, Inc.
910-B South Grant Street
Odessa, TX 79763
(915) 333-4133

The Esteem Machine Teen Theater Repertory Troupe

Contact: Tricia Shelton, Producer/Director

Planned Parenthood of San Diego and Riverside Counties
2100 Fifth Avenue
San Diego, CA 92101
(619) 231-2941

New Image Teen Theater

Contact: Cynthia Burdyshaw, Teen Theater Producer (619) 231-6820

Planned Parenthood of Southeast Iowa
413 Tama Building
Burlington, IA 52601
(319) 753-6209

The Great Body Show

Contact: Cindy Brown, Community Health Educator

NO IS NOT ENOUGH:
TEEN AQUAINTANCE RAPE AND SEXUAL ABUSE PREVENTION
Caren Adams
Jan Loreen-Martin

One in three women will be raped in her lifetime. In more than two-thirds of reported rapes, the rapist is someone the woman knows—a boyfriend, neighbor, family friend. Most victims of acquaintance rape do not report it to the police or anyone else. They consider it very private, personal, and embarrassing. Because artificial lines have been drawn between sex and rape, most young women do not know it is still rape even though they know the guy.

Program Goals

No Is Not Enough provides information for parents about sexual assault of teenagers to enable them to help teenagers avoid rape or sex they don't want. Parents of adolescents are the target audience because teens between fifteen and twenty-five are the most vulnerable.

Both parents and teens may think rapists are likely to be strangers. But many sexual assaults happen during teens' normal pursuit of romantic relationships. Integrating information about sexuality and relationships with rape prevention information can help shift the concern to acquaintances. The goal is to reach parents of boys who might be offenders as well as parents of boys and girls who are possible victims.

Another goal is to bring the cultural definition of rape in line with the legal definition, which says rape is sexual intercourse where lack of consent is clearly expressed. To become integrated into the cultural understanding of rape, consent must be more adequately defined than it currently is. Teens or parents trying to understand "consent" find little to guide them in the conflicting standards of changing sexual mores, the media, and traditional values. Consistent answers about how to behave in romantic relationships and when "no" really means "no" are not available. The primary element of consent is choice. Consent is active not passive. Consent is only possible when there is equal power. Teens need to hear adults say that force is never an acceptable way to gain sexual contact—no excuses, no rationalizations.

To avoid acquaintance rape and sexual exploitation teens need to know: what sexual assault is, what to do if it happens, it's okay to talk about the positive and negative sides of sexuality, rape is never deserved, values should limit our sexual behavior, and force is never justified.

No Is Not Enough covers acquaintance rape, child sexual abuse, sexual harassment, and sexual exploitation. To be legally considered rape, some form of obvious force is necessary. Some forms of sexual exploitation may involve less obvious forms of force such as blackmail, threats, or bribery.

Teens are victimized by adults; child sexual abuse is sexual contact between an adult and a child (age of consent varies from state to state). Child sexual abuse occurs whenever there is enough age difference to give more power to the offender. A friend's parent, a coach, or anyone in authority has such power. Society generally does not see younger children as sexual, so any sexual contact between a child and an older person is considered abusive. As adolescents develop their adult sexual identity, they are involved in kissing, hugging, crushes, and petting. When that or other sexual contact becomes abusive is not as clear as with younger children.

The adolescent developmental stage creates vulnerability. Teens may lack self-esteem, be susceptible to negative peer pressure, take risks, test limits, and challenge rules while pushing for independence and feeling invincible, immortal. Teens also don't know what sexual assault is and push the limits on sexual behavior. They have misconceptions about why and how rape happens. Teens read *No Is Not Enough* voluntarily when it is made available to them through the school library. Classroom presenters find them eager for information about rape, sexual exploitation, and sexual harassment although they seldom call the last by name.

Both schools and parents have roles to play. Parents are powerful sex educators if they provide explicit information and moral guidance about sex, relationships, and abuse. Parents are relieved to see words and phrases they can use as aids to help them start discussions. Many are reminded of painful incidents in their own youth they suffered through alone. They hope family discussions can deter similar incidents and that their teens would not suffer without help. Schools may be most effective presenting information, because teachers and counselors have more credibility than parents at particular stages.

Classroom Discussion

Guidelines for classroom discussion are outlined in *No Is Not Enough*. They include deciding on your own definition of rape in words you can use. The definition should include who is involved, that it may be someone known, the amount and type of force, and that it usually happens during everyday school or social activities. Discussions will go better when you think ahead about strategies to handle discomfort with the topic. Scare tactics divert teens from their own dangers. If you use a stranger situation or a kidnap-murder report in the paper, it will be more difficult to orient teens to everyday reality. Ideas presented as those you wish you had known when you were a teen may be accepted more readily.

Acquaintance rape deserves significant attention because of the enormity of the problem. Although studies differ on the exact numbers of victims, one study estimated that 700,000 to 1 million teenage girls are sexually assaulted each year. Both boys and girls are affected but few girls, and even fewer boys, come forward if they are assaulted. They feel it is their fault. Girls feel it is their responsibility to set the sexual limits, and if forced to have sex (raped), it must mean they failed to set the limits adequately. She shouldn't have been alone with him, let him kiss her, gone on a date, etc. Boys are under different pressures to conceal an assault. The cultural myth is that men are always ready to have sex. A boy who reveals an assault suffers a loss of face that threatens his masculinity. Now that acquaintance rape has been acknowledged as a problem, studies show it to be very widespread. On college campuses one-fifth to one-half of entering female students report unwanted or aggressive sexual approaches in the previous year. Further reason to attend to the problem during teenage years comes from the reports from programs dealing with adult sex offenders. These indicate adult offenders began assaultive behavior as adolescents. If they can be treated as adolescents, genuine prevention results.

No Is Not Enough suggests several prevention strategies dealing with group pressures and setting limits ahead of time. Much teen exploitation may be mutual because neither party understands consent. Evidence suggests that both boys and girls have intercourse for many reasons, including wanting to fit in and be like the others, wanting an affectionate touch, and needing to feel powerful and in control.

Discussions about limits should include dating guidelines, acceptable and unacceptable dating behavior, high-risk dating places, minimum age or conditions for sexual intercourse, and unacceptable reasons for intercourse.

Another prevention strategy is to avoid potential offenders. There are no particular characteristics that identify offenders except they may show behavior that indicates a willingness to ignore what another wants. These can serve as warning signs.

No Is Not Enough also suggests several areas for cultural change, including clarifying touch within the family, changing sex role expectations, and lessening the impact of media.

Programs to prevent rape have discussed curfews for women, self-defense classes, and folk notions about how women could defend themselves from rapists. Few such measures are genuine prevention. They do not change the factors that allow rape to occur.

No Is Not Enough is based on several assumptions about sexual abuse prevention:

1. A successful prevention program will acknowledge the importance of romantic relationships in the lives of teenagers and provide guidelines for pursuing normal activities while avoiding exploitation.
2. An effective prevention program will address both boys and girls as potential victims and potential offenders. About 95 percent of offenders are males, but some girls abuse children, and certainly some girls put sexual pressure on boys. The incidence of rape will not change until force becomes unacceptable, until both boys and girls know it is never acceptable.
3. An effective program will recognize the possibility of higher vulnerability of children in divorcing families, stepfamilies, families with chronic unemployment, and other stresses.
4. Curfews and suggestions that women and children avoid going out alone or at night only limit women or children's freedom. They may be useful safety tips but are not prevention and are particularly unsuccessful with teens.
5. An effective prevention program addresses the problem of securely placing responsibility for an assault on the person who uses force. In order to maintain their sense of invincibility, teens often look for a safety rule the victim broke or what she did that they wouldn't have done. If they believe the victim could have done anything to avoid an assault, they see the assault as her fault. Prevention programs should not add to the belief that it is the victim's responsibility to avoid rape. This cultural belief allows some men to continue to rape without calling it rape.
6. Rape affects everyone because of the fear and distrust generated by the occurrence of rape. Therefore, prevention programs based on fear perpetuate a damaging aspect of rape, without necessarily reaching teens. An effective program will not increase fear.
7. Eventually the interactive nature of substance use or abuse and exploitive, violent behavior must be recognized. One-third to one- half of sexual assaults

involve alcohol. Whether it is used as an excuse, a courage builder, or a guilt reliever, the links must be recognized.

Finally, teens need to hear consistently, from all adults who have influence on them, that pushing, manipulating, pressuring, or exploiting another person for sex hurts that person. They need to hear in many different ways that adults expect their sexual standards to include respect for others, awareness of the problems, understanding that others could try to take advantage of them, and goals for nonexploitive relationships that are nurturing, caring, and fulfilling.

A TEACHER TRAINING MODEL
Peggy B. Smith

Introduction

The lack of strong academic training opportunities in the area
of human sexuality for school instructors is seen as a significant
obstacle hindering the widespread teaching of sex education in
the schools. It is unusual for teachers to have received formal
sexuality education as part of their training experience. Like
parents who have been socialized in a conservative environment,
teachers traditionally have been ill-prepared and poorly supervised
to provide sexuality education to their students. Nevertheless, the
preparation of those who teach the sexuality education curriculum
is crucial. The training of sexuality educators should develop
content and process expertise necessary to impart information in
this area. Teacher preparation should also provide the screening
and training that help allay community apprehension about
instructor credentials. The lack of widespread training
opportunities in college and university settings (Maddock, 1976)
has stimulated creative approaches to continuing education
opportunities in human sexuality (Carrera, 1970; Benjamin, 1971;
Seffrim, 1974).

To meet the need for validated professional training
experiences for the adult population, training models for
educators in the middle and secondary schools in the area of
human sexuality should be reviewed and evaluated. The purpose
of this chapter is to discuss a model teacher training program
developed for middle and secondary public school teachers. It is
assumed that participants in this staff development will experience

and maintain significant knowledge and attitude change. A crucial objective of the model is to increase participants' comfort in the classroom as well as their perceived and actual teaching performance as measured by standardized instruments. The Sex Education Teacher Training and Development Project sponsored by Baylor College of Medicine and the Houston Independent School District was a pilot three-year staff development program in sex education. The primary goal was to develop a training model for middle and secondary school teachers in human sexuality and to evaluate, on a pilot basis, its effectiveness. Inherent in the pilot program was the belief that these instructional specialists or teacher trainers, after participating in an intensive continuing education experience, could, in turn, effectively bring about knowledge gain in teachers who taught in middle and secondary schools. Complementary to the training classes, a training guide was developed as a resource for staff development and other teacher training. Included in this guide were the content, format, and process information necessary to replicate the project for professional educators.

This chapter will review the development, implementation, and evaluation of this three-year project. Student and parent participation will also be discussed as well as the overall sponsorship of the efforts. Recommendations for future efforts will also be mentioned.

Staff Development Overview

The Baylor College of Medicine teacher training program in human sexuality began in January 1979 when a comprehensive continuing education program for the 14 trainers was offered by the medical school staff. The training included 72 hours of class time—nine eight-hour days. Material was presented through lectures, homework assignments, role play, and group process using small and large group discussions. An instructional specialist of the medical school served as facilitator, encouraging group interaction. Since most trainers had an education background, some of the nonsexual content was familiar to them. Group discussion provided participants with opportunities to share their knowledge and experiences and to deal with their personal values. The basis of the content was systems theory and included topics such as human interactions in social systems, interpersonal relationships, the anatomy of sexuality, the control of fertility, diseases of the sexual system, pregnancy and prenatal development, homosexuals in a heterosexual world, divergent sexual behavior, sexual abuse, and sexuality and the handicapped.

Upon completion of the training program, the trainers then taught 44 teachers in a 48-hour class setting—six eight-hour days. Depending on the school, trainers were chosen from either middle or senior high schools. The content and teaching techniques were similar for both groups. Of the total of 44 teachers who originally enrolled in the training, four dropped out; 35 or 87.5 percent completed the course and responded to the pre- and post-assessment questionnaires.

Goals and Theoretical Framework

The primary goals of the teacher training project were for the trainers to be comfortable communicating about sexuality, to understand factual information about human sexuality and social systems, to recognize the influence of their sexual beliefs, values, and attitudes on their behavior, and to comprehend the decision-making systems framework of the training program.

In order to accomplish these goals, the social systems theory included several key concepts that focused on the interdependency of groups and other social organizations and inevitable conflict and stress. Because of this group characteristic, there was a need to maintain a sense of balance to communicate and to maintain the boundaries that define them. The flexibility of this theory allowed a unifying framework within which to view the family, social relationships, society's institutions, and the human body. The theory's principles also placed sexuality in a broad social context and related it to the wide continuum of human needs and behaviors.

Manual Content

The 200-page training manual developed during the project contained the factual information and the audiovisual resources and activities needed to teach adults how to teach sexuality education. The manual chapters were developed to be used independently in whatever order chosen by the requirements of the class. The chapters included: human interaction in a systems perspective; sexuality: an integrated part of human systems; interpersonal relationships; anatomy of sexuality; pregnancy and prenatal development; control of fertility; diseases of the sexual system; homosexuals in a heterosexual world; individual divergent sexual behavior; sexual abuse; and sexuality and the disabled. Discussions provided in the manual centered on human relationships, families, and groups as systems, emphasizing communications processes and problem-solving behaviors.

PROJECT EVALUATION

Method

Two standardized assessment questionnaires designed to measure knowledge and attitudes about sexuality and an assessment questionnaire designed to provide information on the training content and format were used for the evaluation. The two standardized instruments were administered to the teachers three times: one prior to their training, at the completion of the training six weeks later, and six to eight months after the teachers had an opportunity to teach the course. All teachers were asked to complete the two standardized knowledge and attitude instruments at the time of follow-up. Only those teachers who actually taught the course completed the assessment questionnaire about the training content and format.

The participants' responses were anonymous and completed on a voluntary basis. They were instructed not to put their names on the questionnaire. To maximize confidentiality, demographic data were not gathered on the participants at the follow-up. These data had been gathered previously in an independent format. A self-addressed, stamped envelope was provided if the participants preferred to complete the evaluation at home. To assist in analyzing the results, the teachers were instructed to devise a code and place it in the upper-right-hand corner on the questionnaire. The code could be a birthday or a symbol that would be recognized by the participant and would allow pre- and post-responses to be paired and used again on the follow-up. Participants were instructed that they did not have to answer any questions they found objectionable. The teachers were informed throughout the project that the purpose of the evaluation was to measure the effectiveness of the training project and that the evaluation would not be used by the school district to evaluate them. The anonymous coding system helped allay their fears.

Measures

The Sex Knowledge and Attitude Test (SKAT) was originally developed to gather information about sexual attitudes, knowledge, and degree of experience with a variety of sexual behaviors. Only two sections of the SKAT, those measuring knowledge and attitudes, were used in this evaluation. The knowledge portion contains 71 true/false items and yields a single score covering physiological, psychological, and social aspects of human sexuality. The attitude portion of SKAT is composed of 35 five-alternative, Likert-type items that provide scores on the four brief attitudinal scales of heterosexual relations, sexual myths, abortion, and autoeroticism.

The Test for Assessing Sexual Knowledge and Attitudes (TASKA) was the second standardized instrument used for program evaluation. This scale measures basic sexual knowledge about a variety of topics, provides for a measure of attitudes on various topics, and allows for an indication of sexual experience and personal sexual satisfaction. As with SKAT, only the attitude and knowledge portions were used in the evaluation.

The effectiveness of the content and format of the training was also assessed through the process evaluation. The majority of the teacher trainers indicated that they felt either well-prepared or prepared to teach teachers. All of the trainers who provided staff development to the teachers rated their experiences of training as very valuable, and all participating trainers indicated that, if given the opportunity, they would be interested in training other teachers in the district. All trainers recommended a repeat of the training experiences and that additional public school teachers be trained.

The teachers who were taught by the trainers also gave favorable ratings to their training program. As a result of their experience, 77.8 percent of the teachers indicated that they felt prepared to teach the students. Only 22.3 percent felt that they were only somewhat prepared. The training guide received high marks with 94.5 percent of the teachers indicating that the guide was either very useful or useful. Almost all of the teachers indicated that they would recommend a repeat of this training program for other teachers in the school district. Ironically, the only activity that did not receive high ratings was the assignment of homework to both the trainers and the teachers.

In order to assess whether the teachers could translate the knowledge and skills acquired in the staff development, the final evaluation phase consisted of student participation in pilot classes on a voluntary basis (with parental permission) before and after regular school hours. Initially, a total of 206 students enrolled in the program—86.4 percent were in the eighth grade and 12.6 percent were in the tenth grade. To evaluate knowledge gained, a standardized questionnaire was administered at the beginning and again at the end of the program. While only 48.1 percent completed both the pre- and post-questionnaires, both the eighth and the tenth grade students showed significant increase in knowledge. The students also rated the class and teachers at the completion of the program. The students' ratings of their class and teachers and their experience in the program were highly favorable. The dropout rate was attributed to the early hours, transportation problems, competing extracurricular activities, sports, and babysitting obligations. The majority of students indicated that they would attend as well as recommend that their friends attend another program in human sexuality.

DISCUSSION

While the knowledge and attitude changes suggest the potential of a public-school-based staff development program in human sexuality, the proposed model has characteristics that maximize opportunities for future project replications. By utilizing already-employed public school faculty as trainers of teachers, a human sexuality program can be put in place, maximizing its continuation once the pilot phase concludes. In addition, notwithstanding normal staff attrition, the tiered approach of training educational professionals encourages program continuation and expansion from both administrative and direct teaching levels.

This teacher training model also seems to be cost effective in the utilization of staff time and effort. After participating in a 72-hour course, teacher trainers were able to implement a staff development sex education course in approximately one-half the classroom time and still effect changes in knowledge and attitude. The impact of a good staff development program seems to have enhanced change in subsequent participants rather than diminished it. Such a program seems to provide an effective training model in an often difficult subject area.

Trainer Effectiveness

The analysis of both the trainers' and teachers' scores demonstrated significant changes in their human sexuality knowledge as a result of program participation. In addition, their attitudes regarding masturbation changed in a more permissive or liberal direction. Of the four attitudinal categories possible, masturbation measured by the autoeroticism scale may be a common behavior and is probably the one with the greatest degree of guilt. If one accepts cognitive dissonance research that maintains that attitudes follow from behavior rather than vice versa, the sex education training may have, in fact, legitimated a previously taboo behavior for both trainer and teacher, which was then reflected in each group's permissive score change. An alternative explanation for the reported change in masturbatory attitudes should also be considered. The overall change in this attitude score may be accounted for in that some of the participants prior to project participation were actually uncomfortable in reporting attitudes and, therefore, falsely reported a conservative attitude. Program participation, therefore, desensitized them and facilitated their reporting of their original more liberal orientation. In contrast to trainers, teachers also showed a more liberal score in the sexual myth area.

As pre-test scores on both scales indicated, there were no significant differences in attitudes and knowledge between the teachers and the trainers. One may wonder why there was a change in teachers' attitudes on sexual myths but no change for the trainers. One could assume that previous exposure to the content area in other educational experiences might have affected attitudinal change. However, in examining the participants' descriptions of their staff development experiences in human sexuality gathered prior to project participation, no training differences in human sexuality course work were found between the trainers and teachers. Another possible explanation in the apparent differences between trainer and teacher attitudes after project participation may reflect a statistical artifact. Because of the small number of trainers in the first tier of the project, potentially significant statistical trends could not emerge. A larger sample size could have, therefore, yielded significant results.

Teacher Trainer Follow-up

Experiences and data gathered as a result of a teacher trainer staff development project in sex education corroborated what noncontroversial disciplines already confirm—knowledge gained through the academic process, even if assimilated, must be used if it is to be retained. Educational information on human sexuality is no exception. Follow-up administration of standardized instruments revealed that teachers who actively taught human sexuality in the classroom were able to maintain knowledge levels acquired subsequent to staff development participation. On the other hand, their training colleagues did not actively use their knowledge and had significantly lower knowledge scores on follow-up evaluations. Interestingly, participation in the classroom did not increase the knowledge score; it only sustained previous learning.

These results have a variety of continuing education implications for sexuality instructors. Teachers with proven academic performance, whether through an academic or standardized instrument process, can strongly benefit from continuing education. As seen in the comparison of the teaching and nonteaching educator, unless the content is refreshed continually, the basis of knowledge disintegrates, even in an area as interesting to some as sexuality. Periodic staff development not only refreshes basic cognitive material but exposes the teaching professional to new research findings in the field.

While teaching the subject matter to students stabilizes the cognitive domain in sexuality education, it seems to have the opposite effect when attitudes are remeasured. When attitudinal scores were examined following classroom teaching experiences, the participating educators became more conservative than when their attitudes were measured after in-service education. Several explanations can be posed for this apparent conservative retrenchment. Presenting material with sexual content to students rather than discussing the same content with an adult peer group may cause the teacher to retreat to a more conservative position. The teacher, as an authoritarian figure in the school setting, may also want to reinforce a restrictive posture on sexuality. The academic experience seemed to provide psychological support for permissive teacher attitudes. However, the act of instructing adolescents seemed to have a conservative effect. Such an interpretation is supported in that those teachers who did not teach had more permissive attitudes about autoeroticism at the follow-up than in the beginning of the program. However, these nonteaching educators at the six-month follow-up were still more conservative than at the end of the training.

These findings probably indicate that attitudes are difficult to change and that any change may lose its significance over time, with gains in a more permissive direction suffering erosion. Teachers may rather espouse a conservative position than defend a newly gained liberal perspective.

Conclusion

To those people who are intimately acquainted with the urgency and magnitude of the problems of adolescent pregnancy, comprehensive evaluation of their educational activities may seem to be a diversion of scarce resources from needed services and a diminution of efforts that they believe to be successful. While it is easy to sympathize with the principals involved in sex education programs and to recognize the complexity of the problems they face, it is also easy to see a great need for program development and evaluation. In the three-year teacher-training project, knowledge could be inculcated, but conservative orientations could not be significantly altered. This one piece of information should, if anything, assuage community apprehension that individuals will become more permissive as a result of program participation.

In addition, although significant changes were manifested by the teachers and trainers, a limitation of this pilot study should be mentioned. No sexual behavior of teacher or student participants was assessed. Such an assessment could provide additional information concerning the interrelationship of knowledge, attitudes, and behavior. Nevertheless, this pilot study has underscored the necessity for further research comparing teacher trainer scores generated from programs with different formats or from programs serving different populations. A follow-up assessment of this pilot study is crucial to ascertain the long-term degree of attitude and knowledge change and to measure how effectively teachers work with the students.

References

Athanasiou, R. "Review of Public Attitudes on Sexual Issues." *Contemporary Sexual Behavior: Critical Issues in the 1970s.* Edited by J. Zubin and J. Money. Baltimore: Johns Hopkins University Press, 1972, pp. 361-390.

Benjamin, R. "Programs in Sex Education: Use of Clinics in a Community Hospital for Training Graduate Students." *Family Coordinator* 20 (October 1971): 341.

Carrera, M.A. "High School Sex Education: Teaching the Teacher." *Education Project Report* 3 (March 1970): 15-24.

Carrera, M.A. "Training the Sex Educator: Guidelines for Teacher Training Institutions." *American Journal of Public Health* 92 (1972): 233-243.

Elstein, M., K.J. Dennis, and M.S. Buckingham. "Sexual Knowledge and Attitudes of Southampton Medical Students." *Lancet* 2 (1977): 495-496.

Flaherty, C., and P.B. Smith. "Teacher Training for Sex Education." *Journal of School Health* 70 (1981): 261-264.

Gordon, S., and R.W. Libby. *Sexuality Today and Tomorrow: Contemporary Issues in Human Sexuality.* Belmont, Calif.: Duxbury Press, 1976.

Gorry, G.A., and P.B. Smith. "Evaluating Sex Education Programs." *Journal of Sex Education and Therapy* 6 (1980): 17-23.

Hawkins, R., and B. Silberman. "Attitudinal Course in Human Sexuality for the Allied Health Professional." *Journal of Allied Health* 7 (1978): 57-63.

Juhasz, A. "Characteristics Essential to Teachers in Sex Education." *Journal School Health* 40, 1 (1970): 17-19.

Kelly, G. "Sex Education for Counselors." *Personnel and Guidance Journal* 54 (March 1976).

Kent, R.M., J.R. Abernathy, and R.C. Midour. "Teacher Readiness for Roles in Family Life Education: An Exploratory Study." *American Journal of Public Health* 61 (1971): 586-599.

Kilander, H.F. *Sex Education in the School.* New York: Macmillan, 1970.

Kirkendall, L., and R.W. Libby. "Trends in Sex Education." *The Individual, Sex and Society.* Edited by C. Broderick, and J. Bernard. Baltimore: Johns Hopkins Press, 1969.

Lief, H.I. "Preparing the Physician to Become a Sex Counselor and Educator." *Pediatric Clinics of North America* 16 (1969): 447-458.

Lief, H.I., and D.M. Reed. *Sex Knowledge and Attitude Test.* Philadelphia: Center for the Study of Sex Education in

Medicine, Department of Psychiatry, University of Pennsylvania School of Medicine, 1970.

Mace, D.R., R.H.O. Bannerman, and J. Burton. *The Teaching of Human Sexuality in Schools for Health Professionals.* Geneva: World Health Organization, 1974.

Maddock, J.W. "Sex Education in Professional Schools." *Journal of Research and Development in Education* 10 (1976).

Marcotte, D.B., and D. Kilpatrick. "Preliminary Evaluation of a Sex Education Course." *Journal of Medical Education* 49 (1974): 703-705.

Miller, W.R., and H.I. Lief. "The Sex Knowledge and Attitude Test." *Journal of Sex and Marital Counseling* 5 (1979): 282-287.

Munson, H.E. "What Teachers Think They Need to be Sexuality Educators." *Health Education* 7 (1976): 40.

Read, D.A., and H.E. Munson. "Resolution of One's Sexual Self: An Important First Step for Sexuality Educators." *Journal of School Health* 46, 1 (1976): 31-34.

Renshaw, D.C. "Sex Education for Educators." *Journal of School Health* 43, 10 (1973): 645-650.

Ryan, I.J., and P.C. Dunn. "Sex Education from Prospective Teachers' View Poses a Dilemma." *Journal of School Health* 48 (1979): 573-575.

Schiller, P. *Creative Approach to Sex Education and Counselling.* New York: Association Press, 1973.

Schiller, P. "Pilot Training for Professionals in a Multi-disciplinary Approach for Counseling." *Family Coordinator* 42 (1969): 385-390.

Schuck, R.F. "Attitudes of Arizona Educators Toward Specific Content Areas in Sex Education." *Journal of School Health* 42 (1972): 122-124.

Schulz, E., and S.R. Williams. *Family Life and Sex Education: Curriculum and Instruction.* New York: Harcourt Brace Jovanovich, 1969.

Seffrim, J.R. "Teaching Teachers About Human Sexuality." *School Health Review* (November/December, 1974).

Smith, P.B., C. Flaherty, and L.J. Webb. "Training Teachers in Human Sexuality: Effect on Attitude and Knowledge." *Psychological Reports* 48 (1981): 527-530.

Smith, P.B., C. Flaherty, and L.J. Webb. "Human Sexuality Training Programs for Public School Teachers: An Evaluation." *Journal of Sex Education and Therapy* 8, 1 (1982): 14-17.

Smith, P.B., C. Flaherty, and L.J. Webb. "Student Outcomes Associated with Teacher Training in Sex Education." *Journal of Sex Education and Therapy* (1982): 38-43.

Szasz, G. "Sex Education and the Teacher." *Journal of School Health* 40 (1970): 151-155.

Woods, N.F., and A. Mandett. "Changes in Students' Knowledge and Attitudes Following a Course in Human Sexuality." *Nursing Research* 24, 1 (1975): 10-15.

THE SEX EDUCATION COALITION: A MODEL FOR COMMUNITY INTERACTION
Joan S. Benesch

In 1975 approximately 25 sex educators in the Washington, D.C., area began meeting periodically to share information and resources related to their work. That group evolved into an organization that today has 325 members and a mailing list of approximately 4000—most in the Washington, D.C., area but at least a third from other parts of the country and overseas. The purpose of the Sex Education Coalition, "to offer a forum for the exchange of information and resources in education and human sexuality," has attracted a mutlidisciplinary membership including doctors, nurses, teachers, administrators, social workers, health educators, psychologists, and ministers. Because the group does not lobby or take advocacy positions, individuals from diverse political affiliations have joined. Members join as individuals, not as representatives of their agencies or institutions. There are no eligibility requirements for membership. Annual dues (currently $25.00) provide members with a quarterly newsletter (*Coalition News*), notices of meetings, discounts on workshops and publications and free film loan.

The success of the coalition in meeting its stated objectives is demonstrated by the diversity of its membership, the range of programs and services it offers, and by its continued growth and vitality throughout the years.

Background

Washington, D.C., is often cited in professional health education literature as having been the location during the late 1960s and early 1970s of a model program for adolescent mothers (at the Webster school). As federal funding diminished in the early 1970s, a committee of health professionals was established to promote the program's continuation. When that committee began to identify the components of the District's teenage pregnancy problem and to discuss strategies for dealing with it, members' interests were soon divided into two parts—prevention and intervention. While acknowledging the importance of both, most members determined which component was the greater priority for themselves and their agencies.

Those whose primary concern was prevention met separately on several occasions to share information about programs and services for adolescents. Several members subsequently planned local activities during National Family Sex Education Week in 1975. Staff members of Planned Parenthood of Metropolitan Washington, Lutheran Social Services, Preterm Reproductive Health Center, the Unitarian Church, the Washington, D.C., Department of Human Resources, and other agencies organized and implemented a variety of outreach activities, including a hotline for parents. During an evaluation meeting following the week's efforts, several participants indicated a desire to continue working together on a regular basis. At the planning meeting that ensued, the group considered the following basic questions:

1. What common areas of concern could participants work on together?
2. Did participants want to work together in their own geographical areas (by county, for example) and meet once or twice a year to share experiences? Or would they rather work as one group on a metropolitan area-wide basis?
3. Should the group have regular meetings, and if so, for what purpose and with what structure?
4. Who should take leadership? Should there be an elected/appointed board of directors?
5. What about dues, a budget, expenses?

As of that meeting, the group officially adopted the name of the Sex Education Coalition of Metropolitan Washington and decided to meet every two months to learn about ongoing programs and projects; films, books, community resources, curricula, and teaching guides; and professional opportunities in the field. This initial organizational decision is reevaluated periodically to maintain a consensus on goals and objectives.

Development of the Organization

From 1975 to 1977, the Sex Education Coalition functioned informally with no membership fees or by-laws. Its co-chairpersons, Joan Benesch and John Muller, enlisted financial support and agency cooperation from their employers, Planned Parenthood of Metropolitan Washington and Lutheran Social Services. The in-kind contributions of these agencies (for telephone, duplicating, and other communication expenses), coupled with contributions by many others, enabled the coalition to conduct its early work without a budget.

Following three years of a productive, workable network, the coalition decided to adopt a more formalized structure and leadership system. A committee of members drafted by-laws that provided for a non-profit incorporated organization with a leadership structure that includes 5 officers, a 15-member Board of Directors, and the following standing committees: Workshops, Media Fair, Membership, Newsletter, Program, Publications, Public Information, Long Range Planning, Nominations, and By-laws. The board meets bimonthly to review policy, plan programs, and share committee reports. A membership fee of $10 was established to cover the broadening range of membership services. As the membership grew and the coalition's services and activities increased, the board recognized the need to purchase some basic services, and in 1983 contracted for secretarial, phone, computer, and mailing services from the Washington Council of Agencies, an umbrella organization for non-profits.

Programs and Services of the Sex Education Coalition

The major programs offered by the coalition are meetings, the Annual Media Fair, and day-long workshops. Most program events take place during the academic year (September through June) in order to accommodate the work and vacation schedules of the membership, many of whom are educators.

Coalition Meetings. All of the coalition's meetings (3 or 4 per year) include presentations and sharing of resources. At the beginning of each meeting, participants introduce themselves and offer information about their program activities and services. This initial sharing time enables members to develop informal networks that extend beyond the meetings. Another popular feature of regular meetings is a resource table where members are encouraged to display or distribute educational and informational materials.

The major portion of the meeting involves a presentation by one or more speakers, often from within the membership. Recent topics included:

- Evaluation of Sex Education Programs
- Sexuality and Aging
- Developmental Tasks of Adolescence
- Teenage Pregnancy
- Child Sexual Abuse
- Rape Education
- Family Life and Sexual Learning
- Involving Parents in Sex Education Programs
- Sexuality from Some Religious Points of View
- New Perspectives on Homosexuality for Sex Educators

For the past three years the Coalition and the Washington, D.C., chapter of the Society for Adolescent Medicine have co-sponsored a yearly meeting on topics of mutual interest.

Average attendance at meetings is about 50, and each meeting attracts some new people. Meetings are held at centrally located facilities, selected for accessibility to public transportation and parking. All meetings are open to the public and are conducted during the day (9:30-12 noon) or, more often, in the evening (7-

9:30 P.M.). Coalition meetings are publicized through the *Coalition News*, special mailings to members and specific target groups (depending on the subject), and through the community announcement sections of daily and weekly newspapers. However, most participants seem to be recruited by friends and colleagues.

Annual Media Fair. This popular event is held in late June to accommodate teachers, who are then on vacation, and to help all educators plan for the coming year. The scope of the Media Fair has expanded over the past ten years from a two and one half hour film-showing to an all-day fair, and from an initial attendance of 25 to an audience of over 300. Its purpose, however, has remained consistent: to enable educators to preview the latest audiovisual and printed materials in the field of sexuality education and to network informally for the day.

The format includes a plenary session in the morning at which a variety of new films are shown, with some time allowed between films for small group processing or individual assessment and note-taking. Registrants receive schedules and printed information on all previewed films.

After lunch, participants may choose from a variety of activities:

- One-hour seminars on such topics as Producing Low-Cost Audiovisual Materials, How to Select Sex Education Materials, Sexuality Education for Special Populations, and Involving Males in Sex Education and Family Planning;
- Displays of books, filmstrips, and curricular materials in a centralized resource room where exhibits are staffed by a wide variety of community organizations and agencies (Rape Crisis Center, local bookstores, Health Department, March of Dimes, Planned Parenthood, youth clubs, Cancer Society, Gay Activist Alliance);
- Additional film previews in the main auditorium.

The day concludes with a wine and cheese social hour.

An event of this scope could be organized only through the efforts of a large and hard-working volunteer committee. One board member forms and chairs the Media Fair Committee. The committee, in turn, selects a site for the fair (local college, hospital, or school), chooses films and workshop topics, contacts agencies and individuals interested in displaying materials in the Resource Room, publicizes the fair, pre-registers and registers participants, conducts the actual fair, and evaluates it through written questionnaires. The cost of the fair is kept to a minimum. A variety of groups around the country have adopted this Media Fair concept. The coalition used the same format for its "Resource Fair for Special Populations: Focus on Sexuality," geared to professionals working with individuals who are mentally retarded, physically disabled, emotionally disturbed, or learning disabled.

Workshops. In 1979 the Coalition began to sponsor a series of low-cost workshops on Adolescent Sexuality, Health, and Parenting under a small grant from the National Capital Area Chapter/March of Dimes Birth Defects Foundation. Recent topics for these day-long sessions have included:

- Adolescent Development
- Teaching Strategies for Sexuality Education
- Communicating with Adolescents
- Sexuality and Disability
- Homosexuality Today
- Youth and Families
- The Preschool Child
- Developing Culturally Sensitive Programs
- Understanding PMS.

Workshops are open to members and non-members alike, and most workshops have attracted a sizable registration, with some being oversubscribed and subsequently repeated. Individuals employed by over seventy different agencies have participated in the training workshops. Currently the workshops are supported through a registration fee of $30 for members, $45 for non-members. Expenses include speaker honoraria, brochures, mailings, room rental, materials, and light refreshments. The March of Dimes grant was discontinued in 1981. Each year, since the end of the grant, the Coalition has more than recovered its expenses.

Newletter. The Coalition News, a six- to eight-page quarterly, contains articles, reviews, information about workshops, resources, legislation, employment opportunities, and an update on coalition happenings. Most issues focus on a single theme such as preadolescence, parenting education, sexual identity, public policy and the family, adolescent males, training, or research. Some articles are written by members, others contributed by national and international experts in the field of human sexuality. In 1982 the coalition contracted for editorial services to coordinate the publication of the newsletter.

Publications. Coalition members have written, produced, and marketed five publications that are now being widely sold to professionals and parents:

> *Implementation of Family Life Education:Teaching Techniques and Strategies,* a curriculum for junior/senior high levels based on defined objectives;
> *Media Catalog,* an annotated list of FLE audiovisuals available for loan through libraries, health departments, and other private and public agencies in the Metropolitan Washington area;
> *Practical Approaches,* a handbook presenting guidelines and resources for sexuality education with four populations—preadolescents, adolescents, parents, and persons with developmental disabilities;
> *Tips for Parents: Talking with Your Children About Sexuality,*a four-page pamphlet describing "how-to's" for opening and continuing communication about sexuality between parents and children;
> *What is Sex Ed Really?,* a popular pamphlet designed to help the public understand the basic values, philosophy, and approach of responsible sexuality education programs and to encourage dialogue between provider and recipient.

These publications—all resources for program planning, development, and implementation—are marketed through an attractive flyer that is distributed at local and national meetings and through direct mail to individuals and agencies throughout the country. Revenues realized from the sale of these materials are used to support member and community services.

Free Film Loan. The coalition owns copies of more than twenty popular FLE films, which are made available for loan to members free of charge. The paid coordinator of this service receives and schedules requests, mails the films, and handles repairs as needed.

Special Project Grants. Over the years the coalition has received a number of small grants for special projects. The National Capital Area March of Dimes funded the workshops for several years. Subsequently, they supported a two-year Girl Scout Leaders Training Project. The U.S. Department of Health and Human Services provided funds for a two-year Teacher Training Program in the Washington, D.C., public schools. The coalition most recently completed two grants: one through the Council of Governments for Parent/Child Seminars and one through the National Capital Area March of Dimes for work with church groups. All such projects must be approved by the Board of Directors and must be in keeping with the philosophy and goals of the coalition.

Benefits of the Coalition

A small minority of coalition members work exclusively in the area of human sexuality. The majority, however, come from a wide variety of other disciplines. Why, then, do they join this particular organization when they already belong to their own professional organizations? The coalition, besides offering these professionals many needed services, provides a unique opportunity for interdisciplinary linkage, and a diversity of opportunity at affordable costs.

Diversity. The coalition has sought to maintain diversity in its membership and has made deliberate policy decisions to foster this diversity. The focus of the coalition—professional growth of individuals through shared information—allows for a sizeable common ground. The coalition has never been directly assaulted by sexuality education opponents although some opponents have occasionally attended meetings and have voiced strong anti-sexuality education views during selected presentations. Nevertheless, the coalition's Board of Directors has clearly communicated the right of members to hold varying opinions and to work independently to promote various advocacy positions on related issues such as abortion or homosexuality.

Affordable Cost. The coalition has made a concerted effort to serve its members and the larger community through free and low-cost programs and services. Modest fees allow a greater number of people to participate in coalition programs. This is especially helpful during times of limited funding for sexuality education programming.

Linkages and Interdisciplinary/Interagency Collaboration. Although the Coalition was primarily developed as a mechanism for sharing information and resources, its presence has given rise to a great deal of interagency and interdisciplinary collaboration. For example:

- A physician invited a health educator to conduct grand rounds for pediatric residents at a local hospital.
- A social worker was asked to lead parent seminars in a member's church.
- A minister was invited to serve on a local family planning advisory board.

The varied services and programs of the coalition have greatly enhanced the skills and professionalism of its members. Perhaps even more importantly, the existence of the coalition has contributed to an understanding and acceptance of sexuality education in the larger community.

RESOURCES FROM THE
SEX EDUCATION COALITION

Benesch, Joan, Jean Kapp, and Louise Peloguin. *Implementation of Family Curriculum: Teaching Techniques and Strategies.* Washington, D.C.: Sex Education Coalition, 1982.

This 125-page loose-leaf manual presents a curriculum for grades 6 to 12 based on defined objectives. Teaching techniques and learning activities for ten topics are outlined including Communicating about Sexuality, Decision Making, Sex Roles, Anatomy and Physiology, and Sexually Transmitted Diseases.

Cook, Ann Thompson, and Joan Benesch. *Tips for Parents: Talking to Your Children about Sexuality.* Washington, D.C.: Sex Education Coalition, 1984.

This four-page pamphlet contains "how-to's" to opening and continuing communication about sexuality, growth, and development. *Tips* broadens the definition of sexuality, addresses parents' most frequent questions, recommends books for further reading, and offers many practical suggestions for using everyday events to share information, values, and attitudes.

Cook, Ann Thompson, and Mary Lee Tatum. *What Is Sex Ed Really?* Washington, D.C.: Sex Education Coalition, 1986.

This brochure offers a checklist for reviewing sexual education programs and how they can be tailored to meet community needs. It supports "do's and don'ts," topic areas, and addresses the meaning of sexual literacy.

Cook, Ann Thompson, and Pamela M. Wilson. *Practical Approaches to Sexuality Education Programs.* Washington, D.C.: Sex Education Coalition, 1983.

This handbook presents guidelines for developing sexuality education programs for four specific audiences: preadolescents, adolescents, parents, and mentally retarded persons. Each chapter includes program rationale, practical approaches, sample activities, selected resources, and special considerations.

Wilson, Pamela M. *Media Catalog*. Washington, D.C.: Sex Education Coalition, 1986.

The *Media Catalog* is an annotated list of family life films and filmstrips available for loan through libraries, health departments, and private agencies in the Washington metropolitan area. Lending policies and procedures are included.

APPENDIX

Audiovisual Distributors

Agency for Instructional
    Technology
P.O. Box A
Bloomington, IN 47402
(812) 339-2203

Aims Instructional Media
    Service
626 Justing Avenue
Glendale, CA 91207
(213) 240-9300

American Educational Films
132 Lasky Drive
Beverly Hills, CA 90210
(213) 278-4996

John P. Armour
920 Stryker Avenue
St. Paul, MN 55118
(612) 457-6845

Barr Films
P.O. Box 5667
3490 East Foothill Blvd.
Pasadena, CA 91107
(800) 423-4483

Cambridge Documentary
    Films
P.O. Box 385
Cambridge, MA 02139
(617) 354-3677

Carousel Films
1501 Broadway
New York, NY 10036
(212) 354-0315

Centre Films
1103 North El Centro Avenue
Hollywood, CA 90038
(213) 466-5123

Centre Productions
1800 30th Street, #207
Boulder, CO 80301
(303) 444-1166

Centron Films
1621 West 9th, Box 687
Lawrence, KS 66044
(913) 843-0400

Children's Home Society of
    California
Public Education Department
5429 McConnell Avenue
Los Angeles, CA 90066
(213) 390-8954

Churchill Films
662 N. Robertson Boulevard
Los Angeles, CA 90060
(800) 334-7830

Community TV Network
118 West Grand Avenue
Chicago, IL 60610
(312) 467-0425

Coronet/MTI Film & Video
108 Wilmot Road
Deerfield, IL 60015
(800) 621-2131

Direct Cinema Limited
P.O. Box 69799
Los Angeles, CA 90069
(213) 652-8000

Document Associates
211 East 43rd Street
New York, NY 10017
(212) 682-0730

Educational Activities,
P.O. Box 392
Baldwin, NY 11520
(516) 223-4666

Educational Consortium for
    Cable
24 Beechwood Road
Summit, NJ 07901
(201) 277-2870

Fanlight Productions
P.O. Box 226
Cambridge, MA 02238
(617) 524-0980

Film Fair Communications
10900 Ventura Boulevard
P.O. Box 1728
Studio City, CA 91604
(213) 985-0244

Filmmakers Library
133 East 58th Street
Suite 703A
New York, NY 10022
(212) 355-6545

Films Incorporated
5547 N. Ravenwood Avenue
Chicago, IL 60640-1199
(312) 256-4530

Guidance Associates
Box 300
Communications Park
White Plains, NY 10602
(914) 666-4100

Imperial Education Resources
19 Marble Avenue
Pleasantville, NY 10570

Kimberly Clark Audiovisual
    Library
5000 Park St., North
St. Petersburg, FL 33709-9989

Marshfilm
P.O. Box 8082
Shawnee Mission, KS 66208
(800) 821-3303

McGraw-Hill Films
110 Fifteenth Street
Del Mar, CA 92014
(714) 453-5000

Milner-Fenwick, Inc.
2125 Greenspring Drive
Timonium, MD 21093
(800) 638-8652

Arthur Mokin Productions
1600 West 60th Street
New York, NY 10023
(212) 757-4868

Multi-Focus
1525 Franklin Street
San Francisco, CA 94109
(800) 821-0514

National Audiovisual Center
General Services
    Administration Attention:
    Order Section
Washington, DC 20409
(301) 763-1896

National Foundation/March
    of Dimes
1275 Mamaroneck Avenue
White Plains, NY 10605
(914) 428-7100

New Day Films
22 Riverview Drive
Wayne, NJ 07470-3191
(201) 633-0212

New Dimension Films
85895 Lorane Highway
Eugene, OR 97405
(503) 484-7125

ODN Productions
74 Varick Street, #304
New York, NY 10013
(212) 431-8923

The Ounce of Prevention
    Fund
180 North LaSalle
Suite 1820
Chicago, IL 60601
(312) 853-6080

Paulist Productions
P.O. Box 1057
Pacific Palisades, CA 90272
(213) 454-0688

Peregrine Productions
330 Santa Rita Avenue
Palo Alto, CA 94301
(415) 328-4843

Perennial Education, Inc.
930 Pitner Avenue
Evanston, IL 60202
(800) 323-9084

Planned Parenthood Center of
    Memphis
1407 Union Avenue
Memphis, TN 38104
(901) 725-1717

Planned Parenthood
    Federation of America
810 Seventh Avenue
New York, NY 10019
(212) 541-7800

Planned Parenthood of East
    Central Georgia
1247 15th Street
Augusta, GA 30901
(404) 724-5557

Polymorph Films
118 South Street
Boston, MA 02111
(617) 542-2004

Pyramid Films
P.O. Box 1048
Santa Monica, CA 90406
(213) 828-7577

Search Institute
122 West Franklin Avenue
Minneapolis, MN 55404
(612) 870-9511

Serious Business Company
P.O. Box 315
Franklin Lakes, NJ 07417
(201) 891-8240

Special Purpose Films
416 Rio Del Mar Blvd.
Aptos, CA 95003
(408) 688-6320

Stanfield Film Associates
P.O. Box 1983-C
Santa Monica, CA 90406
(800) 421-6534

Sterling Productions
1112 N. Ridgeland
Oak Park, IL 60302
(312) 383-1710

Sunburst Communications
101 Castleton Street
Pleasantville, NY 10570-9971
(800) 431-1934

Tambrands, Inc.
Educational Department
One Marcus Avenue
Lake Success, NY 11042
(516) 358-8300

Texture Films, Inc.
1600 Broadway
New York, NY
(212) 505-1990

Time-Life Video
100 Eisenhower Drive
P.O. Box 644
Paramus, NJ 07653

TRB Productions
P.O. Box 2362
Boston, MA 02107

Bill Wadsworth Productions
1913 W. 37th
Austin, TX 7831
(512) 478-2971

YWCA of the USA
Program Services Division
726 Broadway
New York, NY 10003
(212) 614-2841

INDEX

Abortion
>parents' concern about presentation of, 28-29
>presentation in religiously sponsored programs, 311-312
>in university programs, 151

Abortion counseling
>in school-based health clinics, 172

Abstinence, 100, 257, 258

Abuse, sexual
>defined, 384
>false accusations of, 54
>of mentally disabled, 335
>parents' role in prevention, 53
>prevention efforts, 51-52
>prevention, resources on, 56-66
>and sexuality education, 51-53
>support for abused children, 54

Acquired immune deficiency syndrome. *See* AIDS

Activities
>Feeling Good Workshops, 334
>forced choice, 328
>mother-daughter programs, 321
>participation and risk-taking, 334
>self-esteem, 332
>Straight Talk, 328

Administrators
>enrollment in teacher training courses, 108
>involvement in program development, 167
>and school-based health clinics, 172
>support for independent school programs, 141
>support for school programs, 107-108, 111

Adolescence
        changes in, effects on family, 327
        tasks of, 345
"Adolescent Life and Family Communication" (American Red Cross),
        228
Adolescents
        as "captains of own health team," 363
        invincibility of, 387
        need for AIDS education, 258-259
        need for health care, 169-170
        need for insight into values and selves, 344
        perception of own need for sexuality education, 224
        program attendance under pressure, 313
        range of experience
                teachers' need to recognize, 264
        sexually active
                and AIDS prevention, 259, 260, 261
                use of contraception, 262
        as source of AIDS information for peers and family, 258
        target groups for AIDS education, 259
        vulnerability of, 384
Adultery, presentation to adolescents, 245
Advertising, subliminal effects of, 349
Advisory committee, 131-132
        Catholic response to course content, 312
        community-based programs, 98, 253
        in curriculum development, 108
        family centered sexuality education, 311
        independent schools, 139-140
        role of, 98-99, 102, 311, 313
        school programs, 98
Age appropriateness, curriculum materials, 251, 253, 348
AIDS
        adolescents as source of information for peers and family, 258
        and anonymous sexual experimentation, 40
        assessing risks of, 266
        misinformation on, 258, 259, 260
        presentation in context of healthy sexuality, 257, 264-265
        protection from, 263
        risk groups, 259
        transmission of, 259, 263
AIDS education
        in comprehensive health program, 263

curricula, 257, 264
effectiveness of, 262
lessons from sexuality and health education, 262-263
target groups, 259
The AIDS Movie, 265
Albuquerque, N.M., public schools health education curriculum, 155-160
Alcohol
interaction with exploitation and violence, 387-388
see also Substance abuse
Alexandria, Va., public schools, 105-108
American Red Cross, 228, 356
Anatomy, 149, 157
Anonymity
in middle/high school programs, 123-124
in parent-child programs, 31
in school-based health clinics, 174
Assertiveness
principles of, 348
skill development, 344
teaching, 53
see also Pressure, response to
Attendance
family centered sexuality education, 312
mandatory in school programs, 107-108, 111
mother-daughter programs, 319, 323
as response to perception that parents' values are respected, 310, 313
Attitudes
development of healthy body and gender images, 21
and school-based AIDS programs, 262
Sex Knowledge and Attitude Test (SKAT), 393
shifts of, in teacher training, 395-396, 397, 398
Test for Assessing Sexual Knowledge and Attitudes (TASKA), 393
toward sex, changes in, 6
Audiovisual materials
The AIDS Movie, 265
Bridging the Gap (film), 366-367
distributors of, 415-419
elementary and middle school, 187-194
film loan, Sex Education Coalition, 409-410
high school, 164-212

homosexuality, 49-50
It's OK to Say No Way (YWCA rock music video), 230
parent education, 88-91
Autonomy, 20-21

Baylor College of Medicine, 390
Behavior
     focus on, in AIDS education, 264, 266
     and school-based AIDS programs, 262, 264
     sense of control over one's own, 347
     subliminal effects of advertising, 349
Behavior, sexual
     in AIDS programs, 262, 264
     conflicting messages on, 127-128
     and educational goals, 357
     internal controls, 248
     interrelatedness with other stresses, 375
     morality of, 9, 245
     and risk of AIDS, 258
     sources of pressure on, 344
     understanding appropriate, 326
Beliefs. *See* Values
Berkeley health education curriculum, 156
"Body Works" (Boys Clubs of America), 228
Bonding, 10
Boys Clubs of America, 223, 228
     resources available from, 232
Boy Scouts of America, 223, 356
"Bridging the Gap Between Youth and Community Services"
          (Salvation Army program), 229
"Bridging the Gap" conferences, 363-371
Bridging the Gap (film), 366-367
Bridging the Gap (magazine), 365-366

Calderone, Mary, 225
Campbell, D.T., 276
Camp Fire, Inc., 223, 224, 228, 356
Career planning
     and adolescent pregnancy, 355-357
     as task of adolescence, 345
     women, 355-356
Case study
     American Red Cross, 228

Boys Clubs of America, 228
Camp Fire, Inc., 228
Girls Clubs of America, 224-228
Girl Scouts, 228-229
Health Education Service Project (South Texas Family
        Planning and Health Corporation), 252-256
Planned Parenthood of San Antonio, Tex., 237-241
Salvation Army, 229
YWCA, 229
Catholic Charities of the Diocese of Arlington, Inc. (Arlington, Va.),
        307-317
Center for Health Promotion and Education, Centers for Disease
        Control, 33
Center for Population Options, 223, 360
        resources available from, 232-233
Centers for Disease Control, 33, 155, 257-258
Child development
        in elementary school family life program (New Jersey), 120-
            121
        and homosexuality, 37
        operative principles of, 9-10
        parents' need for information on, 15, 17, 20, 21
        teens' questions on, 127
Child-parent communication. *See* Communication, parent-child
Childrearing, basic principles of, 21-23
Child sexual abuse. *See* Abuse, sexual
Christian Religious Education, 244
Church programs
        course content, 244-245
        laying the groundwork, 248
        method, 244
        models, 246-247
        opposition to, 248
        resources for, 245
        resources on, 300
Class size
        family centered sexuality education, 309
        independent school programs, 141
        mother-daughter programs, 322
        parent-child programs, 29-30
Clearinghouse on Sexuality Education Programs and Materials
        (Planned Parenthood), 69

The Coalition News (Sex Education Coalition, Washington, D.C.), 408-
        409
Cognitive repression, 262-263
Coming out, 35, 40
Communication, differences in methods, 327
Communication, parent-child
        and AIDS, 259
        blocked by parents' feelings, 17
        family centered sexuality education, 310
        and homosexuality, 38
        impact on adolescent sexual behavior, 14-15
        impact of community-based programs, 255
        mother-daughter programs, 321
        need for skills development, 15
        parent-child programs, 27-28, 29
        practice time, 320, 325, 327-328
        and school programs, 262
        about sexuality and values, 307, 308
        teacher as facilitator of, 163-164
        see also Straight Talk
Communication skills
        in AIDS programs, 262
        Bridging the Gap (magazine), 365
        development of, 17, 24, 29, 30
        high school programs, 131
        independent school programs, 142
        parent education, 15
        in teacher training, 101
        university programs, 148, 149
Community activism
        as part of church programs, 247
Community-based programs
        age appropriateness, 251, 253
        development time, 216
        evaluation of, 255
        forms, 216
        goals of, 251, 252
        impact on behavior, 255
        procedures for, 254
        resources for, 254, 283-303
Community involvement in program development, 121, 167
Community organization
        resources on, 218

Community service agencies
    discussion in school programs, 100-101
    referral to by teachers, 133, 239
Condoms
    and AIDS prevention, 258, 261, 266
    opposition to, 261
Consent. *See* Rape
Consistency
    child's need for, 20-21
Consultants
    in community-based programs, 253
    in curriculum development, 308
    as teachers in school programs, 140
Continuing education
    access to via family planning/health agencies, 238
    teacher training, 397
Contraception
    discussion in school programs, 100
    need for, 6
    parents' concern about presentation of, 28-29
    parents' need for information on, 15
    presentation in religiously sponsored programs, 311-312
    in school-based health clinics, 171
    in university programs, 151
    use and continuation rates among students, 176, 262
    use and educational goals, 357
Controls, in program evaluation, 272, 273
Controls, internal, 248
Cost
    "Bridging the Gap" conferences, 369
    family centered sexuality education, 313
    family planning/health agencies teaching in community, 240
    high school programs, 130
    Life Options Strategy, 357-358
    offset by benefits, 271
    and programmatic significance, 279
    school-based health clinics, 176-177
    Sex Education Coalition, 411
    Straight Talk, 329
    teacher training, 109
Counseling
    as part of church programs, 247
    see also Peer counseling

Course content
 AIDS programs, 257-258, 263-264
 "Bridging the Gap" conferences, 367-368
 church programs, 244-245
 community-based programs, 216, 253
 elementary grades, 99, 120, 156-157, 159
 Feeling Good Workshops, 332-333
 health education, Albuquerque, N.M., public schools, 156
 high school, 100-101, 125, 125-126, 126, 131
  family centered sexuality education, 309, 310
 independent school programs, 142
 middle school, 99-100, 121, 125-126, 309-310
  parents' view on, 159
 mother-daughter programs, 320
 parent-child programs, 31
 parents' views of, 159
 Postponing Sexual Involvement Series, 348, 349
 review by advisory committee, 131-132
 revised according to advisory committee response, 311
 teacher training, 392
 TeenAge Communication Theater, 374-375
 understanding and acceptance of, 270-271
 university programs, 148-151
Course dynamics
 high school programs, 132-134
Course format
 "Bridging the Gap" conferences, 368-369
 independent school programs, 141
 Postponing Sexual Involvement Series, 348-349
 Straight Talk, 325, 328-329
 university programs, 151
Credibility
 of family planning/health agencies, 239
 of youth organizations, 230
Curfews, 386, 387
Curriculum
 access to via family planning network of agencies, 238
 age-appropriateness, 348
 church programs, 245
 see also Course content
Curriculum development
 in family centered sexuality education, 308, 309-310
 high school programs, 128, 130-131

independent schools, 137-138, 139
review by advisory committee, 131-132
see also Program development
Curriculum materials
audiovisual, distributors of, 415-419
"Bridging the Gap" conferences, 369
Clearinghouse on Sexuality Education Programs and
Materials, 69
community-based programs, 253, 254
family centered sexuality education, 309, 315
film loan, Sex Education Coalition, 409-410
slow learners (Feeling Good Workshops), 333-334

Dallas, Texas
first school-based health clinic, 170, 176
Data collection for program evaluation, 276-277
Daughters and Mothers/Mothers and Daughters, 319
Decision-making skills
in AIDS programs, 262
Bridging the Gap (magazine), 365
community-based programs, 253
elementary school health program, 157
improving, as goal of school programs, 97
independent school programs, 142
slow learners, 331
Straight Talk, 326
university programs, 151
Desensitization
middle/high school programs, 125, 134
parent education, 24
teacher training, 396
Disabled persons
care providers in social skills training, 334
programs and resources for, 336-341, 409
sexual abuse of, 335
sexuality and social skills education for. *See* Feeling Good
Workshops
as teachers, 332
see also Feeling Good Workshops
Discomfort with discussion of sexuality, confronting students', 124-125
Discussion-leading skills, 164
Discussion rules, 124, 130-131, 133
Dropouts, school-based health clinics, 173

Drug use
        intravenous. *See* IV drug use
        see also Substance abuse

Eleven Million Teenagers: The Problem of Teenage Pregnancy, 353
*Eleven Million Teenagers: What Can Be Done About the Epidemic of
        Adolescent Pregnancies?*, 225
Emory University Family Planning Program, 363
Employment
        and adolescent pregnancy, 355-357
        women, 355-356
Environment
        normative, changing, 262, 349
        sheltered, and development of decision making skills, 331
Evaluation
        administrative. *See* Evaluation, process
        based on existing records, 275-276
        based on new information, 273-275
        "Bridging the Gap" conferences, 370-371
        community-based programs, 255
        data collection for, 276-277
        defined, 270
        family centered sexuality education, 315-316
        family planning/health agencies in school programs, 240
        goals, 270
        high school programs, 134
        interpretation of. *See* Evaluation, methods
        Life Options Strategy, 360-361
        measures, teacher training, 392-393
        methods, 271, 272-276, 392-393
        mother-daughter programs, 323
        outcome, 270, 271
        by participants, Postponing Sexual Involvement Series, 350-
                351
        process, 270-271, 393-394
        resources on, 290-292
        response to, 279-280
        risks of, 279
        sexuality education within health education program, 158-159
        steps in, 271
        teacher training, 164, 393-394
        teacher training guide, 394
        understanding and acceptance of course content, 255, 270-271

youth organization programs, 226-227
Exemption from school programs, moral/religious reasons, 111-112,
121, 144, 158
Experimentation, sexual
media messages about, 6
and parent education, 14-15
parents' reaction to, 20, 22
see also Masturbation
Exploitation, sexual
avoiding, 384
defined, 384
interaction with substance abuse, 387-388
media messages about, 243
mutual, 386
parental guidance, 43
and self-esteem, 331-332
vulnerability of children in stressed families, 387

Facilitation skills, 164, 369
Facts and Reflections on Female Adolescent Sexuality (Girls Clubs of
America), 227
Family
defined, 3
patterns, 5, 20
as system, 325, 326-327
task of, 3
under stress, and vulnerability of children, 387
Family Centered Sexuality Education Associates, 317
Family Centered Sexuality Education (Catholic Charities of the Diocese
of Arlington, Inc. (Arlington, Va.), 307-317
Family centered sexuality education, resources on, 71-91, 309, 315, 317
Family Life Division, New York Medical College, 373
Family Life Education Curriculum Guidelines, including Program
Implementation and a Suggested Curriculum (New
Jersey), 120
Family Life Education for Adolescents (Girls Clubs of America), 226
Family Life Education (FLE) program (Alexandria, Va., public
schools), 105-108
Family Life Educator, 120
Family life programs, 105-108
Family planning/health agencies, 237-242
in community education, 216-217, 237-242
goals of, 252

in school programs
　　mutual benefits, 241
　　opposition to, 240-241
　see also Community-based programs
Family planning professionals
　　as guest speakers in classroom, 238-239
Family service agency
　　clients of, 307
　　preparation for sexuality education, 308-309
　　rationale for sexuality education in, 307-308
　　staff concerns regarding sexuality education, 308
Fantasies, sexual
　　morality of, 9
　see also Thoughts, sexual
Feeling Good About Yourself, 331
Feeling Good Associates, 331
Feeling Good Workshops, 331-335
Feelings
　　homosexual, inability to communicate, 38
　　identifying, 125
　　sexual, normalcy of, 100
　　understanding, 123, 125-126
　see also Discomfort with discussion of sexuality
Fertility, responsibility for, 245
Film loan, Sex Education Coalition, 409-410
Flexibility, in course format, 325, 328-329
Follow-up evaluation, teacher training, 396-397
Follow-up programs, 348-349
Force, to gain sexual contact, 384, 387
4-H, 223, 224
Frustration, children's need to face, 21
Funding
　　based on impact, 255
　　federal
　　　curriculum development, 310
　　　restriction of discussion, 312
　　Feeling Good Workshops, 331
　　Life Options Strategy, 358
　　parent education, 18
　　school-based health clinics, 176-177

Gay bars, 41
Gay men. *See* Homosexuality

Gender, 35
 development of a positive attitude toward, 21
 dignity of, 245
George Mason High School (Falls Church, Va.), 129
Gilchrist, Lewayne D., 346, 347
Girls Clubs of America, 223, 224-228, 356
 resources available from, 233-235
Girl Scouts, 223, 228-229
Goals
 AIDS education, 260-261
 "Bridging the Gap" conferences, 364, 367
 church programs, 248
 family centered sexuality education, 309
 family planning/health agencies, 252
 Feeling Good Workshops, 331-332
 health education, 156
 Life Options Strategy, 353
 middle school program, 157
 mother-daughter programs, 320-321
 No Is Not Enough, 383-385
 Postponing Sexual Involvement Series, 344
 program evaluation, 134-135, 270
 school-based health clinics, 170-172
 of sexuality education, 343
 Straight Talk, 325-326
 teacher training, 389
 TeenAge Communication Theater, 375-376
 university programs, 148, 151
 youth organizations, 225
 see also Objectives
Goals, behavioral, 343-344
 and necessary skills, 344
Goals, educational
 and sexual behavior, 357
Gordon, Sol, 67, 331
Grady Memorial Hospital (Atlanta, Ga.), 363
Groome, Thomas, 244
Group building activities, 309
Group facilitation skills
 in teacher training, 101
"Group Procedures for Helping Adolescents Cope with Sex," 346
Growing Healthy (Bureau of Health, Education and Welfare), 155-156
Guidance, children's need for, 22

Guttmacher, Alan, 223-224

Hammer, Signe, 319
Handicapped Children's Program (Office of Special Education,
          Department of Health, Education and Welfare), 331
Health agencies. *See* Family planning/health agencies
Health care
          adolescents' need for, 169-170
          in school-based health clinics, 170-172
Health clinics, school-based, 169-178
          administration and staffing, 172
          costs and funding, 176-177
          development of, 170
          goals and services, 170-172
          interaction with school, 173
          limitations of, 177
          parental involvement, 173-174
          success of, 174-176
Health education
          course content, 156
          New Mexico mandate for, 155
          sexuality education in, 155-160
Health Education Service Project (South Texas Family Planning and
          Health Corporation), 252-256
Health problems, chronic, detection in school-based health clinics, 175
Health professionals
          participation in group activities, 334
          school-based health clinics, 172
          and sexuality education for slow learners, 332
Heterosexism, defined, 42
Heterosexuality, assumption of, 35
High school programs, 123-135, 158
          anonymity, 123-124
          communication skills, 131
          cost, 130
          course content, 100-101, 125-126, 131, 309, 310
          course dynamics, 132-134
          curriculum development, 128, 130-131
          desensitization, 125, 134
          evaluation, 134
          goals, lack of consensus on, 134
          instructional time, 128-130
Homeless adolescents, as target group for AIDS education, 259

Homophobia, defined, 42
Homosexual adolescents
        as target group for AIDS education, 259
Homosexual feelings
        inability to communicate, 38
        in normal development, 42-43
Homosexuality
        adolescent, and peer groups, 39-40
        causes of, 36-37
        and child development, 37
        early awareness of, 38
        opportunities to discuss, 44
        parents' queries about, 45
        prevalence of, 35, 41-42
        reaction to
                adolescent, 260
                parental, 35, 41-44
                societal, 40
        resources on, 45, 46-50
        young adult, peer groups, 41
Houston Independent School District, 390
Houston, prevalence of AIDS in, 259
Human immunodeficiency virus (HIV). *See* AIDS
Humor
        desensitizing effect of, 125, 134
        as teaching tool, 375

IV drug use
        adolescents involved in, as target for AIDS education, 258
        in AIDS programs, 261, 264
        and risk of AIDS, 258
Identity formation, 101
Implementation of Family Life Education: Teaching Techniques and Strategies, 409
Independence from parents, establishing, as task of adolescence, 345
Independent schools
        as curriculum development lab, 137-138
        sexuality education in, 137-145
Information, personalization of, 347
Information, sexual
        as deterrent to early sexual involvement, 343
        limited effect of, 123, 125-126, 344
Inoculation, psychological, 346

Institute of Family Research and Education, 67
Institutionalization of sexuality education programs, 227-228
Instructional specialists. *See* Teacher trainers
Instructional time, 97, 98
>   in AIDS programs, 257-258, 264
>   family centered sexuality education, 313
>   high school programs, 128-130
>   mother-daughter programs, 322
>   Postponing Sexual Involvement Series, 348
>   Straight Talk, 329
>   teacher trainer instruction, 390-391
>   TeenAge Communication Theater, 374
Intercourse
>   adolescent, and educational goals, 357
>   alternatives to, 219, 260-261, 344
>   consent to, 52, 384
>   delaying, 260-261
>   discussion in school programs, 100
>   parents' concern about presentation of, 28-29
It's OK to Say No Way (YWCA rock music video), 230

Jaffe, Frederick S., 225
Jerome, Elizabeth, 225
Junior high. *See* Middle school programs

Kantner, John F., 224
Kirby, Douglas, 277, 343
Knowledge, gain and retention of, in teacher training, 389-390, 396-397

Language
>   explicit
>   in AIDS programs, 264, 265-266
>   in sexuality education, 53, 265-266
>   homophobic/heterosexist, 44
>   inappropriate, response to, 245
>   marketing programs, 248, 329
Lesbians. *See* Homosexuality
Lewis, R.A., 29
Life Options Strategy, 353-362
"Life Planning Education," 360
"Life Skills and Opportunities," 361
Love, need for evidence of, 22

M.E.N.C.H. (Meaningful Education Now for Citizens with Handicaps)
   Project, 331
McAlister, Alfred, 346
Marijuana, and immune system suppression, 261
Marketing
   "Bridging the Gap" conferences, 369
   community-based programs, 254
   family centered sexuality education, 311
   Straight Talk, 329
   see also Recruiting participants
Masturbation
   parents' concern about presentation of, 28-29
   parents' reaction to, 20
   see also Experimentation, sexual
Matching, 275
Mathtech, Inc., 15, 16, 19, 33, 224
Maturation, university years as critical phase, 147, 152
Media Catalog, 409
Media Fair (Sex Education Coalition), 407-408
Mental disability. *See* Disabled persons; Slow learners
Mental health professionals
   participation in group activities, 334
   and sexuality education for slow learners, 332
Middle school programs, 123-126, 157-158
   anonymity, 123-124
   course content, 99-100, 121, 125-126
      family centered sexuality education, 309-310
      parents' view on, 159
   desensitization, 125, 134
   goals, 157
Missouri, rural, successful parent-child program, 27-34
Mother-daughter relationship
   uniqueness of, 319
   see also Communication, parent-child; Parent-child programs

"National Adolescent Sexuality Brief" (YWCA newsletter), 229
National Center for Family Studies (Catholic University, Washington,
   D.C.), 315
National Coalition of Advocates for Students, 264
National Family Sexuality Education Month (October), 67-70, 377
National Resource Center (Girls Clubs of America), 227
Needles, sharing. *See* IV drug use, 261
New Jersey, family life education curriculum, 120

Newsletters, church
    as part of church sexuality program, 247
No Is Not Enough, 383-388

Objectives
    setting, 271-272
    see also Goals
Opposition to sexuality education
    church programs, 248, 311
    educators' sensitivity to, 217
    family planning/health agencies in schools, 240-241
    and parent involvement, 230
    school programs, 113-117, 240-241

Panhandle Planned Parenthood, 319
Parent-child communication. *See* Communication, parent-child
Parent-child programs, 144, 228, 319-323
    activities, 30
    ages of children, 29-30
    class size, 29-30
    community-based, 217
    course content, 31
    Family Centered Sexuality Education, 307
    goals of, 27-28
    participation patterns, 32, 313
    program structure, 29
    sponsorship, 32
    see also "Postponing Sexual Involvement: An Educational
            Series for Young People"; Mother-daughter programs
Parent education, 16-18
    communication skills, 15
    in community programs, 217, 253, 254
    desensitizing effect of, 24
    educators' views of, 16
    family planning/health agencies, 238
    focus issues, 17-18, 24
    funding of, 18
    goals of, 19
    government support for, 13-14
    impact of, 18-19
    independent school settings, 144
    needs assessment, 15-16
    No Is Not Enough (acquaintance rape), 383

Postponing Sexual Involvement Series, 350-351
problems in, 18-19
reasons for attending, 17
recruiting and retaining participants, 18-19, 23
research on, 14-15
resources for, 24-25, 88-91
and school programs, 16-17, 132, 144
teacher training, 23-24
see also Parent-child programs
Parents
concern for presentation of values, 101, 315
consent to health services in school-based clinics, 173-174
consent to sexuality education, 144, 157, 158
encouraged to share values, family centered sexuality
education, 313
feelings of inadequacy as educators, 13, 17, 27
involvement in curriculum development, independent
schools, 144
involvement in program development, 121, 132, 167
involvement in school programs, 106-107
involvement in youth organization, 230
notification regarding school programs, 111-112
response to homosexual children, 35-45
in sexuality education for slow learners, 332
as sexuality educators, 13, 27, 217, 248, 313, 385
family centered sexuality education, 310
lack of skills, 308
and sexual abuse, 51
support for, 144, 161, 163
in social skills training for slow learners, 334
turnover of, elementary school, 112-113
Participants
ages of, 217
community programs, 216
Partners, sexual, communication between, 261, 307
Peer counselor training, 238
Peer educators, 373, 374, 376
see also TeenAge Communication Theater
Peer groups
homosexual young adults, 41
socialization of heterosexual youths, 38-39
socialization of homosexual youths, 39-40
Peer mediated health programs, 262

Peer pressure
>   interrelatedness with sexual behavior, 375
>   reducing effects of, 157
>   resisting, 343
>   sources of, 344
Peoplemaking, 326
Pilot programs, 103, 143-144, 394
Planned Parenthood, 69
>   leadership in community programs, 216
>   sponsorship of teen communication theater troupes, 378-381
Planned Parenthood of Greater Dallas, 373
Planned Parenthood of San Antonio, Tex., 237-241
Policy statements, youth organizations, 226
Pornography
>   action against, in church programs, 247
>   *see also* Exploitation
"Postponing Sexual Involvement: An Educational Series for Young
>   People," 343-352
Post-test, 273
Practical Approaches, 409
Pregnancy, adolescent, 6-7
>   economic consequences of, 355, 358
>   impact of community-based programs, 255
>   and parent-child communication, 29
>   parents' need for information on, 15
>   prevention of, 19, 175-176, 353, 404
>   reasons for, 131
>   repeat, 176
>   rural Missouri, 27
>   teacher's response, 133-134
Pressure, response to, 126, 347
>   *see also* Assertiveness
Pre-test, 273
"Preventing Adolescent Pregnancy Project" (Girls Clubs of America),
>   227
Printed Matter, Inc., 366
Privacy, need for, 21-23
Private/public rule, in social skills training for slow learners, 334
The Problem That Hasn't Gone Away, 353
Program Guide for Teen Sexuality Education (YWCA), 229
Program to Expand Sexuality Education in Cooperation with Youth
>   Serving Agencies, 223
Prostitution, adolescents involved in, 259

Public/Private Ventures, 361

Raifman, Mark, 170
A Rainbow of Discovery (handbook for early adolescents, Camp Fire,
    Inc.), 228
Random assignment to test groups, 274
Rape
        acquaintance, 385-386
        defining in the classroom, 385
        legal and cultural definitions, 384
        prevalence of, 383, 385-386
        prevention program, 383-388
        reporting of, 383
        responsibility for, 387
        traditional prevention measures, 386
        victim's feeling of guilt, 385-386, 387
Recruiting
        participants
                "Bridging the Gap" conferences, 366
                family centered sexuality education, 310
                mother-daughter programs, 322
                parent education, 18-19, 23
                Straight Talk, 329
        teachers, 110, 162
Relationships
        adult, parents as role models, 22
        development and maintenance of, 148, 149
        discussion in school programs, 100
Reliability, statistical, 277
Religious principles, transferred to sexual life, 243
Reproductive systems, elements of, 8
Reproductivity
        distinguished from sexuality, 7
        onset of, 8
Research
        design problems and solutions, standard, 276
        sexuality education
                Girls Clubs of America, 227
                lack of, 218-219
Results, measuring of, 271, 276-277
        see also Evaluation
Retention
        parent education, 18-19

teen mothers in school, 176
Retreats, in church programs, 247
Risk taking, group response to, 334
Role models
       homosexual, 42
       parents in adult relationships, 22
       parents' lack of, 27
       sexual orientation, 35

St. Joseph, Mo., successful parent-child program, 27-34
St. Paul, Minn., early school-based health clinic, 170, 176
Salvation Army, 229
       resources available from, 235
Satir, Virginia, 326
School board
       involvement in program development, 167
       support of school programs, 106, 107-108
       turnover of members, 113
School Health Project. *See* Growing Healthy
School programs
       AIDS, 257-268
       balancing presentations, 125
       community input to, 98-99
       comprehensive, 97, 156
       content of master plan, 102
       current efforts, 97-98
       development, 117-118, 128, 216
       effects on behavior, 97
       elements of success, 106
       exemption for moral/religious reasons, 111-112, 121, 144, 158
       factors restraining, independent schools, 138
       family planning/health agencies in, 237, 240-241
       family planning professionals as guest speakers, 238-239
       health issues in, 131
       implementation steps, 102-103
       need for flexibility, 239
       opposition to, 6-7, 113-117, 240-241
       overview, 95-103
       parents' consent, 111
       parents' input to, 98-99
       pilot programs, 103
       preschool, 119
       prevalence of, 7

problems, 113-118
rape and sexual exploitation, 383-388
rationale for, 97, 127-128, 157, 158
resources on, 179-212
sexual abuse, 51, 54-55
    see also No Is Not Enough
states requiring, 120
support for, 215
teachers as determinant of success, 101, 109
teacher training model, 389-401
views of, 13
see also Course content; Exemption from school programs;
    Family life programs; Postponing Sexual
    Involvement Series
School programs, elementary grades, 119-121, 119-122, 156-157
School programs, high school. *See* High school programs
School programs, middle school. *See* Middle school programs
Schools
    interaction with school-based health clinics, 173
Seattle health education curriculum, 156
Seattle Rape Relief, 335
Security
    child's need for, 20-21
Self-esteem
    development of, 21, 27, 331-332
    principles of, 332
    and sexual exploitation, 331-332
Sermons, as part of church sexuality program, 247
Sex Education Coalition, 403-411
    resources available from, 407-409, 412-413
Sex Education Teacher Training and Development Project (Houston,
    Tex.), 389-401
Sex Knowledge and Attitude Test (SKAT), 393
Sex offenders, early prevention, 386
Sex, pleasure in, changes of attitudes, 6
Sexual feelings, normalcy of, 100
Sexual identity, establishing, as task of adolescence, 345
Sexuality
    acceptance and exploration of, as goal of parent-child
        programs, 27
    current theology on, 244, 245
    defined, 95
    definition within education programs, 130, 252

distinguished from reproductivity, 7
enhancement of, as goal of education programs, 19
fetal, 7-8
human choices in, 4, 5
infantile, 8
juvenile, parents' reaction to, 8
parents' need for information on, 17
parents' need to understand their own, 16
positive view of, 325-326
in religious life, 243, 245
Sexuality education
acceptability of, 19
adolescent evaluation of, 373-374
as cause of sexual experimentation, 28
in church communities, 243-249
in a conservative community, 360-361
contexts for, 142-143
defined, 3, 96
expected to support itself, 269
family centered, 307-318
goals of, 96-97
operative principles of, 9-10
as part of a basic education, 97, 98
politics of, 217-218
role of TV and print media in, 6
when to begin, 10, 27, 251
see also Community-based programs;School programs; Family
centered sexuality education; Family
planning/health agencies; High school programs;
Middle school programs; Mother-daughter
programs; Parent education; Parent-child programs;
School programs; Youth organizations
Sexuality education movement, 215-219
Sexual learning
defined, 96
histories, 328
Sexually transmitted diseases
impact of community-based programs, 255
in university programs, 150
see also AIDS
Sexual orientation
as part of nature, 245
see also Heterosexuality; Homosexuality

Sexual/reproductive decision, interrelatedness with vocational
        decisions, 354
Sexual response systems, 8
Significance
        of program evaluation results, 271, 278-279
Skills, assertiveness, 344-345
Skills, assertive resistance to pressure, 347
Skill, social. *See* Feeling Good Workshops
Skills training, 346-347
        see also Communication skills; Decision-making skills
Slow learners
        sexuality and social skills education programs for. *See* Feeling
                Good Workshops
        see also Disabled persons
Socialization, 9
        heterosexual adolescents, 38-39
        homosexual adolescents, 39-40, 41, 44
        homosexual young adults, 41
Social workers
        participation in group activities, 334
        and sexuality education for slow learners, 332
South Texas Family Planning and Health Corporation (Corpus Christi,
                Tex.), 252
Spanier, G.B., 29
Sponsorship
        "Bridging the Gap" conferences, 370
        community-based programs, 216, 253-254
        family centered sexuality education, 310
        Life Options Strategy, 358
        mother-daughter programs, 322
        National Family Sexuality Education Month, 68-69
        parent-child programs, 32
        and sense of ownership in program, 311
        teen communication theater troupes, 378-381
Stahler, Gerald J., 315
Stanley, J.C., 276
Sterilization, 151
Straight Talk (Planned Parenthood of Oklahoma City), 325-329
Strangers, 120-121
Students, involvement in program development, 167
Students served, school-based health clinics, 173
Substance abuse
        interaction with exploitation and violence, 387-388

interaction with sexual behavior, 375
Systems theory
family dynamics, 325, 326-327
teacher training, 391

Target groups
"Bridging the Gap" conferences, 368
Life Options Strategy, 354
Postponing Sexual Involvement Series, 347
Task Force on Adolescent Pregnancy in Dallas County, 373-374
Teachers
availability of, 134
challenges for, 220
as determinant of success of school programs, 101
exempting, 110
fallibility of, 218
ideal qualifications, 161
in-house vs. outside, 140
need for self-awareness, 218
recruiting, 110
as referral source, 133
resistance to teaching sexuality education, 138-139, 162
selection, 140-141, 165-167, 389
Teacher trainers, 390
effectiveness, 395-396
Teacher training, 101, 108, 109-111, 238
affective objectives, 162-164
attitude shifts, 395-396, 397, 398
cognitive objectives, 162
community-based programs, 253
continuing education, 397
elementary school teachers, 122
family centered sexuality education, 315
family service agency, 308-309
goals, 389, 391
model program, 389-401
need for, 161-162
parent education, 23-24
Postponing Sexual Involvement Series, 348
primary concern of parents and administrators, 162
problems in, 165
skill objectives, 164
for slow learners, 332

Straight Talk, 329
theory, 391
university programs, 148
youth organization programs, 226-227
Teaching techniques, 164, 320-321
see also Activities
TeenAge Communication Theater (TACT), 373-381
Television, discussion of, in church programs, 247
Test for Assessing Sexual Knowledge and Attitudes (TASKA), 393
Tests, types of, 277
see also Post-tests; Pre-tests
Textbooks, university programs, 152
Thoughts, sexual
guilt feelings for, 53
morality of, 9
see also Fantasies, sexual
Time constraints
in teacher training, 165
see also Instructional time
Tips for Parents: Talking with Your Children About Sexuality, 409
"Today's Girls: Tomorrow's Women" (1978 Wingspread Conference,
Girls Clubs of America), 225
Touching
fear of, 54
permitted, 53
see also Private/public rule
Training manual, teacher training, 390, 392

U.S. Conference of Mayors, 257
University City High School (St. Louis, Mo.), 129, 133
University life, as critical transition, 147, 152
University programs, 147-152

Validity, 277
Values
adolescents' need for insight into, 344
developing, as task of adolescence, 345
presentation of, family centered sexuality education, 314
presentation of, parents' concern for, 28-29
unconscious, 325, 328
Values clarification
in AIDS programs, 262
in family centered sexuality education, 308

independent school programs, 142
in parent education, 17, 20
in teacher training, 162-163
Values, sexual, adolescents' inability to communicate, 131
Victims of Child Abuse Laws (VOCAL), 54
Violence
    interaction with substance abuse, 387-388
    sexual. *See* Rape
Vocational planning
    interrelatedness with sexual/reproductive decisions, 354
    as task of adolescence, 345

Washington, D.C., prevalence of AIDS in, 259
Webster School model program for adolescent mothers (Washington,
        D.C.), 404
What Is Sex Ed Really?, 409
"What's Happening" (conference), 363-364
What's Happening (magazine), 363

YMCA, 223, 356
YWCA, 223, 224, 229
Youth organizations
    and adolescent employment, 356
    credibility of, 230
    health and sexuality education in, 223-231
    pattern of organizational involvement in sexuality education,
        224-228
    resources available from, 232-236
    resources available from, 236

Zelnik, Melvin, 224